Erasmus, Man of Letters

Erasmus, Man of Letters

THE CONSTRUCTION OF CHARISMA
IN PRINT

Lisa Jardine

PRINCETON UNIVERSITY PRESS

PRINCETON, NEW JERSEY

Library of Congress Cataloging-in-Publication Data

Jardine, Lisa.
Erasmus, man of letters : the construction of charisma in print / Lisa Jardine.
  p. cm.
Includes index.
1. Erasmus, Desiderius, d. 1536—Authorship. 2. Authors, Latin (Medieval and
modern)—Netherlands—Biography. 3. Authors and publishers—Netherlands—
History—16th century. 4. Scholarly publishing—Netherlands—History—
16th century. 5. Netherlands—Intellectual life—16th century. 6. Printing—
Netherlands—History—16th century. 7. Authorship—History—
16th century. 8. Humanists—Netherlands. I. Title.
PA8518.J36 1993 878'.0409—dc20 [B] 92-35250 CIP

ISBN 0-691-05700-1

This book has been composed in Linotron Sabon

10 9 8 7 6 5 4 3 2 1

Contents

Illustrations

Acknowledgments

THIS BOOK has been in the making for a number of years, and many people have contributed to its writing. First and foremost, my thanks are due to my friends, colleagues, and students at Queen Mary and Westfield College, who have provided me with a real-life context for my scholarly work, and a pressing set of contemporary intellectual issues to address, which keep me aware, day-to-day, of why scholarship continues to matter. They have sharpened and focused my work on Erasmus in crucial ways. I would like particularly to thank Lorna Hutson and Morag Shiach, whose intellectual companionship I treasure.

The research on which this book is based was carried out during two periods in the History Department at Princeton University: the first in 1988, when I was a Fellow in the Shelby Cullom Davis Center for Historical Studies; the second in 1991, when I was Class of 1932 Professor of History, and a Visiting Senior Fellow of the Council of the Humanities. So many people have made me welcome at Princeton, I have so many debts of intellectual gratitude, that I could not undertake to mention everyone here by name. I owe special gratitude, however, to Natalie Davis, Robert Darnton, Tony Grafton, Lawrence Stone, and Froma Zeitlin. All five of these great scholars set examples of generosity, intellectual scrupulousness, creative energy, and a burning commitment to their chosen field of study which I can only hope to emulate. My fellow Fellows in the Davis Center in 1988 shaped the project in vital ways. In particular, Val Flint taught me to be intellectually courageous, and that even scholarship can benefit from a sense of humour. The librarians and archivists at Firestone Library and the Speer Library of the Princeton Theological College were always patient and helpful.

The staff of the Warburg Institute in London has continued to support me in the kind of studies to which they introduced me when I was a Research Fellow there in the 1970s. Joe Trapp encouraged me as I moved gingerly into areas in which he was an acknowledged expert, and showed his customary tact when dealing with my questions. Charles Hope and Elizabeth McGrath helped me with pictures and slides. Peter Mack, at the University of Warwick, and Kees Meerhoff, at the University of Amsterdam, read parts of the manuscript and made helpful comments (even if they sometimes disagreed with me).

Erasmus had his own *familia*, and I have mine. Bill Sherman has commented meticulously on more drafts of this body of work than I care to own, and he also did the research for the illustrations. Warren Boutcher and Alan Stewart have patiently listened, and given me their comments, including some invaluable suggestions for reorganising the material. My daughter Rachel has grown up over the period of the book's development into a shrewd and alert critic, whose comments I have taken increasingly seriously. Without John Hare's and Daniel Jardine's constant support, good sense, and encouragement, none of this would be possible.

All the errors and omissions that remain are, needless to say, my own.

Abbreviations

Allen   P. S. Allen, *Opus epistolarum Des. Erasmi Roterodami* (12 vols.)
        (Oxford, 1906–1958)

ASD   *Opera Omnia Desiderii Erasmi Roterodami recognita et adnotatione critica instructa notisque illustrata* (Amsterdam, 1969–)

CWE   *Collected Works of Erasmus* (Toronto, 1976–)

Erasmus, Man of Letters

Self-Portrait in Pen and Ink

> What cannot Dürer express in monochromes, that is, by black
> lines only (even though other techniques of his deserve admira-
> tion also)?
>
> —Erasmus, *De pronuntiatione*[1]

IN THE SHADOW OF ERASMUS

For anyone whose education has included the cultural history of the sixteenth century, the name of Desiderius Erasmus is virtually synonymous
with that of the European intellectual Renaissance. For many people, indeed, whether scholars or amateurs, Erasmus's name conjures up a whole
lost world of learning, belief, and, above all, integrity. His were the
golden days, when men thirsted for knowledge, pursued it disinterestedly
and without regard for financial reward, when individual achievement
was first recognised, and when the humanely learned individual was *vir
bonus*—a good man.

Like so many others, I have pursued my scholarly Renaissance studies
in the shadow of Erasmus's reputation. At one of my earliest meetings
with my doctoral advisor, the late Professor Robert Bolgar, he pulled
down a volume of Erasmus's letters from his library shelf, and asked me
to translate a passage. In so doing, he was, I now understand, simply
continuing a tradition in the pedagogic use of Erasmus *epistolae*—exemplary pieces of writing, dense with difficult Latin syntax and rarely encountered eloquence, exercises in retrieving the moral sentiments and
felicitous expression of an antique past. Even then, I knew this was a test
any aspiring scholar of Renaissance thought had to pass—an initiation
test, a rite of passage. And like so many other graduate students in Renaissance studies, I made a mental note not to stumble too closely on Erasmus territory in my own research undertakings in the period—to leave
the study of Erasmus himself to scholars of lofty eminence (and advanced
years).

As a project, therefore, the present book has proved an unexpected
one, both in its conception and in the direction of its development. I never
intended to work on Erasmus. I certainly never expected that researches
which began as a kind of quest for the intellectual driving force behind
what I had identified as a key development in Renaissance thought—

humanist dialectic as the core of the arts educational curriculum—would lead me to Erasmus. And finally, when I uncovered a story of extraordinarily complex and sophisticated manipulations of writing and printing, designed to construct a worldwide reputation both for a movement (Low Countries humanism) and an individual, I was nonplussed that that individual should be that much-idealised figure, Erasmus.

For the trail I followed showed that establishing the stature of the man and making his reputation were an integral part of the strategy that Erasmus and those around him were developing, in the early decades of the sixteenth century. However 'great' the man was in reality, however awesome his talents and his achievements, it came as a shock to watch him, through the pages of his own and others' works, fashioning that greatness himself.

At the same time, there was something historically intriguing about this encounter. Here was a figure generally held up to us as without blemish of worldliness, and as intellectually eminent by virtue of his intrinsic gifts, his relentless dedication to study, his unswerving commitment to truth, and his eschewing of all worldly distractions and (most) rewards. And yet, here I uncovered him shaping his own persisting trace in intellectual history, adjusting his public image, editing the evidence to be left for his biographers, managing the production of 'influences' and contemporary movements to enhance his own posthumous renown. All this with a clear and steady confidence that the importance of the project on which he was embarked justified such activities, that the advancement of learning was so urgent and important a task that it entitled the practitioner to use every ingenious method at his disposal to ensure that the cause prospered.

This last point, I think, needs stressing, to avoid misunderstanding. When, in graphic and textual representations of himself, Erasmus chose to inhabit the familiar figure of Saint Jerome, with all the grandeur and intellectual *gravitas* that might thereby accrue to him, he claimed a role in the secular sphere equivalent to Jerome's in the spiritual. His figural presence was designed to give prominence to the northern humanist movement, to enable it to achieve international prestige and prominence; personal fame was merely a by-product. Jerome stood for the dissemination of true scripture throughout the Western world; Erasmus would stand for the dissemination of humane learning across Europe.

We twentieth-century advancers of learning have altogether lost any such confidence in grand designs. We are painfully aware of an apparently flagging eminence, a diminished stature, a waning of a world in which men of letters made the agenda, and worldly men then strove to pursue it. We have ceased, I suggest, to promote learning as such, because we have lost Erasmus's conviction that true learning is the originator of all good and virtuous action—that right thought produces right government. In fact, of course, we try not to use words like *true, good, virtuous,* and *right* at all, if we can help it. They embarrass us. We are too deeply mired in the relativity of all things to risk truth claims. And on the whole we believe that in all of this, our age is one of loss—that we have lost something which the age of Erasmus possessed.

And yet, apparently, there never was a golden age, when learning self-evidently commanded the attention and admiration of the secular world, or, if there was, it was lost by the time of Erasmus. I argue here that Erasmus's European prominence was something in which Erasmus himself made a considerable investment, in terms of effort and imagination. I shall show how masterfully he manipulated the new contemporary media—the supremely illusionistic painting and the printed book (in particular, the volume of published 'familiar letters')—exploiting their sophisticated use for communication in a thoroughly innovative way. In an age for which the idea of an intellectual reputation at a distance was a strange one, or at least one associated almost exclusively with ancient writers and their texts, his command of publishing and printing in particular worked to produce him compellingly outside his own Low Countries milieu. He invented the charisma of the absent professor—the figure who creates awe by his name on the title page, not by his presence in the classroom. The teacher, indeed, who was *never* present (after his earliest, impoverished years, Erasmus never actually taught), but whose presence was evoked in portrait, woodcut, or published collection of personal letters, set alongside the wildly successful, constantly reissued, revised, and re-edited textbooks, translations, and editions.

What made Erasmus's textual self-presentation so enduringly convincing was the virtuoso use he made of richly signifying, reassuringly current, readily available models. Around the figure of Saint Jerome in his study, I shall show, Erasmus built a multidimensional cultural persona, resonating with verbal echoes and visual allusions, a persona wholly compatible with that of the *auctor* on the model of the Church Father or the civic hero of Greece or Rome. This manufactured 'master' presides magisterially over the text, successfully transmitting its message with an illusion of immediacy which belies the fact that the printed book is in every sense a 'copy', not an 'original'. 'Original', indeed, is thereby made to mean 'infused with a transferrable aura of authority, transmitted from worthy model to worthy emulator'—Erasmus in Jerome's study inspires the reader's confidence. The merging of Erasmus with Jerome is achieved so brilliantly, with such consummate cultural skill, that it is little wonder that that image has endured so convincingly down to the present day.

1. Title page of *D. Erasmi Roterodamus . . . lucubrationes* (Strasburg, 1515).

The extraordinary and apparently commanding stature of Erasmus, captured aptly and permanently in the surviving portraits by Metsys and Holbein with which we are still today so familiar, was then, just as it is now, an illusion. Erasmus himself—the historical, as opposed to the figural Erasmus—was a maverick innovator who in his lifetime achieved limited academic recognition and no significant clerical preferment. He was an itinerant producer of textbooks and translations in multiple copies; he rarely kept a home of his own but lived in the houses of printers, and ran a bustling publishing 'workshop' (*officina*). His works were attacked as unorthodox, denigrated as nonaligned, and banned as politically and doctrinally subversive. The enduring image of Erasmus which seems to stand as some kind of reproach to our own contemporary, fragmented intellectual efforts is Erasmus's own evaluation of his achievement, his own statement of the importance and potential reach and influence of his learning. It is not, and was not, the evaluation of the Europe he inhabited.

LINE DRAWINGS OF ERASMUS

There have been many studies of Erasmus, and many studies of the Low Countries humanist milieu which produced him. Indeed, part of the justification I offer for the present study is that for intellectual historians, the very idea of the international man of letters has been developed, sharpened, polished, and eventually internalised as a set of professional aspirations, under the continuous influence of Erasmus studies. Erasmus is the type and figure of the humanistic man of letters, the model for the detached and disinterested pursuit of learning.

The existing scholarly literature centred on Erasmus may be divided into three fields, each with its own focus and interests. The first, and most extensive (certainly in the English language), is the pietistic history of Erasmus and Erasmian humanism, with particular reference to the dawning Reformation, and to the relationship between humane learning and 'new theology'.[2] Alongside this is the considerable body of secular studies of Erasmus, and Erasmian pedagogy, which in recent years has included some masterly detailed work on Erasmus as an original contributor to the trivium subjects of grammar and rhetoric.[3] Finally, the richest field of all, and the one which has most consistently managed to uncover fresh biographical and textual detail, is the strenuously nationalistic and biographical work by the great scholars of Low Countries humanism, led first by de Vocht, and then by Ijsewijn.[4] This last body of work is invaluable for any study of the lasting impact of a movement which was from first to last self-consciously Netherlandish. But its very terms of reference lead it to stop short of giving detailed consideration to the impact of Low Countries humanism on European culture at large.

There have been fewer, but equally meticulous and scholarly, internal studies of that field in intellectual history designated as the 'history of humanist dialectic'. What first drew me into the exploration which the present book elaborates was the discovery that the story of the emergence of a systematic study of ratiocination shaped by the classical tradition recovered by the humanists (a story in which the name of Rudolph Agricola figured prominently) was not one which could be coherently told in isolation, but was crucially interwoven with the story of Erasmus and Erasmian pedagogy.[5] Indeed, the development of dialectic in the curriculum turned out to be interest-loaded in ways which I believe both make better sense of the history of dialectic and shed light on the brilliant way in which in his later years Erasmus self-consciously shaped the intellectual world we still inhabit. Unlike Erasmus studies, this field has attracted little attention outside the history of pedagogy. Whereas work in Erasmus studies is characteristically about innovation and origins, this field, which takes the backbone of the late medieval curriculum, the trivium, as its field of study, is crucially about continuity. It traces the technical developments, manual by manual, and author by author, from high Scholastic logic to 'rhetoricised' humanistic dialectic.[6] Although this work is virtually inaccessible to the nonspecialist, it mounts a vital argument about developing habits of organising thought, and the patterns of reasoning used by the trained mind, which is clearly intended to have repercussions for any informed study of the northern Renaissance. And recently, historians of logic have begun to recast their field to highlight the importance of this study in tracing the emergence of peculiarly modern patterns or habits of thought. In a deliberate effort to oppose the rigid ahistoricity of the 'history' of formal logic, such studies have laid special emphasis on, and devoted particular attention to, Rudolph Agricola's *De inventione dialectica*.[7]

As a contribution to scholarship, the present book tries to move these fields closer together, to create an interdisciplinary space within which the rich possibilities for cross-fertilisation and mutual enrichment can be cultivated. Out of the mingling of materials from those three rich veins I seek to produce a narrative which is both inclusive and historically precise. My strong claim is that the work which follows opens a discourse that can give coherence and a fixed centre to those previously separated areas of study—areas which, in spite of significantly shared themes and preoccupations, have hitherto proved curiously unreceptive to each other's discoveries.

Thus far for the scholarly story, internal to intellectual history, or the history of ideas. But there is another story here, one with larger dimensions, if one is measuring one's undertaking on the scale of that 'world of learning' which includes both the historical past and our own present cultural awareness. What I offer here is an account of the formation of a peculiarly Western European intellectual self-awareness, which I trace back to that moment, in the early decades of the sixteenth century, when both printing and humanist pedagogy came to maturity, and did so within the charismatic, tirelessly productive person of Erasmus of Rotterdam. I judge the emergence of this highly specific cultural consciousness to be a key European moment—a moment at which it became possible to claim that there *was* something which could be designated 'European thought'. It may be, too, that it is easier to focus intellectually upon such a particular kind of Europeanness, at the moment when the very idea of Europe has become at once an official fact and an evident geographical and political fiction. We learn, in other words, how our own intellectual outlook has been shaped, at the moment when it passes itself into history.

The story I tell is one of Erasmus's consummate mastery of his chosen medium, print. The most vivid way I can find to convey the intellectual thrust of this study is to characterise it as uncovering a fully fashioned *portrait*, cunningly contrived, with all the skill of the accomplished artist, on the printed page—the typographical equivalent to the draughtsman's pen and ink. The sitter for this portrait is Erasmus, his portrait the prototype for a new kind of representation, which features the embodied 'man of letters' as a real (rather than a symbolic) figure.[8] It is Erasmus himself who commissions the work and provides its programme: like Holbein's Tudor court portraits of the same period, the final artifact stands somewhere between portrait and self-portrait, shaped by both the imperatives of the commissioner and the skills of the executer.

We recognise the deft conjunction of the real and the figurative, of the compellingly immediate and the contrivedly enduring, when Erasmus's portrait is produced by Metsys, or by Holbein, or by Dürer.[9] We are apparently more reluctant to do so when the lasting monument in pen and ink is produced as type on the printed page. Yet I shall argue that from the texts of the northern humanists of the first two decades of the sixteenth century, particularly from those 'redundant' prefaces, commentaries, editorial asides, and printed *epistolae* which surround the text proper, we can build the 'type'—the original, the archetype—so as to understand the emergence of northern humanism in a new sense. We need to read the print portrait, in other words, as knowingly, and with as much attention to the conventions of reading in the period, as we do the Dürer.

So I am singling out an individual—Erasmus—in an unfamiliar way. I single him out not as a Renaissance 'self' (however fashioned), but as the centre to which a large, specific part of the print-related activities of a much less well known group of authors, *commendatores*, *emendatores*, and *castigatores* was directed.[10] Here is an individual, therefore, whose trace in history is in a strong sense constructed out of those activities.

2. Map of Erasmus's Europe.

PUTTING THE LOW COUNTRIES ON THE MAP

There is a further shift in intellectual attention which I shall ask of the reader: that is, to rescue the historical Erasmus from an intellectual 'no-place', and reposition him on the geographical map. So firmly is Erasmus established as the prototype of the international man of letters that it is difficult to lose the habit of extrapolating the lingua franca of his Latin (and Greek) into an equivalently nonlocalised place of work, without recognisable institutions, customs, loyalties, and preoccupations. This version of the ubiquitous scholar is supported by the graphic representations, in which, as in every other 'scholar' portrait of the period, Erasmus occupies a study full of the portable apparatus of reading and writing (books, pens, sand-shakers, letters, and papers), but without features which identify it as 'in Basle' or 'in Freiburg'.[11]

Indeed, once again I would argue that it is *because* of Erasmus that such a European intellectual community can be imagined at all—that we believe that a united Europe will effortlessly amalgamate its intellectual activites into a wholly integrated, homogeneous whole, without regard for such parochial details as internally structured degree courses, incompatible models for the disciplines, diverse funding organisations, and so forth. Erasmus himself did indeed put considerable effort into reinforcing this illusion of a cohesive world of learning—a world of like minds, not of separate, insular, local institutions. But that was because his model for the dissemination of knowledge was the diffusion of sacred and patristic texts, his role model for the man of letters the revered Father of the Church. As he pointed out in his *Vita Hieronymi*, each country in Europe claimed Jerome as its favoured son.[12]

The scholarly literature tends to vacillate between 'universal man' and 'local hero' versions of Erasmus, the tensions between which generally become apparent only when specialists of different nationalities converge at international conferences. As I acknowledged earlier, Erasmus studies are profoundly indebted to a specifically Low Countries scholarly tradition, which has provided, and continues to provide, vital resources for all students of Erasmus. We have all gathered our understanding from successive generations of scholarly Flemish/Netherlandish or French language volumes, emanating from the Netherlands and Belgium, containing meticulous study of the milieu, the individual practitioners, and the exchange of ideas of the pre-Reformation years.[13] At the same time, a very particularly British version of Erasmus scholarship has flourished since the beginning of this century.[14] The extraordinary riches tucked into footnotes, header notes and appendices, in Allen's twelve-volume *Opus epistolarum Erasmi*, in particular, have meant that English-speaking Erasmus scholars have had for more than fifty years a considerable head start on their European neighbours. Given Erasmus's early association with England, and the impact of Erasmus on the English Reformation, it is an easy matter for English Erasmus scholars implicitly to claim for him life-long Englishness and, certainly, a lifelong affinity with intellectual life on an English model.

At the height of Erasmus's intellectual influence, however, his affil-iations and preoccupations were in many ways strictly those of a native of the Low Countries, though his interests were in no sense parochial. What I have in mind is that in producing the vivid, contentious, attention-grabbing texts with which his printers were able to flood the markets of Europe, Erasmus relied largely on highly specific, local manifestations of the issues with which he was preoccupied, to colour his writing and make vivid his reader's understanding of the issues. It is, that is to say, a distinc-tive strategy of Erasmus's to give his first-person speaker, in whatever form of publication he is producing, a very local habitation.

In the present work, I try to respond to that specificity of location as part of our 'given' for unravelling the argument, but without retreating into meticulous, antiquarian reconstruction. Such explorations are seduc-tive—there is a real thrill to be got from recovering a tiny fragment which alters a local story of events in the distant past.[15] But for the main purpose of my study, here I make an effort to understand what the telling of the tale (in complex ways, and in varieties of types of text) of all that local activity was conceived of as directed *towards*: how the early practitioners of northern humanism self-consciously represented themselves as con-tributing to some larger movement, some development less provincial than simply 'Low Countries'.[16] Outside the Netherlands themselves, I suggest, scholars have not taken sufficiently seriously the textual clues which direct the reader's attention to Louvain, and to a conscious 'mak-ing of intellectual history' that was going on there, under the auspices of Erasmus in particular. So I also incorporate in my story a key *moment* in that Netherlandish history—the first two decades of the sixteenth cen-tury—in a particular geographic location, Louvain, where Erasmus spent his longest continuous period of residence, from 1517 to 1521.[17]

In 1515, retaliating to his attack on Erasmus, Thomas More wrote to Martin Dorp:

> Erasmus' words gave you no pretext for saying (as you do say) that he charges the Louvain theologians with ignorance, much less all the other theologians of the world. He said he could dispense, not with all theologians, of course—he had already said in the same letter that many of them were outstandingly qualified—but only with those theologians (if some happen to fit the descrip-tion, and some certainly do) who have never learned anything but sophistical trifles. Here you interject, 'I think "those theologians" refers to the ones in

Louvain.' Why so, Dorp? As if it were hard to find some theologians of this stamp, or rather this stripe, anywhere in the world? You certainly do have a pretty impression of those in Louvain if you think that they all, and they alone, fit this sort of description, whereas he neither says so nor thinks so.[18]

I suggest that More's response to Dorp here is deliberately (and characteristically) disingenuous: that Dorp was right in believing that the crux of the dispute lay in Louvain (we shall turn to the exact nature of the dispute later), that struggles between the old and the new learning in Louvain had taken on a representative quality whose implications extended beyond the local and parochial. It was not self-aggrandizement which led Dorp to relate a Europe-wide dispute to his own town and its university; rather, it was Erasmus's astute command of printing, and strategic use of the type-set book, which extended the impact of a local debate far beyond the boundaries of the town and its colleges. It was because he understood clearly the terms and nature of the debate that Juan Luis Vives—even though his attack on traditional logic teaching ostensibly focused on the Collège de Montaigu in Paris—began his own contribution, the *In pseudodialecticos*:

> I am forced to commit my thoughts to a letter, because I am not able (by virtue of my commitments here) to leave Louvain, and thus do not know when I shall be able to see you.[19]

Louvain at a certain crucial historical moment is vital for my story, but we shall need to remember that the scholarly resources I use are those which *circulated*—which reached a Europe-wide audience, for whom (as for us) Louvain was merely a name, a place on a map. And *as* a place on the map, I shall maintain that Louvain stood as centrally for the triumph of Erasmus and northern humanism as Wittenberg stood for Luther and the Reformation. When Shakespeare has Hamlet anxious to return to his studies at Wittenberg,[20] or Marlowe has the chorus introduce the intellectually curious Faustus as having studied there, their audiences knew what a weight of near-contemporary ideological freight that reference carried with it. A 'centre', in both cases, is as much a conceptual as a geographical location—a place looked to, a moment recalled as crucial. And its importance is measured not in terms of numbers of participants, nor of sums of money which supported their activities, nor of buildings and facilities, but of the persisting use of moment and location as a reference point for what comes after: in this case, the grounding of the myth of the northern Renaissance, on which the story of the Reformation was ultimately built.

Just as the portrait of Erasmus on which I focus attention is drawn (like the engraved portrait) in black and white, so, like a map, the journey to Louvain is a journey on the printed page.[21] Indeed, the story I have to tell here is almost entirely a story in print: it is the printed sources which have provided me with my portrait and my location, as they echo from classical text to pedagogic treatise, from prefatory letter to dedicatory epistle, from systematic learned gloss to occasional editorial annotation, shared preoccupations, mutual acquaintances, and a collaborative understanding of the shaping influence of the new learning.

MEN OF LETTERS

Fundamental to such explorations of the printed traces of Erasmus and Louvain are the printed exchanges of letters which began to emerge from a number of European presses, under Erasmus's own supervision (and later, to his annoyance, in unauthorised editions), from 1515 onwards.[22] Erasmus's correspondence was extensive and prolific; by 1521 the *Epistolae ad diuersos* volume was advertised on its title page as 'collected out of huge bundles of papers'. In P. S. Allen's definitive twelve-volume edition, these letters have provided the material on which all subsequent work on Erasmus has been built. De Vocht's *Monumenta Humanistica Lovaniensia: Texts and Studies about Louvain Humanists in the First Half of the Sixteenth Century*,[23] still one of the key sources for biographical information for the Louvain circle, opens with a fulsome testimony as to the crucial underpinning of Low Countries humanistic scholarship provided by Allen and his edition of the Erasmus *epistolae*.[24]

One of the things I set out to do in the present work is to reconsider the role of the published letters in establishing Erasmus's portrait for posterity. For, put back into their respective volumes, into physical books which we can handle and weigh as history, Erasmus's letters seem to shed that 'documentary' quality in which Allen evidently believed. The very earliest letters Erasmus published served a nondocumentary purpose, and displayed a motive other than that of simply leaving a record. In August 1515 Erasmus published three carefully constructed letters praising Pope Leo X, and announcing his intention to dedicate his edition of Jerome to him (at least one of these is carefully backdated to suggest that Erasmus's intention is of some duration).[25] The purpose of these letters is a conventional one: they are designed to bring him to the attention of Leo X, and gain his patronage.[26] I shall suggest that—less conventionally—Erasmus's subsequent published volumes of letters are already intrinsically an exercise in self-portraiture, self-consciously engraving the features of the sitter, Erasmus, with consummate skill:

> He even depicts what cannot be depicted [as Erasmus had written of Dürer's engraving] . . . all the characters and emotions; in fine, the whole mind of the man as it shines forth from the appearance of the body, and almost the very voice. These things he places before our eyes by most felicitous lines, black ones

EPITAPHIVM AD PICTAM IMAGINEM CLARISSIMI VIRI
Hieronymi Buſlidiani, præpoſiti Arienſis,& conſiliarij regis Catholici, fratris reue╱
rendiſſimi patris, ac domini Franciſci archiepiſcopi quondam Bizontini, qui Loua╱
nij magnis impendijs inſtituit collegium, in quo publice tres linguæ doceantur. He
braica, Græca, Latina.

marginal note: Collegiũ Lauaſiẽſe
a quo inſtauratum.

IAMBOI TRIMETROI.

Ο᾽ τήρδε γράψας σώματε μορφὴμ καλῶς,
ωφελες ἄγαλμα ζωγραφῶμ κỳ τῳ νοός.
Ε᾽σίδῶμ ἂμ ἔιν πίνακος ἐμ μιᾶϛ πέδῳ,
Α᾽ρετὴν ἀπασῶμ ἐρατὸμ ἐψύϑεμ χορόμ.
Τὴμ εὐσέβεαμ τⱳ ἱερο πρεπῆ πάνυ,
Τὴμ σεμνότητα, τήμ τε σωφροσώὼ ἅμα,
Τⱳ χρησότητα, τⱳ τε παιδ᾽ειαμ καλήμ.
Και ταῦτα κάλλα μόνος ὑπῆρχ ἱερώνυμ
Ο᾽ βυσλιδίακῆϛ οἰκίας σέλας μέγα.

TROCHAICI TETRAMETRI.

Nominis Buſlidiani proximum primo decus,
Ità ne nos orbas, uirenti raptus æuo Hieronyme?
Literæ genus, ſenatus, aula, plebs, eccleſia,
Aut ſuum ſydus requirunt, aut patronum flagitant.
Neſcit interire, quiſquis uitam honeſte finijt.
Fama uirtutum perennis uiuet uſⱥ poſteris.
Eruditio trilinguis, triplici facunda
Te loquetur, cuius opibus reſtituta, refloruit.

THOMAS MORVS PETRO AEGIDIO   SVO S. D.

I chariſſime Petre ſalue: miſere cupio ecquid tu conualeſcas intelligere:
quæ res non minori mihi curæ eſt, quàm quidúis mei: itaⱥ & inquiro
diligenter, & omnes omniũ uoces excipio ſollicitus. Aliquot mihi me╱
liores de te ſpes renunciarunt, ſeu (quod opto) compertas, ſiue ut deſi╱
derijs meis inſeruiant. Scripſi literas Eraſmo noſtro, eas tibi apertas mit
to, ſignabis ipſe. Nihil opus eſt quod illi ſcribitur, clauſum ad te uenire. Verſiculos,
quòs in tabellam tam inſcite feci, ⱥ illa ſcite depicta eſt, ad te pſcripſi. Tu ſi digna ui╱
debuntur Eraſmo imperti, alioqui Vulcano dedas. Vale. VI. Octobris.

Verſus in tabulam duplicem, in qua Eraſmus ac Petrus Aegidius ſimul erãt ex╱
preſſi per egregium artificem Quintinũ, ſic ut apud Eraſmũ exordientem Paraphra
ſin in epiſtolam ad Romanos, picti libri titulos præferrent ſuos, & Petrus epiſtolam
teneret, Mori manu inſcriptam ipſi, quam & ipſe pictor effinxerat.

TABELLA LOQVITVR.

Quanti olim fuerant Pollux & Caſtor amici,
    Eraſmum tantos Aegidiumⱥ fero.
Morus ab his dolet eſſe loco, coniunctus amore,
    Tam propè quàm quiſquam uix queat eſſe ſibi.
Sic deſiderio eſt conſultum abſentis, ut horum
    Reddat amans animum litera, corpus ego.

IPSE LOQVOR MORVS.

Tu quos aſpicis, agnitos opinor
Ex uultu tibi, ſi prius uel unquàm

Viſos

3. Sixteenth-century marginal annotations in the copy of the *Epistolae D. Erasmi Roterodami ad diuersos* (Basle, 1521) in the Princeton University Library.

at that, in such a manner that, were you to spread on colours, you would injure the work.[27]

When we scrutinise such a self-portrait, we need to balance the artist's own sense of composition and impression to be conveyed against the 'evidence' to be found inscribed upon it.

The readiest way to show the impact of the approach I outline here is to offer, at this introductory stage, a worked example of the way in which such a strategic choice of focus recasts the narrative emphasis, and alters the tale told. For this purpose, I take a sequence of printing 'events' in the early career of the Spanish humanist Juan Luis Vives as it intersects with my present story.

Vives has traditionally been presented as a crucial figure in the history of Renaissance thought—and in particular in the history of dialectic—representing a 'Spanish' development of peculiarly humanistic thought, to set alongside Lorenzo Valla's Italian humanism and Petrus Ramus's French.[28] He received his early education in Spain, and then proceeded to an intensive logical training in Paris; in 1520 he published a virtuoso attack on high scholastic logic, the *In pseudodialecticos*, which won the admiration of humanistically inclined scholars across Europe.[29] This text has always been associated with the Erasmus/More circle.[30] But its precise relationship to that circle has puzzled scholars, and they have chosen, in recent years, to concentrate on key technical elements which suggest co-ordinated thinking about how to point up the absurdity for *eloquentia* of scholastic logic training. Indeed, there is a certain irony in the fact that such recent work has devoted much of its attention to explicating technicalities of formal scholastic logic, so as to make clear to the modern reader what it was that humanists so vigorously and insistently *rejected* in contemporary logic teaching.[31]

Vives was neither in Spain nor in Paris but in Louvain when this provocative early polemic of his was published. There he tutored the teenage William of Croy, nephew of the ambassador to Charles V, William of Chièvres, who engineered his appointment as archbishop of Toledo in December 1517.[32] Croy's education at Louvain was in the hands, at one time or another, of Barlandus and Latomus, as well as of Vives.[33] Erasmus's 1519 *Farrago noua epistolarum* (published by Froben at Basle) includes a studied exchange of letters between Erasmus and Croy—textbook examples of teacher/pupil and pupil/teacher letter-writing—in which Croy names Vives as part of his household ('Viues meus'), and in which he ostentatiously acknowledges tutorial help in composing his letter ('Since I thought you might not be able to read my handwriting, I have made use of an amanuensis').[34] Though a Spanish bishop, Croy never in fact set foot in Spain; he died in a riding accident in 1521. Thus Vives's 'Spanish' milieu at this date is actually quite notional—his location both physically and intellectually at this point in his career was Louvain.[35] The *In pseudodialecticos* was published by the Flemish printer Dirk (or Thierry) Martens in Louvain.

However, if we try to flesh out this link between Vives and an Erasmus circle at Louvain by combing the *Opus epistolarum Erasmi* for further evidence from which to piece together Vives's Low Countries 'life', we are quickly disappointed.[36] Instead, we uncover a publicity campaign, designed to bring Louvain and Vives (amongst others) together to the attention of a larger reading public. We begin, indeed, to see that a 'circle' in the world of Erasmus is precisely a collection of named individuals, linked and cross-linked by exchanges of letters and allusions within letters.

In May 1520, More wrote to Erasmus from England, advising him that he had arranged for tuition of Antony of Bergen, formerly a student of Vives's in Louvain, by 'the famous Louvain scholar', Adrianus Barlandus.[37] Barlandus was, apparently, extremely impressed with the boy's learning (already a tribute to his teacher, Vives). Subsequently, More says, Antony of Bergen showed him some of his former teacher's work:

> I have never seen anything more elegant or more learned [than Vives's works]. How often do you find anyone—indeed have you so far ever found even one— who, at such a young age (for you write that he is still young) has so completely mastered the whole orbit of the disciplines? Indeed, my dear Erasmus, it puts me to shame that my colleagues and I pride ourselves on some rather unpolished book or other, when I see Vives, still so young, producing so many works, based on such thorough investigation, in such fluent language, out of such profound reading. . . .
>
> And while there is nothing in all his work that does not afford me surprising delight, certainly what he wrote against the pseudodialecticians fills me with a peculiar pleasure. This is not only (although partly) because he mocks those silly subtleties with witty banter, opposes them with valid arguments and destroys and knocks them off their base with irrefutable reasoning, but also because I find there certain matters treated with almost the same arguments that I once put together by myself when I had not yet read Vives. These please me now in Vives's little book not only because my reasoning amused me before (for we commonly are pleased if we see others assert what had occured to us earlier), but because I am content with myself, being assured that what I suspected I had expressed rather unsuitably was not at all inept, since it also pleased Vives. Now it captivates and delights me especially because when I see that the same argument occupied both our minds and thought, and then was treated in the same way by both—though at greater length and with more elegance by him, still in many cases we not only asserted the same things but also in almost the same words—it is thus the more pleasantly flattering to me, as if our minds were united with each other in thought by some secret force and harmony of kindred stars.[38]

This is a fine piece of formal letter-writing, designed to make the most of the intellectual credentials of Juan Luis Vives. More's letter employs the fiction that Vives is unknown to him, and that it has been necessary for Erasmus to explain in a previous letter how talented the young man was ('for you write that he is still young'). Vives (like Erasmus himself) had taken no formal university degree, and held no university post, so such an introduction is designed to promote Vives's reputation by accumulating printed testimonials from the best print authorities.[39] In other words, it is calculated so as to build a pedigree in print citations as a substitute for diplomas and degrees—in 1517 Vives required a special dispensation from the University of Louvain to teach publicly there, since he lacked a formal qualification.[40]

In fact, More had known Vives for a number of years—possibly well, since both were in Bruges in 1515.[41] In 1517 we find Erasmus writing to More (in a letter published in the *Farrago* volume, whose publication antedates the first publication of the May 1520 letter):

> Send a *Utopia* at the first opportunity.[42] . . . Dorp's letter to which you replied was copied by your people in such a way that the Sibyl herself could not read it; I wish you would send it me less badly written. . . . If Vives has been with you often, you will easily guess what I have suffered in Brussels, where I have had to cope every day with so many Spaniards come to pay their respects, as well as Italians and Germans.[43]

This letter conveniently establishes Vives's association with Erasmus and More at this date—his being part of the 'circle'—and, incidentally, that Vives was moving between the Brussels court and England, as well as teaching in Louvain; it also announces clearly (and publicly, when it appeared in print in 1519) that Dorp's letter attacking Erasmus together with More's unpublished reply were available in multiple copies in circles in which Vives was moving in 1517.[44]

It is not only More who is misleadingly represented in the May 1520 letter as not knowing the young Vives. The 'famous Louvain scholar' Adrianus Barlandus is also represented as somehow remote from Vives: 'The boy's learning pleases the master exceedingly, and when he heard the boy was recommended to me by you [Erasmus], he asked me to let him take the youth'. But Barlandus and Vives had been colleagues and close friends since Vives's arrival in Louvain in 1517. In Barlandus's *Versuum ex poetarum principe Vergilio proverbalium collectanea* (Paris, Aegidius Gourmont, 1517) he recalls:

> In Louvain at that time it seemed to me that our native studies had been somewhat restored, through the diligence of that friend of mine, most learned Latinist, Juan Luis Vives, of Spanish origin, who by his daily teaching awoke the Latin muses there.[45]

At the end of the same volume Barlandus prints a cordial personal letter from Vives, also dating from 1517.[46]

The letter from More to Erasmus, and Erasmus's reply, appeared in print for the first time in late 1520, in a volume of Erasmus's letters collected and edited by Barlandus himself, *Epistolae aliquot selectae ex Erasmicis per Hadrianum Barlandum*. P. S. Allen argues persuasively that this volume was put together with Erasmus's cooperation and approval, as a schoolbook.[47] It appeared eight months or so before the *Epistolae D. Erasmi Roterodami ad diuersos . . . ex ingentibus fasciculis schedarum collectae*,[48] and contained two letters (both to Barlandus himself from Erasmus) never reprinted. Thus it was at once a 'Barlandus' volume (a testimony to Barlandus's own relationship with Erasmus) and a topical (and pedagogic) volume of Erasmus's own. In this context the careful association of Vives with Louvain, More, and Erasmus takes on something of the air of a propaganda exercise, particularly if it is taken together with Erasmus's reply:

> You speak of Luis Vives' gifts, and I am delighted to find my estimate confirmed by yours. He is one of that band of people who will put the name of Erasmus in the shade. But in none of the others do I take such an interest, and I love you all the more for your open-hearted concern for him. He has a wonderfully philosophic mind. The mistress to whom all do sacrifice, but very few with success, he roundly despises; and yet with gifts like his and such learning he cannot fail of Fortune. No one is better fitted to break the serried ranks of the sophists, in whose army he has served so long.[49]

Barlandus's volume of Erasmus's letters (ghosted, at a distance, by Erasmus himself, who supplies him with corrected copies of some of the letters) is among the most carefully contrived of the many such volumes published in Erasmus's lifetime. Ironically, Allen excludes it from his list of definitive editions, whilst including volumes openly put together by Peter Gilles and by Beatus Rhenanus, thus himself (Allen) conniving in the Erasmian fiction of the absent author. Barlandus's prefatory letter clearly indicates that the compilation of letters is his own, in response to a need for such a volume for teaching (this letter too, significant though it is for Erasmus, does not appear in Allen).[50] It extolls both the printer, Martens, and Erasmus himself for their contribution to *bonae litterae* in Louvain:

> Such is the moral purity and ease of Latinity in these letters, that if you were to remove the personages and the name of Erasmus, they could be taken to have been written by Cicero.[51]

The volume is compiled as an epistolary narrative centred on Louvain, and one which promotes key figures (including Vives) as belonging to a community of which Erasmus is the focus. Vives is 'claimed' as associated with this Louvain circle. Specialist texts produced within that circle, associated with debates (like that surrounding humanist dialectic) with intellectual (and particularly pedagogic) repercussions throughout the educated world, can then be claimed as belonging to a 'school' with a (vague and distant) geographical, rather than institutional, affiliation, and a reality only in print—the 'Erasmian school at Louvain'.[52] The *In pseudodialecticos* itself, far from being a spontaneous 'Spanish' response to the intricacies of logic teaching in Paris, begins to look like a work written to order, as part of a carefully orchestrated bid on the part of Erasmus and his associates to establish the seriousness of their claim to displace logical subtlety with *eloquentia*, as the road to truth.

PAROCHIAL POLEMICS WRIT LARGE

Guerlac and others have drawn attention to similarities in tone, phrasing, and argument between the unpublished More letter to Dorp (written by an Englishman in 1515) and the published Vives letter to Fortis (the *In pseudodialecticos*, written by a Spaniard in 1520). More himself, of course, in the letter we have been looking at, has sanctioned (encouraged, even) such observations.[53] From the case we have just been constructing, we can put the matter more strongly: there is an announced affiliation between More's letter and Vives's text, in the form of a suggestion to the readership at large—that 'community', which in the absence of an institutional affiliation is the 'confraternity' of Erasmianism—that Vives has knowledge of More's text, that the two texts share a point of view and a purpose. The 'point' is not to attack Parisian logic; thus the historian of logic's careful scrutiny of the relationship between Vives's text and technical detail of the Paris school misdirects our attention—it identifies the ties but loses the very historical context which the texts are at pains to establish.[54] The point is to stake a claim (in Louvain) for the Erasmians' ability to provide 'grammatical' teaching which can compete with the technical logic of the Schools as a grounding for liberally inclined theology. The appropriate place to look for the 'actual' activities associated with this confrontation is between the faculties of theology and of arts at Louvain (and that, as we shall see, is indeed where we find Dorp's, More's, and Vives's published texts illuminating historical developments).

When the University of Louvain was founded in 1426 it was not permitted to establish a theology faculty, probably in order that it not compete with the University of Cologne. Within a week of the official opening of the university, the town authorities were petitioning the pope to allow its *studium generale* to include theology as a specialist disci-

pline.[55] It was not, however, until 1432 that their application was successful, and a theology faculty on the model of the one at Cologne was established.[56] By the end of the fifteenth century Louvain was a successful and
popular university, competing self-consciously and satisfactorily with its
powerful intellectual neighbours, Cologne and Paris.[57] Nevertheless,
throughout the fifteenth century, the two 'mother' universities of Louvain—Cologne and Paris—exerted considerable influence over both the
structure of the university and its teaching; and part of such influence
consisted in 'a long-standing antagonism between the Faculty of Arts and
the Faculty of Theology and an uneasy co-existence inherited by Louvain
from the University of Paris'.[58]

There is appealing evidence to suggest that the readership of the
printed collections of letters from the Erasmus circle (on which print resources, remember, we have chosen to concentrate our attention) understood that Louvain and its internal disputes were significant beyond the
local boundaries. A copy of the 1521 Frobenius *Epistolae D. Erasmi
Roterodami ad diuersos*, with marginal annotations, survives in the
Princeton University Library.[59] Prominent amongst these annotations are
references to, and identifications of, Louvain as some sort of crux: a focus
which the reader ought to register, and whose signficance he ought to
take.[60]

On page 143 is the following heading to Greek and Latin epitaphs to
Jerome Busleyden, founder of the Trilingual College at Louvain:

> Inscription for the painted picture of the most worthy Jerome Busleyden some-
> time Provost of Aire and Councillor to his Catholic Majesty and Brother to the
> most Reverend Father in God François late Archbishop of Besançon who
> founded in Louvain at great expense a College in which instruction was given
> publicly in the three tongues, Hebrew, Greek, and Latin.[61]

Against it is the annotation 'By whom the College at Louvain was
founded' ('Collegiu[m] Louaniense à quo instauratum').[62] Thereafter a
number of marginal annotations draw attention (in keeping with the prefatory letter's emphasis) to the centrality of Louvain to Erasmus's epistolary enterprise. On page 147, against a passage in a letter to Janus Las-
caris, is the annotation 'he asks [Lascaris] to look for a native Greek
professor for the Louvain Academy' ('Petit Louaniensi Academiae pro-
spiciendu[m] de professore Graeco nato'), while on page 165, against
another letter to Barbirius, written in 1517, on the death of Jerome Busleyden, is the annotation 'Concerning the success of the Gymnasium at
Louvain' ('De successu Gymnasij Louaniensis'), and two pages later,
'Concerning the appointment of a native professor of Hebrew at the
Louvain Academy' ('De professore Hebraeo nato constituendo Academia
Louaniensi [i.e., a converted Jew]').[63] Louvain is a 'context', a location

both for Erasmus's activities and for making sense of his text (we might recall that the collection of letters which was issued immediately before this one, and which derives its content from it and the 1519 *Farrago* volume, was envisaged by Barlandus and his printer as a volume for teaching purposes).[64]

In any case, as so often in humanistic compositions, there are clues liberally scattered in the text of the *In pseudodialecticos* itself, to alert the reader schooled in Latinity to a family resemblance between More's and Vives's *epistolae*. In that first passage I cited from More's letter to Dorp, in which he took issue with Dorp's localising of the dispute to parochial Louvain, More plays on the phrase 'homines eiusdem farinae' (men of the same grain, or ilk), extending it as 'homines eiusdem farina, seu eiusdem potius furfuris' (men of the same grain, or rather of the same bran).[65] Vives self-consciously 'quotes' the same play in his *In pseudodialecticos*:

> But these individuals, though claiming to speak Latin, not only are not understood by men versed in the Latin language, but often not even by men of the same grain, or should I say, bran [ne ab hominibus quidem eiusdem farinae, seu eiusdem potius furfuris].[66]

A kind of paternity is established for More, in the form of a Latin compliment (More as the authority for an unfamiliar Latin usage) from his intellectual offspring. A year later Erasmus commissioned Vives to produce a commented edition of Augustine's *De civitate Dei*.[67]

If we look in this fashion not simply at the printed texts (though always according those our full and serious attention) but also at the interlocutors in an exchange of letters, the date, provenance, and destination, the editor of the volume in which the works appeared, their *commendatores*, who appended verses or prefatory letters, how surviving marginal annotations suggest the text was read, the story alters. The bare text takes on depth and density. It relocates itself amongst other texts, readers, and readings, so as to offer us a fresh orientation on its meaning to us.[68] The young Vives blends into the Louvain moment—when gifted individual humanists, without formal institutional affiliations or qualifications, boldly claimed a stake in education, and particularly in theological training. And two key texts which intellectual history has kept resolutely apart turn out not just to belong together, but to have been produced with the possibility that readers might *detect* that relationship. And although Vives's *is* ultimately a story on a larger scale, this kind of reconstruction of its origins must surely lead us to tell that larger story differently.

This is the kind of story which I shall be tracing in the course of this book. Here, right at the outset, we find that a supposedly maverick piece of virtuosity, historically recontextualised, has become part of a coordinated programme orchestrated by an exemplary figure (already the 'great' Erasmus), with a precise geographical location, at a particular historical moment. The unique individual intellects cherished by traditional History of Ideas remain individualised, but a network of influences in common, shared projects, mutually inhabited spaces, and collaborative understandings casts a different set of shadows. The questions which local circumstances prompt these groups to ask turn out not to correspond to our own questions; the solutions that satisfy them do not necessarily suit us.[69] But a fresh outlook on Erasmus is there for us to seize, if we allow the shadow of his own age, its issues and interests, freely to fall across, and influence, our own.

THE PRINTING HOUSE AS AN AGENT OF CHANGE

I end where I began, with the key significance for Erasmus studies of the growth of publishing and the printed book. Eisenstein's and Lowry's early studies on this subject are by now classic, and the History of the Book is a field all of its own. I do not propose to recapitulate that literature here, nor the burgeoning of that discipline. But having stressed Louvain and location—the importance of the map—I return us now to the crucially textual nature of Erasmus's shaped reputation, and the way its fortunes are inextricably intertwined with those of the publishing houses with which he associated. Specifically, the later chapters of the present work will unravel a series of publishing episodes in which the Froben publishing house at Basle plays a critical role. The shift from Martens's picturesquely Low Countries printshop in Louvain to Froben's smooth operation in Basle perfectly captures the transition, from his middle to later life, in Erasmus's print production. By the 1520s he had mastered the medium, and perfected any number of strategies (some of which we will trace) for maximising his impact on the world of learning. Erasmus's Basle period, I argue here, is a period of deliberate and, in our own terms, highly sophisticated manipulation of the medium of print, its circulation and marketing.

Here once again I find myself on ground largely untrodden by traditional Erasmus scholarship (certainly until comparatively recently). For in order to follow some of the most telling examples of the way in which Erasmus controlled the production and reproduction of his texts, and thereby (to some extent) the cultural production of their meaning, it is second and third editions of individual works we have to look at, second and third printings of individual letters, later emendations, additions to and deletions from key pedagogic works. Conventionally, editors and bibliographers are most concerned with first appearances, first editions, first printings of single items. Or, ironically, it is the *final* version produced in Erasmus's lifetime to which particular significance is given, as in the case of the *Adagia* or the *De copia*.[70] Indeed, as I scoured libraries in England and the United States for versions of Erasmus's works crucial for my story—particularly the monumental collected editions of secular and sacred classical works edited by Erasmus—I often found that it was smaller libraries which yielded me the second edition I needed, while the major rare books library owned only the (much more valuable) first edition. Similarly, Allen's great compilation of Erasmus's letters makes it extremely simple to identify the first appearance in print of a letter (including, for example, the folio or page reference for that first printing), more difficult to follow where that letter subsequently appeared, and together with what other letters, reprinted or new. But in the case of both Erasmus's *Lucubrationes* of Seneca, and his *Epistolae* of Jerome, it is the *second* edition which turns out to be of vital importance for understanding Erasmus in the sense in which I try to do so here.

There is, I think, a good reason for this. I do not think that Erasmus thought of any of his works as 'definitive' or fixed, in the sense that a modern author might piously hope to have said the (or at any rate, her or his) last word on any subject. Like all good editors, he set considerable store by the accuracy with which a printer produced the text as delivered to him, and the skill with which the printing house subeditors and correctors read the proofs and tidied up the presentation. But beyond that, no work retained for long that fixed and static form which print and a binding apparently, briefly gave it. In spite of the illusion of a detached magisterial figure, isolated in his authorship, Erasmus worked at the centre of an increasingly extensive group of junior editors, pupils, *famuli* and admirers. Each newly issued text became the basis for further, collaborative attention, repersonalising and revivifying the 'dead letter' of the printed page. Master and *famuli* work over and around the text, correcting, adding marginal notes, deleting irrelevances, debating among themselves. The individual volume becomes a personalised copy, a localised classroom; the outcome of reading is a further production (the printed text, its marginal annotations, and, sometimes, looseleaf insertions), from the master-reader Erasmus's *officina*, or workshop.[71]

There is an example of just this kind of 'dialoguing' with, or interrogating, his own text in a copy of the 1522 Froben edition of Erasmus's collected *Apologiae* (*Apologiae Erasmi Roterodami omnes, aduersus eos, qui ullum locis aliquot, in suis libris, non satis circunspecte sunt calumniati*), presently in the *Adversaria* collection in the Cambridge University Library.[72] Throughout the volume, Erasmus and his *famulus* have interacted with the printed text, correcting typographical errors and errors of punctuation, altering page headings and names to clarify the text and the debate it contains.[73] Erasmus expostulates afresh against his adversaries in marginal outbursts; he and his *famulus* add further evidence in support

sententiarū libro tertio.diſtinctione tertia§. Mariá quoꝗ.Poſt con⸗
ſenſum,in quit,ſanctæ uirginis,ſpirituſſanctus ſuperuenit in ipſam,ſe
cundū uerbum domini.quod dixit angelus,purgans ipſam,& poten⸗
tiam deitatis uerbi receptiuam,præparans, ſimul autem & generati⸗
uam. Et tunc obumbrauit ipſam dei altiſſimi per ſe ſapientia & uirtus
exiſtens,id eſt,filius dei,patri homuſios .i. conſubſtantialis, ſicut diui⸗
num ſemen, & copulauit ſibīipſi,ex puriſſimis ipſius uirginis ſanguini
bus,noſtræ antiquæ cōſperſionis carnem, animatam anima rationali
& intellectiua,non ſeminans,ſed per ſpiritum ſanctum creans.Hacte⸗
nus Ioannis Damaſceni uerba recenſuimus. Ad quæ licet non reſpon
deat adamuſſim noſtrū comentū,mihi tamen ſatis eſt, quod hic quo⸗
que per allegoriam fit alluſio ad ea quæ fieri ſolent in coitu coniugali.
Expoſcitur aſſenſus,præparatur uis cōceptiua & generatiua illapſu di⸗
uini ſpiritus, fit mentio diuini ſeminis, opifex ſpiritus hoc agit in hac
cœleſti conceptione,quod in alijs agit ſemen uirile, qui uelut actus eſt
in conceptu,Sed horret Leus dici quicꝗ fuiſſe uice maſculini ſeminis,
in ea cōceptione. Atqui cū legimus: Qđ in ea natū eſt,de ſpiritu ſan⸗
cto eſt,nóne perinde ſonat,quaſi dicas:nō eſt ex uirili ſemine,qđ tu ſu
ſpicaris,ſed ex ſpiritu ſancto? Nōne ſpiritū ſanctū oppoſuit ſemini ui
rili? Rurſus in hymno quē canit chorus eccleſiaſticus:Non ex uirili ſe
mine,ſed myſtico ſpiramine:palā idē fecit Prudētius.Impiū exiſtimat
Leus dicere quicꝗ illic fuiſſe ſeminis maſculini uice.At qd aliud ē hoc
dicere,ꝗ negare illic fuiſſe ſemen maſculinum,ſed quod in uulgaribus
cōceptibus iuxta naturæ curſum efficit ſemen uiri:hoc in Maria ſupra
naturæ ordinem effeciſſe ſpiritū ſanctū/Quæſo te lector, quid hic eſt
quod debeat caſtas aures offendere? Imò quid non potius dignū illo
cœleſti coniugio? At non placet Leo,quod κεχαριτωμένη Græcis ſonat
gratioſam,aut unice charā.Eſt enim participiū à uerbo χαριτόω, quod
eſt gratioſā facio. Sed χαριτόω inquit in meo lexico eſt, gratia impleo.
Quid facias ſi ſic habet lexicū Lei, quod ſuo ære mercatus eſt? Non
opinor licebit refragari.Atqui Homerus Achillē ſic loquentē facit ada
mato ſuo Patroclo ἐμῷ κεχαριςμένε θυμῷ,ſimili nimirū uoce uſus. Dein
de ſtomachatur quod ſibi obijciam Græcum uocabulum,cum proba
bile ſit angelū Hebraice loquutū.Demus iſtud,aut ſi mauult Syriace,
ſed ego tantū tribuo Lucæ,ut uoce illā qua uſus eſt angelus, bona fide
reddiderit Græce,niſi negabit Leus Lucā Græce ſcripſiſſe euangeliū.
Tandē his non ſatis fiſus Leus,ait ſe citaſſe,ut legit eccleſia, cui plus tri
buit, ꝗ Græco meo. Quæſo te lector qs poſſet hæc abſꝗ riſu legere?
An meū Græcū eſt, qđ ſcripſit Lucas?An quod legit eccleſia Latina,
utcūꝗ

4. A page from the copy of the *Apologiae Erasmi Roterodami* (Basle, 1522) in
the *Adversaria* collection at Cambridge, with Erasmus's autograph additions.

of Erasmus's case from texts which they have apparently recently read or reread, on Erasmus's behalf; the *famulus* expands his arguments and deletes imprecise or verbose points made previously.[74] Possibly Erasmus envisaged a further edition, but we should, in my view, understand that this need not be the case.[75] Here is Erasmus as reader and active responder to his own work, vigorously keeping his printed text open and alive, trying to prevent the living text from sliding into dead textbook.[76]

Erasmus, I have come to think, asked a great deal from at least the best of his early readers. He expected them discerningly to follow the trails he laid, to appreciate and take pleasure in the textual deceptions, diversions, entertainments, instructions with which he packed his published works. He anticipated his readers' taking time to read, putting effort into that reading, pursuing his ideas in successive recensions and editions of single texts. We owe him the same kind of expectation of difficulty, with the same determination to follow him through to the text's resolution (for it will resolve). If my reader derives even half as much pleasure from reading these exercises in detection as the pleasure I got from the detective work itself, I shall be well content.

CHAPTER ONE

'A better portrait of Erasmus will his writings show': Fashioning the Figure

WHOSE BOOK? THE QUENTIN METSYS DIPTYCH OF ERASMUS AND PETER GILLES

Early in 1517, Erasmus wrote from Antwerp to Thomas More in London:[1]

> Peter Gilles and I are being painted on the same panel, which we intend shortly to send you as a gift. On my return here, however, I found Peter seriously— indeed, dangerously—ill with some indeterminate sickness, from which even now he has not entirely recovered; as far as the portrait was concerned, this was extremely inconvenient. I myself was in excellent health; but somehow the physician took it into his head to tell me to take some pills to purge my bile, and the advice he foolishly gave me I even more foolishly agreed to take. My portrait had already been begun; but after taking the medicine, when I went back to the painter, he said it was not the same face, and so the painting has been put off for several days, until I look more cheerful.[2]

The joint gift was finally dispatched in September 1517, and More wrote letters of thanks to both donors (who had paid equal shares of the cost of the work). To Gilles he sent a verse tribute (verses which he described as 'as clumsy as the painting is masterly'). The first part of this is a six-line epigram, in the persona of the diptych itself, celebrating the ardent friend-ship between Erasmus and Gilles, as there depicted, and between Erasmus, Gilles, and More, as made vivid by their correspondence.[3] The second, in More's own persona, plays elaborately on the conjunction of portrait-likeness, reproduced handwritings, books and letters, as combin-ing to make the figures recognisable:

> I am confident you will recognise those you see represented here, even if you only saw them once in the past. If you do not, the identity of the first will be revealed to you by the letter which he holds; the other, to enlighten you, is writing his own name; and in any case, even were he not doing so, the inscribed books, which are famous, and read worldwide, will be able to enlighten you . . .

The letter closes with a further enthusiastic outburst on More's part on Metsys's virtuosity in depicting, as it were, the *writing* of the writers:

My dear Pieter, marvellously as our Quintin [Metsys] has represented everything, [your portrait] shows above all what a wonderful forger he would have
made! He has imitated the address on my letter to you so well that I do not
believe I could make a better job if I tried to repeat the original inscription
myself. And so, unless he wants it for some purpose of his own, or you are
keeping it for your own ends, do please let me have the letter back: it will
double the effect if it is kept handy alongside the picture. If it has been lost, or
if you have a use for it, I will see whether I in my turn can imitate the man who
imitates my hand so well.[4]

In spite of the modest disclaimer, this letter and its verses were clearly
intended as a public tribute, and were published the following year.[5]
  Meanwhile, More wrote privately to Erasmus:

Truly, even though this may be a proud thought, I judge it to be thus. I esteem
what you have sent me to mean that you would wish to revive the memory of
yourself in my mind, not just daily, but hourly. You know me so well that I
need not labour to prove to you that although I am not without many short-
comings, nevertheless, I am far from being a common braggart. Yet to tell the
truth, there is one craving for glory I cannot shake off, and I marvel at how
sensuously and sweetly it appeals to me. It is when the thought comes to me
that I shall be commended to the most distant ages because of the friendship of
Erasmus, as testified to by the letters, the books and the pictures, as testified to,
indeed, in every way.[6]

A more fanciful, public offering was published in the 1518 *Auctarium*
volume of Erasmus's letters, however, forming a matching pair with the
letter to Gilles and its verse tribute:

I am delighted that my little verses on the painting pleased you. Cuthbert Tunstall thought the hendecasyllables more than passable, he was lukewarm about
the six-liner. A certain inconsequential monk [fraterculus quidam], however,
dared to take exception to my linking the two of you together as Castor and
Pollux. He said that you ought rather have been joined as Theseus and Pirithous, or as Pylades and Orestes, who were as you are intimate friends one to
the other, not brothers. Since I could not stand the monk, even if he spoke the
truth, I replied to his good intention with a bad epigram, as follows:
    Wishing to show two friends in little verses to be the greatest of mutual
  friends, I had said that they were such as Castor and Pollux once were. 'Your
  comparison of brothers with friends is inept' rejoined a trifling monk [frater-
  culus]. 'What,' I said, 'Is there any closer kind of friendship than that between brothers?' My interlocutor laughed scornfully at such ignorance of
  the obvious on my part, and said, 'In our large and crowded monastery there
  are more than two hundred brothers, but I wager you anything that amongst
  those two hundred you will not find two brothers who are mutual friends!'[7]

The diptych to which this correspondence refers will be familiar to anyone who has ever picked up a volume of Erasmus's selected works or read one of the popular biographies. For the Metsys Erasmus panel alternates with Holbein's portraits to provide the standard likeness of the great scholar, regularly reproduced as book jacket or frontispiece. Together with Albrecht Dürer's engraving and Hans Holbein's late portraits, Metsys's painting has been the subject of a whole sequence of art-historical articles and monographs, whose focus is sometimes Erasmus himself, sometimes Thomas More, and sometimes the genre of scholar-portraits itself.[8]

The exchange of letters between intellectual friends 'frames' the diptych, which is itself a tribute to, and token of, that friendship. The letters provide a setting, an occasion, and a collection of harmonising sentiments which give the graphic representations additional meaning. They contrive an atmosphere of vivid excitement; they dramatise a flurry of delighted exchanges which supposedly attended the transportation from Antwerp to London (via Calais) of the double portrait. The letters—prominently and repeatedly reprinted thereafter—concentrate their own and the reader's attention on the lasting significance of the gift 'likeness' which Desiderius Erasmus and Peter Gilles offer Thomas More. Is what is figured on the wood panels with such consummate skill a permanent record of a particularly humane friendship? Or is it rather an enduring monument to Erasmus, 'man of letters'—a figure whose memorable qualities are those of the Master (*pedagogus* to perpetual student onlookers), the technically superlative translator, editor and circulator in print of the treasures of ancient secular and sacred learning?

I highlight such questions in order to begin to try to revive for us a sense of how thoroughly remarkable it is that the figure of Erasmus should so fully have formed our conception of the European teacher and man of letters. So strongly has Erasmus marked the 'humanities' or the 'liberal arts' that we fail to recognise the strangeness and unfamiliarity of the original figure he shaped in the years around 1520—we miss the virtuoso command of the media he displays as he models graphic and printed representations to his purposes. By 1520, Erasmus was over fifty, and a certain recognisable sort of scholarly 'fame' (academically circumscribed, geographically restricted) was already securely his. He was, that is to say, already a famous intellectual figure in the Low Countries. Yet the self-conscious programme of the gift-portraits, their studied publicising in the accompanying artful letters, suggests that he envisaged some kind of fame on a yet larger scale, with a yet more extensive reach (geographically, and in terms of its duration).

My suggestion is that he aspired to something more like the renown traditionally accorded only to the major ancient authors and teachers of secular and sacred texts—the international acclaim and recognition accorded to a Seneca or a Jerome. We fail to notice the extraordinary presumptuousness of this aspiration on Erasmus's part only, I think, because in the end he was so entirely and consummately successful. The care with which Erasmus composed his version of himself as symbol of enduring success in the domain of 'letters' (or *bonae litterae*), out of available cultural models of timeless, universal scholarly and spiritual achievement, has shaped our own version almost entirely. It has so permeated our understanding of the effectiveness and impact of learning that for centuries since, academics in the humanities have taken it for granted that our professional practice—the professional practice of reading, commenting, and editing—is a source of, and means of access to, limitless power and influence in a world which values our undertakings.[9] Learning elevates individual thought into universal significance, it knows no national boundaries, it can influence world events, it can shape and make political outcomes.[10]

Erasmus's letter to More is studiedly disingenuous about the art of the portrait painter. Quentin Metsys cannot go on with the portrait of Erasmus which he has already started because Erasmus's voluntary purging has left him looking unwell. The sittings cannot continue until Erasmus is once more 'himself'—once more fits the image of himself which Metsys has begun to fix.[11] This little anecdote (much quoted by Erasmus biographers) makes vivid a particular type of resemblance which is to be Erasmus's gift to More—an exact physical likeness, the likeness of *now*, a precious treasure to be sent posthaste to the friend who regrets his absence. We may compare this letter and its anecdote with another intimate exchange of letters, similarly charged with affection, more than ten years later, between Erasmus and Margaret Roper, More's eldest, and intellectually gifted, daughter. That exchange is also about a portrait (or rather, a sketch for a portrait), this time Hans Holbein's group portrait of the More family:

> I can hardly express to you, Oh Margaret Roper, ornament of your native Britain, the deep pleasure I experienced when the painter Holbein set before me the portrait of your entire family. It has captured your likenesses so well that if I were personally with you I could hardly have seen more clearly. How often do I find myself wishing that just once more before I die I could see that group of friends who are so dear to me, and to whom I owe, in large part, my social standing and my fame. (At least I would rather be indebted to you than to any other living soul.) That wish has in large part been granted by the good office of the expert hand of the artist. I have been able to meet and recognise you all once more, and none better than you. I have even believed that I could discover, through that beautiful exterior, the reflection of your yet more beautiful soul.

I congratulate you all on your good fortune, and above all your most dear father.[12]

To which Margaret Roper replied:

We have learned with joy and with infinite gratitude that the arrival of the painter gave you so much pleasure, because he was the bearer of the portrait he had done of my parents and the entire family. Our deepest desire is to see our tutor again one day, and to be able to talk again to him—he whose learned works have taught us everything that we know, he who is also the true and long-standing friend of our father.[13]

In both of Erasmus's letters, intimate friendship is represented as a pleasure taken in a precise physical rendering of the absent friend. The gift he and Gilles offer Thomas More is to be an enduring testimony to the closest of personal commitments; it requires that the representation of the donors be a perfect physical copy of the friends the recipient has known in intimate detail. The sketch of the More family which Holbein brings at Erasmus's request is able, in the meticulous rendering of its originals, to evoke and reawaken the very same deep feelings of affection as their physical presence.[14] And yet, of course, the rhetorical point of such claims is their evident contrivedness—the extent to which the echo of Pliny can be heard behind the extravagant claims for the artist's copy of the real.[15]

In strong contrast, Thomas More's verse response to Gilles focuses not on the bodily but on the textual trace of the friendship—the written instructions in the composition which permit correct identification of the sitters, preserving their memory for posterity:[16]

THE PAINTING SPEAKS

I represent Erasmus and Gilles as as close friends as once were Castor and Pollux. More, bound to them by as great a love as any man could entertain for his own self, grieves at his physical separation from them. So the measure they took, in response to the yearnings of the absent friend, was that loving letters should make their souls present to him, and I [the painting] their bodies.[17]

There is a deliberate distinction being made here between levels of memorial representation. Affectionate letters transport souls to remote locations, paintings make present bodies. And a play is being made on *amans*: the letters are 'loving', yet love yearns for bodies; letters vividly yield 'souls', paintings only the shadowy illusion of (inferior) bodies. This is a formulation we will find cropping up repeatedly in the story this study traces—the compelling yet illusory ability of graphic representation to capture the individual; the extraordinary power of writings to convey the mind, the soul of the great man: 'A better portrait of Erasmus will his

5. Portrait of Peter Gilles by Quentin Metsys.

writings show', as the inscription runs on Metsys's medal representation of Erasmus, and on Dürer's classic engraving.[18]

'Letters' (*litterae*) convey souls, and provide enduring memorials. Images provoke affection, capture the imagination, and are shadowy and enigmatic. In the same letter from More to Gilles, More maintains that the *letter* in Gilles's hand identifies the sitter more securely than his physical traits. While the bodily resemblance can be recognised only by those who have seen the sitters (even if only once), the faithfully forged letter lastingly and precisely records the friendship in a form which can be 'read' by everyone, for all time. And to emphasise that graphic representation as the interpretative centre of the painting, More elaborates on the artifices by means of which he will stun admirers with the virtuosity of the technique which ensures its lasting significance (the retrieved letter set alongside the panel, or More's own forgery of the original set alongside the painterly forgery).

And yet, of course, here too the careful contrivedness of the rhetoric hoodwinks us. It is not writing per se which transports minds and ensures recognition of souls. Like the bodies of the sitters, their handwritings and that of their absent friend are recognisable only to those who know them well. Indeed, the inscription on the letter Peter Gilles holds makes this point elegantly:

V[iro] Il[lus]trissimo Petro / Egidio Amico charissimo / Anverpiae [or Anverpiis].

To that most illustrius man, Peter Gilles, dearest friend, of [or at] Antwerp.[19]

This inscription clearly identifies the *sitter*, in a manner which can be paralleled in other Flemish paintings.[20] The sender of the letter is only 'plain' for someone who can recognise his *handwriting* (and who, indeed, stands close enough to the panel to make that hand out).[21] To any other viewer it is simply a letter to Gilles, and indeed, in the context of the pair of panels (and this is a point to which I shall return shortly), it is most readily interpreted as a letter from Erasmus—famous conductor of a worldwide epistolary correspondence.[22]

The Gilles panel is indeed laden with visual 'clues' which link him much more securely with Erasmus than with More. Behind him, the titles on the books on the shelves identify him not simply as a man of learning but, more specifically, as an up-to-date reader of Erasmus:[23] Plutarch in Latin, Suetonius, Seneca's *Tragedies*, Quintus Curtius, the *Education of a Christian Prince*.[24] One might go further and suggest that the titles identify the sitter as a *student* reader of Erasmus—the titles are all pedagogic works; the somewhat artificial use of Greek transcription for two of the titles (the Plutarch and the *Education of a Christian Prince*) comply with an Erasmian programme of pedagogy grounded in both Greek and Latin. The relationship which the panel therefore clearly defines is not one with the sender of the letter he holds (Thomas More), but with the writer of the books which surround him, Desiderius Erasmus. And although Erasmus had just published his two major contributions to contemporary theology (his *Novum Instrumentum* and his four-volume edition of Saint Jerome's *Letters*), and is shown at work on his first biblical paraphrase, the books which surround Gilles contribute to a representation of a teacher, rather than a theologian or editor. Here is Erasmus *magister*, the *praeceptor obseruantissimus* (most attentive of teachers) of Gilles's most extravagent epistolary salutations.[25]

This still leaves open the question of the ornately bound book under Peter Gilles's hand. For surely the positioning of this book is deliberately designed to invite us to want to ask the question, What book is it? The book is closed; it is elaborately bound, with worked metal clasps; the book protrudes beyond the table edge, thus out of the frame of the painting, towards the viewer (as originally the cup on the shelf behind Gilles did, also).[26] But most strikingly, Gilles points at this book with a ringed index finger.[27] The only reason why art historians have not made more of this gesture, I think, is that Gilles does not look at the book but out of the frame of the picture. But I shall return to that in a moment.

In the Longford Castle panel this book is inscribed *Antibarbari* (in Greek letters) along its outer edge. Erasmus's *Antibarbari* was not published until 1520 (although written much earlier), and Lorne Campbell and others consider therefore that 'the title in the portrait may well be a later addition'.[28] It might be argued that Erasmus had written the *Antibarbari* in 1500, for his paying students in Paris, and that although technically unpublished, it was an extremely appropriate choice to represent the teacher/student relationship.[29] Indeed, Gilles refers to Erasmus as his 'teacher',[30] and the gesture he makes to the book with a ringed forefinger might indicate this very work as one of their exercises.

In the Antwerp copy of the Gilles panel, the book under Gilles's right hand is the only one carrying an inscription, and this reads 'CIS ERAS. R.', a fragment of an inscription, on the basis of which the book has been identified as the *Querela pacis*. On the face of it, this is a plausible identification for the volume, as linking both the two sitters for the panels and the person for whom the gift-panels are executed:

> The first edition of [More's] *Utopia* appeared at Louvain in December, 1516, without [More's] epigrams. This edition was soon exhausted, and as early as May 30, 1517, Erasmus was writing to More that he had sent *Utopia* to Basel to be reprinted, along with the epigrams and with his own *lucubrationes*. Just what these *lucubrationes* represented in his mind at this time is uncertain. In

July he referred again to having sent More's works to Basel. But there were delays. On August 23 he wrote to Froben in Basel urging haste in printing what he had sent 'and especially that More's writings may be diligently prepared'. On the following day he wrote to Angst, a member of Froben's staff, saying that he wished More's *Utopia* and *Epigrammata* to be commended by a preface from the hand of Beatus Rhenanus. Apparently, the *lucubrationes* continued to increase in number, for in December Froben finally brought out a volume of miscellaneous works by Erasmus (headed by his new piece, "Querela pacis") which ran to 643 pages. The Table of Contents included, as the last items, More's two works and Erasmus's *Epigrammata*; but on page 644 there is a notice to the reader by Froben saying that the book has become too large and that he will publish the last three pieces in a separate volume as soon as possible. At last, a year and a half after the first reference to them in More's letter, the *Epigrammata* appeared in print in March 1518, along with *Utopia* and Erasmus's epigrams.[31]

Thus in 1517, the *Querela pacis* inscription might appropriately have designated—under the hand of Gilles—a volume 'in press', in which Erasmus's and More's works appeared together (like the Lucian volume on the shelf behind Erasmus). There are, however, difficulties with this identification (leaving aside the fact that it depends on a version of the painting generally acknowledged to be a copy). The most obvious one, I think, is that gesture of Gilles's. What has *Gilles* to do with this Froben volume? Insofar as Gilles was personally associated with Erasmus-More volumes, it was in his capacity as editor and *castigator* for Martens at Louvain.[32]

In the twinned Erasmus panel, the 'handwritten' inscription also determines—in yet more virtuoso fashion than the More 'letter' does in the Gilles—the identity of the sitter. As the authors of the definitive article on the diptych write, the words on the page before the sitter 'are written in a close imitation of Eramus's own hand'.[33] The inscription reproduces the opening words of Erasmus's *Paraphrase of St. Paul's Epistle to the Romans*:

(IN) EPISTOLAM (AD) RO
(M)ANOS PARIPHRASIS
ERASMI ROTERO
DAME
PAulus ego ille e Sau
lo factus, e turbulen
te pacificus, nup[er] obnox
(ius) legi mosaice. nunc
Moisi Liber(t)us. seruus au
tem factus Iesu.[34]

6. Portrait of Erasmus by Quentin Metsys.

(In case posterity should fail adequately to note this, a letter of Erasmus's to Gilles, published in the *Farrago* in 1519, prompts: 'The paraphrase which I had started in our pictures is now finished, and has begun to be printed'.)[35] And here too the titles on the shelved books identify the scholar-sitter to a somewhat wider audience (though still only those who are already familiar with the figure *as* a famous author): 'HIERONYMUS' (Jerome), 'LOVKIANOS' (Lucian), 'NOVUM TESTAMENT[VM]' (New Testament), 'MOR[IAE ENCOMIVM]' (*Praise of Folly*).[36] As Thomas More writes in his verses to Gilles: even if the identity of the sitter escaped the viewer, 'the inscribed books, which are famous, and read worldwide, will be able to enlighten you'.[37]

Erasmus's editions of Saint Jerome's letters and his New Testament had both been published in 1516. The Lucian and the *Moriae encomium* compliment the recipient of the panel-gift: Erasmus and More had jointly published translations of Lucian's dialogues in 1506, and the punning title of the *Praise of Folly* was (as is well known) a tribute to the two men's close friendship. So whereas in the Gilles panel the inscribed books *set up* a figural relationship between Gilles (identified by his letter) and Erasmus (whose books they all are), in the Erasmus panel the books *frame* the seated figure, redoubling and confirming his identity as theologian-scholar-writer.

Once we are alert to the self-consciousness of the composition, it becomes possible to 'read' it in a fresh way. The book in which Erasmus writes is, after all, elaborately a fiction. He writes the (published) paraphrase of Paul by hand—in that identifiable, forged simulation of Erasmus's own hand. But the published volume is, precisely, a copy of an original, a print reproduction of a hand, a bound replica of an autograph manuscript which was certainly not (if it was to be conveniently handled by the printer) in a bound volume. Once again the 'realism' of the panel misleads the viewer: Erasmus 'writes' his paraphrase, literally, into the volume as if to validate the authenticity of the circulated, printed product. What the reader purchases, far from the presence of the author (and then himself has bound), is represented as produced for him, into his book, by the hand of the author himself.

If at this point we stand back, as it were, from the panels, I think we begin to see what is causing some of the difficulty in 'reading' the visual clues with which they are so liberally provided. There are at one and the same time two single panels and one combined panel. The single panels apparently announce first the physical traits and memorial presence of the individual sitters, and then (less emphatically) a relationship of each sitter with Thomas More (the recipient of the individual, equal gifts, whose cost, they insist, is shared equally between them);[38] the combined gift-diptych, on the other hand, announces a relationship *between the panels*. It is at the altered significance when the two panels are linked as one that we should now look.

The shelves which hold the lovingly detailed books in the two panels are one and the same shelves: they join where the panels are set side by side.[39] The shadows thrown (on the edges of the books and by chalice and scissors/wick-trimmer) imply a single source of light, illuminating the two figures.[40] So when the panels are joined as a diptych, Erasmus and Gilles sit facing one another in a single study-room, at a single desk-table, before an alcove laden with Erasmus's works. As if to insist that something special happens when the separate portraits become a pair, that exaggeratedly foregrounded sandbox in front of Gilles, which we are told (when the Gilles panel stands alone) is the emblem of Gilles's office as town clerk of Antwerp) becomes, suddenly, *Erasmus's* sandbox. Since he is portrayed in the act of writing, with reed pen in hand and ink at his side, the sandbox completes his writing tools. Similarly (if less dramatically), the covered cup behind Gilles (also, we are told, symbol of his office) becomes a covered chalice or goblet placed exactly midway along the bottom of the alcove—a symbol of favour and shared affection between the two figures (or possibly among the three figures; the chalice protrudes forwards out of the panel, over the edge of the shelf, towards More, the recipient of the gift-diptych).[41]

When the panels are united, we have a fresh composition—a teacher and his pupil, a pair of friends, a letter writer and one of his familiar correspondents. Now the representation is of *amicitia* (friendship), in the deepened, classical sense—a relationship of intimacy, trust, and mutual service, captured in the literary heritage with the stories of Theseus and Pirithous, Pylades and Orestes. The graphic representation of intimate friendship is bestowed *in* friendship on the third member of the trio—Thomas More—as token *of* friendship—testifying to 'the most distant ages' the friendship of Erasmus. And at the centre of this testament to friendship rests a book.

The book at which Gilles gestures with his forefinger, in its ornamental binding, occupies the centre of the diptych. Erasmus's eyes are fixed on it (while Gilles's eyes are fixed on Erasmus). It, like the chalice, protrudes forwards, over the edge of the desk-table, towards More, the recipient. In the isolated Gilles portrait it may indeed be any appropriate volume associated with a scholar-student admirer of Erasmus (identified as Gilles by the letter he holds)—either the *Antibarbari* or the *Querela pacis* fits the bill. In the diptych, however, it seems to me irresistible to identify this book as More's *Utopia*, a book with which both Erasmus and Gilles are closely associated—closely enough associated for Gilles to indicate it with an almost proprietorial gesture. More's *Utopia* was seen through Thierry Martens's press in Louvain, in November/December 1516, by Peter Gilles (one of Martens's editors and proof correctors), under the auspices of Erasmus (who regularly published with Martens)—a symbol indeed of the three men's *amicitia*.[42] That symbolic reference is echoed in the diptych: the gazes and gestures of the two linked sitters move the viewer's attention from Erasmus to the book on which he focuses his attention; the book is linked by the demonstrative gesture with the younger, deferentially posed man, whose gaze in turn is fixed on the master, Erasmus.[43]

The gift-diptych is linked—chronologically, geographically, and, as it were, emotionally—with the first edition of More's *Utopia*, published at Louvain in 1516.[44] Not only was Peter Gilles a protagonist in More's fiction, and the addressee of the dedicatory letter which carefully links 'real' life with Hythlodaeus and the occasion of the fiction, but Gilles was involved in the production of the volume at the Martens press to the point of contributing the translation of the 'Utopian' prefatory verses, and at least some of the marginal annotations, for Thierry Martens's publishing house, which produced the volume (and for which, during this period, Gilles regularly did editorial work).[45]

> For the rest, there is nothing I can add to what [More] has written. There was only a poem of four lines in the Utopian vernacular which, after More's departure, Hythlodaeus happened to show me. This verse, preceded by the Utopian alphabet, I have caused to be added to the book. I have appended also some brief annotations in the margins.[46]

The joint portrait project was embarked on immediately after the joint publishing project (*Utopia*). Indeed, one might want to ask whether the search for a suitable artist to provide the woodcut map of Utopia in the 1516 *Utopia* might not have put Gilles and Erasmus in touch with Metsys—a native of Louvain, working in Antwerp.[47] It is hard to imagine that the Metsys diptych is not linked in some way with the publishing history of *Utopia*, and equally hard to resist a 'reading' of the ornate volume, which symbolically links the two panels of the diptych, *and* the recipient of the gift (as it protrudes from the canvas, over the table edge towards him), as a *Utopia*.

PRESENTATION COPIES AND COPIES OF LETTERS

At least one such ornately bound copy of the first edition of *Utopia*, belonging to a member of the close inner circle of friends to which Gilles and Erasmus also belonged, survives. This is a fine copy of the 1516 Louvain edition of *Utopia*, in the Yale University Library. It is bound with other works published between 1508 and 1514 in Reggio, Paris, and Vienna, in an elaborate, near-contemporary Netherlands binding of calf over oak boards. The autograph inscription on the title page of the *Utopia*, the first work in the volume, reads: *Sum Tunstalli* (I am Tunstall's book). These words appear again at the beginning of each of the subsequent works in the volume.[48] It is not difficult to imagine such a precious 'friendship' copy of *Utopia* lying on the table in Metsys's studio, alongside the gift-diptych, just as More imagines his original letter to Gilles lying alongside that same diptych, as it occupies pride of place in the More household. We are meant to keep our gaze fixed upon the book and the letter, I am suggesting. So let us consider one further text-historical detail which might relate to that mysterious letter.

In 1517 a new edition of *Utopia* was published in Paris. It was seen through the press by Thomas Lupset, who had gone to Paris to oversee the publication of Linacre's *De sanitate tuenda* (which is dated August 22, 1517).[49] In many ways this edition is a curious side alley in the history of the publication of *Utopia*, and is treated as such by recent editors of the work. Following the success of the Louvain first edition, after due consultation with Thomas More, Erasmus marked up a copy with corrections and directions for additional material, and sent it to Froben at Basle; from these revisions came the 1518 Basle edition, generally treated as the definitive text for a critical edition by modern editors.[50] The copy from which the Paris edition was produced is considered to have been one marked up by More himself, largely because the 1517 edition contains a single additional letter from More which was not reproduced in any subsequent edition of the work. Apart from the letter of endorsement from Budé to the edition's *castigator*, Thomas Lupset, this second letter to Gilles is the only distinguishing feature of the Paris edition (though one might mention its 'handy' octavo format—the 1516 and 1518 editions are small quarto volumes).[51] Erasmus complained to More immediately after its publication that the Paris edition was 'full of mistakes.'[52]

The additional More letter in this edition (never again reprinted) is addressed to Peter Gilles, and further elaborates the game of truth and falsehood concerning the island of Utopia. The letter opens with a carefully staged 'dilemma', supposedly posed by 'an unusually sharp person', concerning More's relationship to the text (a dilemma characteristic, in its archness and self-consciousness, of the coterie correspondence which surrounds *Utopia*):

> I was extremely delighted, my dearest Peter, with a criticism already known to you, made by an unusually sharp person who put this dilemma about our *Utopia*: If the facts are reported as true, I see some rather absurd elements in them, but if as fictitious, then I find More's final judgment wanting in some matters. Whoever this fellow was, I am very much obliged to him, my dear Peter. I suspect him to be learned, and I see him to be friendly. By this very frank criticism of his, he has gratified me more than anyone else since the publication of my little volume.[53]

In the present context we might wonder whether this is not the very letter Gilles which holds in the diptych, the one which More asked Gilles to return, to display alongside the panel ('unless [Metsys] wants it for some purpose of his own, or you are keeping it for your own ends'). Since all that is shown in the Gilles panel is the outer address on the letter, it is not possible to tell from the published version that it is the very letter, but

More's desire to have that letter bound up with the text with which it is pictorially juxtaposed surely fits the generally self-conscious aura surrounding the exchange of letters, published volumes, and gifts. It is also intriguing that this letter appears only once in *Utopia*'s publishing history, at the precise moment that a letter from More to Gilles is prominently represented alongside a book joining More, Gilles, and Erasmus in friendship (one might want to add that Lupset, too, is part of the 'in' coterie series of exchanges—he solicits from Budé the letter which is the crowning addition to the 1517 (and all later editions) of *Utopia*, as part of the elaborate 'validation' surrounding the published text).[54] The 1517 *Utopia* is an octavo volume, thus not the small quarto shown in the Metsys painting, but then, in that painting, the letter is still separate from the text.[55]

The Paris edition of *Utopia* seems to have been initiated by More himself.[56] Most significantly, the two new epistolary contributions certainly originated in, or were solicited from, England: the second letter to Gilles and the letter from Budé, elicited for the *Utopia* volume while Lupset was actually officially occupied in gaining Budé's approval for Linacre's Galen.[57] This makes these letters distinctive: all the other elaborate prefatory paraphernalia of both the 1516 Louvain and 1518 Basle editions was overseen by Erasmus and Gilles.[58]

Budé's letter is dated July 31, 1517—two months after Erasmus's first letter alerting More to the gift-diptych. Erasmus's letter accompanying the panels when they were finally dispatched is dated September 8, 1517.[59] On September 15, Thomas Lupset told Erasmus that he had just 'finished in these last few days Linacre's book on the preservation of health' and was now 'concerned with the second edition of More's *Utopia*', to be ready by the end of the month.[60] In the 1517 edition of *Utopia*, I suggest, More made his own small contribution to the interwoven graphic and textual fashionings of the portraits of Desiderius Erasmus, Thomas More, Peter Gilles, and the island of Utopia.

'Herakleioi ponoi': Whose Are the Labours?

In a letter to Aldus Manutius, written in 1507, Erasmus compared the great printer's efforts on behalf of classical learning—his energetic retrieval and circulation of ancient texts in Latin and Greek—to the labours of Hercules:

> Your memory in after-time, like your reputation at present, will inspire not merely honour but also affection and love, because, as I hear, you devote yourself to reviving and disseminating good writers, taking infinite pains indeed but failing to receive an adequate reward; and you strive at enormous tasks in the

manner of Hercules, splendid tasks it is true—tasks that will one day bring you undying renown—but which for the time being profit others rather than yourself. I am told that you are printing a Plato in Greek type; most scholars are already eagerly awaiting it.[61]

A year later, however, Erasmus had reconsidered where exactly the 'Herculean labours' lay in connection with the recovery of ancient learning, and had reallocated that effort and exertion to the *editor* rather than the printer. The adage 'Herculei labores'—The labours of Hercules— opens the third book of Erasmus's 1508 *Adages*.[62] We have no problem grasping the meaning of the phrase—it is the *Adages* themselves which have seen to it that such classical tags ring with such an air of familiarity. After his opening preamble, glossing the tag, the example Erasmus chooses to capture the combination of superhuman efforts and undervaluation by those whom those efforts benefit (which he suggests characterises the apt use of this phrase) is the work of textual editors and restorers of ancient works, like himself:

> If any human labours ever deserved to be called Herculean, it is certainly the work of those who are striving to restore the great works of ancient literature— of true literature. While, in fact, they condemn themselves to immense toil, owing to the incredible difficulty of the task, they arouse among the vulgar the greatest envy and ill-will. . . . I should like to know who would not be frightened off . . . from engaging in such work, unless he be a real Hercules in mind, able to do and suffer anything for the sake of serving others?[63]

In the 1515, expanded, Froben edition of his *Adages*, Erasmus added a further digression to the passage on the Herculean labours of the scholar-editor of ancient texts, making yet more vivid the representation of the scholar at work in the printing shop. The additional passage specifies precisely what the Herculean labours are on which Erasmus is currently engaged, vividly embellished with lively detail to hold the reader's attention and interest, exactly in the manner described by Erasmus in his handbook of compelling composition—the *De copia*. It is an account which pushes even further into the background the more literally physical labour of typesetting and printing—the other crucial activities which print production involved:[64]

> When [these 1515 *Adages* were] in process of publication I had beaten all the labours of Hercules. For he, unconquered up to then, could not fight two monsters at once, and thought it better to run away and leave us the proverb ['Ne Hercules quidem contra duos'], than try the contest, preferring to be laughed at in safety than praised when dead. At that time we had a battle on hand with two huge monsters, each of them such a business that it needed many Hercules, instead of both being tackled together by one humble individual. For the print-

ing was going on at Bâle of the *Adagiorum Chiliades*, so amended and increased that the new edition cost me as much trouble as the previous one which had been produced in Venice by Aldus Manutius, and at the same time they were printing the complete works of St Jerome in which I had undertaken the largest and most difficult part, i.e. the Letters. It was no light task, by the Muses! if only for the number of volumes which had to be looked through. Now, heavens above! what a struggle I had with the monstrous scribal errors, which were swarming throughout the text! What a business it was to restore the passages in Greek, which our great author had mixed in everywhere—for mostly they had either dropped out or were wrongly reinserted. Another thing added no little to my labours: those famous Notes [*Scholia*] which we added with their arguments. . . . The task of bringing order into the work of an author who has been so much jumbled by various hands may not redound to one's glory, but it does mean a great deal of trouble. All this mass of work had to be the share of this one poor individual. Except that in dealing with some of the Hebrew, since my acquaintance with that language was only superficial (only a taste, as we say), I did have the help of Bruno Amerbach, a young man as learned as he is modest. We exchanged with each other, he taking over this part of the work and I taking care of the emendations in Greek and Latin. . . . The nature of this kind of work is that it brings profit to everyone, and the only person to suffer hardship is the one who undertakes to do it. The reader who freely runs through all these books does not realise that sometimes we were held up for days by a single word. Nor does he understand, or if he understands he does not remember, what difficulties have gone to create the facility with which he reads, or how many troubles one must go through to save others from trouble. And so it seems to me that I really was born in the fourth quarter of the moon, since by some inexplicable fate I have been plunged into these more than Herculean labours.[65]

This passage gives us Erasmus constructing himself *in* letters—on the printed page—as a particular sort of exemplary scholarly figure for the Renaissance: a symbolic origin of, and focus for, a *renovatio* in learning in which the scholar himself strives for visibility rather than invisibility, textual presence rather than absence. The detail here is at once vivid and immediate, and yet fictionalised and idealised. Here is *work* par excellence—collaborative labour, trouble, struggle, hardship, relieved by friendship and community in learning, work in which the seated corrector and annotater somehow exerts more physical effort than those who operate the heavy presses. Here is a task carried out not for direct profit or fame (or, perhaps, not for those alone), but out of an urge to *set the record straight*, and for the betterment of a world whose boundaries are not national boundaries. The printing-house activity symbolises a kind of internationality of communication, a 'classroom without walls', in which the scholar-editor is the centre of a whirlpool of dramatic activity—a centre at which the struggle with language, meaning, and text becomes a heroic wrestling with the monster, error, to save mankind. There seems to be a project here—a deliberate intensification of an *aura* which will extend beyond the charisma of the individual pedagogue, generating a 'life' for the editor/labourer and his 'works', which can be guaranteed to survive the transposition into print.

Erasmus's scholar-editor-teacher, then, is ostentatiously no model of cloistered selflessness. He is a *heros*, one who heroically and strenuously expends all his energies on tasks worthy of the great heroes of the past. Indeed, he is *more than* a hero: Erasmus, scholar-editor, takes on two superhuman tasks simultaneously, where even Hercules would have quailed at such double labours.[66]

It is, not surprisingly, a representation of the scholar which is somewhat difficult to sustain. In the preface to the 1526 revised edition of the *Adages*, Erasmus is interestingly defensive about the 'labour' of the compiler and editor:

> If God takes me out of the world, I beg and pray the coming generations to
> preserve intact what we have restored with so much labour; and if they light on
> something different from, or better than, what we have handed down, let them
> not do what we see done nowadays in Lexicons, and what was done in the past
> (as we learn) in the Decretals and the Sentences—when the latest person to
> touch up another man's work gets all the praise. No, let anyone who wishes
> write a new book in his own name, or if he has anything to correct or to explain
> let him put it in an Appendix, as we do.[67]

Whereas the earlier 'Herculean' pronouncements are remarkably confident about the unique significance of Erasmus's own efforts at retrieving the texts of the past, now the task has apparently lost that uniqueness, and risks being erased in the emulative efforts of later editors. Erasmus had said that his labours made Jerome his own—here he seems to suggest that his own works too risk being appropriated by those who excerpt and re-edit them. And we might note that this is the period in which Erasmus is himself revising and reissuing a number of his 'definitive' editions— amongst them the Seneca and the Jerome.[68]

In the 1536 edition of the *Adages*, Erasmus takes up Jerome, and his own 'Herculean labours', one last time, in the adage 'To look a gift horse in the mouth'. Jerome uses the phrase, Erasmus says, to refer to those who respond to his unstinting efforts at translating, polishing, and restoring the text of the Scriptures only by carping and criticising. In the same way, Erasmus continues, his own immense labours have been met with vitriol and hostility:

St. Jerome used this proverb in the Preface to his Commentary on the Epistle to the Ephesians. 'So I am not eloquent enough' he says, 'What does this matter to you? Read a more polished author. I don't translate Greek into Latin well? Read the Greek yourself, if you have a knowledge of that language, but if you have only Latin, don't criticise a benefit freely given, and as the popular saying goes, don't look a gift-horse in the mouth.' So far Jerome. But this same ungraciousness of men, which Jerome complains about, I have experienced myself, and marvelled at it. I gave them the New Testament; I emended and explained many passages, at the cost of incalculable toil. It was extraordinary how I was contradicted and shouted down by some theologians, and by the general crowd of monks, the very people to whom that labour of mine was of most use. This diligence of mine was conspicuously lacking to every one of them, but nevertheless they opposed me violently, the ungrateful lot—people who will almost worship anyone who hands them out something in the way of a luxurious meal, which they leave over-fed and tipsy. But the man who freely gives them so useful a possession, established with so much toil—on him they rain abuse.[69]

This is the textual background we need in order to retrieve the programme (either specified by the client, or implicit) behind another graphic representation of the new 'man of letters' commissioned by Erasmus. In 1524, Erasmus sent a gift of a portrait of himself to the archbishop of Canterbury in England, Archbishop Warham. This handsome portrait, now in the Radnor collection, Longford Castle, along with the Metsys Gilles of 1517, shows an enigmatically smiling Erasmus with his hands on a closed book. Behind him, partly hidden by a curtain, is a shelf with more books, and with a transparent glass vase.[70] To his right is a Renaissance pilaster. Along the fore-edge of the closed book is written 'Heraklei[oi] ponoi [in Greek letters]', and 'Erasmi Roter.': 'Erasmus of Rotterdam's Herculean Labours'. Archbishop Warham was the dedicatee of Erasmus's edition of Jerome's *Letters*. It is entirely appropriate, therefore, that the painting Erasmus offers him should depict the author as the saint/ scholar in his study, with a look of achievement on his face, his hands proprietorially upon the Jerome edition on account of which Erasmus had 'been plunged into these more than Herculean labours'.

This was one of two paintings by Holbein which Erasmus sent to England on this occasion. Beatus Rhenanus confirms this in his Pliny *Emendationes*, published by Froben in 1526. Listing Holbein amongst the greatest northern painters of the age, he describes him as follows:

... amongst the Swiss [Rauricos], Johannes [*sic*] Holbein, actually born in Augsburg, but for a long time a resident in Basle, who painted two portraits of our Erasmus of Rotterdam a year ago, beautifully executed and with much grace, which were subsequently sent to Britain.[71]

7. Portrait of Erasmus by Hans Holbein.

The second, now in the Louvre, shows Erasmus in profile, writing his paraphrase of Mark's Gospel, on which he was currently working (published by Froben at Basle in 1524). At the same time a painting was dispatched to France as a gift, apparently for one of the Amerbach brothers. This small painting, now in Basle, shows Erasmus in profile, writing, and is clearly closely related to the 'Mark's Gospel' painting. But in this case the paper on which Erasmus industriously works is apparently a letter.[72]

As in the Metsys diptych, the two Holbein poses show two versions of the scholar in his study, but by 1524 both the writer/author and the bookmaker (the man with his hand proprietorially on the closed book) are one and the same—Erasmus himself. The writer is absorbed in his writing; his gaze is fixed downwards on the paper, the ringed forefinger of his left hand indicates the text he has just completed with the reed pen in his right. The viewer can be relied on also to fix his gaze on that text—paraphrase or letter, depending on the original recipient. In the complete realism of the representation (its apparent loss of symbolic currency), the illusion of the aloneness of the scholar appears complete. And yet that very illusion underscores the paradox: Erasmus's aloneness is seen by everyone. What he writes in isolation is disseminated worldwide. The seclusion of the scholar-scribe masks the diffusion of the printed book.[73]

The Warham portrait provides a further variant on the theme of scholarly labour. Erasmus, again in his study, is depicted not at his scholarly tasks but in repose, with the work completed, under his hands. The credentials of his scholarship are recalled by the books on the shelf, the vase, the Italian Renaissance pilaster. He is depicted as prosperous and content: smiling reflectively, richly dressed in fur-lined robe; in a room with ornate, Italianate decor (recalling the surround in the 1535 Holbein woodcut, described by Boniface Amerbach as 'Erasmus in his house'— 'Erasmus in eim Ghüs').[74] The book bears the title not of its contents, but of the labour it cost its producer/promoter, Erasmus himself.

Here, six years after the Metsys commission, we have a second programme for representing Erasmus to his international supporters. Once again the graphic representation of the author is insistently related to his written production, to produce a deliberate tension between the 'knowledge' of Erasmus to be gained from his writings and the supposedly inferior (or at least less satisfying) representation which is his physical appearance. Yet, as in the Metsys paintings, the *calibre* of the painting undermines the very thing asserted: the physical representation invites the kind of attention which we associate with humaneness—the scholar as model for emulation.

I am suggesting that Erasmus has all of this well in hand, and that he provides the brief for the painter in all its detail. After all, the likenesses between the Metsys and Holbein Erasmuses, given the distinct oeuvres of the two distiguished painters, are most readily attributed to the shared patron—the man of letters, disseminating himself as living icon throughout early modern Europe.

'MORS ULTIMA LINEA RERUM': READING BETWEEN THE ENGRAVERS' LINES

In 1533 and 1535 Holbein produced two woodcuts of Erasmus, completing his series of representations of the great scholar, and returning to the medium in which he had first encountered him. For although Holbein's first portraits of Erasmus were paintings, his early relationship was with Erasmus's works, as they passed through the Froben press, for which, from 1516, he provided elaborate title borders.[75]

Holbein's woodcuts return us to the world of typography, and the repeatable printed text. And at this stage in our discussion, they shed fresh light on the relationship between the graphic image of Erasmus and his portable, movable type, mass-produced works. For what Holbein's engraved borders allow us to recognise is that in the normal run of things, in the printed text, the materiality of writing is deliberately effaced.[76] It is typical, that is, of printed texts, that they seem to encourage us to look through or past the type, to a meaning beyond it—to the mind 'figured' in the text. We do not look *at* the writing, but through it.[77] The border (and, then, the engraved figure with framed accompanying verses) asks us once again to consider the materiality of the writing. In particular, when the More letter to Gilles is framed with Holbein's border, it ceases to be text, cumulatively contributing to the meaning of the work as constructed out of consecutive, artfully contrived, contributions, and becomes once again the *epistola*—the letter sent, the letter held in the hand of the painted figure, the letter which registers enduring friendship.

And this clarifies the way in which written text in the portrait (like the letter Gilles holds in the Metsys panel) similarly asks us to register its materiality, at precisely the moment when we strive to 'read' the inscribed message, made legible by a virtuoso technique which for more than a century is typical of Flemish painting.[78] When we look at the written texts in the paintings, they refer us to the works for the 'true' author; when we turn to the texts, with the particular goal of grasping—entering the presence of—the author, they resist concrete materiality (they are mind, not matter), and we return unsatisfied to the graphic representations for the 'material' presence of the author.

Engraved resemblances (in single-sheet prints) partake of both the 'body' of the painting and the 'mind' of the letter. Conceived of as endlessly repeatable, widely disseminable works, they originate with the function of meditative recall. Single-sheet prints had developed before prints in printed books, and single-sheet printed portraits can be related to woodcut images of saints, purchased for devotional purposes.[79] The portrait print may be purchased, like the book; but it may also be exchanged, like the letter, as a material token of the giver.[80] Dürer's Low Countries notebook records that when he and Erasmus met at dinner at the home of Peter Gilles, Erasmus gave him 'pictures' (presumably prints).[81]

In this discussion of paintings, portraits, and tokens of friendship, we have found ourselves focusing on the concrete reality of 'letters' (*litterae*), and the ability of letters to make physically present the sender/author. Both in the paintings and in the written texts generated around 1517 in the More/Erasmus circle of friends, our attention has been directed towards letters, as bearing the burden of meaning, and the promise of enduring fame: 'loving letters . . . make their souls present to [the absent friend]'; 'I am elated when the thought comes to me that I shall be commended to the most distant ages by the friendship, the letters . . . of Erasmus' (writes More).

The Holbein border which lavishly frames the opening page of More's dedicatory letter to Gilles in the 1518 *Utopia*[82] restores to it some of its original prominence in the volume, even though it is now preceded by Erasmus's letter to Froben, recommending *Utopia* for publication, and by the long letter from Budé to Lupset.[83] Its effect is dramatically to highlight the book's material presence as a gift to Gilles:

> Thomas More to Peter Gilles, greetings.
> I almost blush, my dearest Peter, to send you, after almost a year, this little book, *Utopia*, which I have no doubt you anticipated receiving within a month and a half.[84]

The text surrounded by the engraved border focuses our eye and our attention on the enclosed writing as inscription, retrieving its materiality—the text *bulks* large in its border. Given a deservedly famous border, like Holbein's *Cleopatra*, which uses perspective to simulate three-dimensionality, the enclosed text becomes commemorative, monumental, an inscription, as if in stone.[85] Holbein's portrait woodcuts intensify this focussing: the engraved portrait attests to the physical presence of the great man of letters; the inscription attests to his works, and makes that presence textual.

One of the Holbein portrait woodcuts of Erasmus (a small medallion profile) fronts the 1533 Froben *Adages*; the other is a much-disseminated full-length figure, whose first appearance as the frontispiece to a work of Erasmus's (as opposed to a separate print-portrait) was in Froben's 1540 edition of Erasmus's *Opera*.[86] Erasmus stands with his hand on a bust of Terminus, framed by an Italianate arch which is supported by two *ter-*

mini.[87] The figure of Erasmus, with its Dürer-like draperies, evokes a funeral monument; the echoed *termini* recall the inscription on the Metsys medal, 'mors ultima linea rerum'. Beneath this figure, in the surviving original proof of the print, are two lines of verse by Gilbertus Cognatus (Cousin), one of Erasmus's *famuli.*[88]

> Corporis effigiem si quis non uidit Erasmi,
> Hanc scite ad uiuum picta tabella dabit.
>
> [If anyone has not seen Erasmus in the flesh,
> This likeness, taken from nature, will show him to him.][89]

The complete version of these verses accompanies the smaller medallion print in the *Adages*, and confirms that Cousin's rubric mirrors precisely, in its elegant conceit, More's verses on the Metsys diptych:

> If anyone has not seen Erasmus in the flesh, this likeness, taken from nature, will show him to him. If this talented hand could have reproduced his voice in the same fashion, you would at the same time have been able to contemplate the image of his mind. But what the expert hand has not been able to achieve, Erasmus has done more completely and better. For see how on occasion the portrait of his intelligence appears to you in his books, living and without artifice, more clearly than in a mirror. And this form of the man's appearance deserves far greater attention; that which the painter has represented is only the enclosure of the mind. Consider therefore that you see a portrait of Erasmus each time that you read the products of his genius.[90]

In 1533 Gilbert Cousin, the author of these verses, had completed more than three years of personal service with Erasmus:

> Gilbert Cousin has, for more than three years, been a faithful and devoted *famulus*, whom I have, however, on account of his excellent character treated less as a *famulus* than as familiar friend and colleague in my learned labours.[91]

Erasmus's was, we know, a busy household: a centre of communications for correspondence with scholars and men of affairs across Europe; a resort for a constant stream of visitors; the centre of production from which pedagogic works flowed steadily to the 'classroom without walls' which by this time Erasmus commanded. Cousin nevertheless produces his master once again as the solitary, introspective, cloistered scholar—the man accessible through his works alone, the man of mind rather than of body.

The Holbein engravings, with Cousin's verses, bring us finally to the most closely studied, and probably most familiar, pictorial representation of Erasmus, Dürer's engraving of 1526. In the light of what has been said thus far, the Dürer must appear, I think, as studiedly *monumental.*[92] It bears comparison (as a contrast with the rich pictorial quality of the

8. Engraving of Erasmus by Albrecht Dürer.

Metsys and the Holbeins) with the deliberately statuesque, draped figures of Flemish art, like those on the exterior of the Ghent polyptych. The inscription to Erasmus's left simulates carving on stone, and, like a stone monument, it bears its date prominently.[93] This is one of a group of portrait engravings produced by Dürer in the 1520s, which historians of prints regard as crucially innovative in the marketing and circulation of repeatable figurative art.[94] Featuring prominent and powerful men of affairs (Wilibald Pirckheimer, Cardinal Albrecht van Brandenburg, Frederick the Wise, the elector of Saxony, Ulrich Varnbüler), as well as intellectuals/reformers (Erasmus and Melanchthon), these engravings combine the compelling graphic vividness of the individual prints of saints with the 'worth' of the celebrity status of the sitter, and were apparently hugely popular.[95]

Dürer's Erasmus is studiedly symbolic, and studiedly Jerome (as I shall show more closely in the next chapter). Permanence and the ephemeral are carefully juxtaposed: the statuelike figure alongside the fragile vase of living flowers; the written paper alongside the enduring books; the living man against the inscribed tablet dating when he was 'described from life'. Even Dürer's monogram takes on the quality of enduring sign, closely juxaposed with the paper and pen.

Erasmus went to considerable lengths to persuade Dürer to engrave his likeness, although he was unable to sit for him in person.[96] Once the engraving was completed, he insisted that it did not resemble him. At the same time, he took evident pride in the idea that across Europe scholar-admirers (or even detractors) pinned his engraved image to their study wall.[97] The two attitudes (the urge to be immortalised in an engraving and the insistence that the image was no 'true likeness') are not, however, inconsistent. Erasmus, with his acute sense of the potential of print, both solicits the commemoration and insists on its symbolic, as opposed to 'real', currency. Perhaps what Erasmus conveys here is the fact that in the worldwide dissemination of Erasmus's fame, like/unlike has become a sustaining trope, capturing the paradox, engraved for all time on Dürer's print: 'His works will give a better image of him'. Perhaps, too, the point of both Dürer's and Holbein's engravings is durability—lasting fame. In spite of the ephemeral nature of the individual printed copy, the material of the block for the woodcut, like the medallion, is hard, the image carved out, rather than laid on (as with pigment).[98]

In his verses celebrating the Metsys diptych, Thomas More wrote:

> Oh, Quentin, reviver of an ancient art, . . . why did you choose to inscribe your likenesses, made with so much labour and so competently, of men such as earlier times have rarely produced, still less our own, such as I doubt the future will ever see again, on fragile wood? You should have consigned them to a more durable medium, to preserve them for posterity.

[Quintine O ueteris nouator artis,
... Hei cur effigies labore tanto
Factas tam bene talium uirorum,
Quales prisca tulere secla raros,
Quales tempora nostra rariores,
Quales haud scio post futura an ullos,
Te iuuit fragili indidisse ligno,
Danda materiae fideliori,
Quae seruare datas queat perennes?][99]

In 1519 Erasmus commissioned Quentin Metsys to cast a medallion of his image, with the bust of a young man, on a square plinth, inscribed 'Terminus' (Erasmus's emblem/*impresa*), bearing the motto '*Concedo nulli*' on the reverse. The written inscriptions on this medallion, like those on the Holbein and Dürer engravings (and serving as prototypes for them), stress above all the paradox of the conjunction of enduring record and transient individual physical existence. 'Consider the end of a long life' (in Greek): the boundary stone/Terminus figure marking a physical end; the works of a long life enduring. Similarly, the inscription 'mors ultima linea rerum' contrasts the apparent finality of boundary and engraved line with the inevitability of death, which crosses all lines. When Dürer picks up that inscription in his own, 'Imago Erasmi Roterodami ab Alberto Dvrero ad vivam effigiem deliniata', that *deliniata* draws our attention to the line of the engraving, with its semblance of permanence (of arresting time) and the line which is always crossed by time and death. It also emphasises the monumental, commemorative nature of the engraved image.[100] Thus Erasmus's relationship with the physical reproduction of his image is apparently not vanity (indeed, not *vanitas*), but a curious, and perhaps original, kind of self-symbolism, where the very image of the great man of letters teaches the lesson of the transience of all flesh. Only the engraved line endures: 'a better portrait [of Erasmus] will his writings show'; or rather, 'his works are a more lasting monument'.

Massed in the foreground of Dürer's engraving are books, engraved with quite extraordinary visual illusion of texture, bulk, depth, and density—echoing the lovingly perfect representations of books in northern Renaissance painting of the same period, complete with legible texts displayed to the viewer's gaze, and the compelling materiality of pages and bindings.[101] Dürer's open book is not legible, though it is practically impossible not to believe that it is.[102] Beyond the books lies a handwritten letter, and the sculpted scholar at work on his text; beyond him the engraved 'stone' monument precisely commemorating the 'delineation' of Erasmus *ad vivam*. More monumental than the statue-saint, more permanent (like the stone carving and the engraving itself) than the writing hand, the 'works' are the most true and most enduring version of the man.

9. Medal of Erasmus by Quentin Metsys.

The In(de)scribable Aura of the Scholar-Saint in His Study: Erasmus's *Life* and *Letters* of Saint Jerome

INTELLECTUAL FATHER-FIGURES: WHICH 'GERMAN' SAT AT THE FEET OF GUARINO?

In my opening chapter we began to see Erasmus shaping his transmitted graphic image for a contemporary audience, constructing a 'meaning' for his self-representation which exploits the multiple resonances available in the images of the Church Fathers, the solitary scholar, and the attentive teacher. In the present chapter I want to pursue that theme further. I start, however, not with Erasmus's own writings (or, at least, not with writings which can be safely identified as coming from his own rather than his admirers' pen), but with the early, formative 'lives' of Erasmus. I begin by drawing attention to a textual preoccupation in the early versions of Erasmus's biography—a recurrent desire to provide Erasmus with a genealogy, an intellectual parentage. Here are three fragments, all ostensibly 'biographical', in which a 'father' is identified, a father who sat at the feet of the great Italian humanist Guarino, and who brought humanistic studies back across the Alps with him to northern Europe:

> [Erasmus's father] Gerardus took himself off to Rome. There he made his living by writing (for at that time there was not yet an art of printing): he had a most elegant hand. He lived in a youthful fashion. Soon he applied himself to worthy study. He was well-versed in Greek and Latin. Moreover in knowledge of law he made more than usual progress. For Rome at that time boasted an extraordinary number of learned men. He heard Guarino. He had transcribed all kinds of authors with his own hand. ('Life' of Erasmus, 1524)[1]

> Alexander Hegius of Westphalia presided over that school of humane learning [at Deventer], a man profoundly skilled in 'bonae litterae', and somewhat skilled in Greek literature, thanks to the teaching of Rudolph Agricola, whose friend he became, shortly after Agricola's return from Italy, where he had heard Guarino Veronese lecture at Ferrara and several others distinguished for their erudition. Erasmus's talent soon made itself apparent, since he understood immediately whatever he was taught, and retained it perfectly, surpassing all his peers. (Beatus Rhenanus, 'Life' of Erasmus, 1540)[2]

Sent next to Deventer, we heard Alexander Hegius, student of Rudolph Agricola and of Guarino Veronese, a most pious man, both eloquent and learned,
and a despiser of worldly glory. I was the equal of my contemporaries or colleagues in following and remembering lectures. ('Erasmus', in Johann Herold's
ghosted 'Life', 1542)[3]

In each of these passages, the author is at pains to indicate that Erasmus
is legitimate heir to an Italian humanist tradition, via a spiritual, or perhaps a biological, father. Either Erasmus's father, or the headmaster of
his school at Deventer, Alexander Hegius, or his head teacher's teacher,
the Frisian humanist Rudolph Agricola (whom we will encounter at
greater length later), sat at the feet of Guarino Veronese in Ferrara. One
of these transmitted the authentically humane learning imbibed there to
his 'son', Erasmus.

Rudolph Agricola did study with Battista Guarino, son of Guarino
Veronese, in Ferrara, in the midfifteenth century. There he abandoned
legal studies, the original purpose of his educational journey to Pavia and
Ferrara, and dedicated his life to the *bonae litterae*, becoming an early
link-figure between Italy and northern Europe. By the midsixteenth century, Agricola had come regularly to occupy this figuratively transitional
position in the story of the emergence of northern humanism, as, for instance, in Omar Talon's commentary on Petrus Ramus's *Dialectica*:

Rudolph Agricola made this distinction in the first book of his *De inventione
dialectica*, and Ramus follows him in this, to the extent that he came to rival
Agricola's achievement in this art especially, whom Ramus himself was wont to
rank in logical studies immediately after the ancient school of Socratic logic . . .
and ahead of all subsequent logicians. And he used to say publicly that thanks
to Agricola the true study of genuine [germana] logic had first been established
in Germany [Germania], and thence, by way of its disciples and emulators had
spread throughout the whole world.[4]

The tale is so familiar that we are under the impression that we have
heard it before (even if we have not ourselves heard of Rudolph Agricola,
its supposed hero). The story of the itinerant, gifted intellectual who carries the new learning from its birthplace in one culture to be developed in
crucially original ways within another is an essential component in the
narrative which provides intellectual legitimation for northern humanism—above all, Reformation northern humanism. The spirit of Italy,
transplanted northwards and nurtured by an individual of genius,
germinates there, grafted onto the sturdy indigenous stock to produce a
specifically 'German' intellectual and spiritual tradition. It is a tale of
teaching—of transmitting the Word—from inspired master to gifted
pupil, a genealogy of the chosen who hear and respond to the new learn-

ing's message. Strikingly, this is a narrative in which institutions are not involved. It is the autonomous scholar, unaffiliated to universities, monastic orders, or the households of princes, who is responsible for the transformation of an entire intellectual outlook and the introduction of a revised programme of learning.

The three early, tradition-forming biographies of Erasmus invoke this narrative to suggest that Erasmus is in at the beginning of, and is an active participant in, the building of the intellectual 'bridge' between Italian and northern humanism. The lack of consensus amongst the three versions as to whether it is a natural father or a revered schoolmaster who provides the link between Erasmus and Italy suggests that this is a fiction, or at least a piece of creative rewriting of history. We might prefer to think that the biographers shape Erasmus's early life so as to construct a meaning for his *Vita* (the *Vita Erasmi*), to make Erasmus signify fully in the line of descent from medieval to early modern culture.

The full story of Erasmus's father's trip to Italy, as told in the *Compendium vitae Erasmi*, is not an altogether uplifting one. When Erasmus's mother was pregnant with him (so Erasmus tells us), his father (an ordained priest, or about to become an ordained priest—Erasmus is deliberately vague)[5] fled to Rome, returning only when her family wrote and informed him, falsely, that she had died in childbirth. It is during this ignominious flight that Erasmus represents his father as sitting at the feet of Guarino. The interpolated remarks about Gerardus and Guarino partially recuperate the story. Gerardus may have abandoned his illegitimate son, but he returned with the ultimate legitimating gift—an intellectual heritage, a respectable pedigree for the rest of Erasmus's life. We catch a glimpse here of the ingenuity it took to shape Erasmus's personal history into an exemplary 'Life' (and, perhaps, something of the anxiety behind the effort). The *Vita Erasmi* (autobiography or biography) is the story of leadership and legitimation of an intellectual movement which by the time of his death had spread throughout northern Europe.

From Sanctity to Learning as Model for a Way of Life

Western European culture has customarily preserved and honoured the memory and reputation of its great figures in the verbal oration of praise (the encomium or *laudatio*), in the painted portrait, and the written 'life'.[6] Since it is no longer customary to deliver orations of praise for great men and women on the anniversary of their birth or death, or on their feast day (as, in Renaissance Italy, for example, orations in praise of Saint Jerome were delivered on September 30),[7] these too now preserve the memory of those they celebrate in written form. Here I will combine these with 'lives', as the written memorial (although we shall need to remember that originally the forms were distinct).

The term 'portrait' is conventionally used of both visual and verbal monuments to the famous. Erasmus's letter of 1521 to Justus Jonas, containing the 'lives' of Jean Vitrier and John Colet, offers 'a short life' of Colet, 'a portrait in miniature, as it were'.[8] His celebrated 'life' of Thomas More, contained in a letter of 1519 to Ulrich von Hutten, begins:

> You ask me to draw a picture of More for you at full length, and I wish I were as skilful as you are eager. . . . It is, I suspect, no easier to produce a portrait of More than one of Alexander the Great or Achilles, nor did they deserve their immortality any more than he does. Such a sitter demands the skills of an Apelles, and I fear there is less of Apelles in me than of Fulvius or Rutuba [Roman gladiators]. I will try, however, to do you not so much a picture as an outline sketch of the whole man, based on long-standing and intimate acquaintance, as far as my observation or memory will serve.[9]

Both the painted and the written forms are understood to be creative, to engage the representational and interpretative skills of the artist or writer (as Erasmus here acknowledges). Whilst the figure represented has importantly 'really' existed, the artistic representation moulds, shapes, and colours the original in order to convey something more than the mere physical presence. The portrait may include the sitter's badges of office, or (in the case of a saint) traditional signs and symbols, but it also aims at conveying something of the subject's inner qualities. The 'life' or 'vita' likewise recounts the events which took place (and may even present and evaluate the evidence for believing these to be true), but shapes the narrative so as to give a sense to that lived life, a purpose (an example) beyond the string of recalled incidents. In both cases, indeed, the subject is generally no longer living, and the canvas or printed page may be intended to 'recall' the subject according to understood conventions: those of genealogy or lineage, communal memory, recognisable anecdote, fable.

For a given community, both the 'life' and the portrait function inspirationally, inviting the disciple or follower to emulate, copy, fashion themselves in the image of the great master.[10] To tell again (or read again) the life of the admired saint is to aspire to tread in his footsteps; to make the saint the subject of a visual reworking (or to commission or buy his image for prominent display) is to contrive a permanent vestigial presence, a reminiscence or model for emulation. Responding to Justus Jonas's request for a 'vita' of John Colet, Erasmus takes it for granted that this is likely to be the use to which Jonas will put it:

> You beg me earnestly, dear friend, to write you a short life, a portrait in miniature as it were, of John Colet; and I will do so the more readily because I suspect

you are seeking some outstanding example of piety which you can use as a model for your own way of life.[11]

And he ends his textual diptych:

You have before you, dear Justus, not a portrait but such a sketch as fits the narrow limits of a letter, of two men born in our own day who were in my opinion truly and sincerely Christians. It will be for you to choose out of them both what seems to you to help most towards a really religious life. If you now ask me which I prefer, they seem to me to deserve equal credit, when one considers their different surroundings. . . . If you take my advice, dear Jonas, you will not hesitate to add the names of both to the calendar of saints, although no pope may ever write them into the canon.[12]

In this context, the term 'copy' (either as verb or noun) has richer connotations than mere reproduction, imitation, or mimicry in our modern, generally derogatory, sense. The 'original' is a source of inspiration, energy; blessed by fortune, his reputation has survived the destruction of the body; the contingencies of time and space have been given shape and meaning by a discovered ulterior purpose. All of these characteristics of the representation of 'greatness' invite the disciple or follower to identify, in a full sense, with the creatively structured work—to aspire to *become*, through 'copying', as like its original as he can. To copy, in this case, is to attempt to give meaning to the scattered accidents of an individual life, by in some sense claiming the great precursor as progenitor.[13] To copy is to aspire to a meaning which might itself be carried forward, to become, in its own turn, the basis for future emulation.

The '*vita*' elevates the contingency of lived experience into a pattern to be followed. This chapter traces the way in which Erasmus made his own investment in lived meaning for the future, by way of a collection of portraits and 'lives', and made it, as we know, outstandingly successfully (almost five hundred years later both his portrait and his life continue to serve as models in academic and spiritual communities throughout Europe and the United States). My aim here is to show with what brilliance and originality Erasmus 'copied'—crafted or fashioned—a figure for himself full to overflowing with meaning. And this is a stage in my argument as a whole. For as we watch the strategic recuperation for the charismatic man of letters of the aura which had traditionally surrounded the portrait and the 'life' of the holy man of conventional hagiography, we are, I believe, witnessing the transition from 'sacred' to 'learned' as the grounds for personal spiritual salvation.[14] This claim will require all the evidence I assemble in this book to make it convincing. I ask the reader to keep it in mind, however, during the present discussion. For I am anxious if possible to avoid the most literal interpretation one might want to give Erasmus's self-portraiture—that what we see here is a striking, early example of the kind of academic entrepreneurism and self-promotion which has become a recognised feature of the practice of twentieth-century humanities. It is no part of this study to endorse such a practice in the name of one of its most distinguished founding fathers. But it is a crucial part of my argument that the strikingly original ways in which Erasmus responded to, and improvised around, the novel demands of a Europe-wide pedagogic movement, and the spectacular possibilities for dissemination of knowledge offered by the printed book, made a major contribution to a sixteenth-century spiritual reformation, whose heirs we contemporary academics are.

'In vita sua': Erasmus's Life of Saint Jerome

In 1516 Erasmus's *Life of Saint Jerome* was published in the first of the four volumes of his edition of Jerome's letters, issued from the Froben press.[15] Its opening words challenge the way in which the traditional saint's life fictionalises in order, ostensibly, to instruct. His own biography, he insists, will show that there is no need for such fabrications and embellishments in order to gain the reader's admiration for Saint Jerome:

> I am well aware that many of the old authors were of this opinion: they esteemed it dutiful and proper to make use of appropriate fictitious narratives for the public good, to encourage them to embark on an upright and pious way of life, or to excite their minds towards the study of honourable things, or to stiffen the sinews against any feebleness, or to frighten the impious, whom neither reason can correct nor love move, or to enhance by miracles the glory of saintly men. . . . I hold that nothing is more correct than to describe the saints in just such a way as they actually were.[16]

'To excite [men's] minds towards the study of worthy things', it is only necessary to offer the example of the life of study and contemplation well lived. In place of superstitious anecdotes and fictions, Erasmus announces, he will narrate Jerome's life as a model of learning and piety, and will do so in a way which persuades the reader that the saint is worthy of veneration and emulation. Erasmus's *Life of Jerome* is acknowledged in the Jerome literature to be the first attempt at a biography of the saint purged of the anecdotal and fabulous accretions it had acquired in the Middle Ages.[17]

As the basis for Jerome's exemplary life, Erasmus prefers the testimony of Jerome's own writings to the collections of orally transmitted, communal memories of medieval *vitae*: 'For who knew Jerome better than Jerome himself?' ('Quis enim rectius nouerit Hieronymum quam ipse Hieronymus?')[18] In place of the miracles and prodigies laid before the credu-

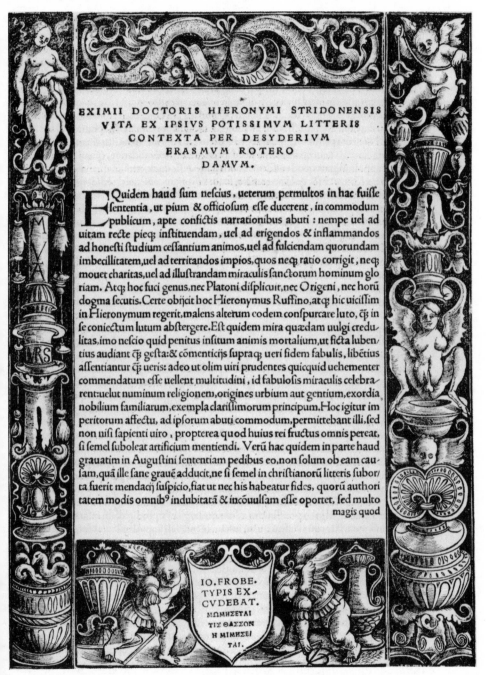

EXIMII DOCTORIS HIERONYMI STRIDONENSIS
VITA EX IPSIVS POTISSIMVM LITTERIS
CONTEXTA PER DESYDERIVM
ERASMVM ROTERO
DAMVM.

EQuidem haud ſum neſcius, ueterum permultos in hac fuiſſe
ſententia, ut pium & officioſum eſſe ducerent, in commodum
publicum, apte confictis narrationibus abuti : nempe uel ad
uitam recte pieqʒ inſtituendam, uel ad erigendos & inflammandos
ad honeſti ſtudium ceſſantium animos,uel ad fulciendam quorundam
imbecillitatem,uel ad territandos impios,quos neqʒ ratio corrigit, neqʒ
mouet charitas,uel ad illuſtrandam miraculis ſanctorum hominum glo
riam. Atqʒ hoc fuci genus,nec Platoni diſplicuit,nec Origeni, nec horũ
dogma ſecutis.Certe obijcit hoc Hieronymus Ruffino,atqʒ hic uiciſſim
in Hieronymum regerit,malens alterum eodem conſpurcare luto, cʒ in
ſe coniectum lutum abſtergere.Eſt quidem mira quædam uulgi credu
litas, imo neſcio quid penitus inſitum animis mortalium,ut ficta luben
tius audiant cʒ geſta:& comenticijs ſupraqʒ ueri fidem fabulis, libẽtius
aſſentiantur cʒ ueris: adeo ut olim uiri prudentes quicquid uehementer
commendatum eſſe uellent multitudini, id fabuloſis miraculis celebra
rent:uelut numinum religionem,origines urbium aut gentium,exordia
nobilium familiarum,exempla clariſſimorum principum.Hoc igitur im
peritorum affectu, ad ipſorum abuti commodum,permittebant illi,ſed
non niſi ſapienti uiro , propterea quod huius rei fructus omnis pereat,
ſi ſemel ſuboleat artificium mentiendi. Verũ hac quidem in parte haud
grauatim in Auguſtini ſententiam pedibus eo,non ſolum ob eam cau
ſam,quã ille ſane graue adducit,ne ſi ſemel in chriſtianorũ litteris ſubor/
ta fuerit mendacij ſuſpicio,fiat ut nec his habeatur fides, quorũ authori
tatem modis omnib⁹ indubitatã & incõuulſam eſſe oportet, ſed multo
magis quod

IO.FROBE·
TYPIS EX-
CVDEBAT.
ΜΩΜΗΣΕΤΑΙ
ΤΙΣ ΘΑΣΣΟΝ
Η ΜΙΜΗΣΕΙ
ΤΑΙ.

10. Opening page of Erasmus's *Vita Hieronymi* (Basle, 1516).

lous in traditional saints' lives, Erasmus offers the miracle of Jerome's oeuvre, and Jerome's erudition:

> Therefore, having examined all those books, we have restored to narrative order the events it was possible to pick out here and there, without adding anything false, because we are of the view that it is enough of a miracle that Jerome presented himself to us in so many outstanding works. And if there is anyone who cannot be satisfied unless by prodigies and miracles, he should read the books of Jerome, in which there are as many miracles as there are thoughts.[19]

At first sight, this move to present the saint's life so that it is the history of the saint as traced through the pages of his own writings ('Hieronymus ex Hieronymo') is simply the commendable, modernising move made by the textual scholar. In its impulse to rid the narrative of its supernatural and superstitious accretions, it is clearly in tune with humanistic piety, with its emphasis on the life well lived rather than on a series of ordeals punctuated by signs of divine intervention. But the move is one which decisively interrupts a familiar tradition of *Vitae Hieronymi*.[20] The wholly 'factual', intellectual biography was certainly not the form of saint's life which had traditionally lent itself to the kind of ritual recall which I earlier described as one of the cultural functions of the '*vita*'. Instead, Jerome's '*vita*' takes its place alongside the lives of Virgil and Petrarch as examples of the growth and development of a mind towards learned seriousness, to be set before every aspiring humanist struggling with the technical detail of Greek and Latin eloquence, holding out the promise that, pursued with virtuous dedication, *bonae litterae* will transform linguistic competence into a whole way of life.

The most immediately evident shift which this produces in the significance of Jerome as culturally exemplary figure is that the meaning of the life becomes inextricably involved with the works, the sense of the works with the life, so that each has to be scrutinised to clarify the other. Traditionally, the aura surrounding the miracle-punctuated '*vitae*' of the Fathers elevated their patristic texts and translations above the reach of 'mundane' text-critical attention.[21] The book, held by the Saint (Jerome, Augustine, Eusebius), conveys this with iconographical clarity: lovingly represented in all its physical detail (often with visible, and sometimes legible, text), it is held in one hand, facing outwards towards the viewer, 'a customary attribute for those who have from the very first moment proclaimed and preached the message of the Gospel: Evangelists, Apostles, and Church Fathers'.[22] Whether accidentally or by design, by discarding the pseudo-biographies faithfully reprinted with the fifteenth-century editions of Jerome's works, Erasmus severs Jerome's writings from the aura of mystical veneration which traditionally surrounded them. These works are now 'miraculous', not in the sense that they represent some acknowledged special relationship between their mundane author and God, but simply in the sense that they have been executed with exceptional scholarly skill, accuracy, and judgement.[23]

In the context of the exemplary life—the life possessed of the power to draw the individual believer to live a life as like it as humanly possible— Erasmus's insistence that Jerome's works themselves are miracle enough to sustain the daily practice of the reader blurs the distinction between, in particular, the kind of attention the pious person gives to the text of scripture and patristics and the kind of attention familiarly asked of the student of *bonae litterae*. A saint may be a scholar, but a scholar is not necessarily a saint. And yet Erasmus's 'Jerome' seems irresistibly to press in the direction of sanctity as it sustains the traditional aura, whilst transferring its narrative attention to the dedication of the exegete, a dedication which it self-consciously depicts as ranging with steady and equal commitment over all *litterae*, both pagan and sacred. Indeed, Erasmus's 'Jerome' is exemplary precisely because it proves impossible to separate secular from sacred letters in his oeuvre. Nor, I suggest, is this choice of Jerome as model Father of the Church other than an extremely careful one. The printed remains which surround the four volumes of Erasmus's *Letters* of Jerome amount to a programme for installing Jerome as a vivid and vital figure—scholar-saint/saint-scholar—at the centre of the canvas depicting a spiritual exegesis in which pagan and sacred are fused in the act of textual attention.[24]

If we take the texts which introduce the first volume of the Jerome *Letters* in sequence, the prefatory letter to Archbishop Warham that stands immediately before the *Vita Hieronymi* sets out clearly an editorial programme, in which Jerome's texts are restored to the kind of pristine integrity and Latin *eloquentia* that makes them an appropriate model for humanistic emulation.[25] The liberal arts are to be the foundation for the enduring worth of any culture. Crucially, antiquity is held up as an example for its commitment to the preservation of great texts rather than to embalming the bodies of its great men—its commitment to a heritage of books, not of relics. Dead men tell us nothing, Erasmus affirms; their written works—their books—are enduring monuments:

> So great was the veneration always accorded to literature even by pagans, . . .
> that they supposed the origins of all the liberal arts should be ascribed to the
> gods alone as their inventors, and the most powerful and prosperous monarchs
> thought no concern more becoming of them than to arrange for the translation
> of works of outstanding authors into various tongues, that more men might
> enjoy them. This was, they thought, the way to secure the truest and most
> lasting renown for themselves and a special ornament to their kingdoms, if they

bequeathed to posterity a library equipped with most accurate copies of the very best authors. . . . And so [great princes] thought it far more appropriate to transfer that solicitude to the books of great men, in which they live on for the world at large even after death, and live on in such fashion that they speak to more people and more effectively dead than alive. They converse with us, instruct us, tell us what to do and what not to do, give us advice and encouragement and consolation as loyally and as readily as anyone can. In fact, they then most truly come alive for us when they themselves have ceased to live.[26]

In emulation of pagan culture's dedicated attention to its own preservation for posterity, Erasmus proposes Jerome's restored works as a more reliable basis for a textually authentic Christianity—a *philosophia Christi*—than any saint's cult. Jerome's works are an exemplum, worthy to be 'copied' by the devout individual. Jerome with his aura of sanctity replaces the pagan Cicero as the unique fount of emulable *eloquentia*, and the cultural product of true *eloquentia* is thereby transformed from 'virtue' to 'piety':

If . . . you are looking for brilliance of expression, on that side Jerome leaves all Christian authors so far behind him that one cannot compare with him even those who spent their whole time on nothing but the art of writing; and so impossible is it to find any writer of our faith to compare with him that in my opinion Cicero himself, by universal consent the leading light of Roman eloquence, is surpassed by him in some of the qualities of a good style, as I shall show at greater length in his life. For my part, I have the same experience with Jerome that I used to have with Cicero: if I compare him with any other author, however brilliant, that man suddenly seems as it were to lose his voice, and he whose language has no rival in my admiration, when set alongside Jerome for comparison, seems to become tongue-tied and stammers. If you demand learning, I ask you, whom can Greece produce with all her erudition, so perfect in every department of knowledge, that he might be matched against Jerome? Who ever so successfully united every part of the sum of knowledge in such perfection? Was there ever an individual expert in so many languages? Who ever achieved such familiarity with history, geography, and antiquities? Who ever became so equally and completely at home in all literature, both sacred and profane? If you look to his memory, never was there an author, ancient or modern, who was not at his immediate disposal. Was there a corner of Holy Scripture or anything so recondite or diverse that he could not produce it, as it were, cash down? As for his industry, who ever either read or wrote so many volumes? Who had the whole of Scripture by heart, as he had, drinking it in, digesting it, turning it over and over, pondering upon it? Who expended so much effort in every branch of learning?[27]

Jerome's command of learning transcends sectarianism. 'This man, single-handed, could represent the Latin world, either for holiness of life or for mastery of theology', Erasmus concludes, drawing secular and sacred traditions tightly together.

The letter to Warham is an extravagant celebration of the enduring worth of pagan culture, and of Jerome's unique combination of that pagan cultural heritage with an equally profound commitment to sacred textual studies. It is irresistibly reminiscent of Lorenzo Valla's celebration of such a Jerome in the preface to the fourth book of the *Elegantiae* (to which I will return in a moment). But whereas Valla's encomium sat perfectly properly in a volume dedicated to secular eloquence, Erasmus's insistence on the close similarity between the range and erudition of Jerome and that of Cicero rings oddly as an introduction to a key work of patristics. For at the heart of any life of Jerome must lie some account of 'Jerome's dream'. As Antin puts it, 'The episode is too brilliantly told for Jerome biographers to fail to take it into account'.[28] The dream occurred during a period in which Jerome was immersing himself day and night in the study of pagan literature (especially Cicero and Plautus—or Plato, as a number of manuscripts have it), to the point that he found sacred texts clumsy and uncouth. Jerome recounts how he dreamed he found himself summoned before a heavenly tribunal and asked to identify himself. 'I am a Christian', replied Jerome. 'You lie', returned the presiding divine figure, 'you are a Ciceronian, not a Christian: for where your treasure is, there will your heart be also'. Jerome's prose is vivid:

> I was asked what I was, and I replied that I was a Christian. And he that was seated in judgement replied, 'You lie, you are a Ciceronian, not a Christian: for where your treasure is, there will your heart be also'. On the instant I was struck dumb, and between lashes—for he had commanded me to be flogged—I was even more greatly tormented by the flame of conscience, reflecting on that verse to myself: 'In the grave, who will give you thanks?' Then I began to cry aloud, and lamenting to say, 'Have mercy on me, Lord, have mercy on me'. This cry rang out above the sound of the blows. At length those watching fell on their knees before the one who sat in judgement, and begged him to attribute my crime to my youth and to give me the opportunity to repent of my error, exacting the full penalty if thereafter I should read any kind of secular literary works. I would have promised anything, under that kind of duress; and swearing assent, I called upon his name, saying: 'Lord, if ever again I possess secular books, or read them, I have denied you.'[29]

Humanists before Erasmus had been at pains to explain that Jerome's passionate promise was figurative rather than literal. As Pier Paulo Vergerio put it, in one of his orations on Jerome, '[Classical works] themselves were not condemned, but rather their too enthusiastic study' ('res ipsa [non] damnata est, sed fortassis eius studium uehementius').[30] In the body of the biographical narrative in Erasmus's *Vita Hieronymi*, the episode of the dream is described with almost laconic brevity:

At that time, as a result of an unrestrained, youthful enthusiasm, and because of a love of the studies of his childhood, he inclined more than he should have in studying and imitating the dialogues of Cicero and of Plato (if I am not mistaken, he was working on these at the time), and he was more intent on imitating them, than emulating the style of the apostles. In a dream sent from God, he was dragged before a divine tribunal, accused of being a Ciceronian rather than a Christian, and then administered a flogging as punishment. After which he awoke, as he himself tells us, in the letter which begins with the words, 'Listen, daughter' [letter 22]. For my own view on this, see what follows, when I come to that point in the narrative.[31]

While in his commentary on the letter to Eustochium itself, in which the account of the dream quoted above occurs, he writes tartly:

This is the story which everyone recalls, even those who have never read a word that Jerome has written. Jerome was flogged because he read Cicero, they say.[32]

Erasmus reserves his further discussion of the dream till the end of the *Vita Hieronymi*, where he devotes a concluding section to justify both Jerome's indebtedness to pagan culture and the classical *eloquentia* of Jerome's works. The model for that discussion is without a doubt Lorenzo Valla's preface to the fourth book of the *Elegantiae*—as vivid a piece of writing in its own way as Jerome's original account of his dream. 'I know there are some', writes Valla, 'especially those who believe themselves to be especially pious and religious, who will dare to maintain that this work of mine is unworthy of a Christian, because it exhorts the reader to read secular works'. He continues:

For having been more attentive to them, Jerome confesses that he was beaten before a tribunal of the Almighty, and accused of being Ciceronian and not Christian, as if one could not be at one and the same time faithful and Ciceronian. He solemnly vowed, however, and that accompanied by the most dire and binding of oaths, that he would never thereafter read any secular works.[33]

This story has contributed in no small part to the 'shipwreck of Latin *litterae*', continues Valla.[34] Yet the story makes no sense at all. Which secular works is one not to read, on Jerome's authority? All the orators, all the historians, all the poets, all the philosophers, all the jurists? Or is one only forbidden to read Cicero? If the ban is only on the reading of Cicero, that is a comparatively straightforward matter (but then, why did Jerome renounce *all* pagan works?); if all ancient authors are forbidden, then not only grammarians and rhetoricians, but all contemporary scholars must be indicted for breaking Jerome's solemn undertaking. But of course, says Valla, answering his own rhetorical questions, it is *eloquentia* which is under attack here. And he proceeds to defend eloquence vigorously as an essential component of all learning, and specifically of 'true theology'—'I consider anyone who is ignorant of eloquence to be utterly unworthy to speak of theology'.[35] As for Jerome:

> Who is more eloquent than Jerome? Who a greater orator? Who, even though he may wish to disguise the fact, is more solicitous, more assiduously studious, more carefully observant of the art of speaking well [bene dicendi]?[36]

Both the letter to Warham and the *Vita Hieronymi* repeatedly echo Valla's *Elegantiae* preface.[37] But the most striking influence on the work is, I think, more fundamental than stylistic emulation and verbal echoing. Erasmus closes the *Vita* with a detailed philological discussion of Jerome's latinity, which takes as its starting point a passage in the *Elegantiae* in which Valla challenges Jerome's derivation of the name 'Jovis Stator' in the *Contra Jovinianum*.[38] This discussion firmly relocates the patristic texts within the body of classical Latin texts available for meticulous textual scrutiny and linguistic analysis. Jerome's *eloquentia* and erudition provide the justification for handling his works as if they *were* Cicero's— retrieving them, purging them of corruptions and accretions, reworking them where necessary, so that they are restored as far as possible to their pristine textual state. The integrity of the *textual* activity, Erasmus maintains, will ensure that the *doctrine* too (the content, as opposed to the style) will be similarly revived, polished, and restored.

As an intrinsic part of the text of the *Vita Hieronymi*, the long section justifying Jerome's *eloquentia*, followed by the philological scrutiny of his Latin usage, surely alters the sense in which the reader is asked to use the *Vita* as original, from which he will make his own 'copy', in pursuit of a Christian life. It is now explicitly the 'books of great men', rather than their physical existence, their lived experience, which serve as example and inspiration, 'the relics of the mind'.[39] The 'copy' is a palimpsest, over-writing and rewriting the textual remains of the exemplary devotional figure. Instead of the figure of the self-mortifying penitent, it is Jerome's library, and Jerome's study, which, in Erasmus's version, most fully *embody* the scholar-saint.[40] It follows that the posture in which the individual Christian most fully partakes of Jerome's example is in the study, in the act of full attentiveness to sacred texts and their exegesis, and that that activity has absorbed from Jerome his 'aura of sanctity'.

LAYING CLAIM TO A RIVER OF GOLD: WORDLY RECOMPENSE FOR THE LABOURS OF HERCULES

At the end of the dedicatory letter to Warham, Erasmus makes an unexpected transition, and claims Jerome not simply as his model, but as his own:

I have followed the example of those who would rather raise a fresh loan than go to prison for non-payment, and have borrowed from Jerome the wherewithal to repay you. Though why should it any longer look like something borrowed rather than my own?—real estate often passes from one ownership to another by occupation or prescriptive right. In any case, in this line of business Jerome himself has laid down a principle for me in his preface to the books of Kings, repeatedly calling that work his, because anything that we have made our own by correcting, reading, constant devotion, we can fairly claim as ours. On this principle why should not I myself claim a proprietary right in the works of Jerome? For centuries they had been treated as abandoned goods; I entered upon them as something ownerless, and by incalculable efforts reclaimed them for all devotees of the true theology.

It is a river of gold, a well stocked library, that a man acquires who possesses Jerome and nothing else.[41]

By painstakingly restoring and correcting, the textual exegete claims the right to the 'work' as his own, as return on the investment of labour (the 'river of gold' is how Cicero described Aristotle's literary legacy). His own efforts elide with those of his original; the two tasks become inseparable in their arduousness and difficulty, and materially indistinguishable. Elsewhere Erasmus discards these wholeheartedly mercantile metaphors for a version of the image of the phoenix; Jerome is reborn in Erasmus, as the scholar is extinguished in the act of restoring the saint's letters:[42]

I have borne in this such a burden of toil that one could almost say I have killed myself in my efforts to give Jerome a new lease of life. One thing I could even swear without hesitation: it cost Jerome less to write his works than it has cost me to restore and explain them.[43]

In either of these two formulations, Erasmus takes on Jerome's role in relation to the exegesis of sacred texts, and becomes his revived physical embodiment. Not, of course, in order to make any claim for himself, but in order to participate in the continuous process of reception and transmission of scripture.[44]

Within the text of the *Vita Hieronymi* there are several points at which the attentive reader might judge that Erasmus is claiming Jerome 'as his own'. The one which Erasmus scholars have found most striking is probably Erasmus's account of Jerome's retreat into the Syrian desert, in which this act of penitence preparatory to the Christian life is reconstructed as an intensive period of humanistic study, following a strikingly Erasmian programme:

He divided his time between study and prayer, devoting a good portion of the night also to these activities. He made the smallest possible provision of time for sleep, even less for food, none at all for leisure. He refreshed himself after the exhaustion of study with a prayer or a hymn; returning instantly refreshed to his interrupted reading. He reread his entire library, he refreshed his memory of all his old studies, he learned the Sacred Scriptures by heart. He meditated on the prophets, paying the closest attention to resolving apparent mysteries in the divine pronouncements. He gathered together the philosophy of Christ [philosophia Christi] from the purest sources—the writings of the evangelists and apostles. For the first step to piety is to know the fundamental tenets of the founders of your beliefs [autores]. He read the other commentators with pleasure and judiciously, he neglected no author whatsoever from whom he could derive something useful, not even pagans and heretics. For he knew, as a man of the greatest discernment, how to collect gold from a dung-heap. . . . Whatever he read, he digested it into 'places' [loci], grouping them under systematic headings according to their similarities and differences, to facilitate the recall of information, and to make it more readily available for use. It is extraordinary how much attention he was prepared to give to all outstanding ability, especially when it was also commended by the endowment of eloquence, to the extent that if it had been possible he would gladly have heaped praise even on heretics, and have forgiven a lapse of faith where there was real erudition (as he did in the case of Origen, whom he called 'his own', and from whom he translated certain homilies in his youth).[45]

It is this passage, I think, which leads both Rice and Olin irresistibly to identify the solitary, intensively studious Jerome of the *Vita* with Erasmus himself (and indeed, with the Metsys panel portrait, the Holbein painting, and the Dürer woodcut). Two other moments in Erasmus's narrative, however, can be more precisely related to his own self-conscious self-formation alongside the scholar-saint. At the very end of the *Vita* Erasmus describes the way in which the revival and restoration via the *bonae litterae* of Jerome's works will result in all Europe's claiming him as their own:

From then on, when humane learning [bonae litterae] had been reborn throughout the whole Christian world, and many discerning people of good faith had begun to reawaken themselves to the ancient and pure theology, everyone embraced Jerome as reborn for our universal studies. Everyone claimed him as their own. Once upon a time seven cities claimed Homer as their own. In the case of Jerome, Dalmatia, Pannonia and Italy all claimed the right of proximity. Stridon congratulated itself on having produced such an shining light. Italy rejoiced on three counts: firstly, because she had educated him; then because through baptism she had produced his rebirth in Christ; and finally she was the repository of the pledge of his sacred remains. France claimed him as hers, because he had travelled there extensively, as he attested expressly in so many of his works. The Spanish laid claim to him, whom he distinguished by certain letters he sent to them. Germany embraced him passionately, even though he taught them and made them known in only a single book. Greece claimed him by double title: firstly, because of his knowledge of her language, and then because she in turn had been of service for his writings as mistress of the world. Egypt embraced him, which made that most learned man more learned. The Arabs and Saracens loved him, who were made famous by his proximity. The Hebrews cherished him whose language and letters he acquired with so much toil. Even Syria claimed him as her own, as the place where he spent most of his life.[46]

Here Erasmus shows an interestingly acute awareness that through the revival of *bonae litterae* it might be possible for the man of letters, though born in comparative geographical obscurity, to find international fame. Because of his writings (in particular, his letters) the man from Stridon is claimed by the nations of Europe and beyond. It hardly needs to be pointed out that this passage—an elaborate forward projection in the case of the reputation which Jerome may retrieve through this edition of his works—is already an appropriate description of Erasmus's own reputation.

One further passage seems directly to touch on Erasmus's own '*vita*'. Erasmus's discussion of Jerome's early education and teachers includes a digression on whether Nazianzenus and Didimus had actually, as he claimed, been his teachers. These sorts of questions are ridiculous, Erasmus comments. When a gifted person claims a respected figure as his teacher, it is of no interest how long he studied with him:

> He called Gregory Nazianzenus his master, and claimed to have learned sacred letters under his guidance. But where or for how much time he studied with him I cannot ascertain. . . . He moved to Alexandria when he was already middle-aged, to perfect the study of sacred texts by studying with Didimus, whom, because he was deprived of sight since boyhood, he called 'the seeing one'. Although Ruffinus accuses Jerome of not having frequented Didimus's circle for more than a single month, that is plainly ridiculous, even if it is the literal truth. For it is of no importance how much time is spent with a teacher, but rather, how much one learned from him.[47]

Erasmus himself consistently maintained that he had had as his teacher Alexander Hegius, and implied that Rudolph Agricola had also taught him.[48] The significance of the latter lay in his having been reputedly the first northern humanist to study at Ferrara, thus being the origin for a genealogy of Italian-influenced northern men of letters. Like Jerome's, these claims do not bear close scrutiny: Hegius taught the top class at Erasmus's school when Erasmus was in the lowest class, and Agricola may once have visited there. Nevertheless, Erasmus is maintaining, even such relatively inconsequential contact may amount to an 'influence'—a model for emulation, an inspirational example.

A year before the publication of the Jerome *Letters*, with their introductory *Vita*, the first of Erasmus's letters ever to be published appeared in a volume in honour of Giovanni de' Medici, Pope Leo X, published by Froben at Basle.[49] Three of these letters relate directly to the anticipated publication of the Jerome edition.[50] Erasmus critics have had some difficulty with these letters, which apparently publicly promise dedication of the Jerome to Leo X; in the end, Erasmus dedicated the *Novum Instrumentum* (his annotated, revised New Testament) to Pope Leo, and the Jerome (as we have seen) to Archbishop Warham.

The letters to Raffaele Riaro (cardinal of San Giorgio), Domenico Grimani, and Pope Leo X in the *Damiani elegeia* volume rework a single central theme—the extraordinary effort which Erasmus is currently expending on extensive enlargement and revisions for the new edition of his *Adagia*, and on the preparation of his Jerome *Letters*, both of which are to be published imminently by Froben. The rhetoric of who should receive the dedication of the Jerome *Letters* is closely bound up with this stress of the arduousness and extent of the task. In all three letters Erasmus conveys vividly his sense that he has earned the right, through his labours, to commercial ownership of the Jerome, and therefore the right to negotiate the profit which might accrue from its publication. The issue of the work's dedication undoubtedly falls within the scope of such a negotiation. Erasmus put the matter frankly when it came to the dedication to Archbishop Warham which eventually prefaced the work:

> Jerome, recalled to the light from some sort of nether region, I prefer to dedicate to you alone, either because I owe you without exception everything I have, or because you always have a special concern for Jerome's reputation. . . . I have one anxiety, that my limited powers may fail to do justice to Jerome's importance or to your eminent position; for nowhere do I feel more clearly how small my talent is than when I am striving to make some sort of response to your exalted virtues and your unbounded goodness to me. But what was I to do, bound to you as I am by so many and such great obligations that if I sold myself into slavery I should not be in a position to repay any part of my debt?[51]

The three letters published in advance of the Jerome *Letters*, by the same publisher who was to issue both them and the revised *Adagia*, provide elaborate advanced publicity—a publishers' marketing blurb which specifies precisely the form which the Jerome volumes will take. The expressed intention to dedicate the Jerome to Leo X, repeated in each of the letters, and culminating in the letter to Leo himself, *is*, therefore, a dedication. It allows Erasmus, in fact, to 'market' the dedication twice, as befits a work (he might say) which had cost him so dearly in terms of effort in the making. The prepublication compilation of letters markets the Jerome as worthy of the pope ('No name is better known than Jerome's, no person more universally acceptable; and yet I see a way to add to his renown, to give more weight to his authority'), and the pope's fame is enhanced by association with the Jerome ('Pope Leo's fame is as glorious as it could be; and yet, if I mistake not, it might be not a little increased').[52] Each of the three letters develops slightly differently the basic theme, each one proposing Leo X as the most suitable recipient of the Jerome, whilst at the same time indicating Erasmus's material indebtedness to Warham (one of his few providers of regular financial support).

Indeed, if we set the *four* letters side by side (the three in the *Damiani elegeia* and the official dedication to Warham), they make up a series of rhetorical variations around a single theme, worked examples of the kind of exercise in *copia* proposed in Erasmus's most popular and well-known work, the pedagogic textbook *De copia*. As an advertising strategy, the impact is considerably stronger than that of the single prefatory letter. Any reader who gives attention to *copia* here is bound thoroughly to absorb the key points around which the embellishments are constructed: the comparative constructions of balanced compliment directed simultaneously to England and Warham, and to Italy and Pope Leo fix both dedicatees' names firmly in the mind; the amplifications on the theme of the arduousness of the Jerome undertaking (and the associated *Adagia* volume) create a convincing atmosphere of expectation for the reader around the promised work. Finally, both powerful patrons gain the satisfaction of the elaborately eloquent exercise—Leo's ensured by the fact that the *Damiani elegeia* is a volume entirely devoted to his celebration; Warham by being the genuine recipient of the volume. There seems no reason to suggest that Erasmus had any change of heart over the dedication of the Jerome. It is simply successfully dedicated twice over, as befits so grandiose a work.[53]

Each of the letters in the *Damiani elegeia* plays a rhetorical variation on the theme of 'the proverbial Hercules', under whose heading Erasmus had also advertised the forthcoming Jerome volume in the 1515 Froben edition of the *Adagia*.[54] In his dedicatory letter to Warham, in the Jerome itself, Erasmus once more compares the effort expended on the saint's writings—effort which is entirely invisible to the reader, who 'never gives a thought to the time and tedium it has cost [Erasmus] to battle with the thorns and briars'—to the labours of Hercules:

> And so I despised all the difficulties, and like a modern Hercules I set out on my most laborious but most glorious campaign, taking the field almost unaided against all the monsters of error. I cannot think that Hercules consumed as much energy in taming a few monsters as I did in abolishing so many thousand blunders. And I conceive that not a little more advantage will accrue to the world from my work than from his labours which are on the lips of all men.[55]

Here the emphasis is still on the superhuman labour undertaken in the Jerome edition; but in contrast to the *Adagia* passage which I quoted in the first chapter, there is also a strong suggestion of the heroic warrior about this scholar-exegete—Erasmus as *miles christianus* (the Christian soldier). This suggestion is taken up again in an extravagently complimentary letter to Erasmus, written in November 1516, and first published in the *Epistolae elegantes* (Martens, Louvain, 1517), by Budé's close friend and collaborator, Francois Deloynes. This letter repeats the conjunction of the Jerome edition and the labours of Hercules, but includes the much earlier *Enchiridion militis christiani*:

> Your *Adagiorum chiliades*, your *Moriae encomium*, your *Miles christianus*, your *Novum instrumentum*, and other things of the same kind launched under such happy auspices from your workshop and received with such applause on their arrival here—all these, as far as my leisure permitted, I have read and re-read. I have in my hands the works of Jerome, a formidable task indeed, and too much for the strength of any but our modern Hercules whose name is Erasmus, in which I fancy I see Jerome himself thanks to your care and diligence and unstinting labour returning to the light of day and forestalling in some sort the day of resurrection foretold in Holy Scripture; for now that the corruptions which abounded everywhere have been cleared away, you have dressed him as it were in a new garment of immortality and restored him to his original and native glory.[56]

In this public statement,[57] Deloynes and Budé (and Bérault, who adds his name at the end of the letter) pledge themselves to support Erasmus's *philosophia Christi*, as represented by the Jerome project. And they add their confirmation to that carefully constructed self-image of Erasmus as scholar-exegete of heroic stature—to that very particular conjunction of piety, scholarship, physical stamina, heroic tenacity, and commercial accumen which emerges, I suggest, in this cultural and historical moment, via Erasmus's self-conscious imaging of himself. Erasmus/Jerome substitutes scholar for saint ('When I read treatises of this sort, on these kinds of men, I can barely restrain myself from saying, "Saint Socrates, pray for us"') as the exemplary European Man of Letters.

LEGIBLE TEXTS: ERASMUS'S PORTRAITS AND THE ECHO OF JEROME

Rice and Olin have both drawn attention to the fact that the portrait of Jerome in the *Vita Hieronymi* is 'disconcertingly' a self-portrait of Erasmus himself.[58] Neither author finds this surprising:

> Erasmus does show his subject 'as a living man, dictating, writing, arguing, consoling and instructing'; at the same time, his portrait of Jerome is a self-portrait, that of a Christian scholar attractively but disconcertingly Erasmian in attitude and personality. This can hardly surprise us. We revive a figure from

the past because he meets a present need, suggests a present strategy, can be used to beat a present enemy and further a present cause, makes legitimate a present call for change and reform. The author of the fourteenth-century pseudographs had emphasized Jerome's devotion to poverty in order to attack contemporary trimmers, his austerities to press for radical monastic reform, his evangelical piety and pastoral concern to show up the wickedness and irresponsibility of contemporary theologians and prelates. What Erasmus admired was not always the same; his tactic was.[59]

What we have now seen, however, is that there is an Erasmian agenda, as it were, which sees to it that the life of the paradigm Christian textual editor and exegete conforms to the expectations of a sixteenth-century humanistic audience. In other words, it is the agenda, rather than any desire on Erasmus's own part to be seen as 'like' Jerome, which draws Jerome's life away from hagiography and towards that cluster of exemplary sacred/secular activities best represented for Erasmus by the combination of Lorenzo Valla's annotations on the New Testament and his *Elegantiae*.

What I am suggesting here is that the Escher-like flicker-effect which Rice and Olin comment upon (as did Ferguson before them, in his edition of the *Vita Hieronymi*)—from biography to autobiography, and from portrait to self-portrait—is neither a side issue nor an accident in Erasmus's treatment of Jerome. At the heart of the Jerome edition—the opus Erasmus produced at the zenith of his international career, and on the threshold of his self-formation as an icon of scholar-piety—is the fusion, or perhaps confusion, of secular and sacred attention. That deliberate redirecting of readerly attention at the text itself, simultaneously *as* text and as true object of pious devotion, is the source of a real critical confusion, to which I think we ought to give serious attention. What is legible in the restored text of Jerome, so Erasmus claims, is the quintessence of piety, that availability for profound and attentive reading by means of which reading transcends mechanical absorption and becomes spiritual education, the very enactment of the *philosophia Christi*.

Because the emphasis here is entirely upon the act of reading, and its relationship to the production of text by the *magister*, somewhere in the recasting of the *Vita Hieronymi*, the lives of Jerome and of Erasmus became subtly intertwined. In the course of the transformation required to reconcile the sanctity of the early Father of the Church with the piety of the northern educator, the aura of the saint modulated into that of the exemplary scholar-translator. If we now turn our attention once more to the fashioned portraits of Erasmus of the last chapter, some of that programme of refashioning saint into scholar can be seen vividly in the iconography of those commissioned and widely circulated graphic images.

Metsys's 1517 portrait of Erasmus is at one level (the one most readily responded to by the modern viewer) a realistic representation 'from the life' of the scholar-translator-commentator in his study. The anecdote with which Erasmus regales More, about the sitting postponed after illness, depends upon an agreed idea of the immediacy, and physical exactness, of the artist's rendering (the impossibility of continuing the portrait when the sitter's illness had supposedly altered his appearance). Yet that letter itself is highly contrived—we shall see in a moment how artfully Erasmus wielded the *epistola familiaris* (familiar letter), as an image-making medium. In other words, a considerable amount of self-consciousness on Erasmus's part is involved in presenting his own 'life' as at once 'realistic' (historically and geographically specific) and as significantly related to other great 'lives' from the classical past (secular and sacred), with their richly accumulated symbolic reference beyond the merely mundane.

When we look more closely at its 'realism', the composition of the Metsys portrait of Erasmus gives prominence to objects and attributes which seem to invite a nonrealist 'reading'—an interpretation which includes their iconographical or symbolic significance: the reed pen, the inkwell, the small lectern, the untidily piled books, the scissors (or wick-trimmer), the signet ring on Erasmus's right-hand index finger, the handwritten page, the capacious, metal-clasped pouch at his waist.[60] We might add the sand-shaker, from the Gilles portrait, which, whilst figuring in the Gilles panel, is reunited iconographically with Erasmus when the two panels are juxtaposed.[61] I propose to respond for a moment to that implied bid for the reader's interpretative attention, and to look at the portrait more closely.

The most striking 'real' item in the portrait, whose symbolic currency we readily overlook, is the scissors which hang from the bookshelves behind Erasmus. A little attention reveals these to be not scissors at all, but wick-trimmers.[62] The candle snuffer/trimmer (with or without an accompanying candle) appears in many late fifteenth and early sixteenth century paintings of Saint Jerome, but its presence in the Erasmus portrait is never commented upon.[63] In her discussion of Carpaccio's *Saint Augustine in Jerome's Study*, Helen Roberts has suggested that 'the scissors, so prominently placed on the saint's writing table, may have a special significance, symbolic of the interpretation of the Scriptures by the Doctors of the Church'.[64] A candlestick is certainly also a regular feature of Jerome paintings, and the scissors/trimmers may rest against or alongside it.[65] Trimming the wick of scriptures so that their light shines out strongly and brightly seems irresistibly to apply to Erasmus's scholarly efforts in his publications around 1517 (the *Novum Instrumentum*, the *Letters* of Jerome, the first of the *Paraphrases*).[66]

If the scissors/wick-trimmers alert us (as I believe they should) to a symbolic function in the 'realistic' study in which Erasmus is seated, then we may need to reconsider the jumble of books on the shelf behind him. Here again, there is a steady iconographic tradition to refer to. In 1456 Bartolomeo Fazio, pupil of Guarino Veronese, wrote a short treatise, *De viris illustribus*, which included a chapter 'De pictoribus' (On painters).[67] In it, he expressed admiration for Jan van Eyck, 'judged to be the leading painter of our time'. And amongst van Eyck's specific achievements, Fazio singled out the representation of books in his painting of *Saint Jerome in His Study*:

> His is a remarkable picture . . . [of] Jerome like a living being in a library done with rare art: for if you move away from it a little it seems that it recedes inwards and that it has complete books laid open in it, while if you go near, it is evident that just their fore-edges are there.[68]

Baxandall (and following Baxandall, Rice and Ridderbos) have identified the painting Fazio refers to as the *Saint Jerome in His Study* of which a copy survives in Detroit.[69] In any case, the Detroit Jerome provides a fine example of virtuoso representation of piled books on the upper of two deep shelves in a recess, partially concealed by a curtain. The books are lovingly and meticulously depicted so as to convey solidity, bulk, and weight, as well as variety of surfaces, textures, types of leather and paper, metal clasps, and cloth ties.[70] The convincing nature of the illusion of depth is enhanced by the comparative flatness of the emblematic objects on the lower shelf (although the stoppered crystal vase stands out for its three-dimensionality). It is not surprising, then, to find later Low Countries painters self-consciously imitating Jan van Eyck's piled books in their own Jerome paintings.[71]

But virtuoso representation of books in the context of learned Fathers of the Church is also to be found in Italian paintings of the late fifteenth and early sixteenth centuries. In Carpaccio's *Visit of Saint Jerome's Soul to Saint Augustine*, books are scattered all around the seated Father. Codices lie heaped on a shelf to his right, and books lie open on a revolving book wheel in the alcove behind him. There are books, closed and open, on his desk, and at his feet are four separate book-based depictions, so meticulously painted that the writing on the open book must originally have been legible, as the sheets of secular and sacred music still are.[72] The books on the pedestal at Augustine's feet, in particular, seem to mediate between the sacred work with which Augustine is occupied (he is writing a letter to Jerome, inquiring on a point of scripture) and the secular world. This mediating role of books can also be seen in Carpaccio's *Disputation of Saint Stephen*, in which precisely similar compositions of books on the pedestal at Saint Stephen's feet mediates between his learning and that of the Jewish elders.[73]

The figure with the precious and lovingly depicted book is a feature of the increasingly convincingly illusionistic portraiture of the beginning of the sixteenth century.[74] I suggest that because of its overload of cultural meaning, the book, in these graphic representations, is ambiguously 'precious'. From the representations of a meditative Virgin and donor portraits of van Eyck onwards, the care with which binding, text, page, illumination, and jewelled bookmark (enhancing their rarity) are depicted focuses the viewer's attention upon them.[75] In the age of print, the book becomes simply part of the scholar's equipment. At the same time, the care taken with the book's depiction means that it retains the freight of 'worth' in excess of any use value, which Natalie Davis has argued is in any case a feature of early attitudes to the printed book.[76]

What the converging Italian and northern traditions give us, I suggest, is a consistent presence of meticulously rendered, scattered or randomly piled books in paintings symbolising the saint-scholar's bringing to bear of the wealth of his pagan-based learning on sacred texts.[77] Incunabula or lavishly bound and ornamented printed books conveniently conserve an aura carried over from the precious manuscript. This aura, visible in the combination of painstaking realism and symbolic lavishness in the volume cradled in the hand of Virgin, saint, or donor in northern paintings from van Eyck onwards, is confused but not lost in 'study' paintings, in which the books are both symbol and tool of the scholar's trade. And as Fazio notes in the case of the van Eyck Jerome, the technical virtuosity makes the shelves of books an object of attention; the viewer's eye passes from the saint's rapt face to the book he studies, then up to the echoed books above him, via the assembled symbols of purity, scriptural exegesis, learning, and devotion on the table alongside the lectern and book and on the lower shelf.

As a number of scholars have noted, the composition of the Metsys Erasmus panel has a number of resemblances with the van Eyck Jerome, foremost amongst which is the arrangement of shelves, and the piled, jumbled books.[78] In the case of Erasmus, the inscriptions on the books themselves identify these works as certainly a mixture of Christian and pagan (edited or translated by Erasmus himself); the scholar works on a paraphrase of scripture, sustained by the presence of this combined cultural heritage.[79] If we are in any doubt as to the relevance to the task in hand (the *Paraphrase of Saint Paul's Epistle to the Romans*), we might compare the Erasmus composition with another Metsys work from the same period, the *Banker and His Wife* (1514), now in the Louvre.[80] In this painting also, the two figures are seated at a table before two shelves in an alcove, on which books and other objects are carefully arranged. Here rather more obviously the objects provide a gloss on the action at the table: the banker's wife turns a leaf of a devotional book (in which a colour plate of the Virgin and child is clearly visible), but her attention is drawn away from spiritual matters to the material objects her husband handles. Behind them are arrayed symbols of the spiritual purity from which she threatens to be distracted, including a a crystal vase, a rosary, books, and rolled papers. These objects recall the van Eyck, as does the convex mirror on the table, reflecting a figure outside the depiction of the painting (as the mirror shows the artist himself in van Eyck's Arnofino marriage painting).[81]

As one might expect, the point is more clearly made in the Holbein portrait of Erasmus presented to Archbishop Warham, in which, as we saw in the last chapter, the Herculean labours of the edition of Jerome's *Letters* is the overt subject of the composition. Behind Erasmus, in this painting, is a curtain, partly drawn. Behind the curtain, above Erasmus's left shoulder, can be seen a shelf, on which rest carelessly piled books and a transparent crystal vase (possibly closed with a paper cover). In front of the curtain, to Erasmus's right, stands an Italianate Renaissance pilaster.[82] Erasmus's hands rest proprietorially, and with an air of satisfaction, on the closed Jerome, inscribed 'The Labours of Hercules'.

The shelf with books and vase are readily identifiable as elements of the iconography of Saint Jerome, partially veiled by the curtain. Probably the most compelling comparison would be Joos van de Cleve's *Saint Jerome in His Study* (ca. 1525), where shelf, books, and vase are remarkably similarly arranged, but the classic reference would be the Detroit Jerome, after Jan van Eyck.[83] In front of the partially obscured Jerome (cut off by the curtain), with Italian Renaissance culture at his right hand, Erasmus appropriates the great Father of the Church and establisher of the definitive text of scripture through his own Herculean labours:

> I doubt if Jerome himself expended so much effort on the writing of his works as they will cost me in the correction. At least I have thrown myself into this task so zealously that one could almost say that I had worked myself to death that Jerome might live again.[84]

On Erasmus's right, the pilaster frames the painting on the left side, as the curtained alcove frames the right. The pilaster refers us to the Italian Renaissance, proudly claimed by Erasmus as the inspiration for his own scholarly activities. There is possibly a suggestion of Erasmus (and Jerome) as 'pillar of the Church', as in Valla's 'Et certi soli eloquentes . . . columnae ecclesiae sunt' (preface to the fourth book of *Elegantiae*). Perhaps, too, it echoes the Herculean theme of the adage—the columns or pillars of Hercules, with their 'terminus' message, *plus ultra*, familiar as

Charles V's chosen emblem.[85] The binding on the book, one might add, is recognisably northern European. Here is the physical presence of the carefully exemplary scholar-editor, strategically located between the old scholarship and the new, the old world of learning and the new, almost to the point of paradox: solitary, but not penitent; pensive, yet looking the onlooker steadily in the eye; sober, yet prosperously dressed; in his study, yet richly housed.[86]

Since we have dwelt so determinedly on the 'Jeromeness' of Erasmus in the Metsys diptych, let us close with a significant difference. Jerome, who gave up all wordly pursuits for the pursuit of godly learning, is consistently represented as modestly attired—the simplicity of his garments ranging from simple, unadorned monastic garb to undress and near nakedness (a tradition which named him 'cardinal' sometimes allows him cardinal's red, but the simplicity is sustained). Although discreetly sober, as befits a scholar, Erasmus, by contrast, is decidedly prosperously dressed. He wears burgher's heavy cloth, elaborate sleeves, and fur.[87] Furthermore, he wears a deep pouch at his waist, so placed that it is difficult not to make it a feature of the painting.[88] The pouch rests in Erasmus's lap, occupying a central space between his head and his book; it connotes both prosperity/profit and mobility.[89] This scholar-exegete occupies a northern mercantile world, the world of business and affairs.[90]

The deceptively 'realistic' portraits, then, are heavy with symbolic significance—heavy, but not steady. The portraits offer layered meanings, retrievable either from the separate panels or from the panels together. Those meanings are sustained and enriched again by the accompanying correspondence, a correspondence which both materially complements the paintings and replicates the contents of the portraits themselves, which contain letters and printed texts as already part of their meaning. The individual, Erasmus, inhabits a visual world dense with meaning, legible beyond the charisma of the mere man. If, as Svetlana Alpers has suggested for the Low Countries of a century later, Erasmus's is a 'visual culture', then here is a thickened meaning for the man of letters, which our intensely text-orientated culture has all but lost.[91]

ERASMUS IN SAINT JEROME'S STUDY

Amongst the northern European (or northern European influenced) paintings whose treatment of the scholar in his study the Erasmus portraits recall, there is one type which seems particularly close, thematically, to the kinds of issue I have been discussing. These are those in which a recognisable contemporary figure is represented as 'Jerome' or 'Augustine', at scholarly work in that saint's study.[92] The van Eyck *Jerome in His Study* (Detroit), generally taken to be the Low Countries prototype for the whole tradition of Jerome-style scholar-portraits, has itself been identified as a portrait of the fifteenth-century cardinal Nicholas Albergati.[93] Antonella da Messina's remarkable *Jerome in His Study*, in the National Gallery, is claimed as a portrait of Nicholas of Cusa.[94] In both cases, the scholarly literature has produced cogent reasons why a formal link between the sitter for the portrait and the saint licensed the portrayal of the one in the guise of the other.

In itself this provides a fascinating insight into contemporary understanding of scholarly 'identity' in the fifteenth and early sixteenth centuries. The fact that Nicholas Albergati had been prior of a monastery dedicated to Jerome, and was himself a zealous scholar of the sacred texts, makes it appropriate for the painter to depict him *as* Jerome, or, rather, as Albergati as Jerome. On Albergati/Jerome's table lies a letter with the inscription:

Reuerendissimo in Christo patri et domino, domino Ieronimo, tituli Sancte Crucis in Iherusalem presbytero cardinali.

[To the Most Reverend Father and Master in Christ, Master Jerome, Cardinal-Priest of the Holy Cross in Jerusalem.][95]

It is Albergati who is cardinal of Santa Croce in Gerusalemme, not the historical Jerome. The ancient scholar has become the 'type' for the contemporary cardinal; in the graphic representation, Albergati inhabits the persona of the great scriptural exegete, and is thus both captured as a personality himself and formally complimented with the likeness.

If such portraits in disguise fascinate us, how much more compellingly 'strange' or 'other' in the conceptual frame they uncover for us are paintings of a type first clearly identified by Helen Roberts in 1959, in a classic article on Carpaccio's well-known painting of an ecclesiastical scholar in an oratory or study.[96] Roberts identified Carpaccio's source for this painting as a spurious letter from Saint Augustine to Saint Cyril, which probably originated in the thirteenth century, and was much reprinted in the fifteenth.[97] In the letter, 'Augustine' describes a miraculous visitation by the spirit of Jerome. Reaching an impasse in his thinking whilst in the process of composing a treatise on the nature of eternal bliss in paradise, 'Augustine' decided to write to his contemporary, Jerome, for expert help. Unbeknown to him, however, Jerome had died at that very instant; 'Augustine' 's study was suddenly flooded with light and 'an ineffable fragrance'. At the same moment, the voice of Saint Jerome counselled 'Augustine' not to put his whole trust in human intellect in order to understand Christian mysteries; he then gave Augustine the help he needed, from his new vantage point as a heavenly soul himself. The spurious letter provides a 'tale', in other words, in which inspiration is authoritatively valued above rational exploration of spiritual truths.[98] Since Roberts's discovery, Martin Kemp has drawn attention to the fact that Botticelli's great *Vision of Saint Augustine* in Florence illustrates the same incident.[99]

In these two great paintings, the scholar-saint sits at work in his study, surrounded by the paraphernalia of learning, intellectual exploration of the heavens (astronomy), and scholarly textual activity, all rendered with compelling meticulousness.[100] The scholar pauses and looks up from these activities, and is painted in the posture of rapt attention, concentrating instead on the 'ineffable' inspirational presence of that other great scholar's insubstantial spiritual presence.

Botticelli's 1480 masterpiece was commissioned together with a companion painting by Domenico Ghirlandaio, *Saint Jerome in His Study*. The paintings remain together in the Chiesa d'Ognissanti in Florence, for which they were produced. Ghirlandaio's painting is fully in the northern, van Eyckian tradition. Behind the saint, seated at his desk, and as if pausing in the act of writing, is an elaborate clutter of books, manuscripts, letters (in the three classical languages, Latin, Greek, and Hebrew), his cardinal's hat, a stoppered crystal flask, a rosary; on his desk are more books and papers, an inkwell, spectacles, an unlit candle and wick-trimmer. The alcove in which he sits is curtained, the curtain half drawn to reveal a two-shelved alcove containing his library.[101] Recently, the original inscription above this painting has been recovered. It reads: '[R]edde nos claros lampas radio[sa] / sine qua terra tota est umbrosa' (Make us bright, radiant light, without which the whole earth is in darkness).[102] In this case, the contrast between scholarly rationality and inspiration apparently lies in the figure of Jerome himself. His direct gaze, out of the painting, at the spectator, figures the transmission of sacred knowledge from one mind to another, mediated by the texts he produces. These texts—in particular, of course, the Vulgate text of the Bible—are the point of exchange of spiritual understanding between past scholar and present reader.

I offer this necessarily curtailed and outline account of this particular genre of scholar paintings to indicate the possible complexity of the figuring of Jerome, or Erasmus as Jerome, which I have begun to uncover. For I want to argue that Saint Jerome is a presence for Erasmus in some more complicated and elusive sense than a mere 'disguise' the scholar might adopt to give himself presence and authority. Erasmus was himself an Augustinian monk; his greatest works of textual exegesis and editing were his own version of the New Testament (for which he claimed the precedent of Jerome) and his edition of the works of Jerome himself.[103] The Metsys Erasmus panel irresistibly asks for comparison with the Ghirlandaio *Saint Jerome*. Equally, the Botticelli *Vision of Saint Augustine* provides an attractive model for the *idea* of one great scholar miraculously inspired by another: Jerome in Augustine; Jerome in Erasmus. And these graphic representations, which somehow make these complex interactions between spirituality, inspiration, and rationality vivid and graspable, in turn offer us a series of footholds into the confusing proliferation of Erasmus's printed works.[104]

'MORS ULTIMA LINEA RERUM': REPRISE

On August 1, 1528, in a letter to Charles V's secretary, Alfonso Valdès, Erasmus attempted to justify his choice of the motto *Concedo nulli* (I make way for nobody), as it appeared on the reverse of the Metsys medallion. He explained that the words were supposed to attach to Terminus, not to himself. And he went on:

> For death is a boundary or limit, which makes way for no one. Nevertheless, the medal is inscribed in Greek, 'hora telos makrou biou', which means, 'do not lose sight of the end of a long life', and in Latin, 'mors ultima linea rerum' [death is the ultimate limit of things]. Someone will object, 'Then you might just as well have had a skull engraved . . .'[105]

Erasmus has been accused of personal vanity, on account of the *concedo nulli* motto.[106] On the contrary, he explains, the obverse of the Metsys medallion carries a *vanitas* motif—it dwells on the inevitability of death, in the midst of life. And for that reason, the Terminus bust might perfectly well be replaced by a death's head, the more conventional *vanitas* emblem.

It may have been Dürer who was responsible for introducing the skull, emblem of the transitoriness of all worldly achievement, into Saint Jerome's study, in northern Renaissance representations of the saint at work.[107] Be this as it may, of all the objects which surround the saint in early sixteenth century versions, the one most obviously missing from the Erasmus portraits is the skull.[108] Erasmus's remark on the interchangeability of Terminus and skull suggests that this *vanitas* motif is indeed pendant to the Metsys Erasmus panel—a reference from one to the other, one more element in the accumulation around the scholar-exegete of the distinctive paraphernalia of the archetypal saint-exegete, Jerome.

Inventing Rudolph Agricola: Recovery and Transmission of the *De inventione dialectica*

THIS CHAPTER takes the form of a scholarly detective story. As I indicated in my Introduction, I first noticed many years ago that the fortunes of Agricola's manual of humanist logic, the *De inventione dialectica*, were historically and textually curious, and in some way tied in with Erasmus and Erasmian pedagogy.[1] The pursuit of the story of the recovery and transmission of that work uncovered a sometimes bizarre tale, in which Erasmus and his circle turned out indeed to be crucially involved. The story of Agricola's *De inventione dialectica* turns out to be the story of a carefully constructed northern European intellectual genealogy, and the emergence of a peculiarly northern curriculum and pedagogy—the construction of pedagogic charisma in print.

Rudolph Agricola's *De inventione dialectica* was the higher-education manual of *argumentatio* (argumentation) most widely specified, bought, and used in schools and universities throughout Protestant Europe, between the early decades of the sixteenth century and the midseventeenth century (when attitudes towards logic/dialectic in the curriculum altered so as to render it irrelevant).[2] The first printed edition appeared in 1515; it was published in Louvain and carried the name of the distinguished theologian Martin Dorp on the title page. Between 1515 and 1600 it went through more than seventy (known) editions (including epitomes).[3]

Not surprisingly, therefore, Agricola's *De inventione dialectica* has been the the object of a considerable amount of attention from intellectual historians (particularly historians of logic), and from historians of education. One might cite three key works as initiating Agricola as a focus for interest: W. J. Ong's extremely readable and influential *Ramus, Method, and the Decay of Dialogue* (Cambridge, Mass., 1958); W. S. Howell's much-cited *Logic and Rhetoric in England, 1500–1700* (New York, 1961); and C. Vasoli's monumental and highly regarded *La dialettica e la retorica dell'umanesimo* (Milan, 1968).[4] I stress the readability and monumental nature of such work in order to indicate that although this was specialist work, it had a considerable impact beyond the histories of logic and 'method', so that Agricola's name crops up (with these bibliographical items attached) quite widely in Renaissance intellectual history and in histories of humanism.

In the standard history of logic, Agricola's name, his textbook, and its influence were already firmly established by Prantl in the late nineteenth century, and the high assessment of his importance (though without a very consistent version of *how* he was important) has been sustained down to the present moment in a whole sequence of 'authoritative' publications, including work of my own.[5] These authorities have tended to divide into two camps: those who have regarded Agricola's *De inventione dialectica* as an integrated part of developing Renaissance logic and dialectic (a camp which includes Vasoli and myself), and those who have regarded it as an aberration or a distraction, diverting 'Renaissance thought' from knotty technical problems of validity and inference (the camp led by the Kneales, who notoriously blame Agricola for 'starting the corruption' in logic but cannot even get his name right).[6]

Who was Rudolph Agricola? He was a distinguished teacher, born in Bafflo, near Groningen, in the Low Countries, in 1444. He trained with Battista Guarino, son of the great Guarino, in Ferrara. He taught Alexander Hegius Greek, who in turn taught Erasmus at Deventer. In addition to being a considerable scholar of Latin and Greek, he was a poet, a musician, and a painter of note. He died in Heidelberg, where he had gone to teach at the invitation of Johann von Dalberg, bishop of Worms, in 1485.[7] All secondary sources are agreed that he was an extremely important influence on the development of northern European humanism.[8]

As early as 1971, however, in an important article, Terrence Heath drew attention to the curious lag of nearly forty years between the completion of Agricola's best-known work, the *De inventione dialectica* (around 1479) and its availability in printed form.[9] Furthermore, Heath suggested that in the first instance, the influence of that text in the early decades of the sixteenth century (its prominence in northern European curricula and university statutes) had to do precisely with its *availability*. It went into print at the moment at which more orthodox Aristotelian and scholastic texts were discarded both because of their explicitly Catholic scholia, and because those commentaries assumed a student body destined for the study of philosophy and canon law, rather than simply gaining an education in the liberal arts.[10]

So we have an author, an acknowledged influential humanist teacher of the late fifteenth century. We have a key text, judged to be a crucial connecting link in a chronological development (assumed linear and direct) of Western European thought, at its logical core. And we have a gap, which is noticed by one such scholar and judged to be significant—the gap between Agricola's writing the work and its appearance in print. That is where this chapter begins.

'WHAT HAS A DOG TO DO WITH A BATH?'

In 1503 Jacobus Faber of Deventer published the *Carmina* and assorted minor works of his and Erasmus's old schoolmaster Alexander Hegius (who had died in 1498).[11] The prefatory letter to the *Carmina* was addressed to Erasmus, and drew attention to the proverb 'Canis in balneo' (A dog in a bath), in the 1500 Paris edition of Erasmus's *Adages* (*Adagiorum collectanea*).[12] (The phrase indicates irrelevance or inappropriateness: 'That is about as appropriate as a dog in a bath', i.e., it doesn't belong there at all.) Faber was anxious to draw the reader's attention to Erasmus's linking of the names of Hegius and Agricola in a digressionary note in that adage.[13]

On the face of it, it seems clear what Faber is doing here. He wishes to enhance the reputation (and historical importance) of Alexander Hegius by pointing out a connection between Hegius and the already well known humanist Erasmus.[14] In the aside in the 'canis in balneo' adage, Erasmus had indicated that Hegius had been part of his own intellectual heritage (though Faber wishes to stress that Hegius's importance is *greater* than that assigned him by Erasmus, thus rhetorically magnifying the eulogy by association).[15] But if Erasmus 'validates' Hegius's reputation in this way, the prefatory letter serves *his* purposes as well. It closes with the following:

> Enough on this subject. For the rest, dearest Erasmus, I fail to comprehend why you have not given me, as we agreed, the Greek oration of Libanius when you have done it into Latin; I am waiting for it. I can glimpse your intention; you have decided to add to my Libanius the books you are now engaged upon: on famous metaphors, on ecclesiastical allegories, on allusions in classical authors, and on witty sayings and replies. This is the one thought I console myself with that I may bear patiently the rather long delay. So now accept our teacher's most important poems, to which will also be added, when I see that it would please you and my other kindly readers, his enquiries into a variety of topics, composed in dialogue form; in this respect he follows the example of Plato, who was most intimately known to him. Finally I shall see to it that any of Rodolphus Agricola's works that come to hand here are sent to you, except those that have been published in previous years and are now in the booksellers' shops.[16]

So the letter provides a 'puff' for Erasmus—in particular his forthcoming Libanius (but also promising a number of other, vaguely specified works, none of which in fact ever saw print under such titles). It also responds, apparently, to Erasmus's tribute to Agricola (in the 'canis in balneo' adage), by indicating that some collection of unpublished Agricola works is also 'forthcoming'.[17]

rare solent,nondum in lucem emerserunt·Quanq̃ hæc ipsa,quæ extant,tametsi ne ædita quidē
ab ipso,plane diuinitatem quandam hominis præ se ferunt.Verum ne uidear homo germanus,
ímodico patriæ studio cæcutire,Hermolai Barbari Veneti,de eo epitaphium subscribam elegā
t·sĩmum profecto,& de quo dubites utrò sit dignius,illo ne,qui scripsit,an hoc,quem eo exor-
nauittEst autē huiusmodi· Inuida clauserūt hoc marmore fata Rodolphū· Agricolam,Fri
sii,spémq̃,decúsq̃ soli· Scilicet hoc uiuo meruit Germania,laudis Quicquid habet Latiú,
Græcia quicquid habet· Quæso quid nostro Rodolpho potuit amplius,aut omnino ma-
gnificentius contingere,q̃ testimonium,tam splendidum,tam plenum,idq̃ redditum non uiuo,sed iam uita defuncto,ne quis ab amore magis,quàm à iudicio profectum causari possit.De
inde non à Germano,nequid patriæ communis studium eleuet testimonii pondus·Deniq̃ ab
eo uiro,qui nõ solum Italiam suam,uerum etiam omne seculum hoc nostrum illustrarit,cuius
tāta est apud omnes eruditos autoritas,ut impudétissimum sit ab eo dissentire,tam insignis in
testituēdis literis utilitas,ut aut à literis omnibus alienissimus,aut certe ingratissimus habeatur,
apud quem Hermolai memoria nõ sit sacrosancta.His itaq̃,tam plenis,tamq̃ absolutis uiri lau
dibus equidem fateor me peculiarius etiam,atq̃ impensius fauere,quod mihi admodum adhuc
puero cõtigit uti præceptore,huius discipulo,Alexandro Hegio Vuesphalo,qui ludum aliquā
do celebrem oppidi Danentriensis moderabatur,in quo nos olim,utriusq̃ linguæ prima didi-
cimus elemēta,uir(ut paucis dicam)præceptoris sui simillimus,tam inculpatæ uitæ,q̃ doctrinæ
non triuialis,in quo unum illud,uel Momus ipse calumniari fortasse potuisset,quod famæ plus
æquo negligens,nullam posteritatis habebat rationem.Proinde siquæ scripsit,ita scripsit,ut rē
ludricam haud seriam egisse uideatur.Quanq̃ uel sic scripta,sunt eiusmodi,ut eruditorum calcu
lis immortalitatem promereantur,Itaq̃ in hanc digressionem non temere sum expatiatus,non
ut gloriosæ Germaniæ laudes iactarem,sed ut grati discipuli uicibᵒ fungerer,& utriusq̃ memo
riæ debitum officiū utcũq̃ persoluerem,pterea,quod alteri ueluti filii debam pietatē,alteri tā
q̃ nepotis charitatem.Nunc ad adagium,quod me quõdam puellum,Græcanicæ linguæ rudē
adhuc didicisse memini,ex epistola quadam longe doctissima !Rodolphi mei,qua quidem ille
Senatui Hantuuerpiensi,summa tum fide,tum facundia suadere conatur,ut ludo literario præ-
ficiant aliquem,qui bonas literas didicerit,nec uti solent,infanti Theologo,aut physico id mu-
neris cõmittant,qui cum se,quacũq̃ de re dicere posse confidat,ipsum dicere, quid sit ignoret.
Quid enim is,inquit,faciet in ludo literario?Nempe,ut Græci dicunt,id,quod canis in balneo.
Lucianus aduersus ineruditū, και τὸν ὁρώντων ἕκαστος εὐθὺς ᵗ προχειρότατον ἐκεῖνο ἐπιφθέγγεται
τι κοινὸν κυνὶ καὶ βαλανείῳ·Atq̃ unusquisq̃ conspicientium protinus illud uulgo tritissimū in te
iacit.Quid cani cum balneo?Quadrabit in eos,qui ad rem quampiam prorsus sunt inutiles,ita
ut in balneo nullus est oĩno canũ usus· Asinum sub freno currere doces· CCCXL·

Asinum sub freno currere doces.Hoc est doces indocilem· Nam equus ad cursum Idoneus·
Asinus ad equestrem cursum inutilis·Horatius, Infelix operã perdas,ut siquis asellum in cam
pum doceat parentem currere freno.Acron admonet prouerbialiter dictum de asino·Est autē
diuersum illi,quod alibi retulimus,τὸν ῖππον εἰς πεδίον·Equum in campum·

Alienam metis messem. CCCXLI·

ἀλλότριον ἀμᾶς θέρος·Alienam metis messem.Duplex est usus huius adagii,quippe quod pa
riter & in eos conuenit,qui cõmoditatibus aliena partis opera potiuntur,& in hos,qui negociū
non suum parũ diligenter curant.Ducta metaphora,a uetusto more,quo uicini rustici in deme
tenda segete,mutuam inter sese operam commodabat· Fit autem hominum more,ut in suopte
quisq̃ negocio longe sit attentior,q̃ in alieno·Id quod elegãter admonet Apologus ille de Cas
sitha,quem non pigeret referre nisi promptum esset,cuilibet apud Aulum Gelliũ legere.Potest
& eo referri,quod aliquoties fit,ut eiectis iis,qui sementem fecerunt alii in eorum locum succe-
dant,citráq̃ laborē,alienis fruantur sudoribus.Vnde Maronis illud,En quis cõseuimus agros.
Aristophanes in equibus,τὰ ἀλλότριον ἀμῶν θέρος·Alienã metens messem.Dictum est in Cleone,
qui in rem paratam,multisq̃ laboribus à Demosthene prius labefactatam ueniens,Pylo capta
gloriam omnem uictoriæ in se transtulit Demostheni præter inuidiam nihil relictum. Cui cõsi
ne est illud Homeri ex Odyssea libro primo,ε πεὶ ἀλλότριον βίοτον νή ποινον ἔδουσιν.Quãdo qui
dem impune uictum comedunt alienum.Eandem sentétiam·Aristophanes in eadem fabula sic
extulit, εγὼ δὲ πιει παι πὸν γ᾽ ἀ π᾽ ὄψ᾽ῃασηεῖον ε ξαντος ἑ πέρου τὼ χυδαῖν ὑφειλόμην.Ego obambulãs
ab officina longius Alio coquente ollam paratam sustuli.

11. Part of the Agricola reminiscence in the 'Quid cani et balneo' adage
from Erasmus's *Adagiorum chiliades* (Aldus Manutius, 1508).

In fact, I think that Faber's prefatory letter to Hegius's *Carmina* is an even more carefully constructed, 'purposive' document than this, and that the final paragraph actually tells us that any 'events' with which the letter deals have to do with books, and in particular with constructing reputations out of genealogies of books.[18] The last paragraph of Faber's letter is, I suggest, a coterie paragraph for a printing community: 'I fail to comprehend why you have not given me, as we agreed, the Greek oration of Libanius when you have done it into Latin. . . . I shall see to it that any of Rodolphus Agricola's works that come to hand here are sent to you, except those that have been published in previous years and are now in the booksellers' shops'. Faber is in Deventer, where the school (at which he teaches) is closely associated with the publishing houses of Paffraet and de Breda.[19] Erasmus is publishing his Libanius with Martens at Louvain. They have 'agreed' to exchange 'in press' volumes. And indeed, as we shall see, a volume of Agricola works largely identical with Faber's was published by Martens (with Erasmus's support) at Louvain in 1511.[20]

In the 1508, much expanded, edition of the *Adages* (*Adagiorum chiliades tres . . .*), published by Aldus Manutius in Venice, 'Quid cani et balneo' (as it now became) contains a much enlarged reminiscence on Erasmus's teachers, and becomes, in effect, an extended, conventional panegyric, addressed in the first place to Agricola and then to Hegius.[21] But in spite of its touchingly intimate tone (on which several Erasmus scholars remark), this long 'digression' (as Erasmus himself calls it) is actually a rather curiously precise account of the published remains of Agricola currently available, of which the following forms the core:

> There are a few literary remains of his work, some letters, poems of various kinds; the *Axiochus* of Plato translated into Latin, and a version of Isocrates' *To Demonicus*. Then there are a couple of lectures given in public session in the University of Ferrara, for it was there he both learnt and gave open lectures. There are lying hidden in some people's possession his treatises on dialectic. He had also translated some of Lucian's dialogues.[22]

These are indeed precisely the works of Agricola which were available at this moment, more than twenty years after his death. The translation of pseudo-Plato's *Axiochus* was printed by Richard Paffraet, around 1480. Hegius lived in Paffraet's house during his time as head teacher at the Deventer school, and Paffraet was the publisher of his *Farrago* (1480–85, 1490, 1495),[23] as well as of Jacobus Faber's posthumous edition of his *Carmina* and *Dialogi*, which carried the prefatory letter to Erasmus discussed above.[24] Isocrates' *Praecepta ad Demonicum* appeared around 1480.[25] The 'Anna mater' poem, and individual letters were in print, generally as additional items in other people's volumes.[26] The juxtaposition of the *De inventione dialectica*, 'lying hidden in some people's possession', and the Lucian translations ('He had also translated some of Lucian's dialogues') suggests Erasmus had not seen the latter, but inferred their existence from one of Agricola's (published) letters, in which he promises to send a Lucian translation to Hegius.[27] And indeed, the information that 'at the very end of his life [Agricola] had bent his whole mind on the study of Hebrew and the Holy Scripture' (one of the few 'facts' the panegyric contains), is found in that same published letter.[28] The lectures (delivered at Pavia and Ferrara in 1473, 1474, and 1476) were widely spoken of and acclaimed.[29] In other words, the additional information about Agricola's life and works, with which Erasmus embellishes the expanded adage, is derived entirely from *printed* remains (rather than from personal reminiscences, though the tone certainly suggests the latter).

In 1508 Jacobus Faber brought out a small (and, contrary to his promise, almost entirely derivative) volume of Agricola's works.[30] Its title page manages to include both Alexander Hegius and the Ermolao Barbaro epitaph around which the *Carmina/Adages* connection had pivoted. It runs as follows:

> Rudolph Agricola's 'Paraenesis', or advice on the method by which study should be pursued, and which authors ought to be studied; together with a letter from the same to Alexander Hegius, headmaster at Deventer school. And Isocrates's 'Paraenesis ad Demonicum', translated from the Greek by Rudolph Agricola. The verses of Ermolao Barbaro on the tomb of Rudolph Agricola of Groningen run:
>
>> Under this stone, the jealous Fates decreed
>> The Frisian hope, his country's light, should come,
>> Rudolph Agricola; in life, indeed,
>> He brought such praise to Germany his home
>> As ever Greece could have, or ever Rome.[31]

But the contents of the volume had largely been available in print before. So the volume makes a *gesture* towards fulfilling Faber's previous, rather grander commitment to Erasmus, that he will 'see to it that any of Rodolphus Agricola's works that come to hand are sent to you, except those that have been published in previous years and are now in the booksellers' shops'. I am arguing that such 'gestures' are 'purposive'—are part of a kind of publishing performance (which appears to fulfil a commitment on behalf of Erasmus, to the public, to make good the deficiency in the available works of the man supposed to be a major influence on northern European humanist pedagogy, but actually provides no new foundation to build on at all).

Erasmus's own next 'press' pronouncement on the subject was more prominently placed. In the new prefatory letter to the 1514 edition of the popular *De copia*, addressed to the printer, Matthias Schürer, he wrote:

We are eagerly expecting at any moment the *Lucubrationes* of Rudolph Agricola (a truly inspired man). Whenever I read his writings, I venerate and give fervent praise to that sacred and heavenly spirit.[32]

This is in fact a fragment of a more extended and rather curious exchange with the Schürer publishing house about an Agricola volume. In February 1514, in the preface to an edition of Pliny's *Letters*, which he had seen through the Schürer press, Beatus Rhenanus had referred to some unpublished *lucubrationes* of Agricola as being in his possession.[33] Erasmus's *De copia* preface is in effect a response to that announcement (placed equivalently prominently).[34] A year later, however, Rhenanus had apparently made no progress, for we find another Schürer corrector, Nicholas Gerbell, telling Erasmus in a letter that Schürer is anxious for Rhenanus to correct the works, so that they can be published without delay.[35] In July 1517 Erasmus was still asking the Schürer printing house 'why the publication of Rodolphus Agricola's papers is so long postponed',[36] and in August Erasmus himself is offering to 'do his duty as a friend', and correct them himself, if Schürer will send them to him.[37] At this point, Schürer himself informed Erasmus that he had mislaid a crucial item from the collection while moving house, but would send the whole thing the moment he could find it ('I have been through the whole house looking for it')![38] *Did* Schürer ever have such a manuscript (no such collection ever appeared)? Or was he hoping to keep Erasmus interested enough in his publishing house to place some of his own works there (as indeed he subsequently did)?[39]

Two months before the publication of the new *De copia* preface, in August 1514, Erasmus had himself published a minor work by Agricola—his Latin translation of Isocrates' *Paraenesis ad Demonicum*—in the edition of his own *Opuscula* published in Louvain by Thierry Martens, thus apparently making his own contribution to the retrieval of the 'truly inspired man' 's works.[40]

However, in spite of the assurance on the title page of this work that nothing in the volume had been available in print before, the Agricola translation from Isocrates did *not* in fact appear for the first time in this volume. It had been printed twice before since 1500 (and several times before 1500), in both cases with Erasmus's own explicit encouragement. In 1508 Jacobus Faber had included it in his Agricola volume.[41] In 1511 it also appeared in a volume of Agricola *opuscula* edited by Peter Gilles and published by Thierry Martens (the publisher of the Erasmus *Opuscula* volume, as of many other of his works) at Antwerp.[42]

There is further evidence that this annexing of an already available Agricola fragment was something of a token gesture, in the prefatory letter which accompanies it in editions from 1517 onwards.[43] In it Erasmus tells the reader that he has 'collated this treatise afresh with the

Greek copies' and has 'found one sentence missing, which in any case [he] suspected might be spurious'. He goes on:

> It has, however, been inserted, with a note [or mark], for fear anyone might suppose it omitted by accident, since it appears in current texts. Further, in another passage Rodolphus seems to have read ψυχῆς where the printed Greek copies have τύχης.[44]

In fact, neither the note nor the emendation is to be found in the printed text. Presumably Erasmus did not have time, or did not care to bother himself with it.[45] Alternatively, it may have been the printer, Martens, who failed to make the proposed changes to his existing text.

In 1505 (or thereabouts) Erasmus had written from Paris to Peter Gilles, urging him to collect together such of Agricola's works as he could for publication.[46] In 1511 Gilles did indeed edit and see through the Martens press such a volume; once again the volume is apparently a compilation of scattered, already published works.[47] We should note that the prefatory letter to this volume is addressed by Peter Gilles to Martin Dorp, a printing-house colleague of his, and another friend of, and proof corrector for, Erasmus.[48]

It was not until 1528 that Erasmus was able himself to lay his hands on and publish a 'first edition' of an Agricola *opusculum* in a volume of his own works.[49] This was the 'Oratio in laudem Matthiae Richili', in a collection of popular Erasmus teaching works, published by Frobenius in Basle, and including the *De recta pronuntiatione* and the *Ciceronianus*.[50] In neither this nor any of the three subsequent editions of this volume does Agricola's name, or the title of his oration, figure on the title page. But Erasmus includes another textual note expressing his earnest desire that more of Agricola's works should be brought to light, and the *Ciceronianus* itself contains another fulsome tribute to Agricola's standing as a Ciceronian and a humanist, in the roll call of great 'modern' figures in humane learning.[51]

But by this time, as we shall see, Agricola publishing had opened up, largely owing to the efforts of Alardus of Amsterdam, another proof corrector for the Thierry Martens publishing house, and another friend and protégé of Erasmus. Alardus, however, belongs in the section on the recovery of the *De inventione dialectica*. He is crucial to our story, and perhaps its picaresque hero.

I have laboured this publishing history in order to insist that Erasmus's published references to Agricola, and his subsequent inclusion of minor works by Agricola alongside his own, constitute a *narrative*—tell a carefully constructed story—to which we need to give attention. As I have tried to develop this narrative, the tale which seems to be unfolding is one of a series of publishing *gestures*, simulating spontaneous tributes to one's (Erasmus's) intellectual antecedents, and matching textual 'discoveries':

EPISTOLA.

ẜ leẟ tes,rumines,exerceas.

Ad tot paranda eloquij compendia
Aphthonius unus ἀφθάνως fuffecerit.

IOANNES PHRISSEMIVS ALAR•
do Aemſtelredamo uiro doƈtiß.ac amico integerimo S. D.

CVM nemo haƈtenus de re literaria ad me ſcripſit Alarde ſuauißime, cuius
mihi literæ inter ſummas etiã occupatiões meas nõ ſingularè aliquã attule•
rint uoluptatem,tum uero tuæ iſtæ,tanto me gaudio, tanta læticia perfuderunt,
ut haud ſciam, ecqua mihi unquã in uita res acciderit æque grata :certe gratior
iucũdiorǭ nõ accidit.Et quid mihi per deũ immortalè gratius,quid iucũdius mo‑
numẽtis Rodolphi?què ego uirũ facio tanti,ita admiror,ita ſuſpicio,ita ueneror,
ut quoties ea de re ſermo incidit Latinũ eum Plutarchũ,hoc eſt,ciuilè quendã ǭ
philoſophicũ oratorè ſolcã appellare.Atǭ huc tu autorè,nõ corruptũ, nõ mendo
ſum,ut haƈtenus,ſed elimatum, ſed integrũ, planeǭ talem,ut germanũ ac γνήσιον
eſſe exẽplar iſtud nõ dubites,ante dies paucos in manus tuas ueniſſe ſcribis,ǯ ut
ǭprimum diligenter emendateǭ in rem oĩm ſtudioſorum ædatur,te cupere. Qua
in re felicitatè an candorè ac liberalitatem iſtã tuã magis prædicem ac demirer,
equidem neſcio, cũ ǯ ſummæ cuiuſdã felicitatis loco mihi ponendũ eſſe uideatur,
quod tibi uni à propitio nimirum numine aliquo datũ ſit, monumẽta uiri tanti ab
interitu uindicare,quodǭ theſaurũ talè ac tantũ , uni Alardo acceptũ referèt ſtu
dioſi oẽs.Sed nõ candidum ac liberale minus qđ rem adeo charã,ǯ quæ ad ſari•
nã quoǭ,ſi huc tu ſpeƈtaßes,facere poterat,nõ ut Aſpẽdius quiſpiã Cithariſta uni
tibi ſeruãdam,ſed in cõmunem oĩm ſtudioſorũ utilitatè publicandã putaris.Quod
inſtitutum tuũ utinã imitarentur hodie multi, qui perpetuo latere,ac à blattis ti•
neisǭ corrodi malint autores bonos , ǭ ſine cõpendio aliquo ſuo in lucè prodire.
Supereſt unũ,ut matures id qđ cœpiſti,ut ǭprimũ huc aduoles,ut ne diu tãti bene
ficij expeƈtatiõe ſuſpenſos teneas animos ſtudioſorũ ut hi non prius benefacere te
uoluiße,ǭ ǯ benefeciſſe intelligãt.Id ſi facies, nemo maiorè unquã gratiã inierit
apud ſtudioſos ǭ tu,nemo maiori illos beneficio ſibi deuinxerit.Quãdo nõ minima
beneficij pars eſt,nõ diu rem diſtuliße.Neǭ dubito ego, quin ſi nõ ſplendida ac te
digna at tolerabili certe cõditione hic tibi futurus ſit locus apud chalcographum
aliquem.Quod ut obtineri non poßit, mihi ſane curæ id erit,ne cum iaƈtura ac di
ſpendio tuo huc te contuleris. Matura modo, ǯ quidem reƈta ad me,ſi non diui•
tem ac magnificum, at beneuolum certe ac liberalem hoſpitem habiturus. Vale
Coloniæ ſexto calendas Aprilis. Anno M. D. XXIX.

EXI•

---

12. Letter from Phrissemius, in Alardus's edition of the works of Rudolph
Agricola (Cologne, 1539).

print pronouncements about the great heritage of Agricola/Hegius; calls for making accessible Agricola's works after the appearance of Hegius's; the appearance of collections apparently answering such calls, sponsored by individuals standing in a direct (printing) relationship to Erasmus (but actually collations of existing incunabulum fragments).

But this is not a linear narrative (at least, I have been unable to think of a way of telling it in linear fashion). So at this point we have to go back to 1503, and that letter from Faber to Erasmus concerning Hegius and what the dog has to do with the bath.

'I THINK IMMEDIATELY OF RODOLPHUS AGRICOLA, THE FORMER TEACHER OF MY OWN TEACHER ALEXANDER'

In addition to the highly specific bibliographical (printer's) material, Erasmus's adage 'What has a dog to do with a bath?' launches two important general themes, championed by Europe's most popular and prolific educationalist. The first is the 'genealogy of teachers' theme—a kind of humanist laying on of hands—Agricola taught Hegius taught Erasmus. The second is the 'can anyone find me the great man's lost works?' theme. As twentieth-century readers, we might feel that as a digression, buried in the body of a compendious reference work, it could hardly be guaranteed the reader's attention. But as we have seen, this textual addition (orchestrated in collaboration with an editor friend from the same academic stable) is only one of a number of careful moves establishing an intellectual pedigree for Agricola (and thereby Erasmus), and advertising for those in possession of Agricola's unpublished works in manuscript to come forward.[52]

Jacobus Faber links Hegius to Agricola, around the tag from Erasmus's *Adages*. When Erasmus expands that reference in the revised edition of his work, he specifies that the link is a letter *from* Agricola *via* Hegius, read to Erasmus (apparently) while he was at the Deventer school:

> I remember having learnt [this adage] from a certain very learned letter of my beloved Rodolphus, at a time when I was a mere child and as yet ignorant of Greek. In this letter he is trying to persuade the town council of Antwerp, with conviction and eloquence, that they should appoint as master of their school someone proficient in liberal studies, and not (as they usually do) entrust this office to an inarticulate theologian or naturalist, the sort of man who is sure he has something to say about everything but has no notion of what it is to speak. 'What good would he be in a school? As much good, to use the Greek repartee, as a dog in a bath.'

Transmission, in other words, is rigorously textual here—not the great man to his pupil, who in his turn passes it on to *his* pupil, but letter from (remote) great man, *sent* to his one-time pupil (not in fact a letter *to* Hegius, but to Barbarianus),[53] and then *read* to the young Erasmus. However, this is not at all the way Erasmus chooses to emphasise the story:

> I quote this adage with all the more pleasure because it refreshes and renews my memory, and my affection, for Rodolphus Agricola of Friesland, whom I name as the man in all Germany and Italy most worthy of the highest public honour. . . . Such full and ungrudging praise of this man has, I confess, a singular charm for me, because I happened while yet a boy to have his disciple Alexander Hegius as my teacher. . . . Now to turn to the adage, which I remember having learnt from a certain very learned letter of my beloved Rodolphus, at a time when I was a mere child and as yet ignorant of Greek.

'A certain very learned letter of my beloved Rodolphus' gives no hint that the letter in question is addressed neither to Erasmus nor to Hegius, but transmitted by the latter to the former in class. What Erasmus emphasises here is above all the bond of affection between master and pupil, a bond which certainly suggests personal contact. And indeed, scholars have expended a good deal of ingenuity on specifying exactly *when* Erasmus had this personal contact with Agricola. What I shall argue in this section is that there was no personal contact—perhaps one brief meeting—but that the *story* of the affective bond is crucial for Erasmus's version of emerging humane studies.

It is interesting to compare the *Adages* digression with a much earlier letter to Cornelius Gerard, written around 1489/90, after Erasmus had entered the monastery at Steyn:[54]

> I am more surprised that you describe [Girolamo Balbi] as the only writer who follows the tracks of antiquity; for, not to mention yourself, it seems to me that I see countless well-schooled writers of the present day who approach quite closely the ancient ideal of eloquence. I think immediately of Rodolphus Agricola, the former teacher of my own teacher Alexander. He was a man not only exceptionally highly educated in all the liberal arts, but extremely proficient in oratory and poetic theory, and moreover as well acquainted with Greek as with Latin. To him may be added Alexander himself, a worthy pupil of so great a master; so elegantly did he reproduce the style of the ancients that one might easily mistake the authorship of a poem by him if the book's title page were missing; and he, too, is not quite devoid of Greek.[55]

Here the intimacy of the *Adages* reminiscence is entirely absent, the link between Agricola and Hegius, conventional and formal: 'the former teacher of my own teacher'; 'a worthy pupil of so great a master'. And the link itself is naturally made by Erasmus around Hegius's ability as a *poet*, and a poet on the written page: 'one might easily mistake the authorship of a poem by him if the book's title page were missing'. At this stage in his life, I suggest, Erasmus's version of a humanistic chain of influence beginning with Agricola and passing via Hegius to himself is a limited one, centring on the production (crucially imitative) of neo-Latin poetry (which we know Agricola *had* published at this date, which Hegius fostered at Deventer school, and in which both the young Erasmus and Cornelius Gerard participated)—a production which nevertheless depended on the circulation of written texts, from Agricola to Hegius and his pupils, and possibly back again for comment.[56]

My crucial point here is that all Erasmus's 'memories' of Agricola are remembered pieces of reading. There are no biographical details to support those memories, and that affection of Erasmus for his 'beloved Agricola', which cannot be traced to a *text* which Erasmus is likely to have encountered. Nothing in fact shows this more clearly than that crucial adage: 'Quid cani in balneo?' For the story about the Agricola letter containing the 'what has a dog to do with a bath?' tag is disturbingly closely related to the *printing* history of Agricola's works (disturbingly, that is, if what one wants to claim is intimacy amongst these three landmark figures in humane learning). The letter from Agricola to Barbarianus about the school at Antwerp, which Hegius read out in assembly at Deventer, was already printed in 1483, in the incunabulum of pseudo-Plato's *Axiochus*.[57] So Erasmus is drawing the reader of the *Adages*'s attention to a letter, which was read to him (but addressed neither to him, nor to the teacher who read it to him), which is available to the reader himself in the (extremely limited) printed works of Agricola (soon to be made conveniently available to the reader in Peter Gilles's edition of Agricola *opuscula*).[58]

That Erasmus *succeeded* in convincing successive generations of readers that he had genuinely had some inspirational contact with Agricola is beyond doubt. By 1539 (the year of publication of Alardus's definitive edition of Agricola's works), Melanchthon had taken up the 'great heritage of Agricola' theme; and by 1557, in his 'Oratio de Erasmo Roterodamo', he had embellished the reference by Erasmus to a brief encounter at Deventer school, so that Agricola singled out the young Erasmus as a boy with a glorious future.[59] Hyma, the author of the classic *The Youth of Erasmus*, provides a perfect example of the intellectual investment generations of scholars have given to this incident:

> A halo of almost supernatural learning seemed to surround those favored beings [early humanists] who told with rapture how they had actually heard the voice of the great Ficino or of the famous Pico. When ambitious boys of twelve or thirteen saw such a scholar, freshly arrived from the land of intellectual giants, they were nearly struck dumb with awe. This happened one day to Erasmus when he beheld the beaming features of Rudolph Agricola, 'who was one of the first to bring a breath of the new learning from Italy.'[60]

As astute a reader as the great Erasmus scholar P. S. Allen, however, is more reticent, but equally revealing:

> As to the meeting with Agricola certainty is not to be attained. Erasmus' estimate of his age quoted above cannot be correct, if 1466 is rightly taken for his birth-year; for Agricola did not return from Italy until 1479. But between 1480 and 1484 Agricola probably passed through Deventer many times on his way to and from Groningen. He mentions a visit in Oct. 1480; and in April 1484 he was staying there, perhaps with Hegius in the house of the printer, Richard Paffraet. From the close connexion which existed in Erasmus' mind between Hegius and Agricola, whom he frequently mentions together, there is some ground for supposing that it was on this occasion that he saw the great scholar, whom he afterwards regarded as the teacher of his own master.[61]

'From the close connexion which existed in Erasmus' mind between Hegius and Agricola' it appears that we can only infer that Erasmus *wished to establish* (canonically) that there had been some crucial meeting with 'the great scholar, whom he afterwards regarded as the teacher of his own master'—some laying on of hands which made him the direct heir to the tradition of humane learning which Agricola had been the first (so the story went) to bring from Italy.[62]

'UNFORTUNATELY IN THE *DE COPIA* WE WERE UNABLE TO CONSULT THE *DE INVENTIONE DIALECTICA*'

I am arguing that the accumulating textual reference to Agricola as intellectual and spiritual ancester to Erasmus of Rotterdam is part of a *purposive* narrative, emanating from Erasmus himself. And I hope you will have noticed that in the story so far the so-called central Agricola text, the *De inventione dialectica*, has been noticeable by its absence. In the systematic search for publishable material (essentially, as we have seen a publishing search, by printers and editors), it had disappeared entirely from sight.[63] But I think it will be clear by now that Erasmus and his 'circle' of correctors and editors were not waiting for a *particular* Agricola work: they were anxious to publish *any* Agricola texts compatible with a version of him as the key intermediary in the transmission of Italian humanism to northern Europe—and of Erasmus as heir to that inheritance.

In fact, if we scrutinise the surviving traces of the *De inventione dialectica* in scholarly correspondence and in prefatory letters, it begins to look as if there was a *problem* associated with that text—a problem of corruption in the text, illegibility, or at the least, serious difficulty for the 'castigator'.[64] And this is where Alardus Amstelredamus comes into the story. Alardus was a scholar in the Erasmus 'circle' who had taught at the school at Alkmaar, who later lived and worked in Louvain (and was, naturally, a corrector for the Martens printing house), and who became the single individual most closely associated with the quest for Agricola's lost works.[65] He came to Louvain from Alkmaar in the second half of 1514,[66] and immediately began to work as a corrector for Martens, which brought him to the attention of Erasmus, who renewed his involvement with Louvain (after an extended period in England) at the same moment.[67]

The publication of the *De inventione dialectica* evidently met with Erasmus's approval: that volume came out with Martens in January, and in June we find Alardus providing a prefatory letter to Erasmus's *Enchiridion militis christiani*.[68] So although the discovery of the lost manuscript of Agricola's treatise on dialectic supposedly antedates Alardus's connection with the Martens press and Erasmus, the editorial work is apparently exactly contemporary with it. Which suggests that in our attempt at unravelling the 'transmission' of the cultural heritage of Agricola, we should go back to that 'discovery' and its consequences. All the detail concerning the pursuit of a manuscript of the *De inventione dialectica* suitable for printing comes from Alardus's dense commentary to his 1539, two-volume edition of Agricola's surviving *Opera*.[69]

Jacobus Faber's volume of Agricola *Opuscula*, published in 1508, had carried a prefatory letter to 'Guillelmus medicus', in which Faber claimed to have in his possession a manuscript of the *De inventione dialectica* 'in six books'.[70] The important thing to notice is that there is a specific reason for Faber's preface including such a boast: the *Opuscula* printed the Agricola letter known as the 'De formando studio', which is indeed an epistolary programme for an education in humane letters. As the culmination of his graded programme of study, Agricola briefly sketches two techniques for ensuring that the body of knowledge acquired is not sterile, but may be redeployed fruitfully, and extended. Both techniques concern the classification of material for easy retrieval: storage under headings or common places to adduce illustratively; and storage under the *loci* of dialectic to facilitate argumentation. On the latter he concludes:

> And if anyone wishes to extend their use [*loci*] through all the dialectical places, as far as the nature of the thing allows, a vast wealth of matter both for speaking and for inventing will certainly become available to him. How, and in what manner this ought to be done is more than can be arrived at in a letter, and I have discussed this matter at length in those three books which I wrote *De inventione dialectica*.[71]

It is because of this direct allusion by Agricola to one of his own (as yet unpublished) works that Faber feels it necessary to include the prefatory information that he has a copy in his possession.[72] The fact that he (*a*) does not include the text in the volume and (b) makes an entirely erroneous remark about the number of books in his copy suggests that there were problems with his manuscript.[73]

Alardus, dedicatedly assembling Agricola's complete works for publication, went straight to Deventer in pursuit of Faber's copy of the *De inventione dialectica*. Although he found that the manuscript was (a) of three books, as all previous reports had suggested, and (b) a corrupt copy, he paid Faber twenty ducats for permission to publish the text with Martens in Louvain.[74] It was another seven years, however, before the edited text appeared, with Dorp's name (and not Alardus's) on the title page.[75]

The only satisfactory explanation for the story (of a wild-goose chase, and a disappointment, followed by a delay in publication),[76] is that neither Faber (who had chosen not to include it in his *Opuscula*) nor Alardus was equipped to put the text they had into publishable form. The most likely reason for this is the state of the manuscript—it was a transcription by several hands, and Agricola's own bad handwriting was notorious.[77] Another is that a good deal of the text was technical, and conceptually innovative. Dorp, by contrast, was both a professional corrector,[78] and a professional theologian and logician by training.[79]

It was another thirteen years before a supposedly substantially revised text became available,[80] and nearly twenty-five before Alardus published his definitive commented edition.[81] There is, moreover, really no plausible explanation for the long delay. Alardus located Agricola's missing papers in 1516, in the possession of the prominent banker Pompeius Occo, nephew of the doctor (and distinguished poet) Adolphus Occo, the close friend to whom Agricola had bequeathed them at his death.[82] In the *Lucubrationes* Alardus claims that the manuscript of the *De inventione dialectica* had been lent by Occo to a passing dignitary, and was not returned until 1528 (when Alardus publicly announced his intention to publish a commented edition). Like other 'colourful' details concerning the retrieval of the text, scattered through the commentary to his edition, this accounts for the dates, without being terribly convincing.[83] And in the meantime, Alardus took employment with Occo, and saw several elaborately illustrated devotional volumes through the press on his behalf.[84]

One of Alardus's problems was, in the end, finding a publisher. It seems significant that after 1519 Erasmus was apparently on more distant terms with Alardus. When, sometime after 1529, Alardus had finally completed his two-volume *Opera*, he could not get Erasmus's support for its publication.[85]

All of which must surely give us pause for thought, when we are considering the 'diffusion' and 'influence' of the *De inventione dialectica* as a key text in the development of humanist dialectic, and humanist pedagogy. For, as far as I am aware, the secondary literature which focuses determinedly on Agricola's *De inventione dialectica* as the significant bridging work between the 'old' dialectic and the 'new' has no anxieties whatsoever about the integrity and authenticity of the text, never alludes to the commentaries or corrections of the *castigatores*, and barely even mentions the name of Desiderius Erasmus.[86]

The tale all this virtuosity tells—this exuberant shuffling of the flash cards to provide self-confirming testimony for northern humanism—is in the end a tale of legitimation. Outside the universities (which cannot, or will not, provide a place for them), *in* print, Erasmus and his circle compose the history of their own intellectual movement: the intellectual pedigree; the testimonies of excellence; the corroborating evidence for and confirming allusions to the seminal influence and lasting impact of a small band of Low Countries educators. Four centuries later the scholarly community still takes them entirely at their word.

EPILOGUE

In 1523, in the polemical *Spongia*, Erasmus once more referred to the 'Quid cani et balneo?' adage, and drew attention to his eulogy of Agricola and Hegius:

> Did not I praise Rudolph Agricola and Alexander Hegius fulsomely, to whom I owed absolutely nothing?[87]

By then, of course, he himself no longer needed to stand on the shoulders of giants. By then the print story of the pre-eminence of Erasmus was already canonical.

Recovered Manuscripts and Second Editions: Staging the Book with the *Castigatores*

IN THE LAST CHAPTER I showed that Rudolph Agricola's reputation as the intellectual figure bridging Italian and northern European humanism was established for a variety of reasons, which did not include the intrinsic merit of one particular text, nor even its known pedagogic value. In the present chapter I shall take this argument a stage further. I move from the print trace of a gathering movement of Erasmian humanists, who claimed Agricola as their intellectual precursor and 'type', and whose common bond was their lack of place in the conventional university system (arts faculty or theology faculty), to another print story. This time I shall follow the clues in successive printed editions of the *De inventione dialectica*, in an attempt to retrieve a convincing narrative to account for the form in which it was 'recovered', and then the form in which it was transmitted.

I have already argued that the 'authentic' text of the *De inventione dialectica* was problematic from the start—that that is the only way we can account for the seven years it took from retrieval to publication. Here I shall show that it is possible to uncover from the text itself something of that process from retrieval to publication. Not only can we piece together who was involved, but, I shall argue, this piece of textual detective work entitles us to look somewhat differently at the intellectual content of the *De inventione dialectica* as finally established.

At the same time, the text of the *De inventione dialectica* became 'fixed' at a curiously early stage (in spite of vigorous claims that additional manuscripts had improved and facilitated the task of cleaning up the text). The 1515 *editio princeps* and the 1528 'revised' Phrissemius text are, apart from trivial differences, the same text. We need to ask why this should be the case (which involves once again piecing together the manuscript history of the text), and why there was apparently a consensus amongst the humanists involved to support the tale of many manuscripts and much emended texts. I shall argue that there is a common set of interests outside dialectic/logic, which is shared by all those who were active around the Agricola treatise. Which will enable me to begin to argue that any interpretation of the text itself must scrutinize rather carefully whatever 'coherence' and functionality one locates there.

The story of the text of the *De inventione dialectica* begins not with Alardus of Amsterdam, nor with Erasmus (who had championed its recovery), but with the Louvain humanist and theologian Martin Dorp. For in spite of Alardus's claims to priority in the discovery and publishing of Agricola's *De inventione dialectica*, the only name the title page of the first edition carried was Dorp's.

Unlike the characters in this story we have encountered thus far, Martin Dorp was an individual who in spite of his commitment to humanism, and in spite of his close association with the Erasmus circle, also had conventional connections with the theology faculty of the University of Louvain; he became bachelor of theology in January 1510, a licentiate in late 1513, and in August 1515, six months after the publication of the *editio princeps* of the *De inventione dialectica*, he became a doctor of theology.[1] There is a long-standing account in the literature of Dorp's relationship with Erasmus which concerns events dating from precisely the period 1514–19 (also roughly the period of the retrieval and transmission of the *De inventione dialectica*); so in reconstructing the Agricola story, we will also need to bear in mind the impact of that story on the established account of that other Dorp/Erasmus tale.[2]

The earliest evidence we have linking Dorp to an Agricola project (of the kind which I argued in the last chapter was part of a promotion venture by an Erasmian circle, on behalf of northern humanism) is the prefatory letter to the second collection of Agricola *Opuscula*, edited by Peter Gilles in 1511.[3] This preface makes three substantial points (of the 'purposive' kind I explored fully in the last chapter). It offers the *Opuscula* as a foretaste of the real significance of Agricola's work.[4] It brings in the name of Erasmus as part of such a project (because of his publicly professed admiration for the Frisian).[5] And it promotes a work of Dorp's himself, edited by Nicolaas van Broeckhoven, which Gilles claims to be a work of major importance, and one which will bring particular credit to the University of Louvain. It closes with an exhortation to Dorp to continue to promote the work of Agricola and Erasmus.[6]

The work of Dorp's which Gilles was so eagerly awaiting, according to this preface, was the printed text of the course he had given at Louvain as *legens* in philosophy, and which van Broeckhoven did indeed publish the following year in Paris: *Introductio facilis . . . ad Aristotelis libros logice intelligendos* (Paris, 1512).[7] So Dorp is here linked, specifically as a distinguished logician of the Louvain theology faculty, with the recovery of Agricola's works 'rescued from the disintegration brought about by mice and worms'. At the same time, most of the preface 'puffs' a forthcoming work on Aristotelian logic—a work deriving directly from the 'respectable' milieu of the Louvain theology faculty, and thus pegging the Agricola *Opuscula* to an existing university context. In addition, it suggests an

Prtrus Egidius Anuerpian⁹. Martino Dor‹
pio Theologo, Amico iucundiſſ. S.D.
Vum nup aliquot Rodolphi Agricolæ Vi‹
ri inſignis doctrinæ opuſcula, nactus eſſem.
Martine feſtiuiſſ. Opereprecium fore exiſtimaui, ſi
a ſoricum tinearumq̃ morſibus prorſus vindicata
typis excuderetur/ vt etiam extrariis gentibus no‹
ſtratiũ ingenia longe lateq̃ innoteſcerent. At pen‹
ſiculanti mihi identide cui nam potiſſimũ cõſecra/
rentur, Tu vel ex oĩbus vnus occurriſti, condignus
ſane cui⁹ ſnb noĩe literaꝝ ꝓceres (nã barbaros de/
generes nihil moror) hoc qualecunq̃ eſt volumen
euoluerent legerentq̃/ Equide qum ꝓpter eximiã
authorisytriulq̃ lingue facultate gratiſſimũ futu/
rũ dubio ꝓcul cognoſcere, tũ nõ parũ noisſibi cõ/
ciliaturũ augurabar ſi nois tui ſpledor in ipſo (vt
ſic dicã) antilogio velut ſtellula quedã ꝑfulgeret.
Et eo certe libẽti⁹effeci, vt te hoc q̃li ſuſcitabulo ad
publicatione ſœture tue inuitare, qppe qui ipſe pri/
dem liquido ex Nicolao Buſcoducen. amico vtriq̃
iuxta charo intellexeri eã iã exaſſeatã ꝓpolitãq̃ ꝑ/
ter formulas chalcographicas affectare nihil. Ac/
cingere igitur & memoriæ vegetandæ gratia, edi/
tione tuã publicitus exoſculandã, in man⁹ doctoꝝ
exire ſinas, nullũ me hercule facinus fuerit glorio/
ſius preſertim quod tibi ſummũ tum decus, tũ fru/
ctus cõpabit. Et p qd viciſſũ Louanien Academie
atq̃ adeo doctiſſimis qbuſq̃ plurimũ nõ tantũ vo/
luptatis, ſed & vtilitatis ſis allatur⁹. Verum vt in/
terim te etiam ad palmatum quendam triũphum

a ii

element of collaboration between the two men (as we saw in the case of Erasmus's prefatory exchange with Jacobus Faber),[8] and there are, indeed, further clues to this effect. The Gilles volume includes Agricola's Latin version of pseudo-Isocrates' *Paraenesis ad Demonicum* (as did the Faber *Opuscula* of 1508). In 1514 Dorp's own edited version of this text appeared (also under the Martens imprint) in Erasmus's *Opuscula* of that date. We seem to be justified in assuming that Dorp, theologian, logician, and *castigator* for Martens (and specifically at this moment, for Erasmus's *Cato*), was part of the team 'rescuing' Agricola's works, with Erasmus's encouragement. The Gilles preface also suggests he would have been particularly committed to a humanist-inspired dialectic text, and the endorsement on the first edition seems further to support this.

So we apparently have a good case for Dorp's intellectual involvement—and investment—in Agricola's dialectic treatise, indeed, for his being primarily responsible for making sense of the text. Furthermore, in the light of the *Opuscula* prefatory letter, this involvement seems to come endorsed by the Louvain theology faculty (to which Dorp is publicly affiliated in that preface). It is therefore with some surprise that we come upon the following, in a life of Agricola, published in 1536 by Gerardus Geldenhauer. Geldenhauer recalls his own involvement in establishing the text of the *De inventione dialectica*:

> There is one thing I cannot refrain from adding. . . . The [manuscript] first book [of the *De inventione dialectica*], in Agricola's own handwriting, had many additional marginal annotations, which needed to be inserted appropriately in the body of the work. But in the text, many things were crossed out, many obliterated, some things annotated with tiny blots rather than with superscript letters, which could only be understood by the use of conjecture and divination. And therefore at the entreaty of a group of most learned men, . . . to please all lovers of learning, I undertook the labour of transcribing the first book in the order in which it is now read, in 1514.[9]

This link between Gerard Geldenhauer (who in 1517 became secretary to Philip of Burgundy, bishop of Utrecht) and the 'authorised' text of the *De inventione dialectica* suggests that the reconstruction of Agricola's dialectic treatise (long lost from sight)[10] was a more complexly collaborative venture than even Alardus's retrospective account allowed.[11]

Geldenhauer was a close friend of Dorp's, and another associate of the Martens press.[12] Like Erasmus, he paid tribute to his schoolteacher at Deventer, Alexander Hegius, as the person who had first introduced him to Agricola.[13] In 1514 (when he specifies he reconstructed the first book of Agricola's *De inventione dialectica*) he and Dorp were collaborating on a Martens volume consisting largely of minor works of Dorp's, but including one of Geldenhauer's own compositions.[14] In itself, therefore,

Geldenhauer's passing remark tells us only that the two men—already working closely at the Martens press—collaborated in the Agricola volume also.[15]

But this aside of Geldenhauer's alerts us to a further, rather more intriguing, possibility. Geldenhauer says that 'at the entreaty of a group of most learned men, . . . to please all lovers of learning, I undertook the labour of transcribing the first book in the order in which it is now read', and we should take him at his word. This raises the possibility that in the 1515 *editio princeps* of the *De inventione dialectica*, with Dorp's endorsement, the first book was reconstructed separately from books 2 and 3.[16] And this in turn raises the possibility that in fact Dorp endorsed the *De inventione dialectica* largely on the strength of the first book (the book he had been directly involved with, via Geldenhauer). In this case, he may well have been insufficiently prepared for the hostility the work aroused, since most of what is contentious for a traditional theologian occurs in books 2 and 3 (that is, Agricola's somewhat cavalier attitude to formal *ratiocinatio*, and his original explorations of informal debating strategies). I shall indeed argue that after the *editio princeps* of the *De inventione dialectica* appeared, Dorp found himself professionally embarrassed by it. Since the setting to rights of the text of book 1 was the work of another theologian, and a close personal friend, Geldenhauer, it seems likely that the problem lay with the later books.[17]

The Text of the First Edition

The first edition of the *De inventione dialectica* is an elegant small folio, with black letter title page and page headings, and a handsome typeface in which the printer Martens evidently takes some pride, since he closes the volume:

> This most exquisite dialectic of Rodolph Agricola's was printed at Louvain by Thierry Martens of Alost in the most highly crafted typeface (as can be clearly seen).[18]

Dorp's commendatory letter forms part of the elaborate black and red title page. At the head of that title page, in red, we have:

> The Dialectic of Rudolph Agricola
> Dorp to the Diligent
>
> [Rodolphi Agricole Phrisij Dialectica
> Dorpius Studiosis]

There follows Dorp's letter recommending the *De inventione dialectica* to all serious scholars (*studiosis*). The centre of the title page is occupied by

Rodolphi Agricole Phrisij Dialectica

Dorpius Studiosis

Vt rectis studiis cōsulatur studiosi,excusa sunt vobis hæc Agricolæ dia
lectica:qbus nihil cēseo vtilius futurū iis:q verā sectātur arte diserte eloquenterq̃ dicē
di:qq̃ nō verbis tm̃ inanibus: sed vberi rerū copia studeant summa cū admiratione p
suadere:atq̃ de re qualibet ex probabilibus apposite:decēterq̃ ratiocinari: quod noster
ille munus esse dialecticū testatur:hic itaq̃ garrula sophistag̃ deliramēta ne expectetis:
verū ea expectate:quæ a multis/sciarum limites cōfundētibus:rhetoricæ tributa:propria
tn̄ sunt dialecticæ:quæq̃ in Aristotelis Ciceronisq̃ libris desiderātur: qbus certe hic li
ber nihilo est inferior: siue elegantiam filumq̃ dictionis spectemus: siue doctrine præ
ceptorumq̃ traditionem. Valete.

❡ Venalia sunt Louanii in ædibus: Theodorici Martini Alustensis
e regione scholæ Iuris ciuilis vbi ab eo sunt impressa.

Cū priuilegio a Max. Aug. z Car. Aust.

14. Title page of the first edition of Agricola's *De inventione dialectica*
(Louvain, 1515).

the Martens crest in black, with the printer's imprint (alternately black and red), followed by the *cum privilegio*, again uniformly in red.

I describe the title page with some care, in order to indicate how prominent is Dorp's endorsing letter, and what a print 'occasion' the volume is—both for the recovery of a much-sought-after work,[19] and for the sophistication and physical beauty of the text (the text also includes single words in Greek font).[20] As for the text itself, however, it displays some curious features. In the first place, there are no chapter divisions as such, and breaks are marked unobtrusively, either by a capital letter (with or without a line break following) or by a discreet paragraph sign. This makes it a difficult work to follow, whilst nevertheless giving it a deceptive kind of integrity: the text runs smoothly and uninterruptedly page by page, without significant breaks, and without commentary or marginal topic headings. It is therefore all the more striking to find, at the end of book 1, the following:

❡ Here ends book one

❡ Gerard Geldenhauer to the reader
Agricola the Frisian instructs you, and throughout many centuries to come
  will instruct others,
Does he live on or has he perished?

[❡ Finit primus liber

❡ Gerardus Nouiomagus Lectori
Te docet, atq[ue] alios per saecula multa docebit,
Viuit an oppetiit? Phrysius Agricola.]

This is followed by a table of comparative lists of *loci*, or topics, from Cicero, Themistius, and Agricola (a feature preserved in all successive editions of the work), and then a bold heading at the beginning of book 2:

LIBER SECUNDUS

❡ RODOLPHI AGRICOLAE PHRISII DE INVENTIONE DIALECTICA
LIBER SECVNDVS .:.

Here we have physical confirmation, in the text itself, of the very thing Gerard Geldenhauer told his readers in his *Vita Agricolae*. Geldenhauer took responsibility only for the first book, and signed off with an appropriate epigram at its close. We might compare the way in which Geldenhauer 'signs off' in another volume whose production he saw through the Martens press, Erasmus's *Parabolae, siue Similia* of June 1515. There, at the bottom of the penultimate page of the entire volume (followed only by a blank page), we find:

tiam:externorum quattuor,cognata applicita: accidentia: repugnantia. In substantia
septem fecimus: definitionem: genus: speciem: proprium: totum: partes: coniugata:
tres circa substantiam:accidentia:actus subiecta.Externos cognatorum quattuor:effi
ciens:finem:effecta:destinata:applicitorum tres:locum:tempus:connexa.Quincப ac
cidentium:contingentia:nomen rei:pronunciata:comparata:similia.Repugnantium
duos opposita: & differentia. Fiunt(ப isti in summa loci viginti quattuor quibus in
omnem rem quacunப erutum inuentumப ratione ducitur argumentum: idப qua
via quoப modo faciendum proximo dicetur libro quoniam iusto maior huius vo
luminis modus excreuit finitப sit: si illud addiderimus Boetium quiப post eum scri
pserumt de locis: singulis locis addidisse quandam vt vulgo loquimur: maximam:
id est pronunciatum quoddam vna sententia multa complexum cui indubitata sit fi
des:vt de quocunப definitio dicitur de eo definitum de quocunப species de eo genus
quod non faciendum mihi non ideo quia id Aristoteles & Cicero non fecissent puta
ui: sed quia in nullum id vsum fieri arbitrabar: primum quod possint istae maxi
me fingi illis in locis qui necessarium prebent argumentum: tamen in eis quae proba
bile faciunt parum conueniet:quorum maior sane pars est. Deinde quod multi sunt
loci in quibus in nullam certam & satis conuenientem formam concludi heae maxi
mae possunt.itaப videas Boetium dum cuilibet loco maximam suam reddere cupit:
in angustias quasdam detrudi. vt quum locus latissime sit fusus: maxima in arctum
prorsus agatur & ne per omnes locos sequamur:quum de efficientibus dixisset sub
iecit maximam:quorum efficientia naturalia sunt eorum effecta sunt naturalia: sic
de materia:cuius materia deest & id quod ex ea efficitur deest:& sic de fine: cuius finis
bonus est ipsum est bonnm:& de forma:tantum quemப agere posse: quantum natu
ralis forma permiserit:quasi vero hi loci quorum amplissimus est ambitus intra hos
conclusi sunt terminos:vt pertineant omnia argumenta ex efficientibus ad esse natu
turale vel non naturale:& ex materia ad deesse velut suppetere.& ex fine ad bonum
vel malum:& ex forma ad agere vel non agere.Adde quod si quis exacte & penitus co
gnitam habuerit locorum naturam,nihil erunt ei opus heae maximae quoni
am vltro fere in animum incurrunt:& apertiores sunt ஞ vt sint di
scendae:aut si quis tam prorsus expers ingenii sit: tam
ஞ a communi sensu rerum abhorrens vt aper
tissima illa & propemodum per se
nota docedus sit: illi ego
nihilo magis
quஞ de lo
cis precipiun
tur pfutura crediderim
ஞ cymeriis quos perpetua nebula
rum caligine opertos tradunt poetae: ea quae
de positione siderum deஞ ipsorum figuris motuஞ tra
duntur.

❧Finit primus liber

❧Gerardus Nouiomagus Lectori
Te docet,atஞ alios per saecula multa docebit,
Viuit an oppetiit?Phrysius Agricola.

15. Gerard Geldenhauer's epigraph concluding the first book of Agricola's
De inventione dialectica (Louvain, 1515) in the first edition.

Gerardus Nouiomagus emendebat. Finis. Louanii, ex Aedibus Alustinis, Mense Iunii, Anno. M. D. XV.[21]

This suggests that we look more closely at books 2 and 3, to see what, if anything, distinguishes these books typographically from the first. And indeed, there do seem to be a number of features of books 2 and 3 which suggest less assiduous editing than that of book 1. In the first place, as the later editor Phrissemius (who worked from the 1515 printed edition to produce his own commentary) complains, these books contain significant numbers of typographical errors, frequent instances of curious punctuation, and grammatical errors in the Latin.[22] They are the kind of errors which would have been corrected as a matter of course by a competent *castigator* like Geldenhauer or Dorp. Or, at least, they suggest that these portions of Agricola's text have perhaps not been worked over with the assiduousness which such correctors could bring to bear on important works. We may contrast, for example, the account of Dorp's activities as a castigator given in a letter to Erasmus from Rutgerus Rescius, engaged in correcting the Martens edition of Erasmus's *Epistolae elegantes*, which appeared in April 1517 (letter dated March 8, 1517):

> In your letter to Wolfgang Faber, O universally learned Erasmus, there is a passage, not far from the end, of which we can make absolutely nothing. It begins: 'Tum audio nonnullos alia quaedam moliri, quae ad Christi cognitionem nihil adferant, sed *funcios* tantum offendant oculis hominum'. I showed it to Desmarez [Paludanus] and Nijmegen [Geldenhauer], and they were stumped by it, just as I had been; but they thought we should make no rash changes, and advised me to show you the passage before printing it. Dorp conjectured that we ought to read 'fumos tantum offendunt [*sic*—should be 'offundant']'. Dirk [Martens] has therefore left this part of the letter to be printed later, and sends you the actual copy, begging you to let him know what you want done about the reading in this place as soon as possible. He would also be glad, if there is anything that could conveniently be added to the preface of the letters, if it might be sent him. He kept for it a whole page blank on both sides, while it will hardly fill half of it.[23]

It appears that less care than this was involved in the correcting the *De inventione dialectica* after Geldenhauer signed off at the end of the first book.[24] We might also note Dorp's own testimony as to his assiduousness as *castigator*, at the end of *Plutarchi Chaeronensis de tuenda bona valetudine praecepta, Erasmo interprete*, published by Martens in November 1513. There, following verses of his own, and before his list of the volume's errata, he tells his studious readers:

> To reduce your labours, you serious scholars, I have assembled here the errors which occurred in these books; not simply those of the typesetters, but also

those of the person who transcribed the copy incorrectly. Unless perhaps that copy itself was not sufficiently flawless. In the majority of cases I have relied upon conjectures, which I am anxious that you should not depend on, as though they were Delphic oracles. For you must be free either to follow them or to reject them, so that you may be conscious of my care in relation to you.[25]

It is difficult to associate this kind of sensitivity and tact in relation to the text in hand with the 1515 version of the later books of the *De inventione dialectica*.[26]

There are two other distinctive typographical features of the 1515 *De inventione dialectica*. At the point in the text which in Phrissemius's allocation of chapter breaks falls as the end of chapter 15 of book 2 (sig. G 5v), there is an inverse pyramidal paragraph, traditionally symbolising a major text break, and the following chapter begins with the only printed ornamental capital. This point in the text marks the end of Agricola's discussion *de argumentatione*, and the beginning of his discussion of affective and persuasive oratory, and of genuinely probabilistic discourse, but it also seems possible that this marks a transition to yet another 'editor'.[27]

At the beginning of what Phrissemius makes book 3, chapter 5, there is a single chapter heading:

❡ Sequitur Capitulum de breuitate copia.:. [*sic*]

The text which follows begins:

Abundance [*copia*] and conciseness [*breuitas*] in speech. It is chiefly by these means amongst other that we delight or displease, and *copia* and *breuitas* are derived by invention. It therefore seems appropriate to our project to say a little about these.[28]

There seems little doubt that this one 'chapter heading', or textual marker, in the entire work is an allusion to Erasmus's *De copia*, which in the revised Schürer edition of 1514 carried that anticipation of the imminent publication of the *Lucubrationes* of Agricola. Within the Martens printing house, apparently, somebody in the Erasmus 'circle' picked up the textual reference to *copia* and introduced the signal to the reader that this should be referred to Erasmus. All subsequent editions of Agricola's *De inventione dialectica* do likewise, and both Phrissemius's and Alardus's commentaries cross-refer from this chapter to Erasmus's *De copia*.[29]

Finally, the 1515 edition makes the break between books 2 and 3 at the end of what becomes book 2, chapter 18 (of 22) in Phrissemius, a break which, as Phrissemius points out in his commentary, produces a number of anomalies in the succeeding four chapters (which refer to book 1 as

¶Sequitur Capitulum de breuitate copia.:.

COpia vero & breuitas in dicendo: quum præfertim iftis inter cætera dele
ctamus & offendimus: conftantœ etiam inuentione ifta: non alienum vi
detur ab inftituto noftro: paucis de his dicere. Conftat autem orationis
vbertas: vel quia pauca quidem: multis tamen eloquimur: vel quamuis paucis di
camus: congerimus tamen multa: atœ vt non magnitudine: aceruo tamen rerum
tendimus orationem: vel quod affluentiffimum eft multa dicimus de multis. fi
oftenderimus autem quomodo multa. & quo modo multis dicatur. tria hæc cu
iufmodi fint facile erit perfpectu. Multa dicûtur & expofitione & argumentatio
ne. Expofitione dicuntur multa: quum nõn tãtum fatis habemus fummas rerum
explicare: fed partes omnes profequimur. Qui dicit enim Iuno quoniam oderat
Troianos: nauigante ex Sicilia Aenæa: claffem eius difiecit: vi tempeftatum qua
rum impulfu delatus ad Africam Aenæas: a Didone hofpitio benigniffime eft ac
ceptus. hoc qui dicit totum primum Eneidos librum complexus videtur. Qui vo
let autem paulo vberius dicere. ille quidem caufas odiorum propter quas infen
fa Troianis erat Iuno recenfebit. Deinde vt e Sicilia nauigarint: follicitatum a Iu
none Aeolum vt tempeftatem claffi immitteret non tamen ille preces Iunonis ef
finget: non pollicita Aeoli: nec quo pacto immiffa fit Troianis aut iactauerit eos
tempeftas profequetur. fufficiet tempeftate difiectos fuiffe demõftrare: atœ diuer/
fos: alium ab alio ad litora portufœ africanos effe delatos. Nec Veneris illæ que
relas nec Iouis refponfa, quibus futurus rei Romanæ ftatus explicatur attinget.
Poft tempeftatem refectis corporibus atœ confirmatis animis fociorum benigno
alloquio Aeneæ: tum vt explorandorum locorum gratia profectus fit Achate
comitatus: cartaginemœ peruenerit. cuius vrbis condende caufam & Didonis ca
fus breuius qui dicet explicabit fuis verbis quã vt defcribenda Venere & quære
lis Aeneæ iactatifœ hinc inde verbis eis effingat. Deinde vt in templo Ilionea &
focios reginæ implorãtes fidem: ne littoribus arcerentur agnouerit agnofcendum
œ fe eis & reginæ præbuerit. nihil hic ad ordinem rerum pertinuerint res Troianæ
pictura in templo expreffæ. nihil Didonis pulchritudo aut templi forma defcri
pta. nihil reliqua multa quæ vt ornandis rebus immenfum ita cognofcendis nul
lum: attulerint monumentum. Poeta enim acerrimi ingenii iudiciiœ: nõn magni
fane putauit: qui fuerint cafus: aut ordo rerum Aeneæ quarum etiam vix teuuis
ad ipfum peruenerat fama: fed fumpta illius perfona: voluit tanœ in fpeculo quo
dam varietatem rerum humanarum vitamœ & mores hominum fpectandos pro
ponere: quæ cuncta vt maiore voluptate commendaret: late fudit: quo orationis
rerumœ decorem & gratiam quæ in anguftioribus delitefcunt: in ipfa amplitudi
ne per omnes poffet numeros explicare. Quin & hæc ipfa multo poterunt effu
fius dici. Nam in caufis odiorum recenfendis: fingulæ caufæ longiffimarum nar
rationum funt capaces. Et quod poftea dicitur. vix e confpectu ficule telluris in al
tum vela dabant. hic & quæ fit Sicilia defcribi poteft & quæ fuerint manendi ibi
rurfufœ difcedendi caufæ & apparatus difceffionis: & iam ipfa exprimetur na
uigatio. Sic videmus in preliis narrandis: tantum quæ acies cui cefferit: & quarum
partium eques pedefue alterius profligauerit equitem aut peditem. fingulorum
rara fit aut perquã breuis mentio: nifi imperatorum aut eorum qui ordines du
cunt: idcirco in anguftum pugnæ apud eos colliguntur: apud poetas fingulæ pu

16. 'De copia' chapter heading in the first edition of Agricola's *De inventione dialectica* (Louvain, 1515).

'the previous book', 'the last book').[30] In general, beyond the 'break' in book 2, paragraphing is unrelated to argument, and indeed, paragraphs get longer and longer.[31]

The evidence is suggestive. In this first printed edition of the *De inventione dialectica*, published nearly forty years after it was written, and more than ten years after the print pursuit of Agricola's lost works had begun with Jacobus Faber's preface to Hegius's collected works,[32] the possibility arises that Martin Dorp, professional theologian, specialist logician, and Erasmian humanist, was closely involved only with the self-contained treatise on topics-theory which makes up book 1.

This is not the place to offer the reader an account, even a condensed one, of the intellectual structure of Agricola's *De inventione dialectica*, as it results from this curious process of recovery and collaborative editing. Such an account would, in any case, according to my own argument, now have to be revised to take account of the fact that the work's 'coherence' (if it can be produced) may well not be the kind of coherence envisaged by its original author, Agricola.[33] However, the reader may find a few remarks here helpful for understanding the next stage in my story.

The first book of the *De inventione dialectica* closely resembles other teaching manuals of the period which present the logical 'places', or *loci*: headings under which the student orator is to group material (propositions, examples, aphorisms, definitions) memorably, for easy retrieval during debate. It is not, however, a convenient work to use in the classroom. Compared with later such manuals, its treatment of the individual places is fuller and less schematic, and its examples extended and textually sophisticated (as befits the work of a practising humanist). This book also carries an important introduction, in which Agricola argues that the purpose of argumentation (*ratiocinatio*) in public debate is to put a convincing case as plausibly as possible, so as to persuade an audience to take a particular course of action. Certain truth (the traditional goal of logic) is not, according to Agricola, of great interest to the orator.

It is this strand in Agricola's thinking which is developed at length in the second and third books. These rehearse, comparatively unsystematically, and often anecdotally, a wide range of persuasive strategies, with worked examples to emphasise the point that most public speaking is concerned to sway, rather than to prove. The emphasis throughout is on the informal validity of practical arguing, rather than on absolutely guaranteed forms. It was Agricola's (and other humanist dialecticians') lack of interest in the traditional formality of the syllogism, and forms of argument appropriate to a rigidly deductive version of religious belief, which infuriated traditional theologians, such as those in the faculty of theology at Louvain. What we have seen in the discussion in this chapter so far is that professional editors (like Dorp) working to reconstruct the unfinished text of Agricola's much-anticipated treatise were reasonably comfortable setting the first book in a recognisable kind of order. But they were more diffident about the second and third books, since these are more idiosyncratic and exploratory (as well as being textually problematic because of the multiple hands and layers of emendations).

I have stressed the fact that Erasmus had represented Agricola's *De inventione dialectica* as a work peculiarly well suited to his own intellectual project, even before its recovery. I have argued that Erasmus was involved, via a dedicated group of younger scholars who customarily assisted him in his own editing undertakings, with the subsequent production of Agricola's key work (as it became for humanistic education, just as Erasmus had predicted). In spite of his affiliation to the theology faculty at Louvain, Dorp associated himself with what seems to have been, for him, an open and provisional establishing of a working text of Agricola. But with the hardening of doctrinal positions between 1515 and 1520, the Agricola text became fixed and closed; Dorp's endorsement of it became an endorsement of a position rather than of a work.

JOSTLING FOR POSITION: THE MARTENS PRESS AND THE ERASMUS/DORP 'QUARREL'

It is at this point that I return to the traditional story of the public print 'quarrel' between Erasmus and Dorp. I propose to ask the question: What was the *point* of the dispute? And in looking for an answer, I direct my attention as usual at the print trace—the official version, authorised for publication (which as we shall see is sometimes, as a certain anxiety in the secondary literature attests, confusingly at odds with the unpublished, private exchanges).

The story of the Erasmus/Dorp quarrel conventionally goes as follows: In 1514, Erasmus and Dorp collaborated in the publication of a collection of minor classical works for Martens in Louvain. Shortly after Erasmus left Louvain, in mid-1514, Dorp wrote him a letter formally outlining the objections of the Louvain theologians to the *Praise of Folly* and their hostility to Erasmus's intended publication of all the discrepancies between the Vulgate translation of the New Testament and the original Greek. According to Erasmus, the letter was never delivered; he first saw it by chance, months later, in Antwerp. Erasmus drafted a hasty response in late May 1515, and expanded and altered it slightly for quick publication with *Damiani Senensis elegeia* (Basle, August 1515). Dorp replied in a letter dated August 27, 1515, reiterating his original criticisms and adding new ones. This letter, too, supposedly never reached its destination. Erasmus claims he first read it in a copy provided by More. Erasmus's close friend and supporter Thomas More replied in Erasmus's defence in the second half of 1515 from Bruges, where he was on an embassy. His reply apparently convinced Dorp not to publish his second letter, nor to take the dispute any further.[34]

Subsequently, there is conflicting evidence concerning Erasmus's relationship with Dorp. Some printed letters suggest reconciliation; others imply a renewed conflict. Dorp's published works after 1516 generally support the Erasmian position on the relationship between the *studia humanitatis* and theology.[35]

A number of scholars have drawn attention to the way in which, in spite of the fact that the ostensible subjects of dispute are the *Moriae encomium* and the correction of the Vulgate, the ensuing correspondence—particularly Dorp's second response and Thomas More's long reply—is particularly concerned with justifying 'humanist' dialectic as a suitable core subject for a revised arts curriculum.[36] The shadow of the freshly 'recovered' *De inventione dialectica*, complete with Dorp's endorsement, falls strongly across this exchange; indeed, I suggest that the debate is unintelligible without our acknowledging its silent presence.

As by now, in the present study, we have come to recognise, the problem with the standard account is its dependence upon a literal reading of Erasmus's published corpus of *epistolae*. The story of the dispute about Erasmian satirical writing, Erasmian theology, and Dorp's more orthodox (and establishment) position is based on a series of letters the sequence of whose arguments is established by the dates at their head (or where there is no date, by Allen's estimated date, based on internal evidence from the letter). But the crucial 'thread' is established, as we learned in the first chapter, by the date when the letters appeared in public, where they were published, who they were addressed to, and with what other works those involved in the exchange were concerned (either as author, or *castigator*, or *commendator*). In other words, the story of the dispute between Erasmus and Dorp is a performance, and is intertwined throughout with Erasmian publishing and textual history. It is a curious 'quarrel', surely, in which one of the protagonists 'personally supervised the publication of his earlier letter and Erasmus's response with the second printing of Erasmus' *Enarratio in primum psalmum* (Louvain, October 1515)'—that is to say, in a volume published by the other protagonist.[37] Dorp, in other words, is still one of Erasmus's official *castigatores* at the height of his 'dispute' with him.[38]

I choose one small piece of printed evidence to illustrate how a shrewd eye kept on the publishing story as part of a historical context (specifically, a network of exchanges between Erasmus, Dorp, and Thierry Martens, centred on Louvain) seems strikingly to alter the story of the public 'quarrel' and, instead, to draw together these threads—the continuing collaboration between Erasmus as author and Dorp as editor and *castiga-*

tor; a self-conscious sense of published correspondence as constituting a narrative (in which once a point has been raised, or a question asked, it ought subsequently to be answered); and the rediscovered *De inventione dialectica* as part of this construction, resonating somehow behind their 'quarrel'.

In the closing stages of the first letter in the published polemic between Erasmus and Dorp, Dorp introduces three thematically related comments which tie his letter to the Martens press, to Louvain, and to Erasmus as the centre for important publishing activity:[39]

> This is a rather lengthy and clumsy letter, but one which cannot possibly cause you offence, since it is prompted by feelings of the deepest affection towards you. Thierry Martens of Alost, our printer, who printed the *Enchiridion* and the *Panaegyricum*, has asked me to remember him warmly to you. He longed to see more of you, and to be able to offer you generous and comradely hospitality. And for that purpose he journeyed to Antwerp. Ascertaining that you were not there, but at Louvain, he retraced his steps thither, and, after travelling all night, arrived the next day at Louvain, barely an hour and a half after your departure. If there is anything whatsoever within his power to do for you, he promises to do it; I do not think there is another man living who loves you more. He has finished printing in correct form the *Cato* which you corrected and entrusted to me, and of which I have corrected the proofs. I have dedicated that work to John de Neve, Principal of the Lily College [at Louvain], as you instructed. He is extremely grateful to you for the honour; you will be able to feel the full lavishness of his gratitude when you return.[40]

Here, at the end of a letter highly critical of Erasmus's recent and projected publishing projects, Dorp shifts tone, and returns to his role as editor/corrector, in order publicly to acknowledge the commitment of the Martens press to Erasmus. He gives a vivid picture of affectionate admiration on the part of Martens for Erasmus, and he does so as part of a precisely specified Low Countries location: Louvain and Antwerp and the great public figure's movement between and around them. At the focus of that map is the Martens Louvain printing house (recently moved there from Antwerp), and the Erasmian educational publishing going on there—the *Enchiridion* and the *Panegyrica*, the Cato *Disticha moralia*, whose printing has just been completed, in Erasmus's absence, under Dorp's editorial superivision. Furthermore, Dorp's remarks suggest that in spite of the critical tone of his letter, the responsibility for directing the dedicatory letter for the *Cato* has fallen to him—however much of that letter had been drafted before Erasmus's departure, its address to John de Neve (regent of the college at which Dorp had studied) is Dorp's.

What I am drawing attention to here is the strongly advertised ongoing collaboration between Dorp and Erasmus which is being signalled at the same time as the supposed theological criticisms. This point can be registered more strongly if we turn to the prefatory letter to de Neve to which Dorp directs his reader's attention. That letter (ostensibly from Erasmus, but tailored to suit de Neve by Dorp),[41] like the first 'quarrel' letter, turns on the issue of the appropriateness of secular humane learning to theology:

> 'But what is this?' I hear some trouble-maker cry. 'You, a theologian, wasting time on such trumpery stuff!' To this I answer, first, that I think nothing beneath our notice, however elementary, that contributes to a good education, not least lines such as these which combine a neat Latin style with the implanting of high moral standards. Although, for that matter, why should I be ashamed to spend a few short hours in a field of literature in which not a few Greek authors have distinguished themselves? . . . And then again, if they think it beneath me to have corrected and explained such modest works, how much more discreditable that they should have been corrupted and that (as is clear from their commentaries) these childish works were not understood by men who thought they knew everything![42]

In other words, the dedicatory letter to which Dorp refers us already begins to answer the criticism he himself voices, in the name of the Louvain theologians, of Erasmus's involvement with secular, and particularly satirical, writing.

The first 'quarrel' letter of Dorp's closes with a request that at some point, if this is at all possible, Dorp would be grateful if Erasmus would make some dedicatory mention of his own patron, Meynard Mann, abbot of Egmond:

> If you have anything to be published that you could dedicate to Meynard, abbot of Egmond, my patron, I know for certain that he will be delighted and will reward you generously. So I beg you earnestly to do this. He is a Hollander and the leading churchman in Holland, a well-read man, but more a man of religion than a scholar, although he has a great affection for all scholars; and he might be helpful to you in many ways, should it so fall out.[43]

Curious, again, that the initiator of a critical 'attack' should end his first salvo by imploring his adversary to dedicate a future work to his current patron (as he has just agreed to dedicate a recent work to the head of Dorp's former college).

Erasmus did not dedicate any work specifically to Mann. However, the 1517 Martens edition of the *Disticha moralia* included the additional 'Erudita . . . epistola . . . Eucherii episcopi Lugdunensis ad Valerianum', with a prefatory letter from Erasmus to Alardus of Amsterdam. This work has previously been erroneously considered a translation from Greek into Latin by Agricola, although in fact the original was a Latin text. Erasmus's prefatory letter sets the matter to rights, and praises Alardus for his efforts in retrieving the works of authors of previous ages, and it also makes a formal gesture towards complimenting Mann in the terms Dorp requested:

I only wish that one engaged in so admirable an enterprise may be encouraged by the favour of the great; though I hear that the venerable figure, your kinsman Meynard Mann, abbot of Egmond, reproduces in this as in all other respects the example of the great prelates of the past.[44]

So a prefatory letter of Erasmus's connected with the Agricola project publicly praises Mann, in a volume closely associated with Dorp as general *castigator* and as personally responsible for the editing of an Agricola minor work contained in it. And that laudatory remark is made in connection with the colleague of Dorp's, Alardus, who was also a key figure in the retrieval of Agricola's papers.[45] The same edition of the *Cato* contains an additional preface by Erasmus to the Agricola translation of pseudo-Isocrates' *Paraenesis*, which carried Dorp's name as *castigator* in 1514, in which Erasmus purports to make alterations to the text (which are not actually made).[46] So carefully constructed a print scenario, in which a second edition confirms and reinforces the tale told in the first, suggests that something quite sophisticated in publishing terms is going on, and that Dorp supports Erasmus in the enterprise.

Allen assigns a date '*circa* September 1514' to Dorp's first letter to Erasmus criticising his *Praise of Folly* and his proposed revisions of the Vulgate New Testament. It is certainly no earlier than that date, since it refers to Erasmus's departure from Louvain in that month, and the publication of the *Cato* volume, for which Dorp was *castigator*.[47] In fact, the published version of the letter (supervised by Dorp, in an Erasmus volume, as we said) leaves the date deliberately vague. Erasmus's published reply (dated 1515, Antwerp) begins, 'Your letter never reached me, but a copy of it—secured I know not how—was shown to me by a friend in Antwerp'.[48] In other words, Dorp's letter could in fact have been written any time between September 1514 and May 1515 (around which time Erasmus reached Antwerp on his way back from London). In the third quarter of 1514 Alardus was in Louvain, as was Geldenhauer, and this is the period in which the *editio princeps* of the *De inventione dialectica* was being prepared for the press.[49] It appeared in January 1515, so at some point during this time, Dorp wrote his commendatory letter:

Dorp to the diligent: this dialectic by Agricola is printed for you, diligent scholars, that good studies may be served. I judge nothing will be more useful than this to those who are pursuing the true art of discoursing fluently and eloquently; and who wish to take pains to persuade by means of the rich abundance of matter with the greatest degree of wonder, not by empty words; and who wish to reason on any matter whatsoever appropriately and fittingly by the most probable means. Our author attests that our dialectic is constructed for that purpose. Here therefore you should not look for the chattering nonsense of the sophists, but truly expect those things which many who confuse the boundaries of the sciences assign to rhetoric, but which are in fact proper to dialectic, and which are lacking in the works of Aristotle and Cicero. To whose works this book is in no way inferior, whether we are looking for elegance and the thread of utterance, or for the communication of erudition and maxims.[50]

This is the full text of the letter which appeared prominently on the title page of the *editio princeps* of the *De inventione dialectica*. There could be no more straightforward and thoroughgoing endorsement of Agricolan dialectic, and it is this letter (and this letter alone) which has led later scholars to attach such importance to Dorp's involvement in the recovery of Agricola's key pedagogic work. But, once again, if this commendatory letter is put back historically in a printing context, the story looks somewhat different. The commendatory letter to the *De inventione dialectica* is one of a series, either by Martens himself or by Dorp, in prose or in verse, which 'sells' volumes being issued from the Martens press in the years around 1515.[51] Such letters, whether they carry the name of Martens, or of a distinguished *commendator*, or of one of Martens's own *castigatores*, are clearly frequently drafted by the *castigator*. We saw in the Rescius letter above that the *castigator* could solicit material from his author, to make up the prefatory letter;[52] on occasion, also, as we have seen, Dorp indicates to Erasmus (and the reader) that he himself has contributed to a dedicatory epistle which will carry Erasmus's own name. Barlandus's *Versuum ex Bucolicis Vergilii prouerbialium collectanea* (Louvain, Martens, March 1514) carries on its title page a commendatory iambic trimeter by Dorp:

> Epigram in Iambic trimeters by Martin Dorp.
> The purchaser speaks, the book replies.

> [Martini Dorpii Epigramma Iambicum trimetrum.
> Emptor loquitur, respondet libellus][53]

Meanwhile, Barlandus's own dedicatory letter to de Spouter, on the reverse of the title page, explains how Dorp and Geldenhauer collaborated in the selection of Virgil material for the volume.[54]

The point I am making is that there is no reason to attach special intellectual significance to Dorp's original gesture of supplying a commendatory title-page letter for the Agricola *De inventione dialectica*. It was a part of the *castigator*'s job to provide a celebration, prominently on the title page of a new volume, of the work issuing from Martens's press. But if the volume offended the theology faculty at Louvain, then that originally merely conventional gesture as in-house *commendator* may have become an embarrassment to the promising theologian starting out on his professional career in the theology faculty.

I suggest that the Dorp letter to Erasmus was written after the publication of the *De inventione dialectica*, and that we should relate it to that other published letter, on the title page of the work Erasmus himself had publicly been awaiting with anticipation for some time.[55] Erasmus's reply is exactly contemporary with the enthusiastic note from John Fisher, bishop of Rochester, in his capacity as a prominent member of the English clergy, 'officially' endorsing the *De inventione dialectica*:

> My dear Erasmus, I have been reading in the last few days the dialectic of Rudolph Agricola, which I found on sale in the bookshops. I was induced to buy it by the praise which you give him in your *Adagia*. For I never could persuade myself that a man could be other than very well worth reading, who was so much praised at the same time by you and by Ermolao [Barbaro]. To put it briefly, I never read anything, as far as that art is concerned, more enjoyable or better informed; he seems to have put every point so clearly. How I wish I had had him for a teacher! I would rather that—and I am speaking the truth—than to be made an archbishop.[56]

In the light of this chronology of interrelated printed *epistolae* and published occasional works from the Martens press, it seems appropriate to reposition the publication of the *De inventione dialectica*—signalled several times in Erasmus's publications as a particularly significant event in the shaping of his own 'movement'—as the centre around which the Dorp/Erasmus debate is orchestrated.

Dorp's second, much more detailed, letter does carry a date; it was written immediately after Erasmus had published his own reply to the first letter (in Frobenius's *Damiani elegiae*), and shortly before Dorp himself saw both his original letter and Erasmus's 'hasty' reply through the Martens press in October 1515.[57] Finally, Thomas More replied at length, and with great eloquence, sometime between August and October 1515. This letter also was not published, but it too circulated widely.

In June 1515, however, Martens published Geldenhauer's *Satyrae octo ad verae religionis cultores*, with a prefatory letter (dated three years earlier) by Dorp. Since the dispute with Erasmus supposedly centres on the admissibility of satire on the clergy (the subject of Geldenhauer's volume), this prefatory letter is of some interest. It begins by establishing clearly Dorp's official affiliation with the Louvain theology faculty, and his consequent defection from humane letters:

My dear Geldenhauer, you have acted so as to give me more pleasure than I can say, in lately sending me your satires. But I am amazed that you invite me to pass judgment on them, who am now a stranger to the entire chorus of the Muses, having transferred my loyalties to holy things.[58]

Nevertheless, the letter expresses restrained approval for Geldenhauer's satires, and closes with an expression of friendship for the author. When Thomas More came to write his defence of Erasmus, he drew particular attention to Dorp's endorsement of Geldenhauer's *Satires*, as evidence of inconsistency and special pleading on Dorp's part, in attacking Erasmus's *Praise of Folly*.

Seen in conjunction, the Geldenhauer prefatory letter, the Gilles dedicatory epistle for the Agricola *Opuscula*, and the *De inventione dialectica* commendatory title-page letter all make explicit moves to position the volumes being produced by the Erasmus circle challengingly in relation to the activities of the Louvain theology faculty.[59] Dorp carries the burden of this symbolic connection. Dorp, newly promoted within the faculty—unique amongst the members of the Erasmus circle we have so far looked at in having a conventional affiliation with the theology faculty—is appropriated by his friends and fellow *castigatores* as spokesman for that part of the university actually most resistant to their attempts at self-promotion. Dorp is annexed as part of the validation for an Erasmian 'movement' (a 'new school of theology', Dorp calls it), and Dorp publicly resists that annexation insofar as it involves invoking him as 'Martino Dorpio theologo eximio' (Martin Dorp, distinguished theologian).[60] This, I suggest, is the point, historically, of the exchange between Dorp and Erasmus, an exchange during which both protagonists actually remained in close contact with one another, and continued to collaborate on volumes of Erasmus's *Opuscula* and *Epistolae* issuing from the Martens press.

'Qui nostra haec nota poterunt esse vel procul dissitis, vel posteris?' (Of what interest are our affairs to those in distant places or to posterity?), asks Erasmus. The centrality (geographically and over time) of Erasmus's attempt to attach an endorsement by the Louvain theology faculty to the publishing activities of his group of extra-university humanists is seen most clearly in the strategic publishing moves made *around* the Dorp/Erasmus exchange, and most particularly from the Martens printing press.[61] And the most well known publication from the Martens press which we can associate with the debate we are looking at is Thomas More's *Utopia*, a work written partly in London, partly in Bruges, by a prominent English public figure with explicit and public links with Erasmus's *Moriae encomium*, but which is issued from Louvain at the end of

1516, at a key moment in the Erasmians' struggle with the theology faculty there.

The importance of More's and Erasmus's selecting Louvain as the place of publication for the *Utopia* lies, of course, in the satirical nature of the work, and the evident association of both the author and the text with the *Praise of Folly*. The prefatory paraphernalia to the *editio princeps* of More's *Utopia* is particularly elaborate, and includes almost the entire cast of the *De inventione dialectica* retrieval drama. The 1516 title page already manages to announce a connection with the university at Louvain:

> A truly golden book, no less beneficial than enjoyable, concerning the best kind of commonwealth and the new island Utopia, by that most celebrated man, Thomas More, citizen and vice-chancellor of the renowned city of London, edited by Peter Gilles of Antwerp, and now published for the first time with the greatest accuracy by the skill of Thierry Martens of Alost, printer of the Academy at Louvain.

> [Libellus vere aureus nec / MINVS SALVTARIS QUAM FESTI- / uus de optimo reipublicae statu, deque noua Insula Vtopia / authore clarissimo viro Thoma Moro inclytae / ciuitatis Londinensis ciue & vicecomite cu- / ra M. Petri Aegidii Antuerpiensis, & arte / Theodorici Martini Alustensis, Ty / pographi almae Louaniensium Academiae nunc primum / acuratissime edi / tus .:.][62]

There follows a pastiche dedicatory poem by 'Anemolius', 'nephew of Hythlodaeus', an epistle dedicatory from Peter Gilles to Jerome Busleyden, a letter from Johannes Paludanus (close friend of Erasmus) to Gilles, verses by Paludanus, Geldenhauer, and Grapheus, a letter from Busleyden to More, and a long letter from More to Gilles.

The sequence of events which produced this collection of commendatory and introductory material (so familiar now to scholars that they barely pause to consider it before proceeding to the *Utopia* itself) may be summarised as follows: On September 3, 1516, More sent the prefatory letter and the *Utopia* to Erasmus and committed all the publishing details to his care. On about September 20, he asked Erasmus to supply written recommendations not only by scholars but especially by statesmen. On October 2, 1516, Erasmus assured his friend that all possible care was being taken with the project. On October 17, he suggested that Peter Gilles address his preface to Busleyden rather than to Erasmus himself; Gilles complied in the Utopian letter dated November 1. The previous day More had expressed to Erasmus his delight at Gilles's approval and wished to know the reaction of Cuthbert Tunstall, Le Sauvage, and Busleyden. On November 9, Busleyden sent his Utopian letter to Erasmus

Libellus vere aureus nec

MINVS SALVTARIS QVAM FESTI-
uus de optimo reip. statu, deq̦ noua Insula Vtopia
authore clarissimo viro Thoma Moro inclytæ
ciuitatis Londinensis ciue & vicecomite cura M. Petri Aegidii Antuerpiésis,& arte
Theodorici Martini Alustensis, Ty
pographi almæ Louaniensium
Academiæ nunc primum
accuratissime edi
tus.∴.

Cum gratia ⁊ priuilegio.

17. Title page of the first edition of Thomas More's *Utopia* (Louvain, 1516).

with a note describing it as difficult to compose, and asking Erasmus to regard his letter as a tribute to Erasmus himself. On November 12, Gerhard Geldenhauer sent the news to Erasmus that Thierry Martens had undertaken to print the *Utopia* and that Desmarais would show him a sketch of Utopia by an eminent artist. On November 18, Erasmus wrote to Gilles from Brussels that the *Utopia* was in the printer's hands. The Utopian letter of Desmarais to Gilles is dated December 1, 1516. About December 4, More told Erasmus of Tunstall's approval, gratefully acknowledged in a personal letter to Tunstall himself. On December 15, More confessed that he was expecting the *Utopia* from day to day.[63]

The self-consciousness of the 'packaging' of *Utopia* is evident. At this crucial moment, Erasmus and More join forces to produce, in Louvain, a volume heavy with authority, whose author was conveniently both prominent and *distant* from the Louvain circle, whilst a publicly acknowledged long-standing friend of Erasmus's.[64] A volume astutely in juxtaposition to the *Moriae encomium*, inserted into the Louvain, Erasmian milieu, but a 'plant', constructed to give the impression of influential support by a collection of prestigious international 'outsiders'. If I am right, there is a fresh reading of *Utopia* to be awaited, which responds to the way in which the work's publication was orchestrated by Erasmus, as part of particular polemic in which he himself was at that moment engaged.[65]

My suggestion is that the Dorp/Erasmus/More exchange of letters performed a double function at the time, both polemical and political, and neither of them much to do with 'quarrels', in our modern, highly personalised sense of fallings-out between individuals. Dorp's first letter is 'Erasmian' in setting out the terms of a discussion of the impact of secular, humanistic text studies on the study of scripture. Indeed, it is exactly contemporary with a prefatory letter to de Neve, ostensibly by Erasmus himself, but 'corrected' by Dorp, which frames the same kinds of question. Since Dorp is a professional theologian, potential criticism is appropriately publicly voiced, within the Erasmus circle, by him.

It was equally appropriate that such a recognisably professional figure should provide the endorsement for Agricola's *De inventione dialectica*, reconstructed by Erasmus's circle to offer a technical grounding for *bonae litterae* to substitute for traditional theology's Aristotelian corpus of logical works. This move, unlike the first, was initially more a matter of form than of a systematically thought-through position, in my view. It was offered as a 'place-logic' manual, with Agricolan additions in its later books (doctrinally nonaligned, and therefore less closely scrutinised by the editors). It appeared an uncontentious move to endorse it on behalf of the *studia humanitatis*. Only as the more disturbingly unconventional undertones of Agricola's works became more apparent (undertones which would be lovingly emphasised by Agricola's later editors, Phrissemius and

Alardus, in the late 1520s and 1530s) did Dorp's support for this particular work become an embarrassment for him. And because it was an embarrassment, because the appearance in print of the *De inventione dialectica* made more of an impact than anyone (except perhaps Erasmus himself) had anticipated, it suited Dorp to be confirmed in print as representing the 'opposition' in Erasmian publications on the issue of seriousness versus frivolity; instruction versus 'literary' amusement; certainty in doctrinal matters versus urbanely probabilistic debate.

CODA: WHO RECONSTRUCTED THE *DE INVENTIONE DIALECTICA*? WHAT THE CORRECTORS SAY

Since so much of this argument has hinged on the claim that Erasmus knew what he wanted to find when he sent out a public message encouraging keen young scholars to find Agricola's *De inventione dialectica*, I end this chapter by assembling some of the internal textual evidence concerning the process of recovery and reconstruction. It points, I suggest, to there having been no reliable 'original' manuscript, and therefore to the editors having had a considerable amount of leeway in deciding what the 'authentic text' of Agricola should be. All editors bring prior assumptions to their editorial work; these editors were all 'Erasmians', in the strong sense that they worked with, and were to some extent dependent for their continuing livelihood on, Erasmus himself, whose reputation was, by this time, considerable. It would not be surprising, then, if their textual reconstructions also were Erasmian.

There are, ostensibly, three versions of the text of the *De inventione dialectica* to be considered: the original 'Dorp' edition (also, in corrected form, the text for the first Phrissemius commented edition),[66] the Phrissemius revised edition of 1528, and the definitive Alardus edition of 1539. There are no major differences between these three texts.[67] However, in spite of the apparent consistency (and therefore sense of security) in the text, the annotations give exactly the opposite impression—that all the editors are in a state of some anxiety about the text they are dealing with.

Johannes Matthaeus Phrissemius, who produced the first commented edition of the *De inventione dialectica* in 1523,[68] taught in the faculty of arts at Cologne (1517–23), and then became a canon lawyer (although his orthodoxy was questioned a number of times). He was chancellor of the city of Cologne from 1525 to 1528, 'representing the city in many legal actions'.[69] Erasmus does not appear to have known him.[70] He died in 1532, before the question of a publisher for the Agricola *Opera* had been resolved, and no trace of him is to be found in Alardus's 1539 edition, beyond a letter of 1529 indicating his willingness to be involved in finding a publisher for the volumes.[71]

Well into the body of his revised edition of the *De inventione dialectica* (published in 1528), commenting on what he takes to be a corrupt passage, Phrissemius gives a vivid description of the Deventer manuscript:

I was about to declare that whatever was erroneous should clearly be attributed to the fault of the printer. But the day before I began to write, the written exemplar was brought to me. It had lain hidden until then in Deventer, first at the house of Jacobus Faber, then with those whom they call the brethren. What more need I say? I believed I had discovered a treasure-house. But when I opened it, when I had begun to study it, I discovered that it was nothing as yet but a kind of compilation [sylva] for a future work—particularly the portions which Rudolphus had written in his own hand. For there were four handwritings, or, if you prefer, scripts. And it was possible to identify the parts written in his own hand from a certain letter of his to Langius, which a certain friend of ours made available to me, the year before. In those parts [written by Agricola] some passages were peppered with obelisk signs, others, on the other hand, were noted in the margin with asterisks. Some things were repeated two or three times, with the words hardly altered; some were changed so much that you could scarcely understand/recognise them. How many entire chapters were either entirely crossed out, or transposed to another place? How many pages were missing altogether? How many passages which had been cancelled were substituted in the margin so that the final words could not be read? How many passages were so confused and altogether scrambled that neither head nor tail could be made of them?[72]

The story of corrupt and unsatisfactory manuscripts and printed editions allows Phrissemius to propose textual variants, and to tinker with the sense in his commentary (on grounds of corrupt transmission), just as if he were dealing with an ancient classical work. In a number of places in the scholia he indicates that he recognises the text he is working with for his commentary (the Martens *editio princeps*) to be seriously corrupt. In the passage above, he further specifies that the only manuscript to which (late in the day) he had access was of little help. He also alerts the reader to the fact that he has made editorial decisions concerning the inclusion of material in one place rather than another in the work. At the very beginning of book 2 of the *De inventione dialectica*, Phrissemius comments, in his gloss to the opening sentence:[73]

I warned in the preceding book that I was led by certain conjectures to believe that the manuscript [exemplar] which the printers at Louvain used was indeed written or at least dictated by Rudolphus himself, but not written or dictated in order that it should be published as it was.[74]

On this basis, Phrissemius proceeds himself to modify the text at this point, and its interpretation.

As an editor, Phrissemius is intelligent and consistent in his response to problems with the Louvain printed text. The account he gives of his access to manuscript evidence to compare with the printed material, however, is not correspondingly consistent. In his commentary on book 1, in a long note to Agricola's definition of *contraria* (contraries) ('Contraria sunt * repugnantia, quorum utrunque potest simul existere, & alterum sine altero esse'[75] Phrissemius struggles with the fact that the text as he has it is, in his view, patently absurd. He is reluctant to seem to insult Agricola's intelligence by suggesting that this is what Agricola intended, and he continues:

> My aim was, by as much consultation as was feasible, to compare my text either with the original manuscript [archetypum exempla] or with a variant emended manuscript [emendatum . . . exemplar]. But in the end my hopes were utterly dashed, nor could I lay hands on any other copy than the one printed in Louvain, which was contaminated with an almost infinite number of errors. For the most part these could be discarded as printer's errors. . . . But . . . some seemed to me to have crept in not out of ignorance or negligence, but because at the outset the text was not sufficiently emended. For it appears that they used a manuscript which Agricola himself either wrote or dictated, but which he did not really write or dictate for publication, but in order that after a month or so it should be returned to to be more diligently emended and hammered into shape. If then there were any little blemishes (as characteristically tends to be the case), they would then be assiduously erased. Thus, to come at last to what is presently at issue, I would not deny that Agricola wrote it, as they have it in the text. But I would dare to maintain at the same time that nothing could be more unlike what Agricola *wished* to write, than what is written there.[76]

Here Phrissemius gives his by now familiar account of the relationship, as he judges it, between the Deventer manuscript on which the editors of the 1515 *editio princeps* had based their text, and what Agricola himself had intended. But here he says he has *not* managed to see another manuscript of the *De inventione dialectica*, to set alongside the manifestly corrupt Louvain edition.

There is still more to this than at first meets the eye, particularly as regards the independence of the editorial activities of Phrissemius and Alardus. Although the editions of Phrissemius and Alardus give the impression that the two editions were produced entirely separately, evidence of collaboration is readily to hand, if we compare the two commentaries. In the description of the state of the Deventer manuscript, with its four distinct hands, which I quoted above, Phrissemius said he identified Agricola's own hand

> from a certain letter of his to Langius, which a certain friend of ours made available to me, the year before.

This turns out to be a very helpfully explicit remark (as I am sure Phrissemius intends it to be). The only extant letter from Agricola to Langius was published for the first time in Alardus's edition of Agricola's *Lucubrationes* in 1539. But we know that that volume was ready for press somewhere between 1528 and 1529,[77] and also that Phrissemius and Alardus were in contact with one another at that time (see the letter to Alardus from Phrissemius at the beginning of the *Lucubrationes* volume, dated April 1529).[78] So the *amicus* who showed Phrissemius the Langius letter in Agricola's own hand in 1527 was in all likelihood Alardus.

Alardus had been involved in the very first, 'Dorp' edition of 1515.[79] In a dedicatory letter to Nicholas Clernardus, which follows the Phrissemius letter, as preface to his 1539 *Lucubrationes* volume of Agricola's works, Alardus describes his disappointment in 1514 at the unsatisfactory state of the manuscript he had found, which went to the Martens press as the basis for the first edition, and his determination even then to produce a better version. The opportunity to do so seemed to have arisen when Pompeius Occo informed him that he had retrieved his own lost manuscript of the work. There follows a long description by Alardus of a *De inventione dialectica* manuscript which bears an uncanny resemblance to the one given by Phrissemius:

> This Pompeius [Occo] advised me secretly by letters . . . that the autograph manuscript of the *De inventione dialectica* had been returned to him after more than twelve years, and not without having been exposed repeatedly to the greatest dangers, and having passed high and low through many uncouth hands, before it came to light. . . . Nor do I think that when Proserpina was abducted to the underworld by Pluto she was more diligently sought after throughout the world by her mother Ceres. Furthermore, when, together with Martin Dorp, I examined more closely the copy [exemplar] which had been sent by that most pious and learned man Jacobus Faber of Deventer to Louvain, I found that the whole text was in ruinous condition: *some passages were obliterated with obelisk signs, others, on the other hand, were noted in the margin with asterisks. Some things were repeated two or three times, with the words hardly altered; some were changed so much that you could scarcely understand/recognise them. How many entire chapters were either entirely crossed out, or transposed to another place? How many pages were missing altogether? How many passages which had been cancelled were substituted in the margin so that the final words could not be read? How many passages were so confused and altogether scrambled that neither head nor tail could be made of them?* I cannot express, nor indeed can it be conceived, with how much joy my soul rejoiced . . . that these *Lucubrationes*, so worthy to be known, had returned at last to friendly hands. [italics added][80]

Here (in a letter virtually contemporary with Phrissemius's revised commentary) we have a vivid narrative which incorporates verbatim Phrissemius's description of the poor state of the Deventer *De inventione dialectica* manuscript (the passage italicized). And just as in the case of Phrissemius, it is syntactically unclear whether the 'mutilated' manuscript to which Alardus refers is the *same* one as that on which the 1515 edition had been based, or a fresh one.

Shortly afterwards in the same letter, Alardus describes how Pompeius Occo has supposedly exhorted Alardus to produce the definitive edition on the basis of his Agricola manuscript collection, with the best scholarly assistance:

> Hasten joyfully to your allotted task [Alardus here supposedly records Occo's direct speech to him], and the work which once first you gave to be printed partly mutilated, partly corrupted, you will now produce set to rights and much more thoroughly and satisfactorily emended, just as you promised in the first edition. Therefore, when you have obtained the original manuscript [archetypum], if after the collation of the various texts amongst themselves, with the application of sober judgment and the exclusion of contention you consider that perhaps something should be altered, the following man of altogether sharp judgment, and thoroughly furnished with every kind of copious discourse [rerum copiam] may be able to help you: Jacobus Volcardus of Bergen. The following will also assist: Hermann of Gouda [Lethmaet] (a man not inferior to him and of the greatest erudition and true integrity); Cornelius Crocus (who is his equal in letters). . . . Others will perhaps suggest others. This is what I think.[81]

The three men proposed (supposedly by Occo) as possible additional editors of the new Agricola material are appropriate both to the humanistic task of emending and commenting Agricola's text, and to ensuring Agricola's reputation as both man of *bonae litterae* and respectable source for theologians. Volcardus was a humanist friend of Dorp's; Lethmaet was a theologian and friend of Erasmus's (named as a beneficiary in his 1527 will); Crocus was a student of Alardus's, a humanist and theologian. All were associated with Louvain.[82] The suggestion of an editorial 'team' also reinforces the idea that the *De inventione dialectica* is a work requiring collaborative effort to decipher—textually and conceptually.

What are we to make of the passage which occurs verbatim both in Phrissemius's and Alardus's editions of the *De inventione dialectica*? One thing is clear, whoever is the originator of the description, the two are in consultation, and it is hardly surprising that the two texts of the *De inventione dialectica* agree. My own (still tentative) conclusion is that the passage describes the Deventer manuscript which Alardus first discovered, on which the Dorp/Geldenhauer/Alardus *editio princeps* was based, and concerning which he describes graphically his disappointment in his commentary to the 1539 edition.[83] I think Alardus includes this passage prominently in the Clenardus preface of 1528 to distract attention from the fact that he has not, after all, found any better manuscript evidence with which to collate the Louvain text for his revised edition.[84] In my view, Phrissemius had seen this letter when he was preparing his 1528 commented edition, and incorporated it in his commentary to distract attention from the fact that he had not had access to any further manuscripts either (as he admits in the note on *contraria* in book 1, quoted above). Indeed, to all intents and purposes, the texts of all three editions of the *De inventione dialectica* resemble one another extremely closely, except for a handful of trivial emendations (by Phrissemius), and alternative chapter breaks, which merely reflect marginally different editorial decisions as to which paragraph breaks to treat as crucial to the sense. I am convinced that there was no better manuscript available on which to base the printed text of the *De inventione dialectica*, and that together the *castigatores* (Alardus and Phrissemius) agreed to retain the original (Dorp) text.[85] Once any further manuscripts turned out to be no more satisfactory than Faber's Deventer one, there was, of course, something to be said for staying with the original printed text, which now had the *authority* of familiarity. In the story of Agricola's influence, authority is very important.

In their commentaries, both Alardus and Phrissemius repeatedly remind their readers of the problematic nature of the text they are editing, and alert them to editorial decisions taken in the text (and then in the scholia), the likelihood that Agricola made a particular 'slip of the pen' (*calami lapsus*), or that his copyist misread one word for another, and other assumptions of this kind, familiar to editors ancient and modern. It is extremely unusual for a sixteenth-century editor to volunteer this amount of detailed information about the unsatisfactory state of his original and the extent of his editorial interventions (indeed, I cannot think of another such case). Possibly they are genuinely perplexed, and at a loss as to how to deal with the *De inventione dialectica* (but the printed text does not really show evidence of such editorial dismay). Or perhaps all this talk about manuscripts and variants may be offered as part of a conscious process of authentication of Agricola in print as an author of the stature of the ancients—a 'past' author whose important works survive in many copies, to be collated, emended, and commented after the manner of Cicero or Demosthenes. We might compare the kinds of remarks they make with those of Erasmus himself, in the preface to his revised edition of the letters of Seneca, where he describes the available texts as 'prodigiously corrupted' through the ignorance and shoddy transcription of copyists.[86] In any case, such clear instructions to the reader are at odds with the extensive twentieth-century scholarly discussions of the transmission and impact of Agricola's work on dialectic, which treat the text itself as unproblematic and intact.

MEANWHILE, WHAT ABOUT ERASMUS?

In all of this story, Erasmus himself is at once present and absent. Behind the *castigatores*, of whose circle he is the acknowledged centre, he prompts and publicises, alerts the reader to Agricola's importance, and then ghosts the publication of Agricola's works. His involvement irresistibly reminds one of his participation in some of the print polemics surrounding Luther and the reformers: his own contributions are ones of indirection, defending without having been seen to be implicated, attacking without specifying the precise occasion of the affront—'ita respondi, ut videar non respondisse' (I have responded whilst seeming not to).[87]

But if Erasmus carefully distanced himself from the production in print of the northern humanist whose mantle he claimed, those in the 'circle' did not.[88] In 1520, Heinrich Bullinger, subsequently to become a key figure in the reformed church, studied for the bachelor of arts at Cologne. He records in his diary that the teachers who introduced him to an alternative approach to humane studies there were Johannes Phrissemius (editor of the first commented edition of Agricola's *De inventione dialectica*) and Arnoldus Vuesaliensis:

> Here Johannes Phrissemius lectured on both books of Erasmus's *De copia*, the three books of Rudolphus Agricola's *De inventione dialectica*, Cicero's oration 'pro lege Manilia', Vergil's *Aeneid*, books 6 to 12, St Paul's Epistle to the Romans, an introduction to Greek, and Plutarch's *Gryllus*. Arnoldus Vuesaliensis expounded Vergil's *Georgics*, Horace's *Odes*, Aristotle on the syllogism, and his *De anima*, etc.[89]

By the 1520s the Erasmian Phrissemius was lecturing on both Agricola's *De inventione dialectica* and on Erasmus's *De copia*, and doubtless drawing the young Bullinger's attention to the affinities between the two works. The careful 'distancing' which Erasmus had effected, interposing between himself and the recently recovered text of the *De inventione dialectica* successive layers of editorial intervention by a circle of correctors, commentators, and editors, had apparently set the stage for precisely such a moment: when an independent scholar and professional teacher would spontaneously bring together that work of the first, legendary Low Countries humanist, Agricola, and the work of the self-appointed centre of the new northern 'world of learning', Erasmus. Lo and behold, the two great figures agree. Agricola apparently perfectly anticipates Erasmus; the mantle of Agricola's humane learning falls upon his countryman Erasmus. And in the history of emerging humanist pedagogy the elaborate stage-managing which produced this piece of intellectual theatre is forgotten with the names of the devoted *castigatores* and *famuli* who made it possible.[90]

CHAPTER FIVE

Reasoning Abundantly:
Erasmus, Agricola, and *Copia*

So FAR the present work has proceeded in two distinctive ways to retell the story of the rise to unprecedented international prominence of Desiderius Erasmus. In my first two chapters I traced the dedicated ingenuity of the redeployment of long-standing images (verbal and visual) of the great text *castigator* and teacher to promote a vivid and durable Erasmus, whose text-persona circulated in the multiple copies of his editions of the ancient classics, the early Fathers of the Church, and the scriptures. In chapters 3 and 4 I showed how, in a complementary move, Erasmus masterminded the recovery, editing, commentary and circulation of the works of Rudolph Agricola—Erasmus's chosen mentor, and the man generally regarded by northern European commentators as having brought humanism from Italy to the north. There is no reason to doubt that Agricola had been a charismatic and inspiring figure. But at his death he left few, and relatively inconsequential, published works, and little (as it emerged) suitable for publication by those concerned to convince an international readership of the eminence and stature of their greatest homegrown humanist.[1] I have argued thus far that Erasmus intervened repeatedly in the publishing history of Agricola's works, to generate, and then to consolidate, the reputation in print which the example of the great Frisian humanist had established during his lifetime. That reputation provided Erasmus himself with an intellectual pedigree, and credentials as heir to a 'tradition' of northern humanistic pedagogy.[2]

The present chapter began as an attempt to understand, in the light of Erasmus's respect for Agricola's *De inventione dialectica*, and his involvement in its emendation (or possibly rewriting) for publication, how we should read Erasmus's own equivalently widely read and influential schoolroom textbook, the *De copia*. What quickly transpired, however, was that once it has been proposed that an intellectual milieu is being consciously stage-managed by assiduous intervention in the editing, publishing, and dissemination of texts, the traditional intellectual-historical concept of a 'context' for a work is altered: transformed from a fixed frame to an animate and active one. In this case, a work like the *De copia* does not simply need to be inserted into a succession of related texts that were printed around the same time by those who read and responded to each others' works. Rather, the *De copia* might depend for its 'meaning' on our restoring it to a setting consisting of a collection of disparate texts, all to a greater or lesser extent sponsored by Erasmus, and published with the conscious intention of creating a network of mutually supporting and reinforcing significance. What makes this version of intellectual historical influence distinctive is that it is quite possible to find that the group of sponsored works which give meaning to a selected work of lasting significance need not lie within a single 'field', in our modern sense—may not all be texts deemed to belong to the 'history of dialectic', for example, in the case of texts giving meaning to Agricola's *De inventione dialectica*. And indeed, what emerged in the case of the *De copia*, as the present chapter will show, was that the meaning of the *De copia* was intimately and inextricably bound up with the publishing history of the prose works of Seneca, rather than that of more obviously 'rhetorical' works.

FINDING A CONTEXT FOR *COPIA*: FOLLOWING THE
PUBLISHING TRAIL AGAIN

In the course of the textual detective work in chapter 3, I drew attention to the fact that one of Erasmus's earliest public remarks linking his own enterprise with that of Rudolph Agricola occurred as the closing paragraph—a kind of afterthought, as it seemed—to a preface to the *De copia*. In the new prefatory letter to the 1514 edition, addressed to the printer, Erasmus wrote:

> We are eagerly expecting at any moment the *Lucubrationes* of Rudolph Agricola (a truly inspired man). Whenever I read his writings, I venerate and give fervent praise to that sacred and heavenly spirit.[3]

As I pointed out then, there is a point of some significance at issue here, concerning the textual transmission of Agricola's works. Erasmus is apparently referring to the small volume of *Opuscula*, edited by Faber, published in 1508 (the first volume to make any works of Agricola available other than as fragmented and isolated items in other people's works). And the link between Agricola and *copia* to which Erasmus is referring is made in a letter—prominently printed there and much reprinted thereafter—known as *De formando studio*.[4]

At the end of the *De formando studio* the following passage occurs, which includes one particular Latin term for the assembling and deployment of linguistic material—*copia*:[5]

> And if anyone wishes to extend their use [of the *loci*], through all the dialectical places, as far as the nature of the thing allows, a vast wealth of matter [*copia*] both for speaking and for inventing will certainly become available to him.

How, and in what manner this ought to be done is more than can be arrived at in a letter, and I have discussed this matter at length [*copiose*] in those three books which I wrote *De inventione dialectica*.[6]

When I looked at this passage earlier, it was in the context of the recovery of Agricola's lost work, the *De inventione dialectica*. Here we shall be concerned with a project on which Erasmus was himself already engaged, the *De duplici copia verborum ac rerum*. In order to understand the significance of that project, and of the resulting volume, I shall argue, we need to return the *De copia* to the historical moment of its conception, and to replace it within the body of works out of which Erasmus was building his classroom without walls.

If this allusion to Agricola as engaged in something like the same project as Erasmus, in the *De copia* preface, is implicit rather than explicit, Erasmus is more direct in a letter to Budé in October 1516, published in the *Epistolae elegantes*, edited by Gilles and published by Martens in 1517. There Erasmus writes:

After [the *De copia*] was published I discovered a certain amount in Rudolphus Agricola.[7]

Here Erasmus is certainly referring to the *De inventione dialectica*, published the previous year, with his own support, also by Martens, at Louvain.[8] And indeed, Dorp's promotional letter which introduces that volume to the reader, at which we have had occasion to look before, explicitly links the two projects—*copia* and dialectical invention—as part of the same larger enterprise.[9]

So we need to take a close and serious look at what might conceivably be considered to be the relationship between Agricola's *De inventione dialectica*, which is persistently characterised in the literature as a revised, humanistic handbook of dialectic for technical *argumentatio*, and Erasmus's *De copia*, which is equally consistently described as a compilation of 'abundant speech'—of creative, and above all unstructured, linguistic virtuosity. Both texts have proved curiously resistant to critical attention. In spite of the efforts of historians of dialectic (including myself), the *De inventione dialectica* has remained cryptic and opaque: put bluntly, no one appears to be sure what the *De inventione dialectica* is about. And Cave seems to come closer to an insight than the entire technical literature when he points out that in book 3, 'the tension between Agricola's preference for disciplined argument and his orientation of dialectic in Book III towards affective modes of discourse becomes increasingly evident', and when he observes that Agricola's treatment of *copia* ultimately succeeds in 'undermining the constraints of dialectic', thus revealing 'a fundamental ambiguity in his project of generating discourse'.[10] I suggest that for us, the *De copia* is correspondingly an unreadable text—we can construe it, we can translate it, we can recognise some of its sources and indebtednesses, but we cannot recognise a purpose for it, beyond the trite one of simple 'resourcing'—accumulating material. Yet Erasmus is insistent that *copia* is abundance without redundancy: we therefore need a reading which allows us to recognise due, apt, or appropriate abundance. This chapter designates a specifically northern Renaissance intellectual genealogy, and identifies associated, familiar texts, which may enable us to reconstruct a context for reading the *De copia*.

'ALIUM PRODIDI SENECAM': REVISING SENECA

Since we have already given a good deal of attention to Erasmus's textual and graphic 'self-fashioning' in the image of Saint Jerome, we should notice that there is a textual link to be made between Jerome and *copia* via the unexpected intermediary of Seneca. In the preface to his *Lucubrationes* of Seneca (1515), Erasmus brackets Seneca and Jerome together, as the two great masters of eloquence—pagan and Christian.[11] As Erasmus pointed out, Jerome himself had expressed the highest regard for Seneca, and considered him worthy of respect as quasi-Christian:

> Jerome is the one author in sacred literature whom we can match even against the Greeks; without him I simply do not see whom we could put into the field who really deserves the name of theologian, if we are allowed to speak the truth. And Seneca was so highly valued by St Jerome that alone among Gentiles he was recorded in the *Catalogue of Illustrious Authors*, not so much on account of the letters exchanged between Seneca and Paul (which, being a critic of keen discernment, Jerome well knew were written by neither of them, though he made thorough use of them as a pretext for praising Seneca [tametsi ad autoris commendationem hoc est abusus praetextu]), as because he thought him the one writer who, while not a Christian, deserved to be read by Christians.[12]

Rhetorically, this prefatory passage offers a strong argument for a Christianised reading of Seneca, and for the suitability of Seneca as a guide to Christian morals.[13] Erasmus's *Lucubrationes* of Seneca looked set to provide the basis for serious collation of pagan and Christian moral thought, and pagan and Christian *eloquentia*.

But, more than any other work for which he had acted as *castigator*, this collection of the prose works of Seneca proved unsatisfactory as an edition. The inadequate nature of the text was already announced on the table of contents;[14] and some extremely shoddy proofreading had resulted in garbled page headers, misnumberings, and other confusions

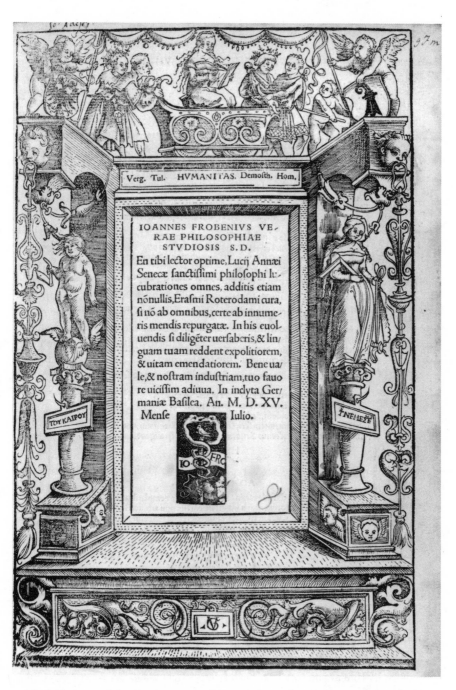

18. Title page of the first Erasmus edition of the works of Seneca (Basle, 1515).

which make the volume difficult to use.[15] In one of his official, retrospective, published letters, Erasmus provided an elaborate story to explain why this had been the case: The inexperienced junior *castigatores* Nesen and Beatus Rhenanus had been left in charge of the volume in Basle while Erasmus was unavoidably elsewhere. As a result, he claimed, the published volume was hopelessly botched.[16] It was, however, Erasmus's standard practice to produce major editions at speed in collaboration with more junior editors and *castigatores*.[17] This arrangement could, however, provide grounds on which publicly to announce a change of heart over a published text.[18] In the present case, as we shall see, between 1515 and 1529 Erasmus had decisively rejected many of the *spuria* which had traditionally formed a significant part of the composite 'Seneca's' oeuvre, and had thereby considerably clarified the significance of Seneca, and improved the standard text.[19]

The 1529 edition was so substantially revised, according to Erasmus, that it was 'an entirely new Seneca'.[20] The features of this volume which distinguish it most strikingly from the first edition are the decisive separation of authentic from spurious texts and the amount of additional material (especially header remarks and commentary), which fully bear out Erasmus's prefatory assurances that *this* Seneca is truly his own.[21] Whereas the 1515 *Lucubrationes* was 'a' Seneca, this volume is definitively 'Erasmus's' Seneca. . . . But it is more than that, as we shall shortly see.

In a number of places in this volume, Erasmus's own magisterial voice directs the reader's attention. In addition to the new preface, Erasmus added introductions to a number of the individual works, including the 'Seneca/Paul' letters. In that introduction he rejects the authenticity of the correspondence vigorously and explicitly, specifying some of the textual grounds on which he does so.[22] To illustrate the glaring anomalies which betray these letters as forgeries, Erasmus singles out for especially contemptuous comment a passage in the ninth letter, from Seneca to Paul. 'It is a sign of monumental stupidity', writes Erasmus, 'when [the forger] makes Seneca send Paul a book *De copia verborum* so that he will be able to write better Latin. If Paul did not know Latin he could have written in Greek. Seneca did know Greek'.[23]

The letter to which Erasmus here refers is extremely brief, and may be quoted in full so that we can imagine its full impact, if one believed (as both Jerome and Augustine appeared to, and as Renaissance readers continued to do) that it was genuinely by Seneca:

> I know that it was not so much for your own sake that you were disturbed
> when I wrote to you that I had read [your] letters to Caesar as because of the

19. Table of contents of Erasmus's revised edition of the works of Seneca (Basle, 1529).

nature of things, which summons the minds of men away from all upright pursuits and practises,—so that I am not astonished in the present instance, particularly because I have learned this well from many sure proofs. Therefore let us begin anew, and if in the past I have been negligent in any way, you will grant pardon. I have sent you a book on facility in using words [De verborum copia]. Farewell, dearest Paul.[24]

Here, apparently, Seneca indicates his approval qua pagan rhetorician and moralist for Paul's Epistles, which has led him supposedly to show them to Nero. And he offers some kind of collaboration with Paul, based on a text of his on the *ars bene dicendi*. However clumsy the letter, its sentiments were such as to make it attractive to a Christian humanist. When, in both editions of the Seneca, Erasmus explains that he includes the spurious works because of their historical importance for the formation of 'Seneca's' reputation in the Christian world, it is these letters which are crucially at issue.

The forcefulness of Erasmus's denunciation of the authenticity of the letters in the 1529 Seneca may be connected in part with his embarrassment that, in spite of his prefatory remarks about *spuria*, authentic and spurious texts were not satisfactorily distinguished in the earlier edition.[25] After all this vehemence, then, it is intriguing to find that the list which Erasmus provides of works of Seneca 'which are no longer extant' ('quae non extant'), below the table of contents of the 1529 *Opera* of Seneca, nevertheless features prominently a 'Liber De copia'.[26] The only evidence for Seneca's having ever written a 'Liber de copia' is the supposed reference to it in one of 'Seneca's' letters to Paul. In spite of his insistence that he has always had grounds for regarding the Seneca/Paul correspondence as a forgery, it appears that the tantalising suggestion found there that Seneca might have written a pedagogic work on *eloquentia* specifically for a Christian writer captured and held Erasmus's attention.[27]

There were other grounds for hoping that a seminal *De copia*, by an author as pivotal as Seneca, might one day come to light, which perhaps kept this hope vivid for Erasmus. In sixteenth-century editions of Quintilian's *Institutio oratoria*, book 10, section 1, carries the heading 'De copia verborum'. And sixteenth-century readers were inclined to link the names of Seneca and Quintilian around the particular rhetorical topic of *Declamationes* and *Suasoriae*.[28] The *Major* and *Minor Declamations*, attributed to Quintilian, and certainly only slightly post-dating the *Institutio oratoria* were grouped with the Seneca *Declamationes* as key examples of taught forensic argument (incomplete, but accompanied in a number of cases by a *rhetor*'s sketch of rules for arguing the case in point, which sheds considerable light on Roman adversarial techniques).[29]

AGRICOLA'S ANNOTATED SENECA: 'NOTED IN THE HAND OF RUDOLPH AGRICOLA'

The new preface to the 1529 Seneca is in fact a full introduction, lavishly furnished with instructions on how the reader is to treat the work. It speaks out with the clear voice of Erasmian authority (as the 1515 edition, to Erasmus's own chagrin, did not). Immediately following the careful rededication—emphasising how entirely new the work is (hence entitled to a new dedicatee, to match), Erasmus specifies his sources for this *renovatio*. Among those sources, Erasmus tells his reader, was a printed Seneca which once belonged to Rudolph Agricola, and carries marginal corrections in his own hand:

> I have produced another Seneca: . . . The efforts of Matthaeus Fortunatus of Pannona helped us a great deal with this labour (a man, as you may see, of precise learning, diligence, and of sober and sound judgement). For he accurately revised and corrected the *Quaestiones naturales*: if only he had executed all the other works as well! Although we followed him freely in many places, we disagreed with him in not a few, above all where the exemplars supported our sense. A codex printed fifty years ago at Treviso, and which belonged to Rudolph Agricola was of great use to us, which he seemed to have read over with great vigilance. This is clear from the annotations in his own hand, where in innumerable places he had corrected the text. In many places he had done so, apparently, by following his own intuitions, rather than by basing his decision on an ancient exemplar. Indeed, it is amazing how much this obviously superhuman man [vir plane diuinus] arrived at by guesswork. For I am not able to sum up Rudolphus's many and extraordinary talents more conveniently. Haio Hermann of Phrysia made the riches of Agricola's codex available to us—a young man born with such a wealth of native qualities that he seems the only one suitable to succeed Agricola's fame, and to maintain the glorious reputation of such a man.[30]

Hermann Phrysius's connection with the project to retrieve the works of Rudolph Agricola is comparatively well documented.[31] Haio Hermann was at the Lily in Louvain with Erasmus in 1519 (and acted as a trusted courier for him between Paris and Louvain). He went to Italy to study, and obtained a doctorate in civil and canon law. On his return north, he married Anna, daughter of Pompeius Occo. Occo, it will be recalled, had inherited Rudolph Agricola's papers from his uncle Adolph Occo, who had attended Agricola during his last illness.[32] In a letter of March 1528, published shortly afterwards in the *Opus epistolarum*, Erasmus congratulated Hermann on his marriage, and urged him to edit the extant works of Agricola.[33]

Hermann published one small translation of Agricola's in 1530,[34] but, in spite of Erasmus's flattery, he did not in the end edit his countryman's works.[35] In October 1528, however, Erasmus wrote to Hermann to final-ise arrangements for the transport of the precious Treviso Seneca, copi-ously annotated by Agricola. So Erasmus's flattery had evidently been successful in establishing access to hitherto inaccessible Agricola texts. The letter (also published in the 1529 *Opus epistolarum* volume) is strik-ingly explicit about the care with which the book is to be transported, and the way in which access to it will be withheld conscientiously from any-one except its intended recipient:

> They have begun the Seneca. For we were fully prepared as far as the *De bene-ficiis*. Meanwhile we have sent this courier at our own cost, for no other pur-pose except to bring back to us your codex. Concerning which you need have no fears whatsoever: apart from myself no one else will touch it. You should wrap it up in numerous coatings made of paper, in such a way that the topmost covering is of linen coated with wax. I will return it with the same care. I will have the opportunity in the preface of commemorating your name with honour, if you will allow. I do not know what codices Vives has seen, unless perhaps yours, or that which a certain friend spent some time collating at the house of Thomas More. In truth, I have accumulated such a collection of anno-tations that I fear neither that codex nor your own.[36]

A letter to Hermann Phrysius when the volume was returned to him, also published in the 1529 collection, *Opus epistolarum Erasmi*, once again emphasises the importance Erasmus attached to the loaned Agric-ola Seneca:

> I am sending back your codex—than which, as you wrote, nothing is more beautiful—together with two printed copies. My contract entitled me to three; I have given you the greater part. If your codex was worth fifty florins, the printed one is worth a thousand [!]. I do not deny that I profited from yours in many places. Nor have we deprived Rudolphus of his due praise, as I can tes-tify. We have mentioned you in the preface, and we have added your name to the *Ciceronianus*. If however this does not seem sufficient to you, what we have begun will be completed out of my own stock. For since the death of Joannes Frobenius the printing house is entirely in disorder.[37]

Evidently Erasmus set enough store by the access given to the annotated Agricola Seneca to pay handsome tribute to Hermann, both with the gift of two of his three publisher's copies of the Seneca *Opera*, and with a commendation in the preface (he also added Hermann to the second edi-tion of his *Ciceronianus*, as one of the *eruditi*).[38] Furthermore, he chose to advertise this fact by arranging for the publication of this expression of emphatic indebtedness, to Agricola and to Hermann, almost simultaneously with the issue of the 'new' Seneca itself. The reader is likely to infer from the two letters together that Agricola's corrections to an early printed Seneca were the crowning glory to the collection of materials assembled to improve the 1515 Seneca, and so, I think, he was intended to do.[39]

Agricola's annotated copy of the Treviso Seneca is no longer extant.[40] It is, however, illuminating for the present story to consult a Treviso Seneca.[41] This handsome slim folio volume opens with the spurious *De moribus*, followed by the spurious *De quattuor virtutibus cardinalibus*, then by Seneca's *Declamationes*, Seneca's *De Ira*, *De Clementia*, and so forth, the spurious *Apophthegmata*, the spurious Seneca/Paul correspondence, and finally the Seneca *Epistulae morales* to Lucilius. It does not contain the *Quaestiones naturales*.[42] This means that the only substantial nonspurious Seneca work for which Agricola's annotated text could have provided Erasmus with emendations and annotations was the *Declamationes*.

The text of the 1529 Seneca documents punctiliously the use Erasmus has made of the Agricola annotations.[43] At the end of the second work, the *De institutione uitae ad Lucilium Balbum, Siciliae Praesidem epistolae*, Erasmus writes:

> When the *Epistolae* to Lucilius were already partially printed, the exemplar arrived from Brabant. By collating this we have rectified whatever errors had fooled us before. Since they could not be inserted into their proper place, we have supplied them in an appendix. We have noted in passing the typical printers' errors, above all if anything seems of any significance.[44]

In case there should be any doubt, Agricola is explicitly and repeatedly named as the annotator whose emendations and annotations to the Treviso text Erasmus gratefully and enthusiastically acknowledges.[45] The *Epistolae* are the second work in Erasmus's volume, preceded by the *De beneficiis*. So the published letter to Hermann accurately specifies the state of affairs: Erasmus received the Agricola Seneca when the printing of the volume was already underway. A six-page appendix of Agricola emendations is inserted after the letters; thereafter, each work is followed by its own section detailing Agricola's comments. As we expect, there are no annotations for the *Quaestiones naturales* (not contained in the Treviso Seneca)—here Erasmus inserts the Fortunatus emendations, from the published edition whose use he had also publicly acknowledged. Nor does Erasmus include any annotations to the *spuria*, now relegated to a section at the very end of the volume. What is more surprising, however, is that no Agricola comments are printed for the *Declamationes* and *Suasoriae*. Since these are texts on the *ars disserendi*, we might well expect that

Agricola had had something to say about them in his personal copy of Seneca.

Here we find, as so often in the present study, that we need to turn our attention to the larger milieu within which Erasmus was publishing, this time at Basle. When we do so, a Basle publication comes into view, of the kind which in the course of the present study we have become used to finding following on the heels of Erasmus's own highly strategic programme of publishing, and filling a gap to which his own printed pronouncements have drawn attention. In 1529 Johannes Bebelius published three of Seneca's *declamationes*, with an introduction and commentary by Agricola, and a prefatory letter by himself: *L. Annaei Senecae . . . Declamationes . . . cum R. Agricolae commentariolis.*[46] According to the Agricola literature, the provenance of this 'commentary' is entirely unknown.[47] The most likely source for this volume seems to be the 'heavily annotated' Treviso Seneca, sent with so much care to Basle by Haio Hermann.[48]

As we saw, Erasmus's published expression of gratitude to Hermann for the loan of the volume elaborately emphasised the care with which the Agricola Seneca was to be packaged and sent, and the fact that he alone would handle the volume. Bebelius says in his introduction that he obtained his Agricolan commentary on Seneca from 'a certain most learned friend', who, on the parallel evidence of the 1529 Seneca, appears to be Erasmus himself.[49] Bebelius had originally been a Froben *castigator*, and Erasmus had given works of his own to him when he set up as an independent printer.[50] Bebelius's prefatory letter to the Seneca *Declamationes aliquot* stresses both the importance of the *Declamationes* for the study of *eloquentia* and the significance of Agricola, in precisely the terms of Erasmus's volume.[51] Whether by design of accident, the upshot was that a further publication saw the light at precisely the right moment to support Erasmus's claim that the *Declamationes* were an important and undervalued teaching text, and that Agricola was the inspirational figure behind the northern European pedagogic movement, of which Erasmus was by now self-appointed leader. And in any case, the 1529 Seneca *Opera* is a major, substantial piece of public testimony to Erasmus's commitment to Rudolph Agricola.

Erasmus's pursuit of, and subsequent use of, Agricola's annotated printed Seneca opens up some further possibilities in this story of the recovery and transmission of the Frisian humanist's works. It appears that the resurfacing of one of Agricola's personal copies of a key work of antiquity, complete with his marginal annotations, was treated as an event as important as the recovery of his minor *opuscula*. Both types of recovery figure as significant moments in the reconstructing of a body of key Agricola printed works, which can be referred to as providing a 'heritage' for the Erasmians—heralded enthusiastically in prefatory letters exchanged between members of the Erasmus 'circle'. Agricola's surviving letters expressed particular interest in manuscripts of the works of Cicero, Quintilian, Seneca, the elder and younger Plinys.[52] It begins to look as if Erasmians embarking on editions of works by these authors naturally included inquiries about surviving Agricola texts and annotations in their preliminary assembling of material.[53]

One of the stories I told in chapter 3 concerned a claim by Beatus Rhenanus, in the preface to his edition of the younger Pliny's letters, that he had in his possession some of Agricola's *lucubrationes*.[54] I suggested that Rhenanus (and then the Schürer press) had no real grounds for making such a claim. But there is one other possibility. The younger Pliny was one of the authors in whom Agricola had a known interest; Rhenanus may well have set out to look for copies of the letters which might be identifiable as having belonged to him. There survive in Stuttgart three incunabula which can be identified as having belonged to Agricola, and which are believed to have come to Stuttgart via his devoted friends, the von Pleningen brothers. The works in question are the older Pliny's *Historia naturalis*, published in Parma in 1476, the younger Pliny's letters, published in Venice in 1471, and a Tacitus, published in Venice around 1473. The Pliny letters bear the marks of Agricola's ownership together with marginal corrections.[55] Two manuscript copies of the Pliny letters made by Agricola himself survive, one in Leiden and one in Stuttgart. In both of these, Agricola incorporates significant textual variants.[56] If Rhenanus had access to one or more of these while he was preparing his own edition of Pliny's letters, he may have hoped, like Bebelius, to produce a volume of Agricola's own *annotationes*; if that was the case, the project apparently came to nothing.

If Rhenanus decided that Agricola's textual variants and marginal corrections did not merit an edition, he may well have been showing characteristic editorial wisdom. The annotations which Erasmus incorporated in his 1529 Seneca justify inclusion only because of the reputation of their author. They rarely consist of more than single-word alternatives to the text, with rare remarks about the beauty of a Senecan sentiment. A surviving autograph manuscript copy of a classical text, like the Leiden Pliny letters, is a precious object, justifiably cherished by its owner.[57] A transcript of his variants conveys practically nothing of the thrill of handling the original.

ERASMUS AND DIALECTIC: STUDIOUS READER OF AGRICOLA

There are no Agricola emendations recorded for Erasmus's texts of the *Declamationes*, *Controuersiae*, and *Suasoriae* in the 1529 Seneca. Instead, these carry a strong introduction, in which Erasmus singles out the

Declamationes as vital for a practical training in *eloquentia*, which begins:[58]

> So far as the needs of scholars are concerned, none of Seneca's works needs a pure text more urgently than these *Declamations*.[59]

It closes with an equally strong endorsement of the classroom usefulness of *declamationes* for a training in 'invention' and 'judgement', and contrasts this with the mere virtuosity (without clear purpose) of 'the dialectic which is currently taught in the schools':

> It is incredible how much usefulness these critical opinions of men excelling in all types of doctrine contribute, not simply to the art of speaking well [ad bene dicendum], but also indeed to good judgement, whether in forensic argument [forensibus causis], or in popular or military public orations, or in assemblies, or in every activity and function of life, in which in some considerable part the use of language is regulated by prudence. That faculty of invention and judgement, if once it is instilled into young boys, seems to me to yield much more fruit that that dialectic which is currently taught in the schools. Which dialectic, however, I do not estimate to be inferior, nor requiring to be done away with, but simply that, once all frivolous niceties have been done away with, it should be taught for practice and use, rather than childish ostentation. If only in some happy case these books of Seneca's [*Declamationes*] could be restored to us in their entirety.[60]

These are unusually explicit words on the subject of dialectic for Erasmus. They are also strikingly similar to sentiments expressed by Agricola in the third and final book of the *De inventione dialectica*, in which he discusses the practical, and above all the forensic and adversarial use of his revised *ars ratiocinandi*. Indeed, subsequent editions of Seneca based on the Erasmus 1529 *Opera* take this introduction to be written by Agricola. They incorporate it into Agricola's *annotationes* on the *Declamationes*, which they reunite with the other Agricola annotations in the *Opera* text (either from Bebelius's edition or from Alardus's *Lucubrationes*).[61]

After 1527–1528, Agricola's *De inventione dialectica* was available in a fully commented version, issued at Cologne by Phrissemius, and the confusion of Erasmus's *Declamationes* introduction with Agricola is not then so surprising.[62] In chapter 14 of the third book of the *De inventione dialectica* (in Phrissemius's version of the text), for instance, Agricola too criticises the dialectical practice in the schools as largely irrelevant, and proposes *controversiae* as a more suitable grounding for practice. And like Erasmus, he both contrasts *controversiae* with the sterile use of logic and argument of 'philosophers of our own age' and maintains that he is not denying a certain place for traditional dialectic in training the novice:

Aristotle and Plato, whose eloquence and erudition are celebrated with equal praise in philosophy, rarely considered that ratiocination should be used naked and plain, as can readily be seen from their works. But in our age you will see that what is explored and argued by philosophers 'firstly and secondly', and has to be noted 'fourthly and fifthly', and derives its consequences in the 'baroco' [figure of the syllogism], and the rest of this kind of ineptitude, is utterly bankrupt and unsuitable for anything we have to say. Nor do I say these things concerning them, because I think they should be condemned. Rather, I would wish them to be learned by beginners in the schools, and indeed, with the greatest care and precision, and to be practised too, as long as they are confined to the schoolroom.[63]

The first passage which Agricola chooses, to show how *controversiae* offer examples of more appropriate and flexible uses of argumentation than 'the dialectic now in use', indicates that, here in book 3, the erudite humanist was exploring neglected manuscript sources in his research into a more humane *ars dicendi*. It is taken from pseudo-Quintilian's *Minor Declamations* (263.2), a work which he was certainly consulting in manuscript:

I estimate argumentation to be as essential to the controversial oration as the nerves without which it is impossible to sustain existence. But just as the body is not merely deformed, but does not even belong to the species 'body', in which the nerves are exposed and devoid of all flesh, so neither do argumentations deserve the form or name in law of 'oration' if they stand out sharply and comprise one uniform, composite type. Amongst the Greeks, indeed, there was a proverb which said: distinguished things come by slow stages [egregia de lente], whenever a small thing was gradually elevated to the heights of a great one. How much more plainly can these things be observed now, when divine things are handled with puerile nonsenses? Therefore the forms of argumentation need to be changed, and their parts need to be organised in a different kind of arrangement. Not, however, that a plain order should be shunned, since we believe that ratiocination should not invariably be entirely revealed. [There follows the example from the *Minor Declamations*.][64]

Uncharacteristically, Phrissemius does not comment on this passage. But in the following chapter Agricola again refers to the *Declamationes minores*, this time explicitly drawing attention to the comparative obscurity of his source, when he discusses extant texts which have dealt richly with *copia dicendi*.[65] At this point, Phrissemius makes it clear that he cannot comment on the *Declamationes minores*, because it has not 'seen the light'—is not available in print:

I am surprised, since nothing has lain so deeply buried up to now that in this our own day it has not been made public, that it should be the case that Quintilian's [*Minor Declamations*] have not up until now been published.[66]

In March 1529, Erasmus wrote to John Lotzer (the letter, yet again, published in the *Opus epistolarum*), to ask him if he would be prepared to loan Erasmus an early manuscript of the works of Quintilian, so that Erasmus could prepare an edition.[67] The reason he gave for wishing to add Quintilian to his list of edited works was that 'we have annotations on Quintilian by various erudite men':

> We have annotations on Quintilian by various erudite men, and we have learned that you possess an extremely ancient manuscript. If you would put this manuscript at our disposal for a few days, I hope that scholars would lack nothing else, with respect to an author of such quality, and your treasure would be returned to you intact and undamaged, and with interest. Furthermore, we would see to it that the whole of posterity would not be unaware to whom they owed this benefit, as you can see we have done in the preface to the recently corrected Seneca.[68]

Lotzer, however, was not as obliging as Hermann had been with his Seneca, and the edition never appeared.

In the terms of a traditional intellectual-historical inquiry, we have come a long way from Erasmus's *De copia*. And yet, the strands which link the Seneca and the Erasmus handbook for the *ars bene dicendi ac scribendi* are all strong. Our quest for a context which gives meaning back to Erasmus's *De copia* has once again produced a story in which Rudolph Agricola has a starring role, and which identifies a carefully laid trail of published works, grouped around the Erasmian work. Here the *Opera* of Seneca provide the ground, as it were, and the *De copia* project the counterpoint. The composite figure, Seneca rhetor/*philosophus*, apparently offers a moral frame compatible with Christian thought, a projected *De copia*, adapting pagan eloquence to a Christian purpose, and a classroom text (the *Declamationes*, which teaches both morals and *eloquentia*). Ironically, however, the period between 1515 and 1529, during which it became clear to Erasmus that the corpus of Seneca's works required drastic reappraisal and reorganisation to reveal the 'true' Seneca, was also the period during which the *De copia* evolved in its published form from a skeleton school text (for Colet's Saint Paul's school) into the key pedagogic work for the *ars bene dicendi*, which he placed first in importance in his catalogue of published works.[69]

The period 1515 to 1529 was also one of growing prominence for Agricola's *De inventione dialectica*, now freely available (thanks to Erasmus's own efforts) in printed (and later, commented) form. Agricola's and Erasmus's rhetorical manuals became increasingly prominent and pivotal in the classroom as the first impetus for reconstructing a Christian-humanist manual of *copia*—the suggestions in Seneca and in Agricola—receded in significance. What remained was the claim that such a work had good classical precedent, and would fill an acknowledged gap in provisions for Christian humanist *eloquentia*. The Europe-wide availability of both manuals in handy, commented, inexpensive printed form (shrewdly backed as usual by Erasmus and his northern European printers) was the practical impetus for a reform (at least in the north) of taught *eloquentia*. With Erasmus's *De copia* and Agricola's *De inventione dialectica* side by side on the reading desk, flanking a copy of Seneca's and Quintilian's *Declamationes*, *argumentatio* was detached from its formal, technical language-based context in the traditional schools. Freed from the rigid and coercive framework of traditional Schools logic, it opened the way to a training in persuasive and affective discourse more appropriate to the civic and forensic context of sixteenth-century education. Already in 1531, in another part of Europe, Thomas Elyot, in his blueprint for effective but uncontentious pedagogy, *The Book Named the Governor*, could cite both works together, and together with Cicero and Quintilian, as if the combination were utterly commonplace:

> After that .xiiij. yeres be passed of a childes age: His maister if he can / or some other studiouslye exercised in the arte of an oratour / shall firste rede to hym some what of that parte of logike that is called *Topica* / eyther of Cicero / or els that noble clerke of Almaine / which late floured / called Agricola: whose warke prepareth inuention / tellynge the places / from whens an argument / for the profe of any mater / may be taken with litle studie: And that lesson with moche & diligent lernyng / hauyng mixte there with none other exercise / will in the space of halfe a yere be perfectly kanned.
>
> Immediately after that / the arte of Rhetorike wolde be semblably taught / either in greke out of Hermogines / or of Quintilian in latine / begynnyng at the thirde boke / and instructyng diligently the childe in that p[ar]te of rhetorike / principally whiche co[n]cerneth persuation: for as moche as it is most apte for consultations. There can be no shorter instruction of Rhetorike / than the treatise that Tulli wrate vnto his so[n]ne / which boke is named the partition of rhetorike.
>
> And in good faythe to speake boldly that I thinke: for him that nedeth nat /or doth nat desire to be a exquisite oratour / the litle boke made by the famous Erasm[us] (whom all gentill wittis are bou[n]den to thanke / and supporte) which he calleth *Copiam verborum et Rerum* / that is to say / ple[n]tie of wordes and maters / shall be sufficient.[70]

And whan a man is comen to mature ye-
res/and that reaſo in him is cōfirmed with
ſerious lerning ⁊ longe experiēce : thā ſhall
he in redyng tragoedies execrate ⁊ abhorre
the intollerable life of tyrantes : And ſhall
contemne the foly and dotage expreſſed by
poetes laſciuious.
Here wyll J leaue to ſpeake of the fyrſte
parte of a noble mannes ſtudie : And nowe
wyll J write of the ſeconde parte/whiche
is more ſerious/and contayneth in it ſondry
maners of lernynge.

The moſte cōmodious and neceſſary
ſtudies ſuccedyng ordinatly the
leſſon of poetes. Cap.xj.

Fter that.xiiij.yeres be paſ-
ſed of a childes age : His
maiſter if he can/or ſome o-
ther ſtudiouſlye exerciſed in
the arte of an oratour/ſhall
firſte rede to hym ſome what of that parte
of logike that is called Topica/eyther of
Cicero/or els of that noble clerke of Al-
maine/whiche late floured/called Agricola :
whoſe warke prepareth inuention/tellynge
the places/from whens an argument/for
the

the profe of any mater/may be taken with
litle ſtudie : And that leſſon with moche ⁊
diligent lernyng/bauyng mixte there with
none other exerciſe/will in the ſpace of halfe
a yere be perfectly kanned.
Immediately after that/the arte of Rhetorike wolde be ſemblably taught/either in
greke out of Hermogines/or of Quintilian
in latine/begynnyng at the thirde boke/and
inſtructyng diligently the childe in that pte
of rhethorike/principally whiche cōcerneth
perſuation : for as moche as it is moſt apte
for conſultations. There can be no ſhorter
inſtruction of Rhetorike/than the treatiſe
that Tulli wrate vnto his ſone/whiche boke
is named the partition of rhetorike.
And in good faythe to ſpeake boldly that
J thinke : for hym that nedeth nat/or doth
nat deſire to be an exquiſite oratour/the litle
boke made by the famous Eraſm⁹ (whom
all gentill wittis are bouden to thanke/and
ſupporte) whiche he calleth Copiam verborum et Rerum/that is to ſay/plētie of wordes
and maters/ſhall be ſufficient.
Iſocrates cōcerning the leſſon of oratours
is euery where wonderfull profitable/ba-
uynge almoſt as many wyſe ſentences as he
hath wordes : and with that is ſo ſwete ⁊
E.iiij. dele-

20. Juxtaposed citations of Agricola's *De inventione dialectica* and Erasmus's *De copia*, in Thomas Elyot's *Boke Named the Governour* (London, 1531).

CHAPTER SIX

Concentric Circles: Confected Correspondence and the *Opus epistolarum Erasmi*

I HAVE ARGUED that comparatively late in Erasmus's life, his reputation as a translator, editor, and pedagogic theorist was consolidated into a solid international reputation as *the* figure of trans-European learning—the quintessential European man of letters. This extraordinary rise to prominence was effected by Erasmus himself, and the tight-knit coterie of scholar-servants, editors, correctors, printers, and publishers, by a combination of more-or-less conscious strategies: self-conscious self-production, on a recognisable patristic model, and assiduous fostering in the publishing houses of publications (by himself and others) which could be promoted as part of a peculiarly northern Renaissance, whose geographical centre was the Low Countries, but in which the subjects and their treatment were 'universal'.

As we saw in the last chapter, this promotion via a conjunction of apt ancient prototypes and reconstructed, near-contemporary humanist mentor could exceed mere strategic 'placing' of an innovative pedagogic text of Erasmus's own. In the case of the *De copia*, it resulted in an unexpectedly original version of *copia*, of lasting importance for *eloquentia*.[1] In the present chapter we return to Erasmus's most enduringly present role model—Jerome—to watch what has come finally to stand as his most lasting monument take on shape and significance: the collected letters, lastingly assembled in Allen's *Opus epistolarum Erasmi*, and the basis for all modern work, not just on Erasmus, but on northern humanism as a whole.

For before we are in a position to engage with what turn out to be the multiple problems of treating the *Opus epistolarum Erasmi*—the greatest surviving resource scholarship has bequeathed to us for the study of Erasmus—as documentary evidence in reconstructing Erasmus's life and work, we need to to take one further look at Erasmus's intense, passionate, and scholarly relationship not just with Jerome, but specifically with Jerome's considerable and vital body of surviving *Letters*. Between 1500 and 1529 Erasmus returned repeatedly to Jerome's *Epistolae*, and the arduous editorial task of organising the surviving letters, identifying and excising spurious material, restoring passages corrupted in transmission, so as to provide the scholarly world with the 'true' Jerome. I shall argue that as Jerome's editor, Erasmus was in the best possible position to understand how wholly our sense of a remote intellectual figure is shaped by his carefully organised and orchestrated correspondence, where such a correspondence exists. Letters, indeed, are irresistibly the familiar, spoken voice of the absent figure who has never been encountered in the flesh, but whose *Opera* are constantly present, read and reread, and integrated into the culture. Jerome's letters made Jerome in Bethlehem present and spiritually effective to a circle of contemporary correspondents; Jerome's letters in Erasmus's printed edition made the saint vividly present to a congregation of those committed to his trilingual learning, and his liberal attitude to biblical textual reconstruction and exegesis. Equally, once we recognise the strategic care with which the successive volumes of Erasmus's own *Epistolae*, edited by devoted followers of Erasmus and published by presses across Europe between 1516 and the end of Erasmus's life, were put together, we have to abandon the idea that they represent the 'real' Erasmus, glimpsed covertly in those fragments of a 'life' which he more or less reluctantly revealed to the public. Instead we uncover an extraordinary resource of a different kind for our understanding of how thoroughgoingly and inventively Erasmus constructed the emerging northern humanist 'world of learning': one which at the same time as being seductively vivid and emotionally charged is as carefully controlled and programmed as the Metsys panel or Holbein painting, and as carefully conceived as a fitting public testimony to lasting greatness in a grand tradition.[2]

We already saw in chapters 1 and 2, in our pursuit of Erasmus's formative influences—the originals for his remarkably poised presentation of himself in print—how Jerome emerged at the most unexpected moments as in a rich sense Erasmus's 'model'. More than simply a canonical figure to be appealed to, the figure of Jerome, as reconstructed from his surviving works, is curiously intertwined with the figure of Erasmus, similarly encountered. Our excavation of the graphic representations of Erasmus revealed these to be heavily laden with reference to that earlier, internationally renowned editor, commentator, and translator of sacred texts. I have argued that these are no mere allusions, no mere gestures in the direction of an intellectual ancestor, but a statement of the deepest affinity, of a shared project and shared understanding which thicken allusion into felt relationship: a taking on fully by Erasmus of a command of both sacred and secular cultural heritages, whose integration into a specifically Christian classical scholarship is the particular legacy of Jerome.

It is therefore inevitable, when, in the context of the present study we come to look at Erasmus's voluminous correspondence, that we should need to recall that it was to Jerome's own *Epistolae* that Erasmus devoted a significant portion of his editing energies, over more than twenty years, to produce the editing tour de force which ultimately made up the opening four volumes of Froben's nine-volume Basle edition of the *Opera omnia*, in 1515.[3] We should recall, furthermore, that it was those letters, painstakingly purged of accreted errors, and separated from the considerable body of *spuria*, which served as the basis for Erasmus's *Vita Hieronymi*—the first biography of the saint to separate 'life' from legend, and to reconstruct a plausibly historical figure worthy to be venerated.[4] Letters provide that authenticity which lies conveniently somewhere between autobiography and biography: first-person testimony, to be reworked by the conscientious scholar into a biographical 'life' perfectly correlated with the 'Works'.[5]

This is a further theme that the present chapter takes up: where are we to ascribe authenticity as we scrutinise the mass of 'data' which Erasmus's voluminous correspondence provides? What would count as sincerity in an oeuvre which conscientiously emulates classical letter-writing, both in form and content? What is the status, finally, of the version of Erasmus's life and work confidently produced by his own editor, P. S. Allen, as he annotates and cross-references the *Opus epistolarum Erasmi* according to his own criteria of narrative reliability? Although such questions will prove difficult to answer, we can be quite clear by now that Erasmus's own virtuoso command of his printed works, of their distribution and circulation, will have to be incorporated.

INTIMATE EXCHANGES: 'AMICORUM INTER IPSOS CONFABULATIONES'

So rich is the surviving store of classical *epistolae*—pagan and sacred—so widely spread in content and style across the whole range of ancient learning and literature, that we are likely to overlook them altogether as a genre. Or rather, we tend to reserve the designation 'letter' for what, both in antiquity and in the Renaissance, was known as the 'familiar letter'—that is to say, the informal and personal letter exchanged with a close friend, to inform, or simply for pleasure.[6] And it is true that in Erasmus's own treatise on letter-writing, published by Froben in 1522, he added the familiar letter to the traditional tripartite division of types of letter into deliberative, demonstrative, and judicial.[7]

To those committed to the classical tradition, however, the letter meant the genre to which many of the major figures of the secular and sacred canon, amongst them Cicero, the younger Pliny, Seneca, Libanius, Jerome, and Paul, had contributed. A form particularly valued by humanists, the letter admitted of so many different and distinctive treatments that some humanists believed that the only shared feature which could be used to define a letter as such was its opening salutation.[8] Erasmus, however, following pseudo-Libanius, preferred the definition: 'As the comedian Turpilius aptly wrote, the *epistola* is a kind of mutual exchange of speech between absent friends' (Est enim [quod scite scriptum est a Turpilio comico] epistola absentium amicorum quasi mutuus sermo).[9]

The prominence of the name of Turpilius in Erasmus's definition cues us to a single source, a short letter of Jerome's on the virtues and necessities of letter writing:

JEROME TO NITIAS

In his treatment of the exchange of letters, Turpilius the comedian said: 'It is the unique way of making absent persons present'. Nor did he give a false opinion, although it achieves its purpose by means of what is not true. For what, if I may speak truly, is more present between those absent from one another, than to address and hear what you value by means of letters. Even before the use of paper and parchment, those primitive Italians, whom Ennius calls 'Casci', who (according to Cicero, in his *Rhetorica*) wished to gain understanding of themselves almost as a way of life, repeatedly sent one another mutual epistolary exhortations, either on writing tablets of smoothed and polished wood, or on the bark of trees. Whence those who carry letters are called 'tabellarii' [tablet carriers], and copyists are called 'librarii' from the bark [liber] of trees. How much the more, now that the world is so sophisticated in arts, should we avoid omitting what they excelled in—whose milieu was raw and rustic, and who were ignorant of all 'humanitas' whatsoever? See how Chromatius, sacred Eusebius's brother by equality of morals as much as by nature, roused me to the task of letters. But you, having departed from us, rend assunder our recently formed friendship rather than dissolving it, which Laelius more prudently prevented in Cicero. Unless perhaps the east is so hateful to you, that you are afraid of your letters coming here also. Awake! Awake! wake from your sleep, produce a scrap of paper, for goodness' sake. Between the delights of your native land and the journeys abroad we shared, breathe at least a word. If you love me, write I beseech you. If you have been angered, you are entitled to write angrily. I will have great solace, and that which I long for, if I receive my friend's letters, even if my friend is displeased.[10]

Here is a letter which both sets out succinctly the abstract rationale behind epistolary exchange and enacts the passionate 'making present of absence' which it extols. It is the only surviving source for such a view of 'Turpilius''s. As Erasmus comments, in his scholia to the letter in his Jerome *Epistolae*: '[Turpilius] has left us no remains of his intellectual activity which are still extant'.[11] So it is what *Jerome* has to say about letter-writing that Erasmus picks up. Here is a vivid characterisation of the effectiveness of the letter: 'Quid enim est (ut ita dicam) tam praesens inter absentes, quam per epistolas & alloqui & audire quos diligas?' (What better way of making the absent writer almost physically present to the recipient?) And here is a letter full of the vivid representation of emotion.[12]

Erasmus's definition (via Jerome) crucially specifies a level of immediacy, as well as of intimacy, which makes the letter as a form a particularly appropriate vehicle for the new mode of 'instruction at a distance' which printing has prompted, and Erasmus himself developed. By definition, epistolary correspondents are known to each other, they address each other as individuals: that knowledge determines the tone and manner of persuasion of the letter. By extension, where the letter is addressed to a general recipient ('ad lectorem studiosum'), or where an apparently fictional addressee is specified (as in a number of Erasmus's longer letters, like the *De contemptu mundi*), there is nevertheless an expectation that the reader will engage with the legible text as an intimate—expecting to be instructed or entertained on a more domestic and private scale than in the oration. As Erasmus puts it in one of his earlier versions of the *De conscribendis epistolis*:

> For this ought to be the character of the letter: as if you were whispering in a corner with a dear friend, not shouting in the theatre, or otherwise somewhat unrestrainedly. For we commit many things to letters, which it would be shameful to express openly in public.[13]

When Erasmus is undecided as to whether particular letters (Seneca's *Epistles to Lucilius*, some of Jerome's longer letters) deserve the designation 'letters', it is on the grounds that they may not be sufficiently emotional to qualify. He is committed to the view that letters convey feeling with immediacy, between a writer and a reader with some kind of mutual investment in the topic treated. This view is clearly expressed in a letter to Beatus Rhenanus which prefaces the 1521 Froben collection of Erasmus's letters (edited by Rhenanus), the *Epistolae ad diuersos*: 'If letters lack real feelings and fail to represent the very life itself of a person, they do not deserve the name of letters'.[14] A closely similar passage occurs in the mature text of the *De conscribendis epistolis*, where both text and examples endorse this generalised view of *epistolae*.[15]

The qualities Erasmus highlights as peculiarly those of the *epistola* are the making present of absent persons in living form, the communication of feeling and relationship publicly, but in the language of intimacy. As the passage from the Siberch edition suggests, it has some of the qualities of stage performance about it—it is an 'intimately theatrical' form. In his gloss on Jerome's letter to Nitias, Erasmus emphasises Jerome's point that *litterae* make present absent persons and feelings in fictional form, but that these fictions are no falsehoods. Rather, they are the means to make truths vivid.[16]

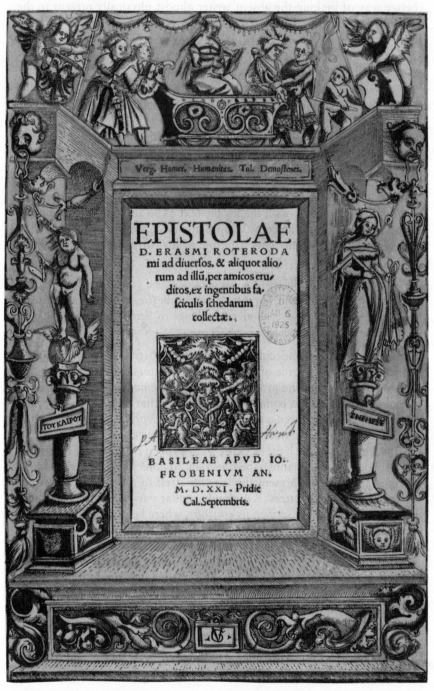

21. Title page of the *Epistolae D. Erasmi Roterodami ad diuersos* (Basle, 1521).

By definition, the letter makes the absent vividly present in writing. Unlike the classic oration or the classic declamation, which are oral, the letter is, necessarily and from the outset, written. *Published*, printed letters provide a virtuoso performance, which is not (like the surviving orations of Cicero or Demosthenes) a written record of an oral presentation, but an original text. There is little doubt that in his own correspondence, Erasmus plays out all possibilities for exploiting the unique version of presence, performance, and originality which are peculiar to the letter. And on top of the individual 'absent presence' which the letter offers, it also makes possible a vivid fiction of a real 'world', a 'world of learning' demarcated by the reach of Erasmus's dense and prolific correspondence. The 'world' thus held together by the bonds of epistolary exchanges which affirm the 'friendship' of writer and recipient is one which is not equivalent to a single institution, or even a single nation. The published letter crosses physical and ideological boundaries, to link separated individuals with shared educational agendas. All their distinctive differences are overlooked; what is specified is the affection implicit in a shared project pursued with intensity—that most cherished of classical bonds (*amicitia*) which ensures communication and understanding.

Opus epistolarum erasmi: Autobiography or Purloined Letters

Recently, a number of scholars have begun to disentangle Erasmus's letters from the seamless chronological continuity and the meticulously uniform textual appearance which Allen's formidable edition of its very nature produces, and have redirected our attention to the remarkably diverse volumes (in arrangement, choice of correspondents, dates of letters, format, typeface, and general presentation) which issued from the European presses between 1515 and 1607.[17] We have begun to accept that each volume of letters issued served some specific publishing purpose. Not, of course, that such a proposition would not ordinarily be readily acceptable. But in the case of the *Opus epistolarum Erasmi*, the whole scholarly edifice is built upon the incompatible assumption that every Erasmus letter is a neutral 'document' offering true insight into the life of the great man of letters.

Any number of citations could be used to make this point (including, inevitably, some passages from the present book, where I, like every other Erasmus scholar, have been lured into citing a letter as reliable evidence for a historical 'fact' of Erasmus's life and thought). One that I find particularly charming comes in the great Low Countries scholar de Vocht's memorial tribute to P. S. Allen himself.[18] De Vocht describes the way in which Allen relived the life of his hero Erasmus, when he visited Louvain:

Epiſtole aliquot illuſtriũ

virorum ad Eraſmum Roterodamum,& huius ad illos
INDEX
Epiſtola Petri Aegidii Antuerpiani ad clariſſimũ virũ
 D. Gaſparum Halmalum iuris vtriuſ{que} doctorem.
Epiſtola Eraſmi Roterodami ad Leonem X. Pon. Ma.
Eiuſdem ad Cardinalem Grymanum.
Eiuſdem ad Cardinalem Georgianum.
Leonis decimi P.M.epiſtola ad Eraſmum Roterodamũ
Eiuſdem ad illuſtriſſ. Angliæ regem Henricum octauũ
 commendans Eraſmum.
Reſponſio Eraſmi ad Leonem P. M.
Epiſtola Andreæ Ammonii, nuncii apud Anglos
 apoſtolici, ad Eraſmum Roterodamum
Epiſtola Archiepiſcopi Cantuarienſis ad Eraſmum.
Epiſtola Henrici Bouilli ad Eraſmum.
Reſponſio Eraſmi ad Bouillum.
Epiſtola Clariſſimi ſenatoris inclytæ ciuitatis Norem≠
 burgenſis viri{que} doctiſſimi Bilibaldi ad Eraſmum.
Epiſtola Gulielmi Budæi Pariſienſis ad Eraſmum.
Reſponſiones Eraſmi ad Budæum.
Epiſtola Ioannis Coleti ſacræ theologiæ doctoris De≠
 cani apud diuum Paulum Londini.
Epiſtola Iacobi Fabri ad Eraſmum.
Epiſtola Vdalrici Zaſii,iuris vtriuſ{que} profeſſoris apud
 Friburgum.
Epiſtola M. Vrbani Regii ad doctorem Ioannem Fa≠
 brum Fpiſcopi Baſilienſis Officialem.
Epiſtola Thomæ Mori ad Eraſmum
Alia epiſtola Vdalrici Zaſii iuris vtriuſ{que} profeſſoris
 apud Friburgum ad Eraſmum.

Uenundantur a Theodorico
Martino Aluſtenſi Chalcographo fideliſſimo.

22. Title page of the *Epistolae aliquot illustrium virorum ad Erasmum Roterodamum* (Louvain, 1516).

Amidst the old buildings in the sinuous Louvain streets, Allen rejoiced: it was as if he lived in the past: as if Baechem and Dierckx and Titelmans were still staying at their convents; as if Goclenius and Rescius were still teaching in Busleyden's *Trilingue*, and as if Vives was still walking in his old garden with the Latin well purling and babbling as it did four hundred years ago.[19]

For Allen, the letters of Erasmus (his life work) were lived out as narrative history in the streets of Louvain. There is absolutely no room here for the possibility that Erasmus's own active and conscious construction of the very history Allen seeks to trace is intrinsic to the composition and circulation of those letters. It is a recurring methodological problem for Allen, recorded in the notes to his edition, that where Erasmus apparently contradicts himself in his letters (particularly as to dates, and occasions of their composition), Allen is committed to treating this as an error.[20] Where the contradictions are Erasmus's, Allen assumes an inadvertent error on Erasmus's part, and never a literary contrivance to heighten the letter's impact, or drive a particular point home.[21] Allen's omission of Barlandus's 1520 *Epistolae aliquot selectae ex Erasmicis* from his checklist of 'authorised' volumes of published letters is symptomatic of a particular standard of transparent 'truthfulness' Allen asks for, in order to judge a publication 'authentic'.

We already saw, in my Introduction, how the Barlandus volume *was* constructed for a particular purpose (a pedagogic purpose which Barlandus himself stated clearly in his preface). We also saw how Erasmus's disclaimer of involvement in the volume is belied by internal evidence: recensions of some of the letters Barlandus publishes depend upon additional corrections made by Erasmus *after* the publication of the edition from which Barlandus is supposedly working without Erasmus's knowledge or support. Barlandus, moreover, prints a letter to himself from Erasmus in the volume (never subsequently reprinted by Erasmus), in which the publication is reluctantly endorsed:

> No doubt you have been careful to choose only those letters which have nothing damaging [aculeorum] about them, for you can see how certain people nowadays take offence at the slightest opportunity. All the same, I could have wished that you had thought of something else; for I am afraid they will be annoyed by the very fact that they see something of mine [aliquid in meum] prepared to be read in schools.[22]

I pointed out before that Allen omits this volume because he apparently felt that here the transparent documentary quality of the letters was tainted by the explicit pedagogic purposiveness of their publication.[23]

As I showed earlier, the Barlandus volume provides a particularly clear version of Europe-wide Erasmianism, in epistolary form.[24] Yet for Allen it differs in no way from other school-textbook reprints of Erasmus's works, like the 1515 *Complures Luciani dialogi*, also published by Martens, with Barlandus as *castigator*. That volume too carries a letter from Barlandus to the 'studious young', in which he describes how he has prevailed upon Martens to publish a volume which will be of the utmost usefulness for their school studies.[25] But by now it must seem clear, in the present study, that there *is* a significant difference between the two publications, and that the irritation that Erasmus regularly shows concerning pirated or unlicensed editions of his pedagogic works is distinct from the real unease which is evidenced in his relations with edited collections of his letters. In order to make this distinction clearer, it is helpful to look at another pair of volumes (edited letters and pedagogic work), this time edited by one of Erasmus's most trusted and personally close *castigatores*, Beatus Rhenanus.[26]

By 1518, when he took responsibility for the *Auctarium selectarum epistolarum* volume of Erasmus's letters, Beatus Rhenanus was one of Froben's most reliable editors and *castigatores* (correctors and monitors of textual emendations), and Erasmus's trusted junior collaborating editor, nominated by him to make editorial decisions for him in his absence. Nevertheless, Rhenanus's preface to the *Auctarium* stresses that the volume is 'purloined'—it has been put together in Erasmus's absence and without his explicit consent. Officially the master has been unaware of the activity of his scholar-servant, as he constructs a version of him *as* master in print:

> By a stroke of luck I chanced upon several bundles of correspondence from Erasmus's library here, out of which I chose forthwith a number of letters, the outstanding letters in fact, of which some are his and some are answers to them from the greatest scholars of our generation. I was encouraged to purloin them by the thought that the very rich who are well supplied with everything do not notice if a few things are actually removed; for I thought likewise that Erasmus who is so richly endowed with all the treasures of the Muses would not detect it if I had removed something. Besides which, that great man loves me so sincerely—little as I deserve it—that even if I do him some serious wrong he will surely make allowances. . . . After Erasmus' departure I handed these letters to Froben to be printed, partly that I might have something to send you, for in your last letter you showed such a desire to be sent something by Erasmus or Budé; partly to be of some use to those who wish to improve, for I know they will gain not a little from the reading of these letters. And, further, the literary circles of this city, as they read them, will be relieved of the sadness they have lately felt because of the great man's departure, or at least will have some consolation. They will think they still hear his voice as they read his letters.[27]

Note that here, just as in the case of the Barlandus volume, it is suggested that one of the functions of such a volume is pedagogic ('partly to be of some use to those who wish to improve [their letter-writing]'). And that that crucial notion of absence made presence—that *epistolae* are 'some consolation' for the great man's departure—is prominent.

In 1519 Rhenanus issued another unauthorised volume of Erasmus's in his master's absence, this time the edited text of an early schoolwork on proverbs.[28] We have Rhenanus's own clear account of the circumstances of his issuing the *Colloquiorum formula* volume without Erasmus's express permission, in his published preface to the volume:

> I obtained, thanks to that learned young man, Lambert Holonius, the *Colloquiorum formulae* which Erasmus twenty years ago or more wrote for amusement to please Augustinus Caminadus, who was teaching certain boys from Zeland (if I am not mistaken), while he was at Paris. I immediately procured its publication in print with Froben, so that just as I had derived pleasure from it first, so this treasure-store should come to other serious students. It had been in the possession of malicious persons until then, guarded exactly like that golden fleece by that watchful serpent, and offered for sale repeatedly by Caminadus himself. The little work itself reflects its author Erasmus in clarity, ease and wit. Besides it contains nothing to give displeasure and nothing trivial, but only the blooms of elegance extracted from the best authors. However, the text was corrupt in many places, many of which we have corrected, some we have retained for the reader, who thought that this work had clearly perished. Farewell, together with William Nesen, your teacher, a man no less upright than erudite.[29]

In this case, Rhenanus represents himself more confidently as performing something like his customary editorial services for Erasmus (though without explicit instructions from Erasmus), on Holonius's assurance that the manuscript was one he would wish published, and in order to prevent its being published elsewhere in a thoroughly 'unauthorised' (and unsupervised) form.[30] For a number of years afterwards, Erasmus expressed public displeasure at the appearance of this early work, without his explicit consent. But his indignation was consistently aimed at 'Holonius', rather than at his *castigator*, and the focus of his interest is insistently the production of 'good texts': Erasmus requires total print control, in order to ensure a consistent quality for the texts circulating.[31] By contrast, Erasmus goes on expressing anxiety about the role of the editor in producing collections of his letters, and the impact of the selectivity which operates, until the end of his life.

My suggestion is that we should take seriously Erasmus's expressed anxiety that 'something of his/himself' is appropriated when the edited volume under scrutiny is a selection of his own letters—his own feelings and his own voice. Even when such a volume is in the hands of someone wholly within Erasmus's own 'circle', the act of editing acquires a significance not usually assigned to such work. Beatus Rhenanus may control Erasmus's work to the point of exercising considerable individual judgement and authority, at the Froben publishing outlet. But when he undertakes the same task in relation to a volume of Erasmus's letters, both editor's and author's response are still uneasy, and the fiction of the master's absence remains obligatory. Evidently there is a distinction to be made between a trusted editor like Rhenanus taking the initiative with Erasmus's edited texts, and taking the initiative with his letters, when 'a few things are actually removed' (something of Erasmus's own is appropriated).

CASTIGATORES AGAIN: WHOSE CORRECT(ED) TEXT?

Not for the first time in the present exploration, the point seems to turn on the sense one gives to the term *castigator*.[32] The term can mean the mere routine print-shop activity of proof correction and copyediting (a capacity in which, as we saw, many of Erasmus's close colleagues and friends worked for the Martens publishing house in Louvain). But it can extend to sophisticated intervention with a text: it has been pointed out by de Jonge that Erasmus consistently describes himself as *castigator* in relation to the text of scripture. In relation to the New Testament, he, like his hero Jerome before him, is *castigator*, restoring a text damaged by the passage of time to its original, pristine state.

In practical terms, Erasmus's own publishing efforts, both his classical and patristic editions and his own pedagogic works, depended increasingly on the teamwork of highly competent younger colleagues, as he undertook more, and more diverse, projects. In general, these *castigatores* remain invisible, that is to say, they remain the invisible assistants to publishing which the term itself implies. But from time to time the *castigator* emerges as formative of a volume: sometimes because he has not had the authority to tamper with a text, sometimes—and this I suggest is the case with Erasmus's own letters—because the act of selection constitutes a real intervention, a shaping influence which determines the 'meaning' of the work. On what occasions do the interventions of the expert correctors and junior editors working in collaboration with Erasmus in his *officina* become visible?

In April 1515, when Rhenanus, with William Nesen, had been left in charge of Erasmus's edition of the works of Seneca, he wrote to Erasmus to notify him of the fact that he had emended a sentence in the *De beneficiis*, 'when that page had already begun to be printed'.[33] With textual work of this kind, 'ownership' was a convenient fiction: in the case of the Seneca, as we have seen, it later suited Erasmus to maintain that

Rhenanus and Nesen had botched the task of completing the editorial work, and that only the 1529 edition was truly 'his'.

But in fact, of course, that edition also was put together in the *officina* Erasmus had set up in the Froben printing house, through the teamwork of *famuli* and *castigatores*.[34] At the end of 1525, Erasmus wrote to Robert Aldridge at Cambridge, with a request for a highly specific piece of editorial help with the Seneca:

> In King's College there is a copy of the works of Seneca on parchment, from which I made a large number of annotations in my copy [in codice meo].[35] . . . What I ask, dearest Aldridge, is that you take a copy of the works of Seneca as published by Froben [Erasmus's first edition], and give it to some reliable persons, who will make a note afresh in the margins, of any discrepant readings. Send that volume, thus annotated, to Thomas More, so that he may dispatch it to me. The books of the *Quaestiones naturales* I know have been edited. I will complete their collation.[36]

Some time later, Aldridge replied as follows:

> In doing this, this is the procedure I followed. The exemplar which is kept in our King's College library only contained the Letters to Lucilius, and the same was true for a copy [of Seneca] which is at Peterhouse. I do not know how it would have been permitted me to borrow the Peterhouse volume, had it not been for the name of Erasmus, such is the solicitous protection required for the custody of the books, laid down also in private decrees. So then I ran through the Letters to Lucilius and compared the published Froben book with the two extremely old codices. Where they differed, I marked in the margins, distinguishing between the two codices in the following way: where the King's copy had something different I have indicated with θ ; where the Peterhouse copy differs I have marked: ꝛ Where those two copies agree, but differ from the Froben, I have marked the variant, but without a sign. Nor have I omitted any variant unless it makes no sense whatsoever. And although in my judgement the Froben printed text was much superior to the others, nevertheless I indicated all variants. . . . I have eagerly carried out to the letter what you asked, and have compared the volumes as you wished. . . . As you requested, I sent the annotated volume to Master Thomas More on May 11, asking him to take care to send it to you as quickly as possible.[37]

In March 1527, Erasmus replied, thanking Aldridge for the annotated Froben Seneca, which had reached him safely, but adding that it was not really necessary to have sent the volume, since everything of value could have been transcribed on slips of paper.[38] Aldridge had, moreover, been misled at King's: there was another Seneca, written on parchment, in the small library, which contained the *sententiae*, arranged alphabetically, and the *De beata vita*. Erasmus had already known that the *Letters to Lucilius* volume contained little of value, and regretted the waste of Aldridge's time in collating it. If Aldridge still had the time, he could check the *sententiae* and the *De beata vita*, indicating variants by the line number on the Froben page.

Here is a delightfully rich and evocative account of collaborative editing. It indicates that Erasmus is prepared to rely heavily on the judgement of others, working at a distance, and acting on their own initiative.[39] For those of us who still spend our scholarly time poring over *codices pervetusti* (ancient volumes), it reveals a world of scholarly exchange entirely like our own—right down to the difficulty of having anyone else inspect a library copy and find the precise thing one is oneself looking for. But in terms of Erasmus's later claim that the new Seneca, unlike the first edition, was entirely his own work, it reveals the customary margin of exaggeration. Erasmus may indeed have learned his lesson. He no longer left the print shop before the pages had been printed (though probably before they had been corrected), nor did he trust the final putting together of a volume to a comparative novice, such as Rhenanus had been in 1515. But editing remained then, as now, an essentially collaborative enterprise.

In 1521 Erasmus himself provided a prefatory letter to a volume of his own letters, once again published by Froben at Basle, once again edited by Rhenanus (but this time with his consent).[40] The volume was an enlarged reprint of the *Farrago noua epistolarum* (1519), and Allen has shown how actively Erasmus was involved in preparing the letters for inclusion in both volumes, in spite of the pretence of absence.[41] In this preface, Erasmus reminds Rhenanus of his dislike for the *Auctarium* volume, and for the subsequent *Farrago* volume, both of which he implies were issued surreptitiously, and without his express consent: 'You know that the *Epistolae* which you first took care in issuing were not a shining success, and that the *Farrago* was even worse, which was dragged from me, partly by the pressure of friends, partly out of necessity'.[42] In this new volume, Erasmus at last hands to a *castigator* full editorial responsibility for the compilation of his letters. But it is as an interestingly *visible* editorial presence that he does so—Rhenanus, Erasmus says, is to act as his 'alter ego', his other self. Absent yet present in this way, Erasmus can finally mastermind his self-presentation to his own satisfaction.

FURTHER UNAUTHORISED EDITIONS: FURTIVE ERASMIAN VOICES

Between 1520 and 1522, as an increasing number of highly successful volumes of Erasmus's *Epistolae* issued from presses in Germany and the Low Countries, three editions of a treatise by Erasmus, *De conscribendis*

FARRAGO
NOVA EPISTOLARVM
Des. Erasmi Roterodami
ad alios, & aliorum ad
hunc:admixtis qui
busdã, quas
Annume *vor li* *ens Simonu*
Henrici Silenni scripsit *Anno 1670.*
ridentem etiã adolescens *mexit dese*
rursse Deus synt.

APVD INCLYTAM BASI,
LEAM EX OFFICINA
IO. FROBENII.

TOY KAIPOY

ΪΝΕΜΕΣΕ

23. Title page of the *Farrago noua epistolarum Des. Erasmi Roterodami ad alios* (Basle, 1519).

epistolis, were published. Two were unauthorised, the third, the 1522 Froben edition, was sanctioned by Erasmus himself. As we trace the story of these publications, as usual, from within the pages of Erasmus's letters themselves, we are provided with an exemplary story of the almost mesmerising interrelatedness of authorship, editorial circles, readership, and market forces. In the shaping of the tale of the *De conscribendis epistolis*, it is hard to decide which is the originating, which the controlling force.

In a brief, tetchy preface to a small volume, *Progymnasmata quaedam primae adolescentiae Erasmi*, published by Martens at Louvain in 1521, containing a collection of poems of Erasmus's—juvenilia which he claimed to be forced to publish because they were already circulating in unauthorised form—Erasmus has the following to say about some further, recent unauthorised volumes:

> They are impudent indeed who make my 'formulae' available in print during my lifetime. Yet more impudent are those who issue my juvenile scribblings. But most impudent of all is the person who ascribes to me someone else's fantasies, which is what someone has recently done in issuing that little book *De conscribendi epistolis* in which aside from the odd verbal echo nothing at all is mine. Nor have I any knowledge of someone called Peter Paludanus.[43]

The most impudent unauthorised publication, according to Erasmus, is the *De conscribendis epistolis*. The reference to a forged prefatory letter to someone called Peter Paludanus, of whom Erasmus has never heard, specifies this to be the *Breuissima maximeque compendiaria conficiendarum epistolarum formula*, which appeared in three separate editions in Germany and the Low Countries in 1520.[44] The letter to Peter Paludanus runs as follows:

> Yes, most humane Peter, you have won: here is the method of writing letters, which you have so often begged me to produce. All the same, notice how many disparaging remarks I have exposed myself to in the course of humouring your whim. For what will the critics say—or rather, what will they *not* say—when they see I have ventured to discuss a subject that has already been handled with skill and thoroughness by so many learned authors? They will say 'Do you then essay to weave Penelope's web? After those great men you must of a surety either repeat what they have written, or write worse; now the former is superfluous for the studious reader, the latter even harmful.' To such persons, among many answers I could make, I will make but this one: I will refuse to follow closely in the steps of another who has written anything on this subject. So accept this most brief and compendious manual for writing letters, and convince yourself of this, they need not words alone but art. Farewell. Salute our friends.[45]

The work in question is slight—a mere eight unnumbered folios long.[46] Probably its most significant feature is that it opens with Libanius's definition of *epistola*: 'Libanius sophista graecus epistolam finit hoc modo Epistola est absentis ad absente[m] colloquiu[m]'. The 'Paludanus' letter is a clumsy reworking, with little alteration, of the dedicatory letter to Robert Fisher (former *famulus* of Erasmus's), which appeared with the other unauthorised published version.

This second text—published in Cambridge by the Low Countries printer Siberch—made no attempt to conceal the absence of authorial approval, but carried an ingratiating (and probably ill-advised) preface to Bishop John Fisher, elaborately insisting on the printer's desire to gain Erasmus's favour, and asking Fisher to intercede on his behalf, should the volume give offence.[47] In the preface to his own edition, it is this Cambridge volume which Erasmus singles out for blame:

> Once that man Holonius was no more in the land of the living, dear Berault, my most learned friend, I supposed I had no one else to fear who might publish to the world the trifles I had written as a young man either to practise my pen or to comply with my friends' wishes, with publication as the last thing I intended. Lo and behold, a second Holonius has suddenly appeared in England, who has printed a book on the art of letter-writing which I began to write in Paris about thirty years ago for the benefit of a friend of dubious loyalty, whom I wished to please with a present on his own level—like lips, like lettuce, as the proverb has it.[48]

The other volume whose unauthorised publication still rankles with him is the one passed to the printer by Holonius—that is, Rhenanus's 1519 Froben edition of the *Colloquiorum formulae*.

In spite of all this insistence on illicit, premature issuing of versions of the *De conscribendis epistolis*, both unauthorised editions answered a real need, a need set up by those very editions of Erasmus's own letters which we looked at earlier. These unprecedentedly successful volumes (emanating from Basle, and much reprinted) emphasised—or, possibly, deliberately constructed—Erasmus's connectedness with a number of European centres of learning, notably Cambridge, Germany, and the Low Countries. It is not surprising that locally, in these centres, there should have been a felt need for a textbook *De conscribendis epistolis* to set alongside the letters themselves. As all the editors, including Erasmus himself, emphasised, these volumes of letters were intended to be educational on a number of levels, one of which was as exemplary *epistolae* themselves.

'Unauthorised' may mean just what is needed in a particular location (England, Germany) to complement some other publication or set of publications of Erasmus's. And this is to leave on one side such relatively straightforward issues as the commercial desirability of multiple editions in different locations in spite of individual publisher's dislike of such arrangements (here also the disclaimers in Erasmus's published and prefatory letters help smooth the way).

'ALIUM PRODIDI HIERONYMUM': ERASMUS'S JEROME AGAIN

Amidst all this orchestrated issuing of texts, confecting of correspondence, and denouncing of imposters and forgeries, Erasmus steadily insisted on his own, special relationship with the published works of the author in whom he had chosen to invest so much of himself. At the end of the dedicatory letter to Archbishop Warham in the original, 1515 edition of the *Epistolae*, Erasmus states plainly that Jerome is not simply the current subject of his scholarly and editorial efforts, nor even his model (a scholar, translator, and editor like himself), but his own:[49]

> I have followed the example of those who would rather raise a fresh loan than go to prison for non-payment, and have borrowed from Jerome the wherewithal to repay you. Though why should it any longer look like something borrowed rather than my own?—real estate often passes from one ownership to another by occupation or prescriptive right. In any case, in this line of business Jerome himself has laid down a principle for me in his preface to the books of Kings, repeatedly calling that work his, because anything that we have made our own by correcting, reading, constant devotion, we can fairly claim as ours. On this principle why should not I myself claim a proprietary right in the works of Jerome? For centuries they had been treated as abandoned goods; I entered upon them as something ownerless, and by incalculable efforts reclaimed them for all devotees of the true theology.
>
> It is a river of gold, a well stocked library, that a man acquires who possesses Jerome and nothing else. He does not possess him, on the other hand, if his text is like what used to be in circulation, all confusion and impurity. [Aureum flumen habet, locupletissimam bibliothecam habet quisquis vnum habet Hieronymum. Atque hunc rursum non habet, quisquis habet cuiusmodi ferebatur antehac vndiquaque confusum et contaminatum.][50]

We are by now so deep into a rhetoric of textual production that it is as well to remind ourself of the contrast between this version of editorial possession and the realities of sixteenth-century editing, as I described them above in the case of Erasmus's edition of Seneca. No edition of Erasmus's of a major classical or patristic author's works is 'his' in the sense that he and he alone did the editorial work necessary to produce it. So that here Erasmus is making the strongest possible claim in relation to the Jerome. He has, he maintains, earned the right to call Jerome's works his, to enter the scholarly persona of Jerome. The labour he had put in, in order to be in a position to make such a claim convincingly, had, we might want to argue, extended well beyond mere editing. It had involved an increasingly self-conscious manipulation of a rich European cultural heritage in Jerome iconography, symbolic reference, and allusion, of the kind I explored in my opening chapter.

In case we should think of this idea of 'ownership', of 'authorship' through editorial labour, as merely a rhetorical flourish, honouring Erasmus's most loyal long-term patron, the point is made more explicitly still in the letter Erasmus wrote to Johann von Botzheim in 1523, which Froben published in revised form under the title *Catalogus novus omnium lucubrationum Erasmi Roterodami* in 1524.[51] Lines 1500–1832 consist of a proposed catalogue of Erasmus's own works, and under volume 9 we find the following:

> Volume nine shall be dedicated to the *Letters* of Jerome, on which I have expended so much labour that I can without impudence add this work to my own list; though Hilary too cost me a lot of work, and so did Cyprian. Of Quintus Curtius I will say nothing; in Seneca I can claim nothing for myself, except that in that field I lost much labour by trusting to the promises of my friends. If Christ grants me life and strength enough to finish my commentaries on the Epistles to the Romans, they will occupy volume ten.[52]

Such statements must, surely, sit somewhat oddly alongside Erasmus's insistence, at every point in the publication of his own correspondence, that the editor (Gilles, Barlandus, or Rhenanus) was never quite up to the task of presenting Erasmus's own letters to the public—that no editor ever made Erasmus his own, that indeed Erasmus exceeded any editor's attempt at capturing him via his *epistolae*. Or perhaps it is Erasmus's fear that the letters do become the editor's own that makes him protest so vigorously that each and every editor has done a poor job.

The strong sense of ownership of the Jerome *Epistolae*, on which Erasmus insists, is not quite reflected in the Froben Jerome as it appeared. The four gathered books of the *Epistolae* are contained as volume 1, and the first part of volume 2, in the bound edition. In part, of course, this reflects Erasmus's collaboration in the enterprise with the Amerbach brothers, and with Gregor Reisch (originally the overall editor).[53] Nevertheless, the arrangement sat somewhat ill with the strong claims in the prefatory letter to Warham: if this was Erasmus himself—Erasmus's Jerome—something rather more distinguished was needed to mark that 'proprietary right'.

Accordingly, in 1524 Erasmus issued a revised edition of a now three-book version of his Jerome *Epistolae*, bound in a single volume, dedicated yet more thoroughly to Warham. The original edition had carried the single dedicatory letter to Warham, with prefaces 'to the studious reader' attached to the three further, individual books. The revised edition carried an additional preface to Warham, and redrafted the prefaces to books 3 and 4 of the original edition, with very little modification, as further dedicatory letters to Warham.[54] The long prefaces to the reader to the two parts of this book are fascinating documents, concerning spurious and misattributed works in the classical and biblical canons, and their crucial importance to the exegetical and interpretative traditions.

Here, finally, we seem to have uncovered the full significance of the handsome volume, inscribed 'HERAKLEI[OI] PONOI', upon which Erasmus proprietorially rests his hands, in Holbein's 1524 gift-portrait for Archbishop Warham.[55] A copy of the elegant folio volume arrived on the heels of the painting—offering the recipient the opportunity to display the physical book alongside the graphic representation of it and its author; just as we saw More expressing the desire to set his own letter alongside its representation in the Metsys diptych:[56]

> You have, I hope, greatest of Prelates, received the portrait, which I sent to you in order that you might have something of Erasmus, should God call me to Him. . . . I send you [herewith] my Jerome [*Epistolae*]—it was not possible to bind it because the ink is too fresh. . . . I am delighted to have successfully completed the Jerome *Epistolae*; for I have corrected many things in it. The other volumes will also follow, if the printers reach agreement; the enterprise is a costly one, and beyond the means of a single individual.[57]

Here is a symbolically sumptuous volume, worthy of Jerome, Warham, and Erasmus himself, recorded and celebrated as a gift of great price. In the Holbein painting the three layers of meaning are brilliantly, simultaneously present: Erasmus's ownership (the proprietorial hands, the look of achievement in the direct gaze out of the picture); Warham's double gift (the painting itself, the volume itself, the enduring worth of both); and the infused, iconographically saturating presence of Jerome.[58]

Erasmus's additional preface at the beginning of the volume, preceding the original dedicatory letter, reads as follows:

> In the first edition such care had been taken that there remained barely a hope, as the proverb runs, of anyone's being able to add anything by subsequent pains, incomparable Prelate. For my part, however, I desired so strongly that this work which I had created as a monument to you (for I hope that it will survive) should be as complete and perfect in every respect, that I took pains to reprint it separately, on superior paper, and in better type. Although Froben had previously printed the complete Jerome so that not only did all agree that it surpassed all others, but also he himself could barely, even on his own authorisation, outclass his earlier efforts. We ourselves could find hardly anything

in the Jerome which required correcting, though we corrected the commentary somewhat, suppressing some things and adding numerous others. There remained certain passages, very few it is true, in which my capacity for insight failed to satisfy me, so that if someone more fortunate than me is able to restore the text, either through ingenuity, or with the help of additional manuscripts, I will gladly embrace his industriousness and thank him warmly for his service to the public.

In the course of this work two things happened which diminished the sum of my entitlement of praise. The first was that languages and *bonae litterae* so flourished throughout the world that my contribution to them no longer seemed so vital. The second is that in the present century the talents of most have been deflected towards those bloody gladiatorial wordmongerings [*logomachias*], and men no longer frequent the wholesome meadows and charming pleasure gardens of the ancient authors. For the rest I would gladly forfeit the praise as long as that did not go along with a general public loss of esteem for studies. Christ will have anticipated the outcome of all this. We at least will have shown our good will, as we shall do to the last day of our life. Farewell.[59]

Characteristically, no emendations have been made by Erasmus to the original dedicatory letter, so that it continues to refer to 'four volumes' of the letters, although these have now been significantly reorganised, and reduced for the time being to three. Nor, indeed, have text and scholia been emended to anything like the extent we might expect from the prefatory promise. Most of what has happened is rationalisation: the dropping of all material which Erasmus had described in his lengthy prefactory discussion for the reader as unworthy of Jerome, and patently obviously not by Jerome; the transferring of editorial material relating to the nine-volume project, rather than the one-volume *Epistolae* to a later volume; the rearrangement of the organisation of header notes, text, and scholia to make better sense for the reader.[60] None of this is particularly surprising—we have grown accustomed to the exaggerated claims of new editions. It should certainly not surprise us in the case of Erasmus, who, as we have consistently seen, tended to have editorial ambitions beyond his resources, both in terms of money, time, and manpower. As in the case of so many of Erasmus's commented editions, the early Jerome letters are by far the most thoroughly commented: early scholia run to several folio pages; later letters sometimes attract only a couple of lines of annotation.

This physical reconstruction of the Jerome means that the opening volume (symbolically issued well ahead of the remaining volumes) can truly be said to be 'Erasmus's own'. With the appearance, two years later, of the remaining volumes of the second edition, the specialness of the 'personalised' first volume is strengthened. The brief preface (also to Warham) with which Erasmus introduces the spurious letters, at the beginning of the second volume, announces that 'in this volume there is nothing of mine except the warnings [of spuriousness]' ('In hoc volumine nihil meum est praeter censuras').[61] And Erasmus adds the intriguing suggestion that in contrast to that first volume, so decisively 'his', this volume is in the hands of the informed reader, to make *his* own:

> If anyone does not concur with my opinion, he has no need to be indignant. For not only does he possess everything which has appeared in other, previous editions, but also many things have been added. He has the same works, more assiduously printed, and better corrected than they have ever been before. Through my efforts everyone can exercise his own individual judgement.[62]

This suggestion that the reader is to make his own contribution to the authenticity of the Jerome *Opera* is further supported by a letter Frobenius adds on the reverse of the title page of the final, nine-volume (in six) issue of the 1526 Jerome *Opera*. Ahead of the 1524 title page to volume 1 ('Erasmus's' volume), Frobenius prints an overall title to the complete edition, and reprints the various indices which had been incorporated into the 1515 volume 1. Then he adds a clear instruction on the reorganisation of items:

> Io. Frob. typographus candido lectori S. D.
> The order of the volumes of letters has been altered somewhat: the second volume, which comprised the misattributed letters, has been moved to the fourth. What was previously the third is thus now the second, and what was the fourth, the third. The book on Hebrew places and names on strong authority we have separated from the fourth volume (which is now, as I have said, the third). We now print those works separately, so that you (the reader) can attach it to whichever volume you judge fit. We have added a new and elaborate index of *sententiae*, which too can be added to whichever volume seems appropriate.[63]

It would be hard to find a more vivid example of the flexibility made possible for the early sixteenth century printer and reader by the fact that books were purchased unbound and bound by the purchaser. Here Froben issues an invitation to his reader to construct the book which best suits his own understanding of the 'true' Jerome.[64]

Textual Theft: A Footnote on Ownership

On the verso of the title page, facing the long dedication to Warham, at the beginning of the first volume of Erasmus's 1515 Jerome *Epistolae*, is an announcement of a five-year privilege, granting Froben exclusive publishing rights, issued in the joint names of Leo X and the Emperor Maximilian. The privilege, set in large type, elegantly reaffirms the panoply of powerful support which Erasmus had extracted for the Jerome project.[65] In 1518 that privilege was broken with the publication of a number of small collections, drawn from the Froben edition.[66] Here, for once, Erasmus's printer really was able to claim ownership of the text for his author, and a lawsuit was brought:

> A certain Eucharius Cervicornus of Cologne has copied some letters of Jerome from our edition. We have taken him to court in Frankfurt for neglecting and indeed despising privileges from the highest authorities. He will pay the penalty, if I mistake not, for his rashness.[67]

Throughout his career Erasmus was plagued by unauthorised and pirated editions of his works; he complained constantly that it was impossible to control the circulation of his works. It seems fitting then that his Jerome should have been sufficiently well designated as 'his' for Froben to be able to take action against derivative publication.

'LITTLE WORKS OF THIS KIND ARE NONE OTHER THAN
CHRISTIAN DECLAMATIONS'

We have, then, a volume evidently particularly close to Erasmus's own heart (which he wishes to claim as 'his' with a real sense of ownership), and that volume is a volume of *epistolae*. And we have a creative project of Erasmus's own: the composition (openly, personally, or by more or less subtle prompting at a distance) of published volumes of his own letters, together with one or more sets of instructions, in the form of a handbook, on how to read those letters.[68] And we have arrived at the moment to put these together, to see whether we learn anything fresh about the *Opus epistolarum Erasmi* from this conjunction.

The opening letter in Erasmus's edition of the Jerome *Epistolae*, 'Ad Heliodorum de laude vitae solitariae', is accompanied not simply by one set of scholia, but by two. The second scholia are preceded by a lengthy introductory note, with the heading 'A Note Concerning Art' ('Annotatio artis').[69] This introduction is followed by detailed annotations on the argumentative and rhetorical structure of the letter—its means of persuasion, and its stylistic creation of intense readerly attention. The suggestion is, apparently, that such scholia could be provided for all succeeding letters (in fact, subsequent letters are followed by scholia which combine exegetical and informational commentary with details of the rhetorical and persuasive strategies Jerome has used). An observation in the *annotatio artis* strikingly goes to the heart of Erasmus's proposal for the rhetorical structure of Jerome's letters:

To begin by touching somewhat upon the genus of argumentation [in this letter]: it is an 'exhortation' [*exhortatio*]. . . . 'Exhortation' has this particularity: that it is more impassioned, and has more praise mixed in with it, which, however, Jerome does not actually use here. For men are goaded on by two things—by praise and by fear of dishonour. And little works [*libelli*] of this kind are none other than Christian declamations.[70]

Here Erasmus unequivocally includes the sacred letters of Jerome in the same category with the secular letters of Cicero, Seneca, and Pliny. All, on appropriate occasions, employ the vigorously persuasive tactics of the *declamatio*—the prepared oration designed to shift the interlocutor's beliefs by means of a wide range of ratiocinative and persuasive devices.

These passages are already in the 1515 edition, that is to say, some seven years before Erasmus reworked his *De conscribendis epistolis* for publication with Froben. Here, then, is Erasmus treating Jerome's letters individually as classical *epistolae*, amenable to classical structural and rhetorical analysis, at the very moment at which he embarked on his own published volumes of letters. And the sense we have of the two projects being related intensifies when we find two passages added to the *De conscribendis epistolis* ('What *exhortatio* and *suasio* have in common', and 'On the *epistola suasoria*') which closely match the passages in the Jerome, and are fuller and more explicit than either of the 'unauthorised' texts of the treatise on letter-writing.[71]

Further confirmation of the close relationship between Erasmus's own published letters and the Jerome letters comes from a work published in 1522, the *De contemptu mundi*. As Dresden points out, in his introduction to the ASD *De contemptu mundi*, the opening words of Erasmus's *exemplum epistolae cohortatoriae*, in the *De conscribendis epistolis*, 'Dici non potest, iucundissime nepos, quanta tum me, tum tuos omnes voluptate affecerit pulcherrimus rumor, nuper hic de rebus fortiter abs te gestis, exortus', recalls the opening of the *De contemptu mundi*.[72] At the end of that *exemplum*, Erasmus explicitly singles out Jerome's letter on the benefits of the solitary life, his 'De vita solitaria' (the letter which opens Erasmus's own edition), as a classic example of the hortative letter:

There is amongst Jerome's letters, the 'exhortatoria to Heliodorus', which comprehends the whole of this type of writing in one example.[73]

This sentence is in the early and late versions of the *De conscribendis epistolis*. In other words, Erasmus's own published letter-writing falls squarely within the period of his close involvement with the letter-writing of his hero, Jerome.

AUTHENTICALLY ERASMUS: 'FOR WHO WOULD HAVE
KNOWN ERASMUS BETTER THAN ERASMUS HIMSELF?'

For the vast biographical literature on Erasmus, P. S Allen's classic twelve-volume collection of Erasmus's letters, the *Opus epistolarum Erasmi*, is the crucial source. Successive biographers have combed the gratifyingly thorough indices of Allen's edition, and correlated their findings with the fragments of further information which survive, sometimes within texts of Erasmus's works themselves, sometimes in letters of friends, colleagues, and *famuli* not contained in Allen. What more impeccably authentic source of information on Erasmus's life than his own testimony? And indeed, as we saw in chapter 2, the use of Jerome's letters as the sole reliable basis for Erasmus's own *Vita Hieronymi* was Erasmus's personal contribution to the period's version of the saint's life. The respectable editor was no longer to rely on legend and hearsay in writing his introductory biography of his author.[74]

Further strengthening this idea that the letter is an essentially unmediated source, which underpins the claim that *epistolae* are the key source for *vitae*, we have Erasmus's definition of the letter, in his treatises on letter-writing, as an original text—a composition which has from its moment of inception been written rather than oral. In the published volumes of Erasmus's letters, particularly the later ones, considerable emphasis is laid upon this highly specific sense of 'original': not a copy, not a secondary redaction, and above all, not a forgery.

Margaret Mann Phillips's elegant account of Erasmus's disappointments and anxieties in later life, based on the *Opus epistolarum* and the successive editions of *Adagia*, draws special attention to his preoccupation with forged letters circulating over his name, and secretarial interventions in the production of his published works.[75] At the end of a 1535 letter to Erasmus Schets, Erasmus writes:

> I have affixed my seal, because some people have begun to imitate my handwriting, so successfully that the forgery can scarcely be detected. This was done at Rome. Erasmus of Rotterdam, with my own hand.[76]

A long letter to Justus Decius of 1533, published with the *De preparatione ad mortem*, includes a graphic account of one 'Sylvius', who 'some twelve years ago' forged letters of introduction from Erasmus, which he passed off on Leo X and on Paulus Bombasius.[77] But in the context of the present study, we need perhaps to ask ourself what such a story is really all about. By 1533 Erasmus's epistolary strategy had entirely succeeded: a letter from Erasmus substituted for the great man himself—circulated in his place throughout Europe, making him genuinely 'international'. For-

OPVS EPISTOLARVM

DES. ERASMI ROTERODAMI, PER AVTOREM

DILIGENTER RECOGNITVM, ET ADIECTIS

innumeris nouis, ferè ad trientem auctum.

FRO BEN.

BASILEAE EX OFFICINA FROBENIANA

ANNO M. D. XXIX.

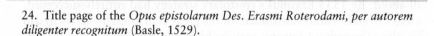

24. Title page of the *Opus epistolarum Des. Erasmi Roterodami, per autorem diligenter recognitum* (Basle, 1529).

gery, therefore, is a grave offence, is impersonation. And Erasmus himself is acutely vulnerable, since he is clearly unable to validate every single letter as it circulates, and as it endows its bearer with additional intellectual 'worth'. Erasmus's own insistence that there exists such a thing as an 'original' Erasmus letter, amid the muddy waters of copies, edited versions, and secretaries' drafts, lays claim to an 'originality' which he can no longer really guarantee. I have already pointed out, in relation to the successive editions of the *Lucubrationes* of Seneca, how deliberately contrived we must judge Erasmus's complaints about Beatus Rhenanus's and William Nesen's editorial incompetence, and the consequent distorting of his 'own' editorial purpose, to be.[78] The letters afford the same opportunity for foregrounding an 'authentic' Erasmus. He is, he insists, the figure constantly present behind the authentic text.

The successive disclaimers, in prefatory epistles and within the published correspondence, in which Erasmus insists that his letters were not conceived of for publication, serve the same purpose. In spite of such insistence, there is ample surviving evidence of Erasmus's care in recalling letters from selected friends for publication and reworking individual letters.[79] Like Jerome's letters themselves, we have a growing corpus of residual texts of the master, caught, apparently at several levels of intimacy away from the 'formal' writings, and thus providing a 'life' or 'vita' with which almost literally to flesh out the author of those works and his authority.

At the same time, in his glosses on the Jerome *Epistolae* we have Erasmus instructing his readers to treat Jerome's letters as *declamationes*—as rhetorical exercises intended to make a particular point of view compelling. And in this case, *Christian declamationes*—*declamationes* written to make the Christian faith, still in its infancy, compelling for a circle of devoted followers. We need to recognise that this idea of the absent member of a 'circle' of the faithful forms part of the 'given' for Erasmus's own *Opus epistolarum*, at least in the letters from 1514 onwards, which Wallace K. Ferguson notes, in his introduction to the CWE translations of the Allen *Opus epistolarum Erasmi*, are manifestly less 'familiar' than earlier letters.[80] Here, at last, we find the project to give prominence to *declamationes*, which I traced in chapter 5, converging with the emphasis on *epistolae* which the present chapter has begun to explore. For Erasmus characterises the *declamatio* also as a form which crucially involves feeling and the persuasive force of affective discourse.

I suggest that we have missed the point if we treat Erasmus's *epistolae* and his many published *declamationes* as attempts at sincerity or authenticity in our own post-Romantic sense. The issue for Erasmus is one of affective *presence*: what are the modes of discourse which will make the absent *praeceptor* a vividly present force, an influential source of learning, wherever his texts are read? In a period and a location (early six-teenth-century northern Europe) which proclaims the value and moral worth of 'plain truth', it is a tricky direction to take. We may ourselves have largely missed its fervour. My hope is that this chapter may have taken the reader to the point where she or he can begin to read the letters of Erasmus afresh, not as factual documents, but as urgently vital, highly contrived examples of a complex sixteenth-century understanding of the textual conjunction of charisma or inspiration and reasoned argument necessary for a convincing version of truth.

'The name of Erasmus will never perish'

Manual Dexterity: The Book Itself as Setting for the Work

One of the most striking features of the reconstructing of Erasmus which has been undertaken in the present study is the way in which the physical book has provided vital clues and crucial evidence in the story. 'Works', we have discovered, are not issued as pristine, isolated texts, waiting to be collected into homogeneous modern editions, with standard critical apparatus. The appearance of an Erasmus work, or works was more like an event—a text accompanied by a narrative frame in which to set it, and supported by a variety of pendant pieces of printing, from title-page woodcut to dedicatory letters. Sometimes, indeed, one text was provided with a setting which included other published works, generally issuing from the same press, which helped shape the reception of the 'centrepiece' work.

The book itself, then is a vital part of the narrative reconstruction of the early modern past. No longer to be seen as a transparent medium, through which the voice of history persists as a trace on the printed page, the book is the physical evidence of assumptions and motives which have to be added to the textual trace on the page, to yield a contextualised reading which in turn we make our own.[1] And what makes this approach so strikingly productive is that Erasmus's generation—for whom the printed book was a fresh and novel artifact—took such constructive reading entirely for granted.[2] The more one explores the northern humanist book, the more compellingly the self-conscious art of self-production of Erasmian humanism, via the book, must strike us.

An Extraordinarily Fine Volume: The Story the Rare Book Tells

In the Rare Books Collection at Yale there is a fine copy of the first edition of Thomas More's *Utopia*, in an early sixteenth-century Flemish binding.[3] This edition was published sometime in November/December 1516 (possibly in order for More to offer it as a 'New Year gift' to friends in England).[4] Some commentators have suggested that the book preserved in the Yale library may have been a presentation copy of the *Utopia*, from More to Tunstall.[5]

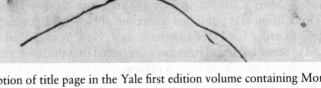

Libellus vere aureus nec

MINVS SALVTARIS QVAM FESTI-
uus de optimo reip. ſtatu, deqz noua Inſula Vtopia
authore clariſſimo viro Thoma Moro inclytæ
ciuitatis Londinenſis ciue & vicecomite cu⸗
ra M. Petri Aegidii Antuerpiēſis, & arte
Theodorici Martini Aluſtenſis, Ty
pographi almæ Louanienſium
Academiæ nunc primum
accuratiſſime edi
tus.⁖

Mori Utopia
Pontici Virunij Hiſtoria Britannica
Aleandri tabulæ græcaru fraʒ traduces
Fran. Tiſſardi Ambacæi fram. Hebr. eʒ Græca
Hocratis, περὶ Cαοιλέιας, ιȷ
πϱὸς Δημόνικον παραίνεσις
Plutarchi opuſcula tria
Jani Pannonij elogiaʒ opuſculi.

Summ Tunſtalli.

J. Hilton

Jn Conſpectu ang⸗lorum

Bodliam tibi domine ſt Adorabo

Ad templum ſanctum

tuum, et conſitebor nomini tua

Cum gratia 7 priuilegio.

25. Inscription of title page in the Yale first edition volume containing More's
Utopia.

The other items bound in with the *Utopia*, however, appear oddly at variance with such a description. They are a brief history of England and a collection of elementary texts for teaching Greek, or (in one case) Greek and Hebrew. This is clearly a classroom collection of texts. And although each text bears the inscription 'sum Tunstalli', these are works far too elementary for a man whom Erasmus praised to Budé as the most proficient Hellenist in England:

> There is a man here called Cuthbert Tunstall, who in England is Master of the Rolls, and is now his king's representative at the court of our Prince Charles; besides a knowledge of Latin and Greek second to none among his countrymen, he has also a seasoned judgment and exquisite taste and, more than that, unheard-of modesty and, last but not least, a lively manner which is amusing with no loss of serious worth.[6]

Tunstall was Thomas More's companion at Bruges on the embassy to the Low Countries of 1515, during which one book of *Utopia* was written. In 1516–17 More was back in England, but Tunstall remained in the Low Countries as English ambassador, where he continued to keep the company of Erasmus and Peter Gilles. He returned to England for short periods, however, at regular intervals, specifically in May 1516, when he was appointed Master of the Rolls. In December, More wrote to Erasmus to say that he had had a letter from Tunstall (still in the Low Countries) expressing his approval for *Utopia*, which he had now read.[7] Evidently he had the *Utopia* bound up with the Greek teaching texts around this time (hence the Netherlands binding).

The character of this 'presentation volume' has altered as we inspect its contents together with the most bibliographically valuable item it contains—the first-edition *Utopia*. It is a teaching volume with a focus on Greek studies, and a geographical focus on England, albeit with a Netherlands link. The title pages of the individual items announce that they 'are Tunstall's', which gives us a provenance, but we know from other such inscribed volumes that this may be only the first stage in a more or less elaborate process of passing on, presenting, or bestowing on others volumes from one significant named individual.[8]

Furthermore, the constitution of this volume redirects our attention in *Utopia* itself to what is, after all, a central theme in book 2: namely, that the Utopians are temperamentally and intellectually allied to Greek culture. Greek culture is the source of the kind of humaneness which Raphael Hythlodaeus presents as the most appropriate model.[9] The presentation *Utopia* volume supports this suggestion by offering the reader the means to access Greek learning, handily packaged together with the encouraging work of fiction.

The strong temptation is to associate this volume with John Colet.

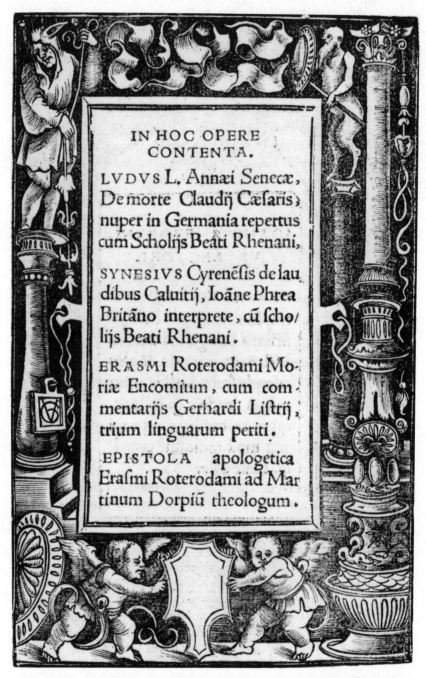

IN HOC OPERE
CONTENTA.

LVDVS L. Annæi Senecæ,
De morte Claudij Cæſaris,
nuper in Germania repertus
cum Scholijs Beati Rhenani,

SYNESIVS Cyreneſis de lau
dibus Caluitij, Ioãne Phrea
Britãno interprete, cũ ſcho/
lijs Beati Rhenani.

ERASMI Roterodami Mo
riæ Encomium, cum com-
mentarijs Gerhardi Liſtrij,
trium linguarum periti.

EPISTOLA apologetica
Eraſmi Roterodami ad Mar
tinum Dorpiũ theologum.

26. Contents page of the volume, edited by Beatus Rhenanus, containing Gerard Listrius's commented edition of Erasmus' *Moriae encomium* (Basle, 1515).

Saint Paul's in London, the school founded by Colet, and for which Erasmus reworked his *De copia* in 1514, was especially committed to teaching Greek alongside Latin.[10] The hand on the flyleaf of the *Utopia* volume (and repeated on each succeeding flyleaf) indeed might even be Colet's own, recording the fact that the volume is Tunstall's and passes as a gift to himself.[11] Perhaps Tunstall offered this volume of up-to-the-moment continental teaching texts for classroom use at Saint Paul's.

But there is another intriguing possibility. In a letter to Erasmus of June 1516 (much published by Martens in early editions of Erasmus's letters), Colet regrets his own lack of knowledge of Greek.[12] Evidently he decided that this state of affairs was not appropriate for the head of a school which prided itself on its competence in Greek and Latin, for in September More wrote to Erasmus:

> Colet is very busy with his Greek, in which he has the voluntary help of my [servant-pupil] Clement. I think he will make progress and achieve his aim by hard work, especially if you encourage him steadily from Louvain, though perhaps it will be better to leave him to his own momentum.[13]

John Clement had himself been a pupil at Saint Paul's School, under the first high master, William Lily. In 1515 he accompanied More and Tunstall on the Low Countries embassy, as More's scholar-pupil.[14] He remained in More's household until 1518. He became a Greek scholar of distinction.[15] Both John Clement and Cuthbert Tunstall figure in *Utopia* itself. Clement is named in the prefatory letter from More to Gilles as having been a participant, along with Peter Gilles, in the dialogue with Hythlodaeus—and he is credited specifically for a talent for the ancient languages.[16] Tunstall is a crucial part of the 'scene-setting' at the opening of *Utopia* itself.[17] Indeed, the 1518 edition of *Utopia* contains a woodcut depicting the occasion, in which John Clement figures.[18]

In this context, the volume we are looking at takes on a stronger significance. The book apparently belongs in a circle of experts and novices in Greek, a circle joining England with the Low Countries in the years 1516–17, and including Thomas More, Erasmus, Cuthbert Tunstall, and John Clement. I suggest that Tunstall's book passed into the hands of Clement (the inclusion of the new and paradigmatically 'northern humanist' text, *Utopia*, providing a compliment to both men), to form part of the grooming of John Colet in Greek studies, which was at that time a project in which the group of friends was taking a lively interest. Like Metsys's Erasmus/Gilles diptych, which we looked at in an earlier chapter, the book, too, presumably carried its friendship message clearly when first dispatched.[19] Lack of recognition mutes our own sense of the volume's purpose-filled construction: the individual Continental teaching texts in their fine Greek fonts, lovingly collected and committed to their fine, Flemish binding, as a personal tribute to the recipient.[20]

Paying close attention to the bound collection of texts—to the physical book in all its specificity—replaces the *Utopia* volume in an active, pragmatic context, and brings it back to life. It also offers us potential ways of enriching our reading of *Utopia* itself. For the possibility arises that the *Utopia* did seem to Tunstall to belong in some crucial way together with texts offered as a means of access to the world of Greek learning. Such an argument is based once again on the reading generated by the physical book as producer of meaning—as 'print event'.

CASTIGATORES AGAIN: MAKING MEANING FOR THE *MORIAE ENCOMIUM*

My second example of 'recontextualising' the text is a work closely associated with More's *Utopia*, Erasmus's *Moriae encomium—Praise of Folly*. And this time the physical book is constructed by the author himself—or at least by his team of *castigatores*.

Erasmus's *Praise of Folly* was first published in Paris in 1511. By 1515 it was both immensely popular and had apparently stimulated public disapproval on the part of the Louvain theologians, who considered it both frivolous and irresponsible in its open and implied criticism of theology and, by implication, the Church. This disapproval was voiced in print in the shape of Martin Dorp's letter of cautious censure, a letter which triggered a vigorous exchange of letters in which both Erasmus and Thomas More were involved. The story as conventionally told is a well-known one, which we already had occasion to look at in chapter 4.[21] Here, in these closing reflections, I take up that story once again, this time as a tale narrated through the succession of published editions of Erasmus's *Praise of Folly*—the work which supposedly first prompted Dorp to criticise Erasmus.

Here I take farther my earlier suggestion that the 'quarrel' is thoroughgoingly a constructed affair, designed indeed to clarify the status of the *Praise of Folly*, but with the cooperation, and indeed collaboration, of all participants in the debate. The story unfolds in a carefully orchestrated sequence of publications, from the Froben and Martens presses, over which, I suggest, Erasmus had influence, if not control. It centres on three individuals intimately connected with the publishing houses, and with Erasmus: the *castigatores* Beatus Rhenanus, Gerard Listrius, and Martin Dorp. In 1515 Rhenanus and Listrius were *castigatores* for Froben in Basle, while Dorp was *castigator* for Martens in Louvain.

Much of Dorp's first critical letter, to which Erasmus responded early in 1515, was devoted to the *Praise of Folly*, as was the major part of Erasmus's first reply. It was these two letters which were repeatedly published from 1515 onwards. Here I want to give attention to where they

GERARDVS LISTRIVS RHENENSIS IOANNI PALVDANO, INCLYTAE LOVANIEN ISVM ACADEMIAE PVBLICO RHETORI S. D.

Quidem nõ in infima felicitatis meæ parte duco, doctif/ sime Paludane, quod mihi contigit cum Erafmo dome/ sticam confuetudinem, menfes aliquot agitare. Tanta est hominis integritas, comitas, festiuitas. Nam eruditionē quid attinet prædicare, tot ipfius editis libris, uel orbi te/ statiffimā? Is mecum de nullo mortalium colloqui con/ fueuit, uel crebrius, uel amantius, uel honorificentius, q̃ de fuo Paluda/ no, nec ego de quoq̃ audiebam libentius. Deum immortalem, quo ore, qua facundia, folet ille referre tuam eruditionē, iudicium, multo rerum ufu collectam prudentiam, incredibile studium erga doctrina præstan/ tes uiros, fingularem ingenij candorem, fummam uitæ comitatem, ciui/ litatem miram, morum inauditam fuauitatem, in amicitia fidem plufq̃ Pyladeam, ut magis te perfpexerim, illo te depingente, q̃ cum Louanij publice profitentem audirem. Hic igitur inflammauit animum meum, licet antea quoq̃ flagrantem, ut aliquo xéniolo Paludanum mihi con/ ciliarem. Neq̃ defuit uotis nostris occafio. Forte fortuna parabatur ad excudendum Erafmi morias encomium, exiguus libellus, & quem ille, quod compertiffimũ habeo, pauculis diebus, lufit magis q̃ fcripfit, fed eiufmodi profecto, ut dubites, plus ne adferat utilitatis, an uoluptatis. Itaq̃ non fine caufa, tantopere placuit, ut iam plus decies fit excufus ty/ pis. Verum funt in eo permulta, quæ non nifi ab eruditis & attentis pof/ fint intelligi. Partim ob græcitatem paffim admixtam, partim ob allufio/ nes, & crebras, & tacitas, partim ob argutiam in iocando, quam non fa/ cile fentiat, nifi qui naris fit emunctiffimæ. Nihil enim ingeniofius, q̃ eru dite iocari. Proinde fuffuratus aliquot horas studijs meis, quæ Græcis & Hebraicis litteris, præcipue uero rei medicæ folitus fum impendere, fcholijs in loco additis, Erafmi mei Moriam, illustraui. Magis placebit, fi magis fuerit intellecta. Et felicius exibit in manus hominum, tui quoq̃ nominis aufpicio. Quare xeniolum hoc tibi dicatum, pro tuo candore libenter accipies. Et in uno libello, duos pariter agnofces, Erafmum ue/ terem amicum, & Liftrium quondam tuum ἀκροατὴν nunc nouum amicitiæ tuæ candidatum, fi non reijcis, nemini tuorum fide, beneuolen tiaq̃ ceffurum. Bene Vale.   a

27. Prefatory letter to Gerard Listrius's commented edition of Erasmus's *Moriae encomium* (Basle, 1515).

were published, under whose supervision, and what the framing provided by the complete volume implies for a reading of the letters. To do so we need to look at Beatus Rhenanus's association with Erasmus, as previously we have looked at Dorp himself, Alardus, and others.

Beatus Rhenanus has had a part to play in my story already. He was an editor of distinction, whom we first encounter working with Erasmus in 1515, when he was left in charge of the Seneca *Lucubrationes*, while Erasmus was in England.[22] The *Lucubrationes* includes Rhenanus's own commented edition of Seneca's *Ludus*—it was ostensibly because Rhenanus was already at work on this text that he was given the task of supervising Erasmus's Seneca. A letter from Rhenanus in Basle to Erasmus in England survives, dated April 1515, in which Rhenanus seeks authorisation from Erasmus for an emendation he has made to the Seneca in proof.[23] Some indication of Erasmus's regard for this young scholar is given by the dedication to the *Ennarratio allegorica in primum Psalmum* ('Beatus vir'), first published in the *Lucubrationes* by Schürer in 1515.[24] Although Erasmus later claimed that Rhenanus and William Nesen had botched the Seneca *Lucubrationes*, I argued in chapter 5 that this had more to do with Erasmus's own altered evaluation of the texts as there printed than with the actual editing of the 1515 edition. At any rate, Erasmus continued to work closely both with Rhenanus and with Nesen.[25]

While Erasmus was in England, Rhenanus was also dealing with the *Moria*. On April 17, 1515, he wrote to Erasmus:

> The *Moria* has only 600 copies left out of 1800, so it will be reprinted straight away, and it will be possible to add, if you like, the *Scarabeus* and *Sileni*, Plutarch's *Gryllus*, and the *Parasitica* and *Praise of the Fly* by Lucian.[26]

Ten days later he wrote to Erasmus again:

> We shall put Plutarch's *Gryllus* with the *Moria*, also Lucian's *Parasitica* and *Fly*, and your *Scarabeus* and *Sileni Alcibiadis*.[27]

In spite of these proposals, the first Froben edition of the *Moria*, issued that year, contained none of the suggested texts, but accompanied Rhenanus's own commented edition of Seneca's *Ludus de morte Claudii Caesaris*—the work he was also preparing for Erasmus's Seneca edition.[28] It did, however, carry for the first time Gerard Listrius's commentary.

Listrius was also a *castigator* for Froben in 1515, associated with Erasmus's works. He was the *castigator* who saw the 1515 *Chiliades adagiorum* through the Froben press—the work, it will be recalled, which together with the Jerome edition (for which Bruno Amerbach was *castigator*) caused Erasmus such 'Herculean labours' in that year.[29] In a carefully formal letter to Jakob Wimpfeling, printed with Schürer's edition of the *De copia* in December 1514, Erasmus listed these three *castigatores* together, as his chosen, select, junior team of textual advisors and editors in Basle:

> Johannes Witz . . . came with me as far as Basle. There I told him not to advertise my arrival, on the ground that I like few friends but rather special and select ones. So to begin with I saw no one except the people I really wanted to see: Beatus Rhenanus, whose unassuming wisdom and keen literary judgment are a great pleasuare to me, nor is there anything I enjoy more than his society every day; Gerard Listrius, a physician of no common skill and a good knowledge of Latin, Greek, and Hebrew besides, and a young man born to be my friend; the learned Bruno Amerbach, who also has the three tongues. I gave Johannes Frobenius a letter. . . . Frobenius's father-in-law [Wolfgang Lachner], after paying all that was owing in my inn, took me together with the horses and the baggage to stay in his house.[30]

The following year, however, Rhenanus saw a volume somewhat resembling the one promised through the press:

> Johannes Frobenius to the reader. Here you have again the Praise of Folly, better emended and corrected than ever. Together with Listrius's commentary and a good many other little works. . . . The *Ludus* of Seneca, *On the Death of Claudius Caesar*, . . . with Beatus Rhenanus's commentary, Synesius of Cyrene's *In Praise of Baldness*, interpreted by John Free of Britain, and Erasmus's *apologia* in letter form to Martin Dorp the theologian.

> [IOANNES FROBENI / VS LECTORI. / HABES ITERVM MO / rias Encomiu[m], pro castiga / tissomo castigatius una cu[m] / Listrij co[m]mentarijs, & alijs / complusculis libellis . . . / LVDVS L. Annaei Senecae, / De morte Claudij Caesaris, /. . . cum Scholijs Beati Rhenani, / SYNESIVS Cyrene[n]sis de lau / dibus Caluitij, Ioa[n]ne Phrea Brita[n]no interprete . . . / EPISTOLA apologetica / Erasmi . . . ad Mar / tinum Dorpiu[m] theologum][31]

Rhenanus supervised the Froben printing of the two adages which he had originally proposed to accompany the *Moria*—*Sileni Alcibiadis* and *Scarabeus*—as a separate volume, in May 1517:

> *Sileni Alcibiadis* by Erasmus of Rotterdam, with Johannes Frobenius's *scholia* added at the end, for better understanding of the Greek words and of certain passages.

> *Scarabeus* by Erasmus of Rotterdam, with *scholia* in which the Greek [words] especially, which are inserted here and there are explained.

> [SILENI / ALCIBI / ADIS. / PER DES. ERASMVM / ROTERODAMVM. / Cum Scholijs Ioannis Frobenij, pro graecarum / uocum & quorundam locorum apertiori / intelligentia ad calcem adiectis.

SCARA / BEVS. / PER DES. ERAS. / ROTERODA / MVM. / CVM SHCOLIIS [*sic*],
IN QVIBVS GRAECA PO / TISSIMVM, QUAE PASSIM INSERTA / SVNT,
EXPONVNTVR. / ⟨v. (BEATVS RHENA / NVS . . ./)⟩][32]

The two letters which publicly constituted the Dorp/Erasmus 'quarrel'
appeared in the Rhenanus volume for the second time as a pair; Erasmus's letter had been published once separately. In August 1515 Erasmus
had added his letter to Dorp to the three *encomia* letters to Leo X in the
Damiani elegeia volume; Dorp himself had supervised the printing of
both letters in a volume issued by Martens in 1515, which carried a letter
in which Martens 'puffed' the volume for its convenient bringing together
in one volume of texts otherwise available only in separate publications,
and which students might wish to own:

> The contents of this volume are as follows:
> *Enarratio* on the first Psalm, especially concerning figurative matters, by Eras-
> mus of Rotterdam, Professor of sacred theology and altogether most learned.
> The letter of Martin Dorp, in like manner Professor of sacred theology to that
> same [Erasmus], concerning the *Praise of Folly*, and concerning his emendation
> of the New Testament from the Greek codices.
> *Apologia* of Erasmus to Dorp, defending his works most copiously and
> elegantly.
>
> [Contenta in hoc libro
> D. Erasmi Roterodami sacrae Theologiae Professoris vndecunque doctissimi
> Enarratio in primum Psalmum Dauidicum, potissimum iuxta Tropologiam.
> Martini Dorpii itidem sacrae Theologiae Professoris ad eundem Epistola, de
> Moriae Encomio, deque noui testamenti ad Graecos codices emendatione.
> Erasmi ad Dorpium suos labores defendentis copiosa et plaena eloquentiae
> Apologia.][33]

The story of the putting together of the 1516 Froben *Moria* volume by
the *castigatores* seems to suggest a series of decisions about communicat-
ing some message which will be recognised by the reader, concerning
Erasmus's satirical text. And since the Dorp/Erasmus exchange of letters
consistently accompanies the volume thereafter, let us assume that the
volume which Rhenanus proposed putting together for Froben represented some kind of response to the criticisms of the Louvain theologians,
as voiced by Dorp. What are we entitled to infer?

Listrius's learned commentary brings the *Moria* into line with the
Greek texts, translated and commented by Rhenanus and Free, which
now accompany it. The *Moria* acquires the 'weight' of an ancient text,
dignified with the attention of a learned scholar in the three ancient languages, who has festooned the satirical text with explanatory notes and

cross-references to other texts in the genre of established antiquity and status.[34] The effect is one of anchoring the *Moria* in a textual past whose topography provides Erasmus's work with a place in the landscape.

There is nothing unusual about the *castigatores'* activities in this respect, except that the text is not a curriculum work, but a work written ostensibly for entertainment. Listrius provided an exactly analogous commentary for his *Commentarioli in dialecticen Petri Hispani* of 1520, and Rhenanus's commentary on Seneca's *Ludus* matches the one on Erasmus's *Scarabeus* adage.[35] What is unusual is the sense we get that it is how the volume *appears* which is of vital importance here—that the *castigator* is to furnish the *Moria* with its respectability in the form of its 'customary' academic framing. And this framing is further contrived by the textual juxtaposition of ancient texts—both Latin and Greek—which similarly lavish eloquence on apparently absurd or trivial themes: Seneca's *Ludus* (conveniently available for publication in Rhenanus's own commented edition) and Synesius's *In Praise of Baldness*, a classic text in eulogising the absurd.

Furthermore, if we return to Rhenanus's proposed volume, as opposed to the volume which was finally put together, we may conclude that this construction of a frame of comparable ancient texts was a pragmatic compromise, in order to get the volume out whilst fulfilling Rhenanus's ambitious wish to complement the *Moria* with exemplary, commented ancient texts in the same idiom or mode. Rhenanus wanted Plutarch's *Gryllus* and Lucian's *Parasitica* and *Fly* (as well as Erasmus's own *Scarabeus* and *Sileni Alcibiadis* adages). Not only are these texts, like those finally published, classic eulogies of trivial subjects, but they are by a pagan and a Christian Greek author. If we include the two Erasmus adages, for which he and Johannes Frobenius provided the necessary learned commentaries to compliment Listrius's for the *Moria*, they feature the same two themes as emerge from the Lucian and the Plutarch. The first is the theme of eloquence ostentatiously produced in the service of the trivial or absurd; the second is a consistent highlighting of Greek culture, particularly for a kind of arcane exoticism.[36]

Rhenanus could not, apparently, complete his *Gryllus* translation and commentary to be published without holding up the volume. Some time in 1516 Nesen wrote to Erasmus from the Froben printing house:

> I will strive to see to it that the *Copia* sees the light of day as speedily and at the same time as handsomely as possible, printed by Froben. Your *Praise of Folly* is now pronounced almost blameless by more intelligent theologians everywhere. Beatus Rhenanus has been delaying . . . for some time in putting the finishing touches to his *Gryllus*, which he has translated into Latin and hopes to publish with it. Schürer has printed your *Enchiridion* again. . . . Frobenius

ut pueri caueant hos magiſtros,& pſertim qui in Academijs ꝗs̃
uniuerſitates uocant,has magno conatu magnas nugas effutiũt,
(Cur em̃ manifeſta diſſimulem̃?)magna mercede nihil ſcire docē
res,utꞯ contemnant tandem, has Crambas toties recoctas,quoↄ
uis Aconito uirulentiores,

❡ Incipiunt Tractatus Petri Hiſpani a Li/
ſtrio caſtigati.

DIALECTICA eſt ars artiũ,ſcien/
tia ſcientiaꝫ, ad omnium methodoꝗ
principia,uiam habens. Sola em̃ diale/
ctica ꝓbabiliter diſputat de principijs
oim aliaꝫ ſcientiaꝫ.Et ideo in acquiſitiõe ſcientiaꝫ
dialectica debet eſſe prior. Dicitur aũt dialectica a dia
qd̃ eſt duo,& logos,ſermo,uel lexis ratio,quaſi duoꝗ
ſermo,uel ratio,ſcilicet opponentis & reſpondentis in
diſputatione.Sed quia diſputatio non poteſt fieri niſi
mediante ſermone,nec ſermo niſi mediãte uoce,nec
uox niſi mediante ſono,Omnis enim uox eſt ſonus,
Ideo a ſono,tanꝗ a priori inchoandum eſt.

Magis placet mihi diffinitio dialecticæ ſupra poſita,quam ab
Agricola mutuati ſumus.Ars eſt collectio multaꝗ de ũna re cõ
ꝓhenſionum,ad finem aliquem utilem uitæ,uel Ars eſt recta ra
tio rerum faciendaꝗ,talis autem eſt dialectica, nam & multas cõ
prehenſiones colligit,quo pacto inueniendum ſit argumentum
& quomodo iudicandum ubi inueneris , & faciendi iſtoꝗ rectã
tradit rõnem,eatenus, quatenus uerbum faciendi,poteſt eis apↄ
plicari,Et ſcientiam hic pro arte capio,ut pueris non faceſſant
negocium magiſtri,cum ſcientia illa Ariſtotelis,quam dicit eſſe
habitum concluſionis demonſtrationis,quæ ut a pueris intelliↄ
gatur , id quod perdifficile fuerit, hic certe ſic capi non poteſt.
ſtultum etiam eſt dicere,notitiam huius concluſionis, dialectica
eſt illatiua cõſequentis ex antecedente,eſſe dialecticam,quod ſo
phiſtæ dicunt,

B

28. A page from an annotated copy of Gerard Listrius's *Commentarioli in dialecticen Petri Hispani* (Basle, 1520) in the British Library.

implores you, that if you have anything which you have either newly corrected or newly written, you will send it to him, and he will thank you with diligence, work and money.[37]

But the *Gryllus* never, as far as we know, appeared. The Synesius will probably turn out, as usual, to have been conveniently available. One thing which seems to be consistent about these composite volumes is that the editorial discipline and application which went into a work in the Erasmus workshop was not forthcoming for the 'peripheral' or framing works. This ought to remind us what a very considerable feat Erasmus's publishing activities represented—a superhuman effort in control and organisation, vividly captured in that thumbnail sketch of the editor/ translator at work, in the *Herculei labores* adage.

The two final letters in the Dorp/Erasmus 'quarrel' were never published. Allen refers to Erasmus's reply to Dorp's second letter as 'suppressed'.[38] Dorp's reply, and the letter from More to Dorp in defence of Erasmus, survive bound up together at the end of Erasmus's *Farrago*, among Rhenanus's books at Sélestat.[39] At the end are the words 'Exscrip: Basileae 1518'. Did Rhenanus perhaps consider publishing a further volume to orchestrate a more acceptable response to the *Moriae*? By 1518 the moment had probably passed.

CONCENTRIC CIRCLES: ECHOES OF ERASMUS

There is one final component in this print picture on which I would like to touch here, although the detailed work necessary to substantiate what I am about to say is beyond the scope of the present study. We have seen how the paraphernalia which surrounds the published texts of Erasmus's works evidences an excess of collaboration and consultation amongst editors and preface-writers: the work is stage-managed in its setting; the appended pieces of writing locate it, intellectually, geographically, and ideologically, in ways which, I have argued, Erasmus himself is in a position to control. The same, I suggest, is true for the letters—not just the letters published, but also letters which, according to Allen, survive only in the so-called Deventer manuscript. Correspondents are overeager, apparently, to indicate in their letters to the great exponent of letter-writing that they are as closely familiar with his own writings as a humanist was customarily expected to be with the works of antiquity.[40] In addition, correspondents are intriguingly closely connected with one another, to form a 'network' which contemporary sociology would consider overdetermined.[41]

Letters 495, 500, and 504 in Allen's *Opus epistolarum* are all from Lister to Erasmus, and all survive only in the Deventer manuscript. All are written from the school at Zwolle at which Listrius taught. They are brief, well-constructed exercises in familiar letter-writing, with expressed admiration for Erasmus as their focus. They cross-refer, internally, to other correspondents, and friends of Erasmus's, including junior associates of Erasmus's: Dorp and Longicampianus.[42] They express eager anticipation of the arrival of Erasmus's commentary on Paul's Epistles. Such letters are surely set pieces, to be read at the Zwolle school (as we saw Erasmus was read Agricola's letter to Barbarianus at Deventer, by his master Hegius), or to circulate amongst the 'circle' of closely connected followers of Erasmus's fortunes.[43] And if this is the case, and these are epistolary exercises, it is not surprising that their distribution throughout the corpus of Erasmus's *epistolae* results in a strong impression of textual *magnification*— the amplifying of key themes and ideas in the corpus as a whole by contrived reiteration, citation, and recapitulation.

I offer two simple examples of this amplification. In the first of the letters I refer to, from Listrius to Erasmus, around 1516, Listrius compliments Erasmus as follows:

> What could Listrius either do or attempt without your support? Everything I produce, of whatever kind, I refer to you for approval. For since you have obliged all posterity, not to speak of the present age, with so many *lucubrationes*, so many labours of Hercules, you are thoroughly entitled to the most singular and personal gratitude from me.[44]

A year after Erasmus expanded the *labours of Hercules* adage in the *Chiliades adagiorum*, to transform it into the studiedly autobiographical vignette figuring the intensity of thankless labour involved in the scholar-editor's recovery of ancient and patristic texts, Listrius alludes to the adage as part of his staged compliment to Erasmus. A further touch of elegance is added when we note that Listrius was the *castigator* at Froben who saw that 1515 edition of the *Adages* through the press. Listrius supervised the production of the text from which he 'samples' to confect a recognisably Erasmian, erudite compliment; and he participates *as castigator* for that edition, in the very Herculean print-shop labours Erasmus there captured for posterity.[45]

My second example of such epistolary staging is taken from a letter from John Colet to Erasmus, also written around 1516. Again it is elaborately complimentary of Erasmus, again it refers to key works by Erasmus, recently published or about to be published. At line 43 it too interpolates a formal compliment to Erasmus:

> Long-windedness in you is brevity in others. The appetite grows (as long as the stomach is in good health) among lovers of Scripture as they read you. You have opened up the sense, which no one could do better than yourself, you will

have conferred a great benefit upon mankind and will have recommended your name for immortality. What am I saying, for immortality? The name of Erasmus will never perish [Nomen Erasmi nunquam peribit].[46]

'The name of Erasmus will never perish' is, of course, a version of the central, virtuoso example of *copia*—the production of abundant but not excessive speech—in Erasmus's *De copia*. Colet elegantly turns Erasmus's own example, presented in the *De copia* as an extended compliment to his friend Thomas More, into a renewed and amplified compliment (on Erasmus, of Erasmus, by Erasmus).

'The name of Erasmus will never perish': this seems a fitting place to close the present study. In precisely the way suggested in the *De copia*, Colet's formulation remains as true today as it did when first committed to the page, thus confirming the heavily ironical implications of such virtuosity: 'As long as Erasmus lives, the name of More will never perish'.[47] By setting that sentence down in print, it is at once perpetually true and locally false: the statement contributes to the enduring name of More; but the sentence itself endures beyond the moment at which it is strictly true as a statement—*beyond* the death of Erasmus. What I have begun to trace here is the complex, and correspondingly virtuoso, ways in which Erasmus, master of print, masterly producer of himself as European man of letters, has come to stand, for all posterity, as the archetype and exemplar of the European scholar.

Appendices

APPENDIX TO CHAPTER THREE

Letter from Jacobus Faber to Erasmus, 1503

Jacob to his Friend Erasmus, an accomplished scholar in Latin and Greek and a Canon regular, Greetings

The writings of that excellent scholar, your teacher and mine, dearest Erasmus, are well worth my editing with your blessing; and I shall take every possible care to see that as far as in me lies they are reproduced in elegant characters. I could justifiably be held guilty of disloyalty, indeed of malice, towards studious youth, if, observing as I do that none of his close friends is undertaking this charge and that they shrink from the toil it involves, I were to fail to rescue those products of his pen, filthy with dust and buried in darkness, from the devouring worm; for they are works that deserve to be preserved by the cedar oil of Pallas Athene, drawn by our Hercules from an inner shrine. I recognize how much I am indebted to the teacher under whom you and I served, though at different times. Who has ever responded worthily to all he did for us? I have even more for which to be grateful, inasmuch as he was closer to me personally. How loyal you yourself have been to him the Greek adages which you translated some time ago show very clearly; for near the beginning of that work, in the adage called, as I remember, 'Quid canis in balneo', you did not forget to mention him in these terms: Rodolphus Agricola, 'whom I name to the general honour of the entire German nation; and name all the more gladly because as a boy I had for my own teacher his pupil Alexander [Hegius] of Westphalia, so that I owe to the latter filial duty, to the former as it were a grandson's affection. But, in case I as a German should arouse resentment for singing the praises of my fellow-countryman Rodolphus, I shall add the epitaph composed by Ermolao Barbaro, whom everyone, I think, must agree to have occupied the preeminent place among Italians, both for personal honour and for scholarship:

> In this cold tomb hath envious fate sealed up
> The hope and glory of the Frisian name;
> Whate'er of praise to Rome or Greece belong,
> He, living, won for Germany that same'.

How highly Agricola himself respected Hegius is made clear by the following: he was convinced that by virtue of his intense enthusiasm for study and his sincere goodwill, such as he himself longed to possess, our master was most effective in evoking, prompting, and assisting others' studies. With him he loved to share whatever he discovered by reflection, or created in writing, or learned by reading, or marked as deserving either praise or censure. And these things he poured into our master's ears, just as Hegius did into his. He always made some relevant point, or expressed reluctance or hesitation, or debated the matter, sometimes chiding carelessness with an outspoken rebuke and sometimes encouraging an attempt with kindly words of praise, but always both able and willing to speak and to listen. And therefore there was nobody with whom he would have preferred to spend his life than with our master; and he was very sorry that their circumstances made it impossible.

Who could easily chronicle all our master's good qualities? Though he surpassed others in rank and authority, he showed exceptional affability in condescending to men of low estate. He was extremely energetic, and always preferred a busy life to a quiet and restful one; he was extraordinarily anxious to find the best way of serving the interests of studious youth, and his life-story shows that he regarded it as his destined task to educate youth well. He took infinite pains to achieve what would be most pemanent without calculating what struggles it would cost him; for in order to deserve well of youth and win its affection, he thought no kind of fatigue was of any consequence, and when he sought hard work, he did so not under the spell of foolish Midas's hidden gold, but out of a longing to do good. In fairness he would not allow those who were obviously poor to be disappointed by others who claimed the same benefits in return for fees, and was very ready to admit them, regarding Heaven as his recompense; and he taught the liberal arts to them with the same careful attention as to the rich. Thus whole he was alive he did all that one could do to live a virtuous and unselfish life; he relied on God, and did not hope in vain; indeed he lived up to his own hopes in generous measure, for he was filled with goodness and made perfect in goodness. He was most assiduous in encouraging the pursuit of virtue, to the exercise of which he earnestly called his pupils; he preached and praised virtue, exhorting them to abandon vice, which he hated. The extent of his hostility is shown with perfect clarity in the many deeply serious poems he published each year, as was his custom; these I have deliberately decided to issue in advance of his other productions, even though the latter are far more accomplished, for I shall thereby come to know what reception they can expect. When I perceive that they have won approval (and they are sure to receive a warm welcome from every educated person with any taste for literature, both for their profound learning and for their restrained moral exhortations), I shall then be more ready, without suffering the printer's importunate insistence as I do now, to send his other works to the press to be printed. They consist of the following:

An enquiry in the form of a dialogue on the true method of determining the date of Easter, which depends upon the Bible; this he evidently derived from the Greek, Isaac Argyros; together with a lengthy treatment of the mystery of the incarnation.

On knowledge and [that which can be] known; against the philosophers of the academic school

On philosophy

On the tripartite soul: vegetable, sensory and rational

On ability and its absence

On rhetoric

On morals

On sensation and its object; also several other writings

And thus, as treasures of the mind are finer than transitory and ephemeral possessions, so may his glory ever grow greater from his enduring achievements; for by his teaching he deserved excellently well of his pupils, whom he never teased with circumlocutions, obscurities, or vain and petty cleverness of no relevance to the subject; who never learned the art of adding light to the sun; who did not wrap up in thick veils matters that were clearer than daylight, blunting the understanding with useless additions. On the contrary, he set whatever was obscure in the clearest possible light, in such a way that anyone save he whose 'blood within his breast did coldly run' [*Georgics* 2.484] could understand it with the greatest ease. For this reason he deserves to enjoy eternal remembrance among posterity through the literary memorials he has left.

Enough on this subject. For the rest, dearest Erasmus, I fail to comprehend why you have not given me, as we agreed, the Greek oration of Libanius when you have done it into Latin; I am waiting for it. I can glimpse your intention; you have decided to add to my Libanius the books you are now engaged upon: on famous metaphors, on ecclesiastical allegories, on allusions in classical authors, and on witty sayings and replies. This is the one thought I console myself with that I may bear patiently the rather long delay. So now accept our teacher's most important poems, to which will be added, when I see that it would please you and my other kindly readers, his enquiries into a variety of topics, composed in dialogue form; and in this respect he follows the example of Plato, who was most intimately known to him. Finally I shall see to it that any of Rodolphus Agricola's works that come to hand here are sent to you, except those that have been published in previous years and are now in the booksellers' shops. Also I thought it not inappropriate to add a rough-and-ready dirge that I composed in honour of our departed friend, which touches on certain admirable qualities in him, which may ever serve to commend him to your friends.[1]

Erasmus, Adages *(1508)*, *'What has a dog to do with a bath?'*

What has a dog to do with a bath? I quote this adage with all the more pleasure because it refreshes and renews my memory and my affection, for Rodolphus Agricola of Friesland, whom I name as the man in all Germany and Italy most worthy of the highest public honour: in Germany, because she gave him birth, in Italy, because she made him a great scholar. No one was ever born this side of the Alps more completely endowed with all literary gifts; let it be said without prejudice. There was no branch of fine learning in which that great man could not vie with the most eminent masters. Among the Greeks he was the best Greek of them all, among the Latins the best Latin.[2] As a poet you would have said he was a second Virgil; as a writer of prose he had the charm of a Poliziano, but more dignity. His style, even extempore, had such purity, such naturalness, you would maintain that it was not a Frisian who spoke, but a native of ancient Rome herself. Such perfect eloquence was paired with the same degree of learning. He had delved into all the mysteries of philosophy. There was no part of music in which he was not accurately versed. At the very end of his life he had bent his whole mind on the study of Hebrew and the Holy Scripture. In the midst of these efforts he was snatched from the world by the envy of the Fates, not yet forty years old, as I am told. There are a few literary remains of his work, some letters, poems of various kinds; the *Axiochus* of Plato translated into Latin, and a version of Isocrates' *To Demonicus*. Then there are a couple of lectures given in public session in the University of Ferrara, for it was there he both learnt and gave open lectures. There are lying hidden in some people's possession his treatises on dialectic.[3] He had also translated some of Lucian's dialogues. But since he himself cared little for glory, and most mortals are, to say the least of it, careless in looking after the work of others, none of these have yet seen the light. But the works that are extant, even if not published by him, give plain proof of something divine about the man.

Let it not be thought that I as a German am blinded by patriotic feeling; to avoid this I will transcribe the epitaph written for him by Ermolao Barbaro for Venice. It is superb, and one might find it difficult to decide whether it was more worthy of the man who wrote it or the man it was written about. Here it is:

> Under this stone, the jealous Fates decreed
>   The Frisian hope, his country's life should come,
> Rudolph Agricola; in life, indeed,
>   He brought such praise to Germany his home
>   As ever Greece could have, or ever Rome.

What ampler or more magnificent tribute could be paid to our dear Rodolphus than this splendid testimony, so complete, and offered not to a living man but to one already dead—so there is no question of its proceeding from affection rather than from judgment? and to a German so there is no possibility that love for a country they both shared could diminish the weight of the testimony? And it came from that man who had brought glory not only to his native Italy, but to this whole age of ours; whose authority is such among all learned men that it would be most impertinent to disagree with him; whose work in restoring literature is so outstandingly valuable that anyone would have to be utterly impervious to culture, or at least utterly ungrateful, who did not hold the memory of Ermolao as sacrosanct.

Such full and ungrudging praise of this man has, I confess, a singular charm for me, because I happened while yet a boy to have his disciple Alexander Hegius as my teacher. He was headmaster of the once famous school of the town of Deventer, where I learned the rudiments of both languages when I was almost a child. To put it in a few words, he was a man just like his master: as upright in his life as he was serious in his teaching. Momus himself could have found no fault with him except one, that he cared less for fame than he need have done, and took no heed of posterity. If he wrote anything, he wrote as if he were playing a game rather than doing something serious. And yet these writings, so written, are of the sort which the learned world votes worthy of immortality.

So it was not without thought that I plunged into this digression; not to boast of the glory of Germany, but to perform the duty of a grateful pupil, and acquit myself of the debt I owe to the memory of both these men, because I owe one the loving respect of a son, and to the other the affection of a grandson.

Now to turn to the adage, which I remember having learnt from a certain very learned letter of my beloved Rodolphus, at a time when I was a mere child and as yet ignorant of Greek. In this letter he is trying to persuade the town council of Antwerp, with conviction and eloquence, that they should appoint as master of their school someone proficient in liberal studies, and not (as they usually do) entrust this office to an inarticulate theologian or naturalist, the sort of man who is sure he has something to say about everything but has no notion of what it is to speak. 'What good would he be in a school? As much good, to use the Greek repartee, as a dog in a bath'.

Lucian, *Against an Ignoramus*: 'And each one of the onlookers immediately voices that very handy proverb: what do a dog and a bath have in common?' Again in the *Parasite*: 'But to my way of thinking, a philosopher at a drinking-party is just like a dog in a bath'. So this is to be applied to those who are totally useless for certain purposes, just as there is no use for dogs in a bath.[4]

Early Printing History of Agricola's Works

The following account is based on a search of L. Hain, *Repertorium Bibliographicum, in quo libri omnes ab arte typographica inventa usque ad annum MD*, 2 vols. in 4 (Paris, 1826–38), and W. A. Copinger, *Supplement to Hain's Repertorium Bibliographicum, or Corrections towards a New Edition of That Work*, 3 vols. (Milan, 1950). I have also made use of G. van Thienen, *Incunabula in Dutch Libraries: A Census of Fifteenth-Century Printed Books in Dutch Public Collections*, 2 vols. (The Hague, 1983), with additional information from J. C. T. Oates, *Catalogue of the Fifteenth-Century Printed Books in the University Library Cambridge* (Cambridge, 1954). Finally, as always, I have derived a good deal of guidance by careful reading of P. S. Allen's header notes and footnotes in his edition of Erasmus's letters, *Opus epistolarum Des. Erasmi Roterodami*, 12 vols. (Oxford, 1906–58), as well as from his 'Letters of Rudolph Agricola', *English Historical Review* 21 (1906), 302–17.

The only original work of Agricola's published in his lifetime seems to have been the long Latin poem 'Anna mater' (Alardus, *Lucubrationes*, 297–309), and a small number of individual letters. The 'Anna mater' was published by Richard Paffraet: 'On 7 April 1484 Richard Paffraet and his wife Stine were honoured by a visit to their home by the great man Agricola. In his luggage the humanist had a panegyric to St. Anne, the mother of the Virgin Mary. Paffraet hastened to his workshop and returned with Agricola's *Anna Mater* in ten pages of print. Agricola, in a hurry to continue his journey, had to overlook the printing errors'.[5] This volume is recorded in Copinger as item 133 as follows:

> Agricola (Rodolphus) Anna mater.—Epicedion, epitaphium et epigramma [Daventriae, Rich. Paffroet, 1485.] 4°. Goth. . . . 10ff.

It corresponds to Huisman 141 (where it has strayed ito a post-1500 bibliography):[6]

> S.A. (Deventer. R. Paffraet.)
> 4°.a[10].
> a2 Rodolphi Agricolae / Anna mater incipit
> a7 Rodolphi Agricolae / Mauricio comiti spegelbergi epicedion.
> a10 Epitaphium. / Eiusdem epigram[m]a

The 'Epicedion' is printed in Alardus, 314–19; the epitaph to the same is printed in Alardus, 319. Copinger 134 is another edition of the 'Anna mater', 'Carmina in divae Annae laudem' [Swollis, Petr. Os de Breda, 1500] (also 10ff.).

Hain 15923 gives the following:

Vegius (Maphaeus) Vita divi Antonii. F. Ia: Uita diui Antonii a Mapheo Vegio Laudensi viro si quisq[ue] fuit etate nostra eruditissimo tam vere quam eleganter conscripta unacum suauissimis quibusdam carminibus de Sancte Marie et beate Anne laudibus pucherrimis. . . . Impressum Liptzk per Gregorium Werman et per magistrum Ioannem Cubitensem diligenter emendatum. 1492.

I take it this is Huisman 140 (also pre-1500):

1492. s.l. s.n.
In Annam matrem carmen.
1492.
in: Mapheus Vegius: Vita Divi Antonii.[7]

The 'de Sancte Marie' poem here suggests a link with Copinger, item 5753, Jodocus Beysselius, *Rosacea augustissimae christiferae Mariae corona* (Antwerp, Govaert Bac, [1493–]), which van Thienen lists as 'with other tracts' (item 808), and which Oates indexes as containing 'Anna mater' (Oates, item 3980 and page 702).

In addition to prefatory letters in his own volumes, two Agricola letters, to Rudolphus Langen and Antonius Liber (Vrye), were published around 1477 in a volume edited by Liber, *Familiarum epistolarum compendium* (Cologne, J. Koelhoff, ca. 1477).[8]

Two of Agricola's translations from the Greek (at least) were also published during his lifetime. His translation of Isocrates' *Praecepta ad Demonicum* appears as item 3328 in Copinger as follows:

Isocrates. Praecepta ad Demonicum. *Sine notâ* [1480.] 4°. . . . 8ff. Praecepta Isocratis per eruditissimum virum Rudolphu[m] agricola[m] e graeco sermone in latinum traducta.

It was apparently reprinted in Heidelberg (Heinrich Knoblochtzer, about 1495) and Nuremberg (Friedrich Creussner, about 1497).[9] His translation of pseudo-Plato's *Axiochus de contemnenda morte* appears as item 4766 in Copinger as follows:

Plato Axiochus de contemnenda morte. Daventriae, In platea episcopi [Rich. Paffraet, ca. 1480] 4°. Goth . . . 6ff.

In a characteristic printer's move, Paffraet later used this six-folio work to fill the end of another publication. Copinger 2953 gives the following:

Hieronymus s. Epistolae duae ad Athletam et Heliodorum etc. [Deventer, Rich. Pafraet, ca. 1500] 4°. Cont. Hieronymus s. Epistolae duae ad Athletam et Heliodorum—Marcus Tullius Cicero: Epistolarum ad familiares libri tres ultimi—Basilius Magnus s.: De legendis libris gentilium—pseudo-Plato: Axiochus, seu

De contemnenda morte.—Quintus Flaccus Horatius: Satirae, seu sermonum liber primus.

Copinger item 4768 is a more interesting volume for my purposes, since it includes, in addition to the *Axiochus*, Agricola's translation from French of the letter 'de congressu Imperatoris Friderici et Caroli Burgundiorum ducis' (Alardus 2, 221–27), and the letter to Barbarianus containing the *canis in balneo* tag, as well as some *carmina*:

> Plato. Dialogus de contemnenda morte qui Axiochus inscribitur, vertit Rodolphus Agricola.—Rod. Agricolae Traductio in epistolam de congressu Imperatoris Friderici et Karoli Burgundiorum ducis etc. [Lovanii, Joh. de Westfalia, ca. 1483] 4°. Goth. . . . 28ff. including 1st and last blank.

Oates's version of the same volume runs: 'Traductio in epistolam de congressu Friderici et Karoli. Epistola ad Barbirianum. Carmina. [Louvain, J. de Paderborn]' (Oates, item 3777 and page 702).

Copinger item 4767 is also an edition of the *Axiochus*, listed as follows:

> Plato [Moguntiae, P. Friedberg, 149–.] 4°. Goth. . . . 8FF.
>
> F.1ᵃ. (Title) Axiochus Platonis de con \\ temnenda morte. \\ Infracto ut possis animo contemnere morte \\ ad nomen cuius vugus mane tremuit: Divini Socratis verba haec lege quis moriente \\ Axiochus monuit: illico tutus eris \\
>
> F.1ᵇ (Text) Jacobus Canter Phrysius artiu[m] ingeniaru[m] p[ro]fessor: \\ Poeta Laureatus . . . \\ End. Finit dialogus de contemnenda \\ morte qui Axiochus inscribitur Feliciter. \\

According to Allen (1:126), Jacobus Canter's preface to this edition can be dated as after March 26, 1496 (death of Hermann Rinck), thus confirming a publishing date in the 1490s (after Agricola's death). Canter corresponded with Erasmus around 1489 (see my discussion of the neo-Latin poetry link between Erasmus as possibly the original stimulus for his interest, above).

Hain item 6692, lists the following, undated and without place of provenance:

> Eucherivs Episcop. Lugduneus. Epistola ad Valerianum de Philosophia Christiana.

Allen identifies this as the 'Epistola Valerii episcopi ad propinquum suum ex Greco in Latinum sermonem per magistrum Rodolphum Agricolam traducta' (J. de Breda [Deventer, ca. 1485]) (Allen 3:98 [introduction to ep 676]). In 1517 Erasmus printed this work in an edition by Martens of his *Disticha Catonis*. In his prefatory letter to Alardus, he identifies the letter as being from Eucherius to Valerianus, rather than vice versa, and points out that it was a Latin original and not translated from the Greek, but he used Alardus's text (possibly the edition just described) to prepare his own edition.[10]

Finally, in pursuit of the elusive Lucian, A. F. van Iseghem (*Biographie de Thierry Martens d'Alost, premier imprimeur de la Belgique* [Alost, 1852]) refers to a record of a volume *Rodolphi Agricolae varia* (Martens, 1511) which supposedly contained Agricola translations of two Lucian dialogues, but there appears to be no trace of this work apart from this one citation.[11]

APPENDIX TO CHAPTER FOUR

Preface to Agricola Opuscula *(Antwerp, Martens, 1511)*

PETRUS EGIDIUS ANTUERPIAN[US] MARTINO DORPIO THEOLOGO, AMICO IU-
CUNDISS. S.D.

Quum nup[er] aliquot Rodolphi Agricolae Viri insignis doctrinae opuscula, nactus essem. Martine festiuiss[ime] Opere pr[a]ecium fore existimaui, si a soricum tinearumq[ue] morsibus prorsus vindicata typis excudere[n]tur / vt etiam extrariis gentibus nostratiu[m] ingenia longe lateq[ue] innotescerent. At pensiculanti mihi indentide[m] cui nam potissimu[m] co[n]secrarentur, Tu vel ex o[mn]ibus vnus occurristi, condignus sane cui[us] sub no[m]i[n]e literar[um] p[ro]ceres (na[m] barbaros degeneres nihil moror) hoc qualecunq[ue] est volumen euoluerent legerentq[ue] / Equide[m] q[u]um p[ro]pter eximia[m] authoris vtriusq[ue] lingue facultate[m] gratissimu[m] futuru[m] dubio p[ro]cul cognoscere[m], tu[m] no[n] paru[m] no[m]i[n]is sibi co[n]ciliaturu[m] augurabar si no[m]i[n]is tui sple[n]dor in ipso (vt sic dica[m]) antilogio velut stellula queda[m] p[rae]fulgeret, Et eo certe libe[n]ti[us] effeci, vt te hoc q[ua]si suscitabulo ad publicatione[m] foetur[a]e inuitare[m], q[ui]ppe qui ipse pridem liquido ex Nicolao Buscoducen[sis] amico viriq[ue] iuxta charo intellexeri[m] ea[m] ia[m] exasseata[m] p[er]polita[m]q[ue] p[rae]ter formulas chalcographicas affectare nihil. Accingere igitur et memoriae vegetandae gratia. editione[m] tua[m] publicus exosculanda[m] in man[us] doctor[um] exire sinas, nullu[m] me hercule facinus fuerit gloriosius pr[a]esertim quod tibi summu[m] tum decus. tu[m] fructus co[m]p[ar]abit. Et p[er] q[uidem] vicissim Louanien[sis] Academi[a]e atq[ue] adeo doctissimis q[ui]busq[ue] plurimu[m] no[n] tantu[m] voluptatis. sed et vtilitatis sis allatur[us]. Verum vt interim te etiam ad palmatum quendam triu[m]phum prouocem. Nosti eni[m] vt noster hic Rodolphus vti antesignanus quispiam. cum ipsa etia[m] et Gr[a]ecia et Lati[n]o de doctrinae fastigio conte[n]derit, multosq[ue] militi[a]e literariae scientissimos. no[n] dico equauerit sed et longe vicerit. Id q[uod] satis sup[er]q[ue] ex operibus liquet / et que[m]admodu[m] Elephantu[m] a dentibus. Ita ex iis totum licebit estimare Rodolphum. Quod si fas est et alios recensere. Age Erasmum Roterodamum Viru[m] vndecunq[ue] doctissimum hoc in albo non secus ac Hanibalem que[n]dam collocemus, qui vt ille cu[m] Romanis super libertate. Ita hic de arce regin[a]e eloquentiae certauit. Cuius quidem laus tanta est vt nullis praeconiis indigeat. ip[s]a abu[n]de vel p[er] se sit apprime illustris, Sed quorsum h[a]ec inquies ta[m] multa? Etenim vt te ad hor[um] imitatione[m] quasi classico quodam animarem incendereq[ue] Et ne patereris opuscula tua diutius a scrineis strangulari / Quinetia[m] vt Germania que dudu[m] mera Romana mera Cecropis atq[ue] Attica facta est. Itali[a]e scrupulum iniciat, et velut olim imperiu[m] / ita longe et gloria[m] et decorem tollat surripiatq[ue], Macte igit[ur] et ta[m] magnifico tropheo consulens, non prius quiescas q[uam] opera tua in vulgu[m] protruseris. vt vel exotici intelligant magis atq[ue] magis Italie iactura[m] / et ruinam. Necq[ue] est q[uod] vereare Barbaroru[m] interim assultum, q[u]um habeat et Louaniu[m] co[m]plusculos viros neutiq[uam] vulgariter eruditos. sub quoru[m] tutamine. vti sub Paliados Aegide latitans Meduseos etia[m] vultus intuebere. Vale Doctissi[me] Martine Anuerpie pridie Idus dece[m]bris.[12]

APPENDIX TO CHAPTER FIVE

IO. BEBELIUS CANDIDO IECTORI [sic] S.D.

EN habes Lector Lector studiose, Rodolphi Agricolae co[m]mentaria quaedam in aliquot Annei Senecae Declamationes, parua quidem illa, sed quae docti iudicauerunt non indigna, ut in publicum ederent[ur], quod nihil sit eius uiri tam exiguum, quamuis extempore scriptum, quod non admirabilem quandam ingenij uim praese ferat. Non enim obscuru[m] est, in tanta scriptoru[m] turba paucissimos esse, qui illius uiri eloquentiam & in docendo felicitatem assequuntur, etiamsi propositum exemplar aemulari conentur. Volui itaq[ue] hac gemmula ab amico quodam doctissimo mihi oblata, & Senecae Declamationes ornare, & uestra studia, quantu[m] nunc quidem licuit, reddere splendidiora. Neque enim aut purpura ulla, aut ullae gemmae sic orna[n]t hominem, ut uel mediocris facundia, quae quum ex omnium autorum libris, tum uero maxime ex eoru[m] monumentis paratur, qui declamandi artem aut exemplis nobis tradiderunt, aut scholijs aliorum in declama[n]do peritiam dilucide ob oculos posueru[n]t. Si uero munusculum hoc nostrum tibi gratum, & paratis ulnis amplexu[m] sensero, curabimus & alia quaedam addere, tuo studio usui futura. Interim Bebelij opellam boni consulas uelim. Vale feliciter. Basileae, Calen. Septemb. Anno M.D.XXIX.[13]

Table of Contents at End of Treviso Seneca

In hoc volumine continentur infrascripti libri Senecae. Primu[m] liber vnus de moribus. Liber vnus de formula honestae vitae: vel de quattuor virtutibus cardinalibus. Liber vnus ad Gallionem de remedijs fortuitorum. Libri decem declamationum. Libri duo de Claementia ad Neronem. Libri septem de beneficijs ad Eburtium Liberalem. Libri tres de Ira ad Nouatum. Liber vnus de mundi gubernatione diuina prouidentia: & quare multa mala bonis viris accidant. Liber vnus de beata vita ad Gallionem. Liber vnus de consolatione ad Martiam. Liber vnus de consolatione ad Albinam matrem suam. Liber vnus de tranquillitate vitae ad Serenum. Liber vnus quomodo in sapientem non cadit iniuria. Liber vnus de breuitate vitae ad Paulinum: cui continuatur liber vnus de consolatione fratris ad Polybium sine inscriptione & interuallo ex incuria famuli compontentis: qui incipit Nostra comparas firma sunt. Prouerbia Senecae. [Prologus beati Hieronymi: super epistolis Pauli ad Senecam: & Senecae ad Paulum. Epistolae Senecae ad Paulum & Pauli ad Senecam.] Vltimo eiusdem Epistolae ad Lucillum [*sic*] centumuigintiquinque.

Impressum Taruisij per Bernadum de Colonia
Anno domini M.cccc.lxxviij.

Table of Contents, Erasmus, Seneca Opera, *1529*

Catalogus eorum, quae hoc volumine continentur . . .
Falso Senecae tributa
De quatuor uirtutibus moralibus lib. I.
De moribus lib. I.
Epistolae Senecae ad Paulum, & Pauli ad Senecam.
Mimi Publiani falso hactenus Senecae inscripti, cum alijs aliquot sententijs.
Quae non extant
Intercidit magna pars Declamationum.
Item lib. de terrae motu, quem ipse citat in naturalib. quaestionibus.
Liber De copia.
Libri complures De ritibus sacrorum ethnicorum.

Erasmus 'ad lectorem': Preface to 1529 Declamationes *(p. 485)*

Inter omnes Senecae lucubrationes, nullum opus extare integrum & inuiolatum magis referebat publicae studioru[m] utilitas, quam hos declamationum libros, quos eruditus aliquis contraxit in compendium, delectis quae uel intelligebat, uel minus erant deparauata, ac distinctis partibus, tum ex adiectis, quae extra controuersiam dicebantur a censoribus. Quod ipsum si paulo copiosius ac dexterius praestitisset, operam sumpsisset haud quaquam aspernandam. Certe quisquis hoc aggressus est, eo consilio fecisse uidetur, ut opus alioqui diffusum ac uarium, deinde corruptissimum, postremo multis Graecis sententijs interlitum, in scholis praelegi posset. Quod honoris omnibus pene huius uiri monumentis praestitere quondam Christiani. Quin in hanc epitomen extant iusti commentarij, morem scholasticum prae se ferentes. Nec mihi in hoc labora[n]du[m] arbitror, ut doceam hos libros nihil aliud esse quam epitomen, quum aliquotie[n]s praefatio sit propemodum libro prolixior, nec praestetur in libris quod pollicentur exordia. Id magis etiam perspicuum fit, ex aliquot controuersijs, quas habemus superstites, in quibus deprehenduntur quae hic co[m]pe[n]diarius decerpsit, quamq[ue] interdu[m] sibi permisit quasda[m] uoces de suo uel addere uel immutare. Opus ipsum Seneca diuiserat in controuersias & suasorias. Sic enim aliqua[n]do loquitur in controuerijs, de quo plura dicemus, quum ad suasorias uenerimus. Nunc uidemus inuersum ordinem. Priore loco posuerunt paucas suasorias, sed primam *akephalon*, reliquas ite[m] truncas ac mutilas, adeoq[ue] deprauatas, ut alicubi uix ipse Seneca, si reuiuiscat, diuinaturus sit, quid scripserit. Posteriore co[n]trouersias aliqua[n]to plures, sed imperfectas aeque et me[n]dosas. Graecis autem p[ro]rsus omissis, aut tam inepte notatis, ut a nullo deprehendi lectio germana possit. In his tamen multa restituimus ex hac epitoma: no[n] pauca diuinauimus, plura reliquimus. Huius igitur op[er]is si quod exe[m]plar integru[m] & emendatu[m] inueniatur, nescio quid amplius desiderari posset sapientis eloquentiae candidatus. Hic enim uelut in speculo licet intueri, quomodo doctissimi uiri, defensionis colore[m] inuenerint, quomodo causae summam in propositiones diuiserint, deinde singulas in alias subiectas partiri soleant, quibus argumentis unamquanq[ue] confirment, tum quas sententias adhibuerint, quae schemata, quos affectus monuerint, quam uarie idem thema a diuersis ingenijs tractari potuerit, & in his quae perperam inue[n]ta, aut ineptis schematibus siue uerbis explicata, quae stulta & causae officie[n]tia, quae *asustata* secu[m]q[ue] pugna[n]tia, quae *aprosdionusa* & extra causam dicta. Hae censurae hominu[m] in omni doctrinae genere praecellentiu[m], incredibile dictu, quantu[m] utilitas attulissent, non solu[m] ad bene dicendu[m] ueru[m]etia[m] ad iudicandu[m], siue in forensibus causis, siue in concionibus popularibus militaribusue, siue in co[n]sessibus, siue in omni uitae functione, quae maxima ex parte, linguae prudentis officio temperatur. Ea inuenie[n]di iudicandiq[ue] facultas, si statim pueris tradatur, mihi uidetur multo plus fructus allatura, quam quae nunc in scholis traditur dialectica, qua[m] tamen nec improbo, nec submouendam censeo, modo resectis nugalibus argutijs, ad usum potiusquam ad puerilem oste[n]tationem tradatur. Adq[ue] utinam felix aliquis casus hos Senecae libros nobis integros restituat. Ex his tamen qualibuscunq[ue] fragmentis non parum emolumenti capient, qui sagaci praediti ingenio non grauabuntur huc animum intendere.

Prologus beati Hieronymi super epistolis Pauli ad Senecam et Senecae ad Paulum

[Treviso text identical with Erasmus 1529 Seneca, apart from the single bracketed *autem* (omitted by Erasmus) and tidied-up punctuation]

Lucius Anneius Seneca Cordubensis: Fotini stoici discipulus: patruus Lucani poetae: continentissimae vitae fuit. Quem non ponerem in catalogo sanctor[um]: nisi me illae epistolae prouocare[n]t: quae legu[n]t[ur] a plurimis: Pauli ad Senecam: & Senecae ad Paulum. In quibus: cu[m] esset Neronis magister & illius temporis potentissimus: optare se dicit eius esse loci apud suos: cuius sit Paulus apud Christianos. Hoc ⟨aute[m]⟩ ante bienniu[m] q[uam] Petrus & Paulus martyrio coronarentur: a Nerone interfectus est.

Preface to Rhenanus's edition of Pliny's Letters (1514)

Beatus Rhenanus Io. Rusero Novientano S. D. P.

Matthias Schurerius, conterraneus noster, qui bonos authores cotidie procudendo rem literarium mirum in modum adiuvat, epistolas Plinii Secundi nunc sub incude habet, quas fere ad umbilicum perduxit, summopere conatus, ne ab archetypo Aldino transversum, quod aiunt, digitum uspiam aberraret. Quidni enim id nunc faceret, quod foecit semper? Debet profecto multum Schurerio Germania propter emissos hactenus libellos, ob emittendos et id in brevi longe plus debebit. Tu vero, mi Ioannes, quod Pliniarum epistolarum lectioni tam deditus sis, ut ab illis te nullus avulserit, quodque illas in manibus semper gestes, quo menti tenacius inhaereant, non meo solum, sed etiam Rhodolphi Agricolae, polyhistoris illius, iudicio rectissime facis. Qui cum in Heidelbergensi academia studia humanitatis profiteri vellet, Plinii epistolas primo interpretari coepit, quod crederet Plinium succi plenum, brevem, sententiis densum, nitidum, accuratum et cum meditatione scribentem, eloquentiae studiosis tam utilem quam qui maxime. Hunc legendem suadebat, si quispiam se rogasset, quem pro adipiscenda eloquentia ducem sequeretur. Hunc denique tanto studio perlegerat Rhodolphus, ut suum vocaret, velut ex eo carmine clarum evadit, quod ego nuper inter varias eius viri lucubrationes vulgo adhuc invisas reperi et hic tui gratia ad epistolae calcem adscripsi. Neque tibi tantum illud perplaciturum scio, sed et studiosis omnibus, non modo quum Plinianos Panegyricos extollat, sed vel

ob solam Rhodolphi authoritatem, et quum sit elegantissimum neque minus festivum. Bene vale et Plinium lege, lege et Rhodolphi hendecasyllabum carmen, quod proxime sequitur.
Ex Selezia XII Kalendas Martias ann. MDXIIII.[16]

APPENDIX TO CHAPTER SIX

Siberch's preface to 1521 Cambridge edition of the
De conscribendis epistolis

R. P. ac D. Domino Ioanni Fischero Forrensi episcopo, Io. Siberch Cantabrigiensis typographus, S, D, P.

Obtulit mihi haud ita pride[m] amicus quidam meus libellu[m] hu[n]c, quem habes, Praesul optime, doctissime, Aiebat sese ex ipso Erasmi *autographo* olim eum descripsisse. Rogabat ut imprimerem, Persuasit, si id facerem, non aliam commodiorem patere uiam, memet in Erasmi amicitiam insinuandi. Quem heroa tantum abest, ut uoluerim, uel in re minima, unquam offendere, ut nunq[uam] unq[uam] in uotis quidqu[uam] magis fuerit, q[uam] ut ansa olim praeberetur mihi aliqua quanq[ue] uia gratificandi Erasmo. Quanq[uam] ut ingenue fatear praesta[n]tiae tuae, uix quiuit perpellere me uir alioqui amicissim[us] iuxta ac eruditissimus, ut hanc prouinciam capesserem, cu[m] ob alia permulta, tum ob illud imprimis, quod non eram nescius, q[uam] male sit Hollandus [for 'Holonius'] quida[m] ob non dissimile negotiu[m]. Ne[m]pe is qui Colloquioru[m] formulas, non consulto prius Erasmo, eius nomine inuulgarit. Adeo nisi tu in tam ancipiti consilio, ueluti deus aliquis ex insperato interuenisses, no[n] potuisset sane fieri, ut libellus hic formulis hisce me is excusus, nunc in publicum prodijsset. Veru[m] eni[m]uero quum iterum atq[ue] iterum animo uersabam meo summam illam morum, uitaeque integritatem tuae, quae facit ut omnes in tui admirationem, tuamque sententiam facile pelliceas. Rursum quum cogitabam insignem illam tuam prudentiam, neque non eruditionem pene incredibilem, pro quibus apud omnes omnia, apud Erasmum uero tuum nihil non potes. Confidebam fore, si hic libellus, istis tuae amplitudinis manibus Britannis tuis, sed & exteris quoq[ue] porrigeretur, non solum obuijs, quod aiunt, manibus ab omnibus acceptum iri, sed etiam Erasmum ita temeritatem hanc meam laturum, ut non succenseret saltem mihi hoc nomine, etiam si non probaret factum, & quod in alijs solet, hic quoq[ue], si quid fortasse offenderit, uel in tua[m] gratiam, suprema[m] manu[m] operi usq[ue] adeo multu[m] diuq[ue] desyderato, uellet imponere. Id quod si per te effecerit, praesul ornatissime, n[on] paru[m] sane co[n]suleris eruditionis uirtutu[m]q[ue] tuaru[m] gloriae. Quae etsi tot ta[m] preclare abs te gestis clarissima, illustrissimaq[ue] iam olim sit, hac tamen haud dubie uia, multo maximus, & claritatis, & splendoris cumulus illi est accessur[us]. Siquide[m] no[n] crederes quantu[m] ab omnibus iuxta applaudebatur, quu[m] pri[mu]m coept[us] e[st] rumor i[n] uulg[us] spargi de libello hoc. Deinde non facile est explicatu[m], quantu[m] a me quotidianis pene conuitijs efflagitabatur. Quem quum absoluissem tande[m], miru[m] q[uam] certatim in amplexus occurebant, q[uam] auide emptitabant, emptumq[ue] desuauiaba[n]tur, Te bonorum studiorum parentem, te moecenatem, te reparatorem subinde praedicantes, admirantesque. Quam ob rem quum par sit credere R. libellum hunc apud posteros quoq[ue] plurimum laudis, gloriaeq[ue] pariturum tibi, amplectere obsecro hos clientuli tui labores, quos non nisi tua benignitate, certissimosque praesidio fretus, fuissem aggressus. Amplectere, & libellum ipsum, quem olim cuidam tuorum cognatorum, ipse dicauit Erasmus, Apud quem te eum mihi patronum praestes oro, ut nolit mecum iniuriarum agere, quod illius iniussu ediderim, sed ut interpretetur potius, in hoc a me excusum esse, ut illi, pariter & tibi, neq[ue] non bonarum literarum studiosis omnibus gratifiarer. Quod si effeceris abunde laboribus meis satisfactum putabo. Quid enim praeterea desydere[m], si mihi duo usq[ue] adeo praeclara numina, Te dico, & Erasmu[m], ullis laborib[us], aut officijs, aut obsequijs de[n]iq[ue] meis co[n]ciliare liceat, Bene ualeat R. D. T. meq[ue] i[n]ter illos nu[m]era, qui tuae amplitudini serio sunt addictissimi, Cantabrigiae decimo Calendas Nouembris.[14]

Candido lectori

Ignosces candide lector iam primu[m] experienti mihi, & pro tuo candore lapso facile uenia[m] dabis. Equide[m] ingenue fateor, & foedae quide[m], & saepius (quod enim manifesta negem?) in hoc excudendo libello a me erratum esse. Veru[m] id non tam mea incuria admissum putabis, q[uam] ob exemplaris quod mihi contigit longe deprauatissimum, describendi, emendandiq[ue] difficultate[m], Praesertim quu[m] nec Erasmu[m] ipsum co[n]sulere, nec doctu[m] alique[m] adhibere licuit. Quanq[uam] tu, quae tua est sapientia prude[n]s lector, etia[m] si illa quoq[ue] in parte uel maxime a nobis peccatum fuisset, Homericu[m] illu[d] facile cogitasses scio [Greek text]. Quare quum non sit, cur iure mihi uelis succensere optime lector, ut esset, quam ob rem me amares, laudaresq[ue] plurimu[m], decreui erratoru[m] quantu[m] praestare [no[n]] abseq[ue] Theseo tamen) potuerim, emendam facere, Et si quid esset qu[od] tua[m] lectionem offenderet, morariue posset, sequenti indice te ama[n]ter, libereq[ue] admonere. Quod reliquu[m] est, Hercule[m], i[d] est] Erasmum ipsum desyderat, iuru[m] in eiusmodi negotijs & inuictissimu[m] & pote[n]tissimu[m], Vale.[15]

Notes

Introduction

1. 'Durerus, quanquam et alias admirandus in monochromatis, hoc est nigris lineis, quid non exprimit?' (ASD I-4, 40).

2. A good part of this considers Erasmus and his long-standing English friend Thomas More together. We may take as a synthesis of such work the Toronto edition of the *Collected Works of Erasmus* (CWE), in conjunction with the *Yale Edition of the Complete Works of St. Thomas More* (New Haven, 1963-).

3. The most invaluable of these is J. Chomarat, *Grammaire et rhetorique chez Erasme* (2 vols.) (Paris, 1981).

4. See H. de Vocht, *Monumenta Humanistica Lovaniensia: Texts and Studies about Louvain Humanists in the First Half of the Sixteenth Century* (Louvain, 1934), and his monumental history of the Trilingual College at Louvain, *History of the Foundation and the Rise of the Collegium Trilingue Lovaniense, 1517–1550* (4 vols) (Louvain, 1951–55); J. Ijsewijn, *Humanistica Lovaniensia*, passim.

5. See my 'Inventing Rudolph Agricola: Cultural Transmission, Renaissance Dialectic and the Emerging Humanities', in A. Grafton and A. Blair (eds.), *The Transmission of Culture* (Philadelphia, 1990), 39–86.

6. See, for convenience, the sections on logic and dialectic in N. Kretzmann, A. Kenny, and J. Pinborg (eds.), *The Cambridge History of Later Medieval Philosophy* (Cambridge, 1982); and C. B. Schmitt, E. Kessler, and Q. R. D. Skinner (eds.), *The Cambridge History of Renaissance Philosophy* (Cambridge, 1988), section 2.2. See also, for example, A. Seifert, *Logik Zwischen Scholastik und Humanismus: Das Kommentarwerk Johann Ecks* (Munich, 1978); W. Risse, *Die Logik der Neuzeit* (Stuttgart, 1964).

7. For an interesting account of the interrelated developments of the histories of dialectic and of formal logic in the twentieth century, see the following contributions in *Atti del convegno di storia della logica (Parma, 8–10 ottobre 1972)* (Padua, 1974): E. Agazzi, 'Attuali prospettive sulla storia della logica', 3–23; C. A. Viano, 'Problemi e interpretazioni nella storia della logica antica', 25–36; F. Alessio, 'Prospettive e problemi della storia della logica medievale', 37–59; C. Vasoli, 'La logica europea nell'età dell'Umanesimo e del Rinascimento', 61–94; F. Barone, 'Sviluppi della logica nell'età moderna', 95–112.

8. I have in mind the contrast not only with medieval manuscript representations of the Fathers of the Church at work on the texts of scripture, but also with the quite similar representations of Petrarch and other early humanists. I am grateful to James Marrow, who discussed early scholar drawings in manuscripts with me.

9. For a brilliant account of the self-consciousness of the Erasmus portraits, see A. Hayum, 'Dürer's Portrait of Erasmus and the *Ars Typographorum*', *Renaissance Quarterly* 38 (1985), 650–87.

10. I shall return frequently to the individuals designated by these technical terms from printing in the period. The most important of these here is the *castigator*, literally a person who physically chastises, or 'corrects'; in printing, the corrector of the text, the subeditor and proof corrector. On Latin printing terms in general, see J. W. Binns, *Intellectual Culture in Elizabethan and Jacobean England: The Latin Writings of the Age* (Leeds, 1990), appendix A, 'The Printing of Latin Books in England', 399–435.

11. On 'scholar' portraits, see Jan Białostocki, 'Renesansowy portret pisarza', in *Portret: Funkcja—Forma—Symbol* (Warsaw, 1990), 89–115. I am extremely grateful to Tom Kaufmann, for drawing my attention to this invaluable survey article, and for translating it for me from the Polish. For the local unspecificness of the 'study' in the case of Erasmus, see the engraving of Erasmus and Cognatus at work, reproduced in L. M. Tocci, *In officina Erasmi* (Rome, 1989), figure 24. Though Tocci maintains that this is Erasmus's 'real' study at Freiburg (because of the 1530 date on it), its details are common to all such portraits.

12. See below, chapter 2.

13. I have in mind in particular the sixty years of publications in the *Humanistica Lovaniensia* series, initiated by the great studies of H. de Vocht, and continued under the able guidance of J. Ijsewijn. The present study would have been quite impossible without the extraordinary resources these published volumes contain.

14. E.g., F. M. Nichols, *The Epistles of Erasmus, from His Earliest Letters to his Fifty-first Year* (3 vols.) (London, 1901–17); F. Seebohm, *The Oxford Reformers: John Colet, Erasmus and Thomas More* (London, 1911); P. Smith, *Erasmus: A Study of His Life, Ideals, and Place in History* (London, 1923). For a slightly whimsical account of this sudden flowering of interest in Erasmus at Oxford, see H. C. Porter's introduction to D. F. S. Thomson and H. C. Porter (eds.), *Erasmus and Cambridge* (Toronto, 1963), 4–8.

15. I do in fact do something like that in chapters 3 and 4.

16. I am not, of course, suggesting that the humanism of the Netherlands was not intrinsically of importance. See most recently Ijsewijn's survey article on Humanism in the Low Countries in A. Rabil, Jr. (ed.), *Renaissance Humanism: Foundations, Forms, and Legacy* (3 vols.) (Philadelphia, 1988), 2:156–215.

17. See M. Nauwelaerts, 'Érasme à Louvain: Ephémérides d'un séjour de 1517 à 1521', in J. Coppens (ed.), *Scrinium Erasmianum* (2 vols.) (Leiden, 1969), 1:3–24.

18. 'Sed ad epistolam tuam reuertor, ut ostendam nullam ex Erasmi uerbis ansam tibi datam, qua eum (id quod facis) diceres, Louanienses Theologos multoque adhuc minus caeteros omnes imperitiae damnare, Si quidem quum ille dixisset se ualere sinere, non omnes quidem Theologos, ut qui prius in eadem epistola multos dixerit esse prestantissimos, sed eos tantum (si qui tales sunt, ut certe sunt) qui preter sophisticas nugas nihil didicerunt, Hic tu statim, "theologos istos puto" (inquis) "Louanienses designari." Quid ita Dorpi? quasi uero difficile sit, huius farinae, immo istius furfuris, aliquos ubique reperire? Belle profecto sentis de Louaniensibus, si eos, et solos, et omnes, putas eiusmodi descriptione cognobiles, quod ille neque sentit, neque dicit' (D. Kinney [ed.], 'Letter to Martin

Dorp', in *The Yale Edition of the Complete Works of St. Thomas More* [New Haven and London, 1986], 15:38–39).

19. '. . . quae (quoniam per occupationes meas non licet mihi Louanio egredi, neque sat scio, quando istuc ibo) litteris sum modo necessario commissurus' (C. Fantazzi [ed.], *Juan Luis Vives, "In pseudodialecticos": A Critical Edition* [Leiden, 1979], 27).

20. *Hamlet* 1.2.112–17: 'For your intent / In going back to school in Wittenberg, / It is most retrograde to our desire, / And we beseech you bend you to remain / Here in the cheer and comfort of our eye, / Our chiefest courtier, cousin, and our son'.

21. See Svetlana Alpers, *The Art of Describing: Dutch Art in the Seventeenth Century* (Chicago, 1983), chap. 4, 'The Mapping Impulse in Dutch Art', for the centrality of maps and mapmaking to Dutch culture; in particular her discussion of Vermeer's *Art of Painting*, and the map of the Netherlands depicted there.

22. Allen 1, appendix 7, 593–602; 3, app. 12, 627–29.

23. (Louvain, 1934).

24. Allen had died in 1933.

25. See 'The Early Publication of Erasmus' Letters', in CWE 3:348–53.

26. The letters, together with Erasmus's letter countering Martin Dorp's 'attack' on the *Moriae encomium*, were published in the Frobenius volume, *Iani Damiani Senensis ad Leonem X pont. max. De expeditione in Turcas elegiae*. See 'The early publication of Erasmus' letters', in CWE 3:348–53, 348.

27. *De recta . . . pronuntiatione*, cited in Hayum, 'Dürer's Portrait of Erasmus', 685–86.

28. The classic account comes in E. Cassirer, *Das Erkenntnisproblem in der Philosophie und Wissenschaft der Neueren Zeit* (4 vols.) (Berlin, 1922–57) 1:351; see R. Guerlac (ed.), *Juan Luis Vives Against the Pseudodialecticians: A Humanist Attack on Medieval Logic* (Dordrecht, Holland, 1979), 2–3: 'Cassirer groups Vives with Valla and Ramus as representing three separate stages in which humanism was progressively accepted by three great national cultures'.

29. See Fantazzi, *In pseudodialecticos*, 1–4. For Vives's biography, see P. G. Bietenholz and T. B. Deutscher, *Contemporaries of Erasmus* (3 vols.) (Toronto, 1985–87) 3:409–13.

30. The most succinct account, which alone of all those I have read includes a mention (although a somewhat obscure one) of the *De inventione dialectica* as somehow involved in the story, is H. de Vocht, *History of the Foundation and the Rise of the Collegium Trilingue Louaniense* 1:232–34.

31. See both Fantazzi's and Guerlac's editions of the work. A similar tendency in relation to Thomas More's related letter to Dorp, defending Erasmus, is shown in D. Kinney, 'More's *Letter to Dorp*: Remapping the Trivium', *Renaissance Quarterly* 34 (1981), 179–207.

32. Vives tutored Croy from early in 1517. See J. Ijsewijn, 'J. L. Vives in 1512–1517. A Reconsideration of Evidence', *Humanistica Lovaniensia* 26 (1977), 83–100, 92.

33. See Allen 3:68.

34. 'Quoniam existimaui te haud facile meum characterem lecturum, idcirco vsus sum amanuensi' (Allen 3:568 [ep 958]). This letter is dated 1518, and I think

that is correct for this exchange of letters, which are real classroom exercises. Allen wants them later, because of the 'intimacy' they evidence between Erasmus and Croy, but that is part of the teacher/student genre.

35. Croy's early death was a great misfortune for Vives, depriving him of a prestigious patron at a crucial moment in his career. His personal crises (deriving largely from his Jewish origins—curiously effaced by twentieth-century Vives scholars until recently) are recorded in his own correspondence (particularly with Cranevelt) and in the *Opus epistolarum* of Erasmus. He was invited to take up Antonio de Nebrija's chair at the University of Alcalá in 1522, but at the same moment his father was arrested by the Spanish Inquisition 'on a charge of resuming Jewish religious observances. In 1524 the elder Vives was convicted and handed over to the secular arm for execution. Although Vives' mother had died in 1509, she too came under the scrutiny of the Inquisition and after a trial in 1528 and 1529 her body was exhumed and burnt' (Bietenholz and Deutscher, *Contemporaries of Erasmus* 3:410). Vives himself never risked returning to Spain. For Vives's correspondence with Cranevelt, see H. de Vocht (ed.), *Literae virorum eruditorum ad Franciscum Craneveldium, 1522–1528, Humanistica Lovaniensia*, vol. 1 (Louvain, 1928). See especially Vives's letter to Cranevelt from London, December 2, 1524: 'Res meae Hispanicae sunt tristissimae; quae cogunt me saepenumero moerori vela dare; vel quum haec scriberem, allatum est auunculum quemdam interijsse mihi charissimum; & qui non secus domum nostram curabat ac suam ipsius' (352).

36. This is, nevertheless, what a number of unsuspecting Vives scholars have tried to do.

37. For the letter, and some biographical details, see Guerlac, *Juan Luis Vives Against the Pseudodialecticians*, 218. Rita Guerlac's edition of Vives's *In pseudodialecticos*, which came out in the same year as Fantazzi's edition and translation of the same work, contains additional material which includes the More letter to Erasmus, and passages from the letter from More to Dorp, replying to Dorp's criticism of Erasmus. It is thus intriguingly close to putting together the sort of story I offer here, whilst somehow avoiding the implications of the juxtaposed texts. Since Guerlac's volume was taking shape whilst the two of us were participating together in a seminar at the Society for the Humanities at Cornell (see Guerlac, *Juan Luis Vives Against the Pseudodialecticians* xiii) I would like to think that we were moving together towards an account which fitted the disparate pieces of the puzzle into a whole, but were still failing to make the crucial connections.

38. Guerlac, *Juan Luis Vives Against the Pseudodialecticians*, 161–5. Latin in Allen 4:266–69 (ep 1106).

39. See Ijsewijn, 'J. L. Vives in 1512–1517', 87–88: 'Neither the Dutchman [Erasmus] nor the Spaniard [Vives] had an academic degree and they could rely upon their pen alone to win a place in the learned world of their time'.

40. Bietenholz and Deutscher, *Contemporaries of Erasmus* 3:409. Alardus Amstelredamus was similarly stopped from teaching publicly in 1519 (A. J. Kölker, *Alardus Aemstelredamus en Cornelius Crocus: Twee Amsterdamse Priester-Humanisten, Hun Leven, Werken en Theologische Opvattingen* [Nijmegen-Utrecht, 1963], 35–36), but he failed to overcome the ban, possibly because he was less well connected, but also because of the sensitive nature of his attempt to move Erasmian teaching into the faculty of theology (see below).

41. For the evidence concerning Vives's movements during this period (he took up permanent residence in Bruges in 1512) see Ijsewijn, 'J. L. Vives in 1512–1517', 82.

42. More and Erasmus were jointly revising the text for publication; see Allen 2:494–95 (ep 543).

43. CWE 4:274–75. Allen 2:496–97: 'Mitte Vtopiam vbi primum licebit. . . . Epistola Dorpii cui tu respondisti, sic a tuis descripta est vt ne Sibylla quidem possit legere: vellem mitteres minus male scriptam. Quaeso te vt scribas de omnibus diligenter, cum primum licebit. . . . Si Viues crebro fuit apud te, facile coniectabis quid ego passus sim Bruxellae, cui cotidie cum tot salutatoribus Hispanis fuerit res, praeter Italos et Germanos'.

44. In the revised, printed form, Vives's name is replaced by 'Pollio'. Cranevelt argued (on the strength of the 1520 More letter, taking it at face value) that 'Pollio' could not be Vives, and de Vocht reiterates this view equally confidently (*Monumenta Humanistica Lovaniensia*, 1). But later editors agree that the evidence is conclusive for the identification, and tacitly assume as I do that the 1520 letter's 'ignorance' is rhetorical. In its published form, the 1517 letter does not need Vives's name, since its 'purpose' is apparently to circulate the information that Erasmus and More were in communication over the Dorp/More correspondence, and furthermore that the letters are being widely read.

45. 'Lovanii hoc tempore videntur mihi studia hec nostratia ex parte sibi aliqua restituta, diligentia Latine doctissimi amici mei Ludovici Vivis, Hispani generis, qui quotidie docendo dormienteis excitavit hic Latinas Musas' (cited in Ijsewijn, 'J. L. Vives in 1512–1517', 90).

46. See Ijsewijn for the dating of this letter, ibid., 88–89. On Barlandus, see Bietenholz and Deutscher, *Contemporaries of Erasmus* 1:95–96.

47. Allen 3, appendix 12, 627–29. See especially: 'In the preface Barland states that Martens had requested him to select some of the shorter letters "ex magno epistolarum Erasmi volumine", for publication as a schoolbook. The "magnum volumen" is, of course, the *Farrago*, which had appeared on October 1519. Of the 123 letters which the selection contains, 115 are derived from *Farrago*, 6 are not in [*Farrago*] but appear in the *Epistolae ad diuersos*, Aug. 1521, and two [letters to Barlandus] are not found elsewhere than in this volume'.

48. Allen 1:600. The title boast, 'collected out of huge bundles of papers', should surely alert us to Erasmus's self-promoting intentions in publishing such a collection of letters.

49. CWE 7:295. See Allen 4:269–70 (ep 1107): 'De Lodouici Viuis ingenio gaudeo meum calculum cum tuo consentire. Is vnus est de numero eorum qui nomen Erasmi sint obscuraturi. Nec aliis tamen aeque faueo, et te hoc nomine magis amo, quod huic tam candide faues. Est animo mire philosophico. Heram illam cui sacrificant omnes, litant perpauci, fortiter contemnit. Et tamen tali ingenio, talibus litteris non potest deesse fortuna. Non alius magis idoneus qui profliget sophistarum phalanges; in quorum castris diu meruerit'.

50. It is printed in A. F. van Iseghem, *Biographie de Thierry Martens d'Alost, premier imprimeur de la Belgique* (Alost, 1852), 311–12.

51. 'Barlandus lectori: Reflorescentibus iam pulcherimme literarum studijs, Theodoricus Alostensis primus apud Louaniu[m] typographus, cupiens prodesse bonae spei adolescentibus me rogavit vt ex magno epistolarum Erasmi volumine

breuiores colligerem sibiq[ue] traderem excudendas. Id quod feci duas ob res ita libe[n]ter, vt nihil vnquam fecerim in vita libentius. Primum quia non dubitauerim eloquentissimi doctissimiq[ue] viri epistolas ita selectas plurimum profuturas eloquentiae candidatis. Deinde quod sperarem fore, vt has quoq[ue] sic in Enchiridion redactas ludimagistri commissae & creditae sibi iuuentuti praelegere atq[ue] enarrare inciperent. Quod si fecerint maximo & suorum & suo bono fecerint, Ea enim Latini sermonis castimonia & facilitas est in his epistolis, vt si personas & nomen Erasmi sustuleris, videri possint ab ipso Cicerone conscriptae. Nunc igitur optime lector a me tibi collectas, & a Theodorico qui noctes diesq[ue] publicae vigilat vtilitati, cuiq[ue] nu[n]quam exhausi satis est, impressas vere aureas epistolas eme, euolue, fruere, & feliciter vale' (*Epistolae aliquot selectae ex Erasmicis per Hadrianum Barlandum* [Louvain, Martens, December 1520], t–p^v).

52. Two further, long letters dated June 1520, in the *Epistolae ad diuersos* of 1521 (Allen 4:270–76, 280–83 [eps 1108, 1111]) make fully explicit the implications of the letters in the Barlandus volume. In a long set-piece letter, Vives claims that the *In pseudodialecticos* has met with approval, even from the Paris logicians, and couples this with a full and eulogistic description of the approval with which all Erasmus's published works met in Paris (specifying the theologically contentious New Testament edition). Erasmus replies by claiming the *In pseudodialecticos* as a significant victory for Erasmian humanism in universities worldwide, and contrasting (again with specific detail) the precarious position of Erasmianism in Louvain.

53. See, e.g., Guerlac, *Juan Luis Vives Against the Pseudodialecticians*, 157: 'The *Adversus pseudodialecticos* was published at Selestat in April 1520. At the end of May More wrote Erasmus the letter included here [the May 1520 letter]. His praise of the young Vives is warm and generous, but the particular interest of the letter lies in his reaction to the treatise against the pseudodialecticians. Vives, he says, treats the same subjects on which he himself had once written, and in almost the same words, which gives More a strong feeling of intellectual kinship with the younger man'.

54. Both Guerlac and Fantazzi spend a good deal of their commentary on lining up passages from Dullard and Lax with Vives's examples of logical quibbling.

55. See E. J. M. van Eijl, 'The Foundation of the University of Louvain', in J. Paquet and J. Ijsewijn (eds.), *Les universités à la fin du moyen age, Actes du Congrès international de Louvain, 26–30 mai 1975* (Louvain, 1978), 29–41; 35–6; 'De stichting van de theologische faculteit te Leuven', in E. J. M. van Eijl (ed.), *Facultas S. Theologiae Lovaniensis, 1432–1797, Bibliotheca Ephemeridum Theologicarum Lovaniensium*, vol. 45 (Louvain, 1977), 19–36.

56. A. G. Weiler, 'Les relations entre l'Université de Louvain et l'Université de Cologne au XVe siècle', in van Eijl, *Facultas S. Theologiae Lovaniensis*, ibid., 49–81; A. L. Gabriel, 'The Universities of Louvain and Paris in the 15th Century', ibid., 82–132, 88.

57. A. van Belle, 'La faculté des arts de Louvain', ibid., 42–48, 46–48.

58. Gabriel, 'The Universities of Louvain and Paris', 132.

59. Since I wrote this, I have inevitably encountered a number of other volumes heavily annotated by student readers, notably those in the British Library

and Cambridge University Libary, whose annotations correspond closely in character to those described here.

60. Call number Ex.2949.32.32g. The prefatory letter is to Beatus Rhenanus. The opening letter of the collection, whose first page is surrounded by an elaborate ornamental border, is addressed to Petrus Barbirius, and begins: 'Amantissime tu quidem mi Barbari, subinde me prouocas ad amicitiam cum theologis Louaniensibus adglutina[n]dam, sed planè currentem, quod aiunt, incitas. Nemo me uiuit amicitiae uel cupientior, uel tenacior sed nescio quid malus genius in causa sit, ut cum his aut no[n] coëat, aut coëat infirma. Ego meapte natura simplici sum animo, & amicos diligo magis quàm colo. Cuius rei tu potes optimus esse testis, qui uideris quàm indiligenter coluerim eximiu[m] illu[m] uiru[m] Ioannem Syluagium, Caesaris cancellarium, tibi mecum communem Moecenatem' (6). This letter is dated 1521, and is inserted ahead of a letter to 'Eximio theologo Guolphango Fabritio Capitoni Hagenoio trium Linguarum peritissimo', also with an ornamental border to its opening page, and evidently intended originally to begin the volume.

61. 'Epitaphium ad pictam imaginem clarissimi viri Hieronymi Buslidiani, praepositi Ariensis, & consiliarij regis Catholici, fratris reuerendissimi patris, ac domini Francisci archiepiscopi quondam Bizontini, qui Louanij magnis impendijs instituit collegium, in quo publice tres linguae doceantur Hebraica, Graeca, Latina'. On Busleyden and the Trilingual College, see H. de Vocht, *Jerome de Busleyden: His Life and Writings, Humanistica Lovaniensia* 9 (Turnhout, 1950).

62. Ibid., 143.

63. 'Erasmus Rot. Aegidio Buslidio suo s. d.', 167.

64. The copy I have used in the British Library (call number c.66.c.10[1]) is annotated by an English-speaking reader, providing evidence that Barlandus's self-consciously Low Countries volume was used by those elsewhere.

65. Kinney, 'Letter to Martin Dorp', 38.

66. Fantazzi, *In pseudodialecticos*, 34–35. Fantazzi notes: 'The play on words is difficult to reproduce, for it depends on a late Latin idiom, in which *homo eiusdem farinae* has the meaning of "a man of the same ilk or paste" to use the closest English equivalents. Vives substitutes for *farina* the alliterative *furfur*, "bran", the coarse part of the grain, which was proverbially accounted as useless'. Guerlac (whose edition includes an abridged version of the More letter alongside the Vives text) unfortunately omits the passage in which More uses the phrase, though she comments on Vives's use of it. The proverb is in Erasmus's *Adagia*.

67. Bietenholz and Deutscher, *Contemporaries of Erasmus* 3:410.

68. On the relationship between 'meanings for us' and 'meanings then', in terms of a history of reading, see R. Chartier and P. Bourdieu 'La lecture: Une pratique culturelle' (Reading: A Cultural Practice), in R. Chartier (ed.), *Pratiques de la lecture* (Paris, 1985), 218–39.

69. See N. Jardine, *The Scenes of Inquiry* (Cambridge, 1991), for a History of Science version of this point.

70. Margaret Mann Phillips's work is an exception to this general rule. Her meticulous treatment of the successive editions of the *Adagia* is fully aware of the continuous process of development, which matches equivalently continuous de-

velopment of Erasmus's own outlook. See *Erasmus on His Times: A Shortened Version of the 'Adages' of Erasmus* (Cambridge, 1967).

71. For a stimulating recent account of Erasmus at work on his own texts in this way, see Tocci, *In officina Erasmi*.

72. Call mark Adv.a.5.1. On this volume, and the two hands in it, see H. J. de Jonge, 'Aantekeningen van Erasmus in een exemplaar van zijn *Apologiae omnes* (1522)', *Nederlands Archif voor Kerkgeschiedenis* 58 (1978), 176–89. I agree with de Jonge that this volume is not the source of the 1540 Basle edition of the *Apologiae*, but I do not agree with him that the annotations in the second hand, which de Jonge correctly describes as 'niet door Erasmus zelf aangebracht', are 'het resultaat van een collatie van het onderhavige exemplaar van de editie Bazel 1522 met [de Bazelse *Opera* (1540)]' (189). Tocci's explanation of such double annotating agrees with my own.

73. For a similar combination of annotations in Erasmus's handwriting and in the hand of a *famulus*, see the reproductions in Tocci, *In officina Erasmi*.

74. Tocci shows how, where such annotation did result in a further edition (the case with the *Adagia*), typographical corrections and Erasmus's own annotations are incorporated; the *famulus*'s contributions, however, generally do not make it into the new printed text.

75. Tocci too points out that the copy of the *Adagia* he has studied is not the one which with its emendations and corrections eventually provided the text for the new edition, but an intermediate 'work in progress' volume.

76. Compare Ramus's constant reworkings of his textbooks in the next generation. See also my work on Gabriel Harvey as reader in A. T. Grafton, L. Jardine, and W. Sherman, *Reading in the Renaissance* (forthcoming).

CHAPTER ONE

1. I am trying not to use the 'dates' of letters as offered by Allen, because they often prejudge the status of the letter, and allocate a date on the basis of reconstructions with which I am trying not automatically to concur.

2. Allen 2:576 (ep 584). This letter was first published by Froben, in the *Farrago* volume of Erasmus's letters, in 1519.

3. 'Such friends as once were Castor and Pollux, / Such I present Erasmus and Gilles to you. / More grieves to be separated from them, / Joined as he is to them by as great a love / As anyone could have for his own self. / He reflects with such ardent longing on those absent ones, that as I render their beloved bodies, he restores their souls in a loving letter [?]' Allen 3:106 (ep 684).

4. Allen 3:105–7 (ep 684); cited in Gerlo, *Erasme et ses portraitistes: Metsijs, Dürer, Holbein*, 2d ed. (Nieukoop, 1969), 14–16. CWE 5:151 (letter 684); I have preferred my own prose translation of the verses, rather than the CWE's verse one.

5. The original of this letter no longer survives, but copies soon circulated, and it was printed in one of the early collections of Erasmus's letters, the *Auctarium selectarum epistolarum* (Basle, Froben, August 1518). There the verses are given a descriptive heading, describing the identifying handwritten inscriptions and titles on books. See Lorne Campbell, Margaret Mann Phillips, Hubertus Schute

Herbrüggen, and J. B. Trapp, 'Quentin Matsys, Desiderius Erasmus, Pieter Gillis and Thomas More', *Burlington Magazine* 120 (November 1978), 716–24, 717, appendix A, 724.

6. Allen 3:104 (ep 683): 'Nam sic ipse certe—satis pol superbe, sed tamen sic—interpretor, quod istud abs te missum est mihi quo non in dies modo sed in horas etiam tui apud me memoria renouetur. Equidem scio me sic perspectum tibi vt non sit in eo mihi valde laborandum, me vt tibi probem (quanquam multis alioquin ineptiis non vaco) vacare saltem longissime ab Trasonicis adfectibus. Sed tamen, vt verum fatear, vnum hunc pruritum glorie excutere profecto non possum, quo mirum quam suauiter titillor, quoties animum subit sere demum posteritati me Erasmi amicitia litteris, libris, tabulis, omnibus denique modis contestata commendandum'. See also Allen 3:111 (ep 688). A copy of this letter survives in the Deventer manuscript. It was not pubished in any of the editions of Erasmus's letters issued during his lifetime.

7. 'Gaudeo versiculos meos in tabellam tibi placuisse. Tunstallus endecasyllabos plus satis laudauit, hexastichon moderate. Sed id fraterculus quidam ausus est etiam reprehendere quod vos Castori et Polluci conferebam, quos dicebat potius comparari debuisse Theseo ac Pirithoo aut Pylади et Oresti, qui, quod vos estis, inuicem erant amici, non fratres. Ego fraterculum ne vera quidem dicentem potui ferre, resequutus hominis bonam operam malo epigrammate. "Duos amicos versibus paucis modo / Magnos volens ostendere, / Tantos amicos dixeram quanti olim erant / Castorque Polluxque inuicem. / *Fratres amicis* ait *inepte comparas* /Ineptiens fraterculus. / *Quid ni?* inquam. *An alteri esse / quisquam amicior / Quam frater est fratri potest?* / Irrisit ille inscitiam tantam meam, / Qui rem tam apertam nesciam. / *Est ampla nobis* inquit *ac frequens domus / Plus quam ducentis fratribus, / Sed ex ducentis pereo si reperis duos / Fratres amicos inuicem*"' (Allen 3:133 [ep 706]).

8. See in particular J. B. Trapp, 'La iconografía de Santo Tomás Moro', *Ephialte: Lecturas de historia del arte* (1990), 45–59; J. B. Trapp, 'Thomas More and the Visual Arts', in *Essays on the Renaissance and the Classical Tradition* (Variorum [1990]), 27–54. The definitive article resolving the matter of which of the surviving versions of the Erasmus panel is the original, and establishing the Longford Castle Gilles and Hampton Court Erasmus as the original panels (together with convincing arguments for the relationship with these of the Rome Erasmus and the Antwerp Gilles), is Campbell et al., 'Quentin Matsys'. See also J. B. Trapp, 'Postscript', *Burlington Magazine* (1979). For the arguments prior to the detailed and technical research done by the authors of that article (on which, inevitably, some secondary work on the likenesses tends still to depend), see A. Gerlo, *Erasme et ses portraitistes*; G. Marlier, *Erasme et la peinture flamande de son temps* (Damme, 1954). The original article establishing the Hampton Court Erasmus as the original version was M. Mann Phillips, 'The Mystery of the Metsys Portrait', *Erasmus in English* 7 (1975), 18–21. See Gerlo, *Erasme et ses portraitistes*, for a similar argument for the authenticity of the Longford Castle Gilles portrait (16, note 19): 'L'importance historique de cette lettre [Ep. 684] doit à peine être soulignée; elle a evidemment largement contribué à identifier les portraits conservés. Grace à la description minutieuse de Morus, on est notamment parvenu à déterminer que le portrait de Pierre Gilles a Longford Castle est

la moitié du diptyche original de Metsijs'. See also the classic article by Erwin Panofsky, 'Erasmus and the Visual Arts', *Journal of the Warburg and Courtauld Institutes* 32 (1969), 200–227.

9. Such a view was also fostered by cherished ancient works, like Xenophon's *Cyropedia*, of course, which suggested that the greatest rulers inevitably had scholars at their right hand to advise them on policy and morals.

10. For the argument that our professional activity as academics in the humanities is 'the practice of reading', see Pierre Bourdieu and Roger Chartier, 'La lecture: Une pratique culturelle', in Chartier, *Pratiques de la Lecture*, 218–39.

11. Tony Grafton adds (personal communication, May 1991): 'Actually, the text is more problematic. The likeness must be of now but can't be because now isn't good enough'.

12. Allen 8:274 (ep 2212); cited by Gerlo, *Erasme et ses portraitistes*, 54–55.

13. Allen 8:300 (ep 2233); cited by Gerlo, *Erasme et ses portraitistes*, 55–56.

14. It would be nice to think that this was the line drawing now in the Basle Art Museum (reproduced by Trapp, 'La iconografía').

15. On the Pliny see *Natural History*, 35; for Erasmus's close use of Pliny in his eulogy of Dürer in the *De recta pronuntiatione*, see E. Panofsky, 'Nebulae in pariete', *Journal of the Warburg and Courtauld Institutes* 14 (1951), 34–41.

16. Gerlo (*Erasme et ses portraitistes*, 16, note 19) cites Marlier, *Erasme et la peinture flamande de son temps*, 90: 'A l'époque d'Erasme, la critique d'art n'est pas née: nul ne songe a traduire en paroles plus ou moins éloquentes ce qu'il éprouve à la vue d'une oeuvre.... La vérité, c'est qu'en dehors de l'action, assurément profonde, que l'oeuvre d'art exercait sur les hommes de ce temps, ceux-ci étaient particulièrement amusés par certains détails, par cetains effets de trompe-l'oeil que les peintures flamandes réussissaient mieux que tous les autres'. I am arguing that the 'trompe l'oeil' of the identifiable letter, manuscript, and books is the vital and central 'message' of the diptych, and that More responds in precisely the terms Erasmus and Gilles intended. It is nevertheless of interest that this kind of trompe l'oeil was a Flemish specialist technique.

17. Allen 3:105–7 (ep 684); cited in Gerlo, *Erasme et ses portraitistes*, 15. On the peculiar efficacy of *epistolae* (letters) to make absent friends present, see below, chapter 6.

18. Compare Ben Jonson's lines 'On the Portrait of Shakespeare, to the Reader': 'This figure that thou here seest put, / It was for gentle Shakespeare cut, / Wherein the graver had a strife / With Nature, to out-do the life: / O could he but have drawn his wit / As well in brass, as he has hit / His face; the print would then surpass / All that was ever writ in brass: / But since he cannot, reader, look / Not on his picture, but his book'. The same sentiment is invoked in Erasmus's letter to Margaret Roper above: 'I have been able to meet and recognise you all once more, and none better than you. I have even *believed* that I could discover, through that beautiful exterior, the *reflection* of your yet more beautiful soul' (my emphasis).

19. See Campbell et al., 'Quentin Matsys': 'The letter that Gillis holds in Lord Radnor's picture, though so overpainted that the hand can hardly now be identified with any confidence as More's, is at least clearly directed to Gillis. A century ago, Alfred Woltmann read: ⟨V[iro] Il[lus]trissimo Petro/Egidio Amico charissimo/Anwerpiae⟩ (or *Anverpiis*). Now one can make out V[iro], followed by a

meaningless jumble from which the letters *erasimo* stand out, with other shadowy letters behind them. Perhaps they were originally *illustrissimo* or *litteratissimo*. then, clearly visible, *Petro Egidio*, followed by what may be *Am[ico charissimo] An[twerpiensi]* (or *An[twerpiis]*)' (718).

20. See, for instance, the Detroit panel, after Jan van Eyck, where the letter lying on Saint Jerome's desk contains the inscription: 'Reuerendissimo in Christo patri et domino, domino Ieronimo, tituli Sancte Crucis in Iherusalem presbytero cardinali' (To the Most Reverend Father and Lord in Christ, Lord Jerome, Priest-Cardinal of the the Church of the Holy Cross of Jerusalem). See B. Ridderbos, *Saint and Symbol: Images of Saint Jerome in Early Italian Art* (Groningen, 1984), 27–28.

21. It is because More insists rhetorically on the ease of identification, I think, that Lorne Campbell et al. evidence some anxiety about the possibility of identifying the hand ('though so overpainted that the hand can hardly now be identified with any confidence as More's' ['Quentin Matsys', 718]). If, as they suggest, the letters 'erasimo' are now all that can be read clearly in the repainted inscription, this suggests that the restorer produced an inscription suggesting 'to Erasmus', resolving (erroneously, if we trust More's account) the difficulty.

22. In the Antwerp Gilles panel, Gilles holds the letter rolled, in a much less contrived fashion than is required in order to display the handwriting in the Longford Castle panel. Because of this difference in composition (amongst other alterations of detail), Campbell et al. suggest that this second panel might have been a contemporary copy, made either for Metsys himself, or for Erasmus (ibid., 724). If this was the case, then it might well have seemed appropriate to delete the compliment to a foreigner, and leave the letter to be interpreted as one of the many Gilles received from Erasmus.

23. These titles have been overpainted. See ibid., 718–19.

24. 'All are works written or edited by Erasmus, and recently at that. . . . There is no obvious explanation for the use of Greek in two of the book titles . . . ; it is probably a mere humanist flourish. As for the other volumes, Erasmus's edition of Plutarch's *Opuscula* first came out in 1512 and his Seneca's *Tragedies* in 1513. His Quintus Curtius and his Suetonius were not printed until 1518, though the epistle dedicatory of the first is dated 4th November 1517 and of the second 5th June 1517' (ibid., 719).

25. Allen 3:340 (ep 846).

26. See Campbell et al., 'Quentin Matsys', for the retouching of the shelf in the Radnor Gilles painting.

27. I follow Michael Baxandall in wanting to take seriously such gesture-instructions, in all their historical specificity. See, most recently, *Patterns of Intention: On the Historical Explanation of Pictures* (New Haven and London, 1985), and classically, *Painting and Experience in Fifteenth-Century Italy* (Oxford, 1972).

28. Campbell et al., 'Quentin Matsys', 719.

29. See R. Pfeiffer, *History of Classical Scholarship from 1300 to 1850* (Oxford, 1976), 80.

30. Allen 3:339 (ep 846).

31. L. Bradner and C. A. Lynch (eds.), *The Latin Epigrams of Thomas More*

(Chicago, University of Chicago Press, 1953), xiii. Campbell et al. call this possibly 'an informed attempt to correct a blunder [the *Antibarbari* inscription]' ('Quentin Matsys', 719).

32. See chapter 4, below.

33. Campbell et al., 'Quentin Matsys', 719. See also note 34: 'Professor T. Julian Brown, who kindly compared the inscription, at our request, with facsimiles of Erasmus's hand, thought the resemblance "compelling". There is a facsimile of Erasmus's hurried hand in 1517 in Allen, Vol. iii, facing p. 339; and a more formal specimen from 1524 in Georg Menz: *Handschriften der Reformationzeit*, Bonn etc. [1912], Pl. I. See also *Erasmus en zijn Tijd*, Catalogue of the Exhibition, Rotterdam [1969], No. 235, Pl. 130'.

34. Ibid., 719. The painting has now been cleaned. 'Parentheses represent letters no longer visible; italics represent the expansion of a contraction'. For the text of the first words of the paraphrase see CWE 42. In a recent lecture on 'Portraits of Petrarch', J. B. Trapp suggested that Petrarch is the first secular author to be represented graphically in the act of writing the first lines of his own work (as customarily is the case for the Gospel writers and Fathers of the Church).

35. CWE 5:156 (letter 687).

36. Accepting the evidence of Campbell et al. that the 'HOR' now visible overpaints 'MOR' ('Quentin Matsys', 720). They also report that 'infra-red photography shows that, of the two books now apparently unlabelled, the topmost on the lower shelf was once inscribed' (719).

37. Allen 3:105–7 (ep 684); cited in Gerlo, *Erasme et ses portraitistes*, 14–16; Campbell et al., 'Quentin Matsys', appendix A, 724.

38. Allen 3:76 (ep 654).

39. See Campbell et al., 'Quentin Matsys', for figure and comments on restoration. Also see Trapp, 'Postscript'.

40. I am extremely grateful to John Hare for noticing this.

41. In Dürer's *Nemesis* engraving, Nemesis holds a very similar goblet/chalice and a bridle, 'symbols of favor and castigation'. *Albrecht Du[e]rer: Master Printmaker* (Museum of Fine Arts, Boston, 1971), 82, plate 60. See Campbell et al., 'Quentin Matsys', on the retouching of the bottom shelf in the Gilles panel, so that this is no longer evident.

42. The letter from Erasmus to More with which I opened this chapter continues with an explicit reference to the fact that Erasmus is at that moment (early 1517) seeing through the press a planned further edition of More's *Utopia* together with their joint *Epigrammata*: 'I have sent your *Epigrammata* and *Utopia* to Basle by my own servant, whom I had maintained here for several months for that purpose, together with some things of my own'. In the end, the two publications came out separately.

43. For such careful use of eye direction in Flemish paintings linked in diptychs or polyptychs, see, e.g., the angel and the Virgin Mary in Jan van Eyck's Ghent polyptych: the angel looks at her; she looks upwards towards heaven. Similarly, the donor's wife looks at the donor; the donor looks heavenwards. Adam and Eve look at one another (neither looks at the apple, though Eve holds it up, demonstratively). John the Baptist looks at (and blesses) Christ; the Virgin looks at her book; Christ looks at the viewer.

44. See below, chapter 4.

45. See Iseghem *Biographie de Thierry Martens*. He may well have composed the 'utopian' verses.

46. 'In caeteris igitur nihil est, quod illius scriptis queam adijcere. Tantum tetrastichum uernacula Vtopiensium lingua scriptum, quod a MORI discessu, forte mihi ostendit Hythlodaeus apponendum curaui, praefixo eiusdem gentis alphabeto, tum adiectis ad margines aliquot annotatiunculis' (E. Surtz, S. J., and J. H. Hexter [eds.], *Utopia*, vol. 4 of *The Complete Works of St. Thomas More* [New Haven and London, 1965], 22–23). See also clxxxiii: 'On September 3, 1516, More dispatched the prefatory letter and the *Utopia* to Erasmus and committed all the publishing details to his care (Eras. *Ep.*, 2, 339). About September 20, he asked Erasmus to supply recommendations not only by scholars but especially by statesmen (ibid., 2, 346). On October 2, Erasmus assured his friend of the expenditure of all possible care (ibid., 2, 354). On October 17, he suggested that Giles address his preface to Busleyden rather than to himself (ibid., 2, 359), a request with which Giles complied in the Utopian letter dated November 1 (20/10 f.). The previous day More had expressed to Erasmus his delight at Giles' approval and wished to know the reaction of Tunstall, Le Sauvage, and Busleyden (Eras., *Ep.*, 2, 372). The last-named, on November 9, sent his Utopian letter (32/1 f.) to Erasmus with a note describing it as difficult to compose and as a tribute to Erasmus himself (Eras. *Ep.*, 2, 375). On November 12, Gerhard Geldenhauer joyfully sent the news to Erasmus that Thierry Martens had undertaken to print the *Utopia* and that Desmarais would show him an eminent artist's sketch of Utopia (ibid., 2, 380). On November 18, Erasmus wrote to Giles from Brussels that the *Utopia* was in the printer's hands (ibid., 2, 385). The Utopian letter of Desmarais to Giles is dated December 1, 1516. About December 4, More told Erasmus of Tunstall's approval (ibid., 2, 413–14), gratefully acknowledged in a personal letter to Tunstall himself (*Corresp.*, pp. 84–85). On December 15, More confessed that he was expecting the *Utopia* from day to day (Eras., *Ep.*, 2, 421)'.

47. Surtz and Hexter, *Utopia*, have the following to say about the woodcut of the island in the 1516 first edition: 'The *tabula* in its 1518[m] form is the work of Ambrosius Holbein. . . . The original artist for the *figura* in 1516 . . . is described as *quidam egregius pictor* by Gerard Geldenhauer (November 12, 1516, Eras. *Ep.*, 2, 380) but remains unidentified. [There follows a series of suggestions of minor artists who might be associated with the woodcut.] But an artist whose identity exhaustive research fails to reveal hardly merits the epithet *egregius*. Consequently, one suspects deliberate concealment either from a sense of modesty or as a contribution to the general hoax and humor. Just as Giles had added the Utopian alphabet to the edition, has another person involved in it offered a sketch of Utopia to enrich it? If so, the latter could be none other than Gerhard Geldenhauer, the first two letters of whose name appear on the banner as NO[uiomagus?]. Cr. H. de Vocht, *Literae virorum eruditorum ad Franciscum Craneveldium* (Louvain, 1928), p. 133, for a letter to Cranevelt signed "Gerardus Geldenhouerus No⟨uiomagus⟩" ' (276–77).

48. On pages 152, 153, and 497. The copy measures 8 1/4 × 5 1/2 inches. See Surtz and Hexter, *Utopia*, clxxxiv.

49. Ibid., clxxxv.

50. Ibid., clxxxvii.

51. Ibid., clxxxiv, clxxxv, clxxxviii.

52. Ibid., clxxxv.

53. Ibid., 248, 249. For the full text of this letter, see Appendices.

54. On this and on the self-conscious assembling of the prefatory material for the early editions of *Utopia*, in general, see P. R. Allen, '*Utopia* and European Humanism: The Function of the Prefatory Letters and Verses', *Studies on the Renaissance* 10 (1963), 91–107, especially 97–98.

55. For a fascinating discussion of the way Erasmus himself used presentation copies of his works, and accompanying letters—sometimes separate, sometimes bound into the personalised binding of the presentation volume—see J. Hoyoux, 'Les moyens d'existence d'Érasme', *Bibliothèque d'Humanisme et Renaissance* 5 (1944), 7–59. Hoyoux mentions the Metsys diptych, and suggests that the letter Gilles holds is a dedicatory letter from Erasmus, to accompany the *Antibarbari* on the table. Whilst this is no longer acceptable (because of the identification of the letter as one from *More* to Gilles), it does allow the conjunction: dedicatory letter from More to Gilles, presentation copy of *Utopia* on the table.

56. P. R. Allen suggests that editors have wanted to make More ignorant of the edition (presumably because Erasmus—who was preparing the Basle edition himself—disparaged its accuracy) (98). But More was a friend of Linacre, on whose behalf Lupset travelled to Paris with both Linacre's Galen and More's *Utopia*. See the letter from More to Erasmus, February 1516 (CWE 3:236 [letter 388]): 'Linacre, my dear Erasmus (take my word for it), both thinks of you and speaks of you everywhere in a most proper spirit, as I have lately heard from people who were present when he was speaking of you to the king at dinner on a most affectionate and warm-hearted way'. I take it that the 'take my word for it' refers to More's personal experience with Linacre, and the 'I have lately heard', to the particular occasion when Linacre praised Erasmus to Henry VIII.

57. For a clear account of these events see Budé's letter, Surtz and Hexter, *Utopia*, 5.

58. See Allen, '*Utopia* and European Humanism'.

59. CWE 5:106 (letter 654).

60. CWE 5:125–26 (letter 664).

61. CWE 2: 131 (letter 207). CWE reproduces a photograph of the original, autograph letter (130), which is inscribed on the back, in Aldus's hand, 'Erasmus Roterodamus. Ex Bononia Kal. November 1507'. On Aldus Manutius and his printing house, see the classic work by M. Lowry, *The World of Aldus Manutius: Business and Scholarship in Renaissance Venice* (Oxford, 1979). Most of Lowry's book is extremely relevant to the present study.

62. 3.1.1; LB. 707 D. Translated by Margaret Mann Phillips, *Erasmus on His Times: A Shortened Version of the 'Adages' of Erasmus* (Cambridge, 1967), 18–31.

63. Mann Phillips, *Adages*, 20–21. In the *De copia*, Erasmus repeats this highly specific version of 'Herculei labores': attempting and suffering anything *for the sake of serving others*. CWE 24:611: 'In some instances it is not particularly difficult to grasp the sense of the allegory: . . . the labours of Hercules tells us that immortal renown is won by effort and by helping others'.

64. On digression for emphasis see *De copia*, book 2.

65. Mann Phillips, *Adages*, 30–31. For discussions of Erasmus's textual editing itself which give some idea of how much 'labour' it entailed, see H. J. de Jonge, 'Vann ist Erasmus' Übersetzung des Neuen Testaments entstanden?' in J. Sperna Weiland and W. Th. M. Frijhoff, *Erasmus of Rotterdam: The Man and the Scholar* (Leiden, 1988), 151–57; D. F. S. Thomson, 'Erasmus and Textual Scholarship in the Light of Sixteenth-Century Practice', in Sperna Weiland and Frijhoff, *Erasmus of Rotterdam*, 158–71 (especially the section on Jerome, 165–66).

66. Erasmus uses the tag 'Not even Hercules against two adversaries' again in the 'Sileni Alcibiadis' adage (Mann Phillips, *Adages*, 292): 'It is hardly possible for one man to be equal to two different forms of administration, like Hercules with his two monsters'.

67. Cited ibid., 162.

68. See below, chapter 5.

69. Cited in Mann Phillips, *Adages*, 126–27.

70. This shelf, books, and vase are uncannily like the same composition elements in Joos van Cleve's *Saint Jerome in His Study* (ca. 1525), reproduced in E. Rice, *Saint Jerome in the Renaissance* (Baltimore, 1985), 148, fig. 37. They seem to be a topos of northern European Jerome paintings of this period. See also the reproductions in Ridderbos, *Saint and Symbol*, and in Helen Roberts, 'St. Augustine in "St. Jerome's Study": Carpaccio's Painting and Its Legendary Source', *Art Bulletin* 41 (1959), 283–97.

71. '. . . apud Rauricos Ioannes Holbenius, Augustae Vindelicorum quidem natus verum iamdiu Basiliensis civis, qui Erasmum nostrum Roterodamum anno superiori in duabus tabulis pinxit felicissime et cum multa gratia, quae postea sunt in Britanniam transmissae' (cited in Gerlo, *Erasme et ses portraitistes*, 49). See also Allen 5:470 (ep 1452); cited in Gerlo, *Erasme et ses portraitistes*, 49.

72. Its upper right-hand corner appears to show the creases of a folded paper, i.e., a letter. Campbell et al., 'Quentin Matsys', assume that in it also Erasmus is writing his paraphrase of Mark, but this identification 'is impossible from photographs of the Louvre [Basle?] picture' [I think these are the wrong way round, or Gerlo has them identified the wrong way round!] Actually, I would have thought that the painting dispatched to Paris might have been sent to the king, to whom the Mark paraphase was dedicated. Erasmus writes: 'My portrait has also been taken to Paris. The King asks for me again' (Allen 5:470 [ep 1452]; cited in Gerlo, *Erasme et ses portraitistes*, 49).

73. In his study of Erasmus's *familia*, Bierlaire notes this discrepancy between the graphic representations of Erasmus as solitary and isolated (by Metsys, Holbein, and Dürer), and the circle of amanuenses, *famuli*, admirers, and friends amongst whom Erasmus lived and worked. F. Bierlaire, *La familia d'Erasme: Contribution à l'histoire de l'humanisme* (Paris, 1968), 101–2.

74. Gerlo, *Erasme et ses portraitistes*, 60–61. For a similar suggestion of prosperity or 'success', see the fat purse at Erasmus's waist in the Metsys (below, chapter 2).

75. Hyatt Mayor, *Prints and People: A Social History of Printed Pictures* (New York, 1971), plate 214 and surrounding text (volume unpaginated).

76. I take this formulation from Michael Fried, in the introduction to *Realism,*

Writing, Disfiguration (Chicago and London, 1987), xiii–xiv. I am extremely grateful to Nicole Plett, for directing me to the Fried for a methodology appropriate to the relationship between written and graphic representations just when I needed it.

77. See, however, Erasmus's comments on particularly wanting Aldine italic, or Froben's exquisite type.

78. See Alpers, *Art of Describing*, and Schama, *Embarrassment of Riches*, for the persistence of this tradition in the seventeenth century.

79. Some of this 'devotional' association surely survives in the circulation of prints of Erasmus and other 'great leaders' of the early sixteenth century (Luther, Melanchthon, Emperor Maximilian, etc.). See *Prints and People*, Mayor, plates 136–37, 141–44, 282–85. The *worth* of engravings was significantly less than that of painted canvases or panels.

80. There are a number of instances, in Erasmus's letters, of Erasmus's sending either print or medallion to a correspondent.

81. On the other hand, Dürer himself is reputed to have used his own prints like travellers' cheques, to pay his way in his travels around Europe. See Jane Hutchison, *Albrecht Dürer: A Biography* (Princeton, 1990).

82. Not the letter of the Paris edition, but the original one offering him the tale as a personal gift.

83. Surtz and Hexter, *Utopia*, clxxxviii. No such border yet frames the title page in the edition. This may, of course, be because at the time of designing the border for the opening page, this letter was still expected to be the beginning of the volume, the additional material being added later. Erasmus's printers regularly altered the physical structure of the volumes right up to publication.

84. 'Thomas Morus Petro Aegidio S. D. Pvdet me propemodum charissime Petre Aegidi libellum hu[n]c, de Vtopiana republica, post annum fermè ad te mittere, quem te no[n] dubito intra sesquime[n]sem expectasse' (reproduced Surtz and Hexter, *Utopia*, plate II^v, following 253).

85. Reproduction, Hyatt Mayor, *Prints and People*, plate 324 (title page of Erasmus's *Paraphrase of Saint John's Gospel*).

86. See Gerlo, *Erasme et ses portraistises*, 60–61. On the rapid development of the 'exactly repeatable pictorial statement' during the late fifteenth and early sixteenth centuries, see W. M. Ivins, *Prints and Visual Communication* (Cambridge, Mass., 1953); and Mayor, *Prints and People*.

87. On 'termini', and for the Italianate detailing on the arch, see Franz Sales Meyer, *Handbook of Ornament* (Carlsruhe, 1888; Dover, 1957), 225–27. See also the facade of the Palazzo Negro in Genoa (attributed to Castello, ca. 1560), for stone ornamenting, including termini and swagged fruit very reminiscent of the Holbein woodcut (reproduced in J. Shearman, *Mannerism* [Harmondsworth, 1967], plate 39).

88. On Cousin and Erasmus's *familia*, see Bierlaire, *La familia d'Erasme*, 97–100.

89. Reproduced in Gerlo, *Erasme et ses portraitistes*, facing 41.

90. Ibid., 61. These Latin verses are followed by the following in Greek: 'Whoever contemplates this portrait of the aged Erasmus sees only the old hide, not the man' (ibid., 62).

91. 'Gilbertus Cognatus mihi iam plusquam triennium fidelem et commodum praestitit famulum quem ego tamen ob mores liberales non tam pro famulo habui quam pro convictore et in studiorum laboribus socio' (Allen 10:331 [ep 2889]; cited in Gerlo, *Erasme et ses portraitistes*, 97–98).

92. Notice the epigraphic capitals.

93. On the Dürer and Erasmus, see Hayum, 'Dürer's Portrait of Erasmus', 650–87. Hayum's brilliant article greatly influenced my thinking about Erasmus and printing; but in the present context I am focussing somewhat differently on the engraving (as opposed to Erasmus's eulogy).

94. Mayor, *Prints and People*, plate 283.

95. Reproduction (plates 213, 214) from *Albrecht Du[e]rer: Master Printmaker.*

96. Allen 6:2 (ep 1536); cited by Gerlo, 25, *Erasme et ses portraitistes* 34–35: 'I too would like to be depicted by Dürer, for who would not like to be by so great an artist? But how could that be achieved? He began the work in charcoal in Brussels, but he probably mislaid that work long ago. If something could be done with the help of the medallion [Metsys's?] and his memory, let him do for me what he did for you [Dürer had engraved Pirckheimer already], and add a certain embonpoint'.

97. Allen 9:226 (ep 2466); cited by Gerlo, *Erasme et ses portraitistes*, 26.

98. Woodcut blocks are more durable than the metal plates which superceded them, according to Ivins (*Prints and Visual Communication*, 29).

99. Latin taken from Campbell et al., 'Quentin Matsys', 724.

100. Pliny has 'imaginem [deliniatam] in pariete carbone' (35.10.36). The medal itself (rather than in photographic reproduction), has a massy solidity which seems to underline this inscription. I was surprised by how *weighty* it was, when I saw it in the 1991 Henry VIII exhibition at Greenwich.

101. See next chapter.

102. Contrast his early Jerome engraving, in which three texts, in the three ancient languages, can be easily read. The open volume here evokes the *Adages*, perhaps, by the typographical layout—the visible paragraphing and indented quotations on the double page. It is also tempting to set this feature of Dürer's engraved book alongside a phrase in Fazio's description of the virtuosity of Jan van Eyck's representation of books in Jerome's study (below, chapter 2): 'Bibliotheca mirae artis, quippe quae, si paulum ab ea discedas, videatur introrsus recedere, & totos librose pandere, quorum capita modo [just their fore-edges] appropinquanti appareant'. Elizabeth Holt (like Panofsky before her) renders 'quorum capita modo' as 'only their main divisions', which aptly matches what happens when we view the Dürer (*A Documentary History of Art* [Doubleday, 1957], 1:200. Baxandall prefers 'just their main features' (M. Baxandall, *Giotto and the Orators: Humanist Observers of Painting in Italy and the Discovery of Pictorial Composition, 1350–1450* [Oxford, 1971], 106, note 140).

Chapter Two

1. 'Gerardus [pater] Romam se contulit. Illic scribendo, nam tum nondum erat ars typographorum, rem affatim parauit. Erat autem manu felicissima. Et vixit

iuueniliter. Mox applicauit animum ad honesta studia. Graece et Latine pulchre calluit. Quin et in iuris peritia non vulgariter profecerat. Nam Roma tunc doctis viris mire floruit. Audiuit Guarinum. Omnes auctores sua manu descripserat' (*Compendium vitae Erasmi*, Allen 1:47–48). On the authenticity of this biographical sketch see Allen 1, appendix 1, 575–78.

2. 'Praeerat illuc ludo literario tum Alexander Hegius Vestphalus, homo bonarum literarum minime expers et Graecarum nonnihil peritus, Rudolpho Agricola communicante; cuius amicitia familiariter vtebatur nuper ex Italia reuersi, vbi Guarinum Veronensem Ferrariae profitentem et alios aliquot eruditione celebres audiuerat. Ingenium Erasmi mox eluxit, quum statim quae docebatur perciperet et fideliter retineret, aequales suos omnes superans' (Beatus Rhenanus to Charles V, prefatory letter to *Erasmi omnia opera* [1540], Allen 1:57).

3. 'Deinde Daventriam deductus, Alexandrum Hegium, Rodolphi Agricolae, et Guarini Veronensis Discipulum, Virum sanctum, facundum aeque ac eruditum, gloriae humanae contemptorem audiuimus, nullo coaetaneorum, aut soldalium [*sic*] inferior in percipiendis aut retinendis pralectis' (Johann Herold, *Philopseudes, sive Prodes Erasmo Roterodamo v.c. contra Dialogum famosum Anonymi cuiusdam, Declamatio* [Basle, 1542]; in M. Mann Phillips, 'Une vie d'Erasme', *Bibliothèque d'Humanisme et Renaissance* 34 [1972], 229–37, 233).

4. 'Hanc differentiam Rodolphus Agricola docuit I. lib. de Inventione, quam P. Ramus sequutus est, sic ut aemulatus in hac arte in primis industriam illius viri, quem in studio logico, post antiquam illam Socraticorum Logicorum scholam . . . omnibus postea natis Logicis anteponere solitus est, dicereque palam ab uno Agricola verum germanae Logicae studium in Germania primum, tum per ejus sectatores et aemulos, toto terrarum orbe excitatum esse' (Petrus Ramus, *Dialectica A. Talaei praelectionibus illustrata* [Basle, 1569]; cited in N. Bruyère, *Méthode et dialectique dans l'oeuvre de La Ramée* [Paris, 1984], 305–6). As Bruyère points out, this edition of Talon's commentary on Ramus's *Dialectica*, revised well after Talon's death by Ramus himself during his stay at Basel, reproduces Ramus's own version of the significance and intellectual origins of his works.

5. The vagueness has a point to it. Hyma cites the following assessments of the circumstances of Erasmus's birth, which assume that Erasmus's father was in holy orders at the time: 'Et deinde, licet defectum natalum patiatur, ex illicito et, ut timet, incesto damnatoque coitu genitus' (Pope Leo X); 'Nunc populares tui, aliquot etiam vicini, viri boni, nobilis, te aiunt ex incesto natus concubitu, sordibus parentibus, altero sacrificulo, altera prostituta' (J. C. Scaliger, *Epistola* 15, in A. Hyma, *The Youth of Erasmus* [Ann Arbor, Mich., 1930], 53, 57).

6. On the *laudatio* see J. W. O'Malley, *Praise and Blame in Renaissance Rome: Rhetoric, Doctrine and Reform in the Sacred Orators of the Papal Court, ca. 1450–1521* (Durham, N.C., 1979); S. Camporeale, 'Lorenzo Valla tra medioevo e rinascimento: Encomion s. Thomae—1457', *Memorie Domenicane* 7 (1976), 11–194. There is an extensive literature on the absence of 'lives' as a genre in the Middle Ages, and the rediscovery of the form with early humanism. I have learned most from L. Panizza, 'Biography in Italy from the Middle Ages to the Renaissance: Seneca, Pagan, or Christian?' *Nouvelles de la republique des lettres* 2 (1984), 47–98. See also Margaret Mann Phillips, 'Erasmus and biography',

University of Toronto Quarterly 42 (1972–73), 185–201, 186: 'The consensus of opinion seems to be that such a conception [of the unified portrait of an individual] was foreign to the mediaeval mind. In the Middle Ages we find a number of kinds of descriptive writing: in poetry (epic and romance), in the chronicles, in the lives of saints. None of these are productive of biography in [the modern] sense'. See, however, D. A. Stauffer, *English Biography before 1700* (Cambridge, Mass. 1930), for a modified view. On portraits, see below.

7. Rice, *Saint Jerome*, 95; O'Malley, *Praise and Blame*, 85–87.

8. CWE 8:226, letter 1211.

9. CWE 7:16, letter 999.

10. On this feature of saints' lives, and the way textual devices encourage and sustain such participation, see, for instance, A. M. L. Fadda, 'Sulle traduzioni altomedievali di testi agiografici: Considerazioni in margine alla versione anglosassone della "Vita" di Sant'Egidio abate', in S. B. Gajano and L. Sebastiani (eds.), *Culto dei santi, istituzioni e classi sociali in età preindustriale* (Rome, 1984), 11–35; M. G. Bertolini, 'Istituzioni, miracoli, promozione del culto dei santi: Il caso di Clemente III antipapa (1080–1100)', ibid., 69–104; C. Bologna, 'Fra devozione e tentazione: Appunti su alcune metamorfosi nelle categorie letterarie dall'agiografia mediolatina ai testi romanzi medievali', ibid., 261–363; C. Frugoni, 'Il linguaggio dell'iconografia e delle visioni', ibid., 527–36; O. Redon and J. Gélis, 'Pour une étude du corps dans les récits de miracles', ibid., 563–72.

11. CWE 8:226, letter 1211).

12. Ibid., 243–44. Jonas's letter requesting the portrait of Colet does not survive; Erasmus's letter was published in the *Epistolae ad diuersos*. Two previous letters to Jonas apparently respond to requests for guidance on living a Christian life (876, 967A). Letter 876 contains another interesting comment on biography: 'You have sent me not so much a letter as affection undiluted, all the warmth of a very loving heart. In heaven's name, what breathing life, what power it has to move one and touch the heart in many ways! You try to draw a picture of me, but all you produced is a reflection of yourself, and while exalting my eloquence you exhibit your own' (145).

13. It is striking how consistently a claim is made for some kind of connection with the original emulated, as Erasmus claimed Rudolph Agricola as his intellectual teacher and mentor (see below, chapter 3). See also Augustine's *Confessions*. See J. Swindells, *Victorian Writing and Working Women* on working-class autobiography and high fiction, for a modern counterpart.

14. Here I find Victor Turner's distinction between 'liminoid' and 'liminal' rituals helpful (in spite of the ugliness of 'liminoid'). Liminal rites are those which an individual is obliged to perform in order to make a transition recognised by the community (for instance, from childhood to adulthood); 'liminoid' or 'quasi-liminal' rites share features with liminal rites (for instance, the function of acknowledged transition from one state to another), but are more flexibly situated in relation to normal social practice. Turner designates 'pilgrimage', for instance, as 'liminoid': 'Pilgrimage has some of the liminal phase attributes in passage rites: release from mundane structure; homogenization of status; simplicity of dress and behavior; communitas, both on the journey, and as a characteristic of the goal, which is itself a source of communitas, healing, and renewal. . . . But since

it is voluntary, not an obligatory social mechanism to mark the transition from one state or status to another within the mundane sphere, pilgrimage is liminoid rather than liminal' (V. Turner and E. Turner, *Image and Pilgrimage in Christian Culture: Anthropological Perspectives* [New York, 1978], 253–54). This is certainly how Erasmus represents the choice of the *bonae litterae* as the basis for a life—as a voluntary but transformatory rite of passage.

15. The *Vita Hieronymi* was issued separately by Frobenius in 1517; I have used the copy of this edition in Firestone Library, Princeton University. See W. K. Ferguson, *Opuscula Erasmi* (L'Aia, 1933), and now A. M. Guerra (ed.), *Vita di san Girolamo: Edizione critica e traduzione* (Rome, 1988). The *Vita Hieronymi* and Erasmus's commentaries on Jerome's letters will form volume 61 of the Toronto *Complete Works* (J. C. Olin, 'Erasmus and Saint Jerome: An Appraisal of the Bond', in Weiland and Frijhoff, *Erasmus of Rotterdam*, 182–86; 182).

16. 'Equidem haud sum nescius veterum permultos in hac fuisse sententia, vt pium et officiosum esse ducerent, in commodum publicum apte confictis narrationibus abuti; nempe vel ad vitam recte pieque instituendam, vel ad erigendos et inflammandos ad honesti studium animos, vel ad fulciendam quorundam inbecillitatem, vel ad territandos impios, quos neque ratio corrigit neque mouet charitas, vel ad illustrandam miraculis sanctorum hominum gloriam. . . . Ego nihil arbitror esse rectius quam eiusmodi describere sanctos, cuiusmodi fuerunt ipsi' (Guerra, *Vita*, 33–35).

17. See F. Cavallera, *Saint Jérôme: Sa vie et son oeuvre* (2 vols.) (Louvain and Paris, 1922), 2:145; Guerra, *Vita*, 11–13. See also Rice: 'The life of Jerome with which he prefaced his edition is a saint's life written to an unprecedented standard of accuracy and critical skepticism and a turning point in Renaissance hagiography' (Rice, *Saint Jerome*, 130).

18. Guerra, *Vita*, 38.

19. 'Ex huius igitur libris omnibus lustratis, quod sparsim annotare licuit in narrationis ordinem redegimus, nihil admentientes, quod arbitremur abunde magnum esse miraculum ipsum Hieronymum tot egregiis voluminum monumentis sese nobis exprimentem. Quod si cui nihil absque miraculorum portentis placere potest, is legat Hieronymianos libros in quibus tot pene miracula sunt quot sententiae' (ibid.).

20. For a discussion of *Lives of Jerome*, including Erasmus's, see Cavallera, *Saint Jérôme* 2:135–45.

21. See Peter Brown, 'A Debate on the Holy', in *The Making of Late Antiquity* (Cambridge, Mass., 1978), 1–26; 'The Rise and Function of the Holy Man in Late Antiquity', in *Society and the Holy in Late Antiquity* (Berkeley, 1982), 103–52; 'Society and the Supernatural: A Medieval Change', ibid., 302–32; *The Cult of the Saints* (Chicago, 1981); 'The Saint as Exemplar', *Representations* 1 (1983), 1–25 (also in J. S. Hawley [ed.], *Saints and Virtues* [Berkeley and Los Angeles, 1987]).

22. Ridderbos, *Saint and Symbol*, 1. See the early Jeromes in Ridderbos.

23. This verbal sleight of hand is not original to Erasmus, though I think he is the first fully to take advantage of the move. A century before Erasmus, in one of a series of orations in praise of Saint Jerome, P. P. Vergerio had already called his eloquence prodigious, his knowledge miraculous: 'Is it not obvious that there was

something divine about this man?' (cited in Rice, *Saint Jerome*, 99). Between about 1392 and 1408, Vergerio delivered ten panegyric orations to Saint Jerome on his feast day, September 30 (O'Malley, *Praise and Blame*, 85–86; Rice, *Saint Jerome*, 95–99). Valla uses the same formulation to establish Thomas Aquinas's claim to the status of saint and martyr, in his *Encomium sancti Thomae Aquinatis* (in L. Geiger [ed.], *Vierteljahrsschrift für Kultur der Renaissance* [Leipzig, 1886]; reprinted in E. Garin [ed.], *L. Valla: Opera omnia* [Turin, 1962], 340–52). See Camporeale, 'Lorenzo Valla tra medioevo e rinascimento'.

24. See below for Carpaccio's corresponding installation of Bessarion (humanist man of letters) as Augustine inspired by Jerome in *Saint Augustine in Saint Jerome's study*.

25. As usual, here, I consider the original volume as an integral cultural artifact for the purposes of 'reading' what Erasmus offered his sixteenth-century reader.

26. CWE 3:256 (letter 396).

27. CWE 3:259 (letter 396).

28. P. Antin, 'Autour du songe de S. Jérôme', in *Recueil sur saint Jérôme* (Brussels, 1968), 71–100, 75.

29. Ep. 22, 30 (383–84), to Eustochium, cited from Antin, 'Autour du songe', 74–75 (my translation). For the textual provenance, see Antin, 'Autour du songe', 71.

30. Cited in Antin, 'Autor du songe', 75.

31. 'Inter haec vero dum immodico quodam et iuuenili calore et puerilium amore studiorum plus satis indulget exprimendis M. Tullii Platonisque dialogis, nam id tum, ni fallor, agebat, et hos magis nititur effingere quam sermonem apostolicum, somnio diuinitus immisso, raptus ad tribunal Dei, accusatus quod Ciceronianus esset non Christianus, denique plagis emendatus, sibi redditus est, vt ipse refert in epistola cuius initium "Audi filia." Qua de re quid sentiam fortasse nonnihil dicturi sumus, cum ad eum locum erit ventum' (Guerra, *Vita*, 54).

32. 'Haec est illa fabula quam memoriter tenent omnes etiam ii qui ne uerbum quidem unquam legerunt in scriptis Hieronymianis. Vapulabat, inquiunt, Hieronymus quod Ciceronem legerit' (cited in Antin, 'Autour du songe', 91). Erasmus continues: 'Ac mira quadam religione sic ab omnibus bonis abstinent literis ut nec sacras attingant, ne forte imprudentes incidant in aliquod uerbum Ciceronis & cum Hieronymo uapulent & tum sibi uidentur Apostolis proximi, si quam spurcissime loquantur. (. . .) Nec hoc unquam sensit Hieronymus Ciceronem non esse legendum, sed in hoc duntaxat ut diuina rectius intelligamus & commodius tractemus. Alioqui quid sibi uult quod scribit ad oratorem Magnum? (Ep. 70) . . . Vnde recte statuit Leo decimus, qui cum haec scriberem Romanam tenebat sedem, ne quis in scholis publicis quas Vniuersitates uocant, ultra quinque annos sic in rhetoricis aut poeticis literis studium omne consumeret, ut nihil attingeret grauiorum studiorum. Verum quod uetuit in poeticis, idem uetuit in philosophicis. Nos quoque pueri quondam libris aliquot istorum stolidam superstitionem explosimus, qui praetextu religionis politiores literas, quia non didicerint, insectantur. His acceptum ferimus, quod autorum ut quisque est lectu dignissimus, ita deprauatissimum habemus. Horum opera factum est, & ut in restituendo Hieronymo, doctis aliquot plus sudoris impensum sit quam ipse insumpserit scribendo.

Quin insuper sacrilegi tantum ac tam sacrum uirum audent uocare poeticum parumque religiosum, quod non scribat quaestiones Scotico stilo. Quasi uero Paulus aut prophetae aut omnino quisquam ueterum ac uere Christum spirantium theologorum, ad istum scripserit modum. Ne ipse quidem Aristoteles homo ethnicus, nec inter philosophos admodum probatae uitae, qui tantum auri reliquerit ut a Plinio inter Croesos et Crassos referatur, deinde talium argutiarum pater unquam tam sophistice nugatus est quam nugantur isti qui se diuinarum literarum doctores & interpretes uocant' (ibid., 91–92).

33. 'Scio ego nonnullos, eorum praesertim qui sibi sanctiores et religiosiores uidentur, ausuros meum institutum hoc laboremque reprehendere, ut indignum christiano homine, ubi adhortor ceteros ad librorum saecularium lectionem, quorum, quod studiosior esset Hieronymus, caesum se flagellis ad tribunal Dei fuisse confitetur, accusatumque quod ciceronianus foret, non christianus, quasi non posset fidelis esse et idem tullianus. Eoque spopondisse, et id diris execrationibus, libros saeculares postea se non esse lecturum' (E. Garin [ed.], *Prosatori latini del quattrocento* [Milan and Naples, n.d.], 612).

34. Ibid., 612.

35. Ibid., 620.

36. Ibid., 618.

37. In the preface to Warham, in addition to the more obvious stylistic similarities (like the repeated rhetorical questions, and the listing of Jerome's outstanding talents), see the comparison of Jerome with a bee, 'collecting the best of everything to make the honey stored in his work' (CWE 3:261), and Valla's 'These ancient theologians seem to me like bees which fly to distant pastures, to bring together the sweetest nectar and softest wax' (Garin, *Prosatori latini*, 622). In the *Vita*, Erasmus specifies Valla amongst those who have written on Jerome's eloquence; he also picks out Peter and Paul, as Valla does, as outstandingly eloquent.

38. Guerra, *Vita*, 87.

39. CWE 3:256.

40. For representations of Jerome as penitent, see Rice, *Saint Jerome*, and Ridderbos, *Saint and Symbol*. Both authors indicate a fairly precise period during which paintings and engravings of *Jerome in His Study* were in vogue—running roughly from the 1430s to the early seventeenth century.

41. CWE 3:265–66 (letter 396).

42. It might be worth pursuing Erasmus's use of the phoenix image for himself in later life.

43. CWE 3:108 (letter 335). I shall return to this letter to Leo X shortly.

44. There are precedents for this re-embodiment of the scholar-saint. Art historians consider the Jan van Eyck, Detroit Jerome panel to be, in all probability, a portrait of Cardinal Nicolò Albergati (Rice, *Saint Jerome*, 108). Rice continues: 'Van Eyck has given Cardinal Albergati's features to St. Jerome, an early example of the kind of travesty portraiture that would become fairly common later on: St. Antonino, archbishop of Florence (d. 1459), Cardinal Nicholas of Cusa (d. 1464), the French humanist and philosopher Jacques Lefèvre d'Etaples (d. 1536), Cardinal Albrecht von Brandenburg (d. 1545), even Martin Luther, are other examples of churchmen and scholars portrayed as St. Jerome. The practice was at once a flattering testimonial that the sitter possessed at least some of Jerome's

titles and merits and an act of sympathetic magic by which the devotee declared his special veneration for Jerome and sought to secure his blessing and protection' (and particularly references, 239, note 77). See also Ridderbos, *Saint and Symbol*, 109.

45. 'Tempus omne studiis et orationibus partiebatur, bonam etiam noctium partem his operis addens; minima portio dabatur somno, minor cibo, nulla ocio. Studii lassitudinem recreabat deprecatio, aut hymnus: mox velut integer ad intermissam lectionem redibat. Relegebat vniuersam bibliothecam suam, veterum studiorum memoriam sibi renouans; sacras litteras ad verbum ediscebat. Meditabatur in prophetis, in eruendis oraculorum mysteriis vigilantissimus. Ex euangelicis et apostolicis litteris, velut ex purissimis fontibus, Christi philosophiam hauriebat. Primus enim ad pietatem gradus est, scire autoris tui dogmata. Ceteros interpretes adhibito delectu iudicioque legebat, nullum omnino scriptorem praetermittens, vnde non aliquid decerperet, non ethnicos, non haereticos. Nouerat enim vir prudentissimus ex sterquilinio legere aurum. . . . Quoque certior esset memoria et paratior vsus, quicquid legerat, id in locos digerebat, compositis singulis vt affinitatis aut pugnantiae ratio postulabat. Felicibus ingeniis dictu mirum quantopere fauerit, praesertim quae facundiae quoque dos commendabat, adeo vt haereticos etiam laudibus ornaret, libenter, si licuisset, fidei vitium eruditioni condonaturus: cum primis autem Origenis, quem suum appellat, et cuius homilias aliquot adolescens adhuc Latinitate donauit' (Guerra, *Vita*, 52–53).

46. 'Posthac quando per vniuersum orbem Christianum reuixerunt bonae litterae, et non pauca bonae spei ingenia ad veterem illam ac germanam theologiam expergisci coeperunt. Hieronymum veluti renatum communibus studiis complectamur omnes: hunc singuli sibi ceu peculiarem vindicent. Olim Homerum septem vrbes sibi certatim asserebant. At Hieronymum vicinitatis iure rapiat hinc Dalmatia, hinc Pannonia, hinc Italia. Stridon sibi gratuletur, quae tam eximium orbi lumen produxerit. Triplici nomine sibi gratuletur Italia; primum quod erudierit, deinde quod per baptismum genuerit Christo, postremo quod sanctissimi corpusculi pignus apud se seruet. Hunc vt suum agnoscant Galliae, quas omnes sic peragrauit, quasque tot libris nominatim dedicatis instituit. Hunc sibi vindicent Hispani, quos aliquot epistolis ad illos scriptis illustrauit. Hunc exosculetur Germania, quam vnico licet volumine satis et docuit et nobilitauit. Hunc gemino nomine complectatur Graecia, primum ob linguae commercium, deinde quod orbis magistra huius viri litteris vicissim adiuta sit. Complectatur Aegyptus, quam toties inuisit, quaeque ex doctissimo nobis reddiderit doctiorem. Amplectantur Arabes et Saraceni, quos sua vicinitate reddidit claros. Hunc colant Hebraei, quorum sermonem et litteras tantis sudoribus pararit. Hunc omnis quidem rapiat Syria, in qua magnam vitae suae partem exegit' (ibid., 90–91).

47. 'Gregorium Nazianzenum praeceptorem suum appellat, et hoc interpretante se sacras didicisse litteras testatur. Verum vbi nam audierit hominem, aut quanto tempore parum mihi compertum est. . . . Alexandriam sese contulit iam semicanus, quo videlicet ex Didymi consuetudine, quem quod a puero captus esset oculis "Videntem" appellat, summam imponeret manum studio sacrarum litterarum. Etiamsi Ruffinus calumniatur Hieronymum non plus mense Didymi consuetudine vsum fuisse, sed ridicule tamen, vt iam vere. Nec enim refert quanto tempore verseris apud praeceptorem, sed quantum proficias' (ibid., 62–63).

48. See below, chapter 3.

49. See CWE 3:348: 'In the summer of 1515, when [Erasmus] arrived in Basel from England and found Froben printing *Jani Damiani Senensis ad Leonem X pont. max. De expeditione in Turcas elegeia*, 4°, August 1515, he seems (the suggestion is Allen's) to have taken the opportunity to circulate four important letters written earlier that year, Ep 335 addressed to Leo X and two associated with it (Epp 344 and 333), and his long answer to Maarten van Dorp's strictures on the *Moria* (Ep 337), which was in future to be printed regularly with the *Moria* and not with the *Epistolae*. These letters had no preface; they seem to have been reprinted, perhaps at Louvain by Thierry Martens later in the same year and at Leipzig by Valentine Schumann in 1516'.

50. The fourth is Erasmus's answer to Dorp's criticism of the *Moria*, and of Erasmus's scriptural emendation, which I discuss in chapter 4.

51. CWE 3:264–65.

52. CWE 3:109 (letter 335).

53. In the dedication of the *Novum Instrumentum* to Leo X, Erasmus once more manages to include Warham. One might regard this as the fifth letter in the series. For Erasmus's pattern of dedications, including multiple dedications, see J. Hoyoux, 'Les moyens d'existence d'Érasme', *Bibliothèque d'humanisme et renaissance 5* (1944), 7–59, 34–41.

54. See chapter 1.

55. CWE 3:263.

56. CWE, 155 (letter 494).

57. And in letter 493, from Budé to Erasmus, which refers to the Deloynes letter, and which appeared in the same volume of letters in 1517.

58. Rice, *Saint Jerome*, 132–33; J. C. Olin, 'Erasmus and Saint Jerome: The Close Bond and its Significance', *Erasmus of Rotterdam Society Yearbook 7* (1987), 33–53; 'Erasmus and Saint Jerome: An Appraisal of the Bond', in Weiland and Frijhoff, *Erasmus of Rotterdam*, 182–86.

59. Rice, *Saint Jerome*, 132–33.

60. Throughout this discussion, as in that of the diptych in the last chapter, I am assuming that Erasmus played a large part in determining the composition. If one compares the diptych with the rest of Metsys's oeuvre, these appear more complex and studied in their arrangement of figures, and their attributes.

61. See the sand-shaker in the 'van Eyck' Detroit Jerome.

62. Particularly in the infra-red photograph of the Hampton Court original. See the reproduction in Campbell et al., 'Quentin Matsys'.

63. See Rice, *Saint Jerome*, and Ridderbos, *Saint and Symbol*, for convenient reproductions of comparable Jeromes, e.g., Colantonio, *Jerome in His Study* (Ridderbos, *Saint and Symbol*, 45); Dürer, *Saint Jerome in His Study* (Rice, *Saint Jerome*, 110; Matteo di Giovanni da Siena, *Saint Jerome in His Study* (105); Pieter Coeck van Aelst (attrib.), *Saint Jerome in His Study Meditates on the Four Last Things* (167); Joos van Cleve, *Saint Jerome in His Study* (148).

64. See Helen Roberts, 'St Augustine', 295: 'Scissors are prominent also in Dürer's engraving of *St. Jerome in His Study* of 1514 . . . and Ghirlandaio's *St. Jerome in His Study.* . . . Aside from their place in writers' equipment, they were in at least one instance given a symbolic meaning in connection with use of them

in the Church. The thirteenth century Bishop of Mende, Guilielmus Durantis, in his *Rationale Divinorum Officiorum*, included the following symbolism: "the snuffers or scissors for trimming the lamps are the divine words by which men amputate the legal titles of the law, and reveal the shining spirit, according to that saying, 'Ye shall eat old store, and bring forth the old because of the new' " (William Durandus, *The Symbolism of Churches and Church Ornaments*, tr. John M. Neale and Benjamin Webb, London, 1906, p. 54). If this interpretation had been a part of general Church symbolism, the scissors could conceivably refer to the exegetical function of both Jerome and Augustine'.

65. See Rice, *Saint Jerome*, 160: '[Molanus] noted that painters often put a candle on Jerome's work table when they showed him in his study. He allowed it no symbolic meaning. It refers to a passage from the preface to his *Commentary on Ezekiel* where he complained in his old age that his sight was so dim that he could no longer read his Hebrew books by candlelight'.

66. Domenico Ghirlandaio's *Saint Jerome* (1480), in the Chiesa d'Ognissanti, Florence (which contains a prominent lighted candle, with adjacent wick-trimmer), originally bore the inscription: 'Redde nos claros lampas radiosa / sine qua terra tota est umbrosa' (Make us bright, shining light, without which the whole earth is in shadow). Candle and wick-trimmer (to restore clarity to the guttering flame) perfectly capture this version of Jerome. See Martin Kemp, 'The Taking and Use of Evidence: With a Botticellian Case Study', *Art Journal* 44 (1984), 207–15; 215 (note 24, text corrected), and chapter 1, above.

67. See Baxandall, *Giotto and the Orators*, 98–111, 163–68.

68. Ibid., 106; Latin text, 165: 'Eius est tabula . . . Hieronymus viventi persimilis, biblioteca mirae artis, quippe quae, si paulum ab ea discedas, videatur introrsus recedere et totos libros pandere, quorum capita modo appropinquanti appareant'. *De viris illustribus* was not printed until the eighteenth century; there are manuscript versions in the Vatican Library and the Biblioteca Nazionale, Rome (ibid., 99).

69. See ibid., plate 10(b) for the appropriate detail; Rice, *Saint Jerome*, 107, for the complete work.

70. Books are equally meticulously represented in other van Eyck paintings, notably those in the Ghent polyptych.

71. See the paintings indicated in chapter 1, note 70, above.

72. On this painting see definitively Roberts, 'St. Augustine'.

73. For a reproduction of this painting, see P. Fortini Brown, *Venetian Narrative Painting in the Age of Carpaccio* (New Haven, 1988), 129, plate 15, as well as for relevant discussion of Carpaccio's narrative paintings. Is what is on the open book more legible now than that in the *Saint Augustine?*

74. Whilst this style is called 'mannerist', its precisely and three-dimensionally rendered representation of the human body gives the viewer the confusing sense that portraiture, in particular, is 'real', rather than symbolic. See, for example, the portrait of a young man with a book, *Portrait of A Youth*, by Bronzino (reproduced in M. Lowry, *The World of Aldus Manutius*).

75. See the many reproductions of the Ghent altarpiece.

76. Natalie Davis, 'Beyond the Market: Books as Gifts in Sixteenth-Century France', *Transactions of the Royal Historical Society* 33 (1983), 69–88.

77. For another striking rendering of shelves of books in juxtaposition with a pensive Jerome and his own text of scripture, see Colantonio's *Jerome in His Study* (Ridderbos, *Saint and Symbol*, 45).

78. Also striking is the collection of objects around the small lectern at which both scholars work: sand-shaker (if we agree that the sand-shaker in the Gilles panel 'belongs' to Erasmus), inkwell, and brush (if it is a brush).

79. The scissors appear to direct our attention from *Novum Testamentum* to *Hieronymus*. Are we entitled to do anything with 'GRATIA' on the facing page?

80. Reproduction, A. Smart, *The Renaissance and Mannerism in Northern Europe and Spain* (London, 1972), 135.

81. For a convenient representation of this detail see Baxandall, *Giotto*, plate 10(c).

82. For the pilaster panel see Meyer, 212, *Handbook of Ornament*, plate 131, 1 ('Italian Renascence'); for the figure on the pilaster capital see plate 67, 5 ('relief, Italian Renascence').

83. Reproductions, Rice, *Saint Jerome*, 148, 107.

84. CWE 3:89–90 (letter 333 to Cardinal Riario).

85. On *plus ultra*, the pillars of Hercules, and Charles V, see E. E. Rosenthal, 'The Invention of the Columnar Device of Emperor Charles V at the Court of Burgundy in Flanders in 1516', *Journal of the Warburg and Courtauld Institutes* 36 (1973), 198–230. Possibly, additionally, the pilaster stands for Rome/Italy, and the Greek lettering of the inscription on the book for Greece—Erasmus's double cultural heritage.

86. For these tropes of studiousness in relation to Jerome, see Rice, *Saint Jerome*, and Ridderbos, *Saint and Symbol*. For the prosperity compare Holbein's portrait of George Gisze.

87. This is particularly clear in the infrared photograph in Campbell et al., 'Quentin Matsys', where the carefully rendered fur, obscured by restorations, reappears. In the Holbein Warham portrait, Erasmus's dress is even more discreetly lavish.

88. That this *is* a pouch can be clearly seen in the Hampton Court panel; in the Louvre version it looks like a metal ornament around Erasmus's neck.

89. In Dürer's *Flight into Egypt* woodcut (1504), Joseph wears a closely similar pouch at his waist (reproduction, *Albrecht Du[e]rer: Master Printmaker*, 107, plate 78). Here, of course, the Holy Family are travellers. In other Dürer prints, like *Ecce Homo* (1498–99), ibid., 70, plate 51, burghers and Pharisees wear prominent pouches.

90. For Dutch graphic representation of this mercantile world in the seventeenth century see Schama, *Embarrassment of Riches*.

91. On the 'visual culture' of the Dutch, see Alpers, *The Art of Describing*, xxv: 'For art to have a history in [the] Italian sense is the exception, not the rule. Most artistic traditions mark what persists and is sustaining, not what is changing, in culture. What I propose to study then is not the *history* of Dutch art, but the Dutch *visual culture*'.

92. In what follows I have had the benefit of the able guidance of Patricia Brown, of the History of Art Department at Princeton, to whom I express my great gratitude for sharing her current work on the Carpaccio painting *St. Augustine in St. Jerome's Study*, with me.

93. See Ridderbos, *Saint and Symbol*, 26–29.

94. Ibid., 41–62.

95. Ibid., 28.

96. Roberts, 'St. Augustine'.

97. We will need to notice that it still appears in the 'Vita et transitus Hieronymi', reprinted among the *spuria* in Erasmus's edition of Jerome's *Opera*.

98. The letter is reprinted in Roberts, 'St. Augustine'.

99. Kemp, 'Taking and Use of Evidence', 207–15.

100. See the details reproduced in Roberts 'St. Augustine', and Kemp, 'Taking and Use of Evidence'.

101. These details, as we have seen, are remarkably faithfully rendered in the Erasmus portraits too. See above, chapter 1.

102. Kemp, 'Taking and Use of Evidence', 215.

103. By contrast, the edition of Augustine's works, produced late in his life, was a collaborative enterprise, in which he acted only as a figurehead.

104. See also the sumptuous fifteenth-century miniatures of Jerome in his study which preface the *epistolae* in Florentine manuscripts of the period, reproduced in A. Garzelli (ed.), *Miniatura Fiorentina del Rinascimento, 1440–1525* (2 vols.) (Florence, 1985), plates 826, 828, 830, 832, and 923.

105. Allen 7:431 (ep 2018); cited in Gerlo, *Erasme et ses portraitistes*, 25.

106. Does anyone tell us so, however, apart from Erasmus himself?

107. Rice suggests that Dürer initiated the tradition when he included a skull in his Jerome engraving of 1514 (*Saint Jerome*, 111, 165).

108. See the Joos van Cleve and Pieter Coeck van Aelst paintings, and the Dürer engraving; see Rice, *Saint Jerome*, reproductions, 110, 148, 167, 168; and text, 165–66. The Joos van Cleve *Saint Jerome in His Study* carries the motto, pinned to the wall, 'respice finem' (think on your end).

CHAPTER THREE

1. See above, Introduction.

2. For the case for the persistence of a more traditionally scholastic view of logic/dialectic, however, see J. M. Fletcher, 'Change and Resistance to Change: A Consideration of the Development of English and German Universities during the Sixteenth Century', *History of Universities* 1 (1981), 1–36; J. K. McConica, 'Humanism and Aristotle in Tudor Oxford', *English Historical Review* 94 (1979), 291–317.

3. G. C. Huisman, *Rudolph Agricola: A Bibliography of Printed Works and Translations* (Groningen, 1985). This work replaces W. J. Ong, *Ramus and Talon Inventory* (Cambridge, Mass., 1958) and W. Risse, *Bibliographia Logica: Verzeichnis der Druckschriften zur Logik mit Angabe ihrer Fundorte. Band I, 1472–1800* (Hildesheim, 1965), for Agricola editions, since Huisman incorporates these authors' work.

4. Inevitably one's view of precisely who were the influential originators of the sustained study of Agricola will be subjective, and in my case probably related directly to my own initiation into the subject. One should probably add N. W. Gilbert, *Renaissance Concepts of Method* (New York, 1960), and W. Risse's *Die Logik der Neuzeit*, vol. 1 (Stuttgart, 1964).

5. C. Prantl, *Geschichte der Logik im Abendlande* (Leipzig, 1870) vol. 4, chap. 21; W. and M. Kneale, *The Development of Logic* (Oxford, 1962) (though they cite him as 'Agrippa'!); Risse, *Die Logik der Neuzeit*; Vasoli, *La dialettica*; Vasoli, 'La retorica e la dialettica umanistiche e le origini delle concezioni moderne del "metodo"', *Il Verri* 35, no. 6 (1970), 250–306; L. Jardine, *Francis Bacon: Discovery and the Art of Discourse* (Cambridge, 1974), chapter 1; 'The Place of Dialectic Teaching in Sixteenth-Century Cambridge', *Studies in the Renaissance* 21 (1974), 31–62; 'Humanism and the Sixteenth-Century Cambridge Arts Course', *History of Education* 4 (1975), 16–31; 'Lorenzo Valla and the Intellectual Origins of Humanist Dialectic', *Journal of the History of Philosophy* 15 (1977), 143–63; 'Humanism and the Teaching of Logic', in Kretzmann, Kenny, and Pinborg, *The Cambridge History of Later Medieval Philosophy*, section 43, 797–807; 'Humanistic Logic', in C. B. Schmitt, E. Kessler and Q. R. D. Skinner (eds.), *The Cambridge History of Renaissance Philosophy*, section 2.2 (Cambridge, 1988).

6. Kneale and Kneale, *Development*, 300.

7. Agricola biographies tend to be in Dutch. The standard such ones are: H. E. J. M. van der Velden, *Rodolphus Agricola (Roelof Huusman) een Nederlandsch Humanist der vijftiende Eeuw* (Leiden, 1911); M. A. Nauwelaerts, *Rodolphus Agricola* (Den Haag, 1963). Such detail as there is concerning his life (and much of this paper will be concerned with the *sources* of such detail) is to be found in the following places: F. G. Adelmann, 'Dr. Dietrich von Plieningen zu Schaubeck', *Ludwigsburger Geschichtsblätter* 28 (1976), 9–139; R. Pfeiffer, *History of Classical Scholarship from 1300 to 1850* (Oxford, 1976); J. E. Sandys, *A History of Classical Scholarship* (3 vols.) (Cambridge, 1903–8), vol. 2; R. Radouant, 'L'union de l'éloquence et de la philosophie au temps de Ramus', *Revue d'histoire littéraire de la France* 31 (1924), 161–92; P. S. Allen, 'The Letters of Rudolph Agricola', *English Historical Review* 21 (1906), 302–17; K. Hartfelder (ed.), *Unedierte Briefe von Rudolf Agricola: Ein Beitrag zur Geschichte des Humanismus*, Festschrift der Badischen Gymnasien, gewidmet der Universität Heidelberg (Karlsruhe, 1886); P. Pfeifer (ed.), *Commentarii seu index vitae Rudolphi Agricolae Phrisii . . .*, *Serapeum* 10 (1849), 97–107. On Agricola as a painter see M. Baxandall, 'Rudolph Agricola and the Visual Arts', *Institution und Kunstwissenschaft: Festschrift für Hans Swarzenski*, 409–18. See also L. W. Spitz, *The Religious Renaissance of the German Humanists* (Cambridge, Mass., 1963), 20–40; de Vocht, *History of the Foundation and the Rise of the Collegium Trilingue Lovaniense*, especially vol. 1.

8. For a good example of this type of generalised argument for Agricola's importance see Spitz, *Religious Renaissance*. The classic, influential account, of course, is W. H. Woodward, *Studies in Education during the Age of the Renaissance, 1400–1600* (Cambridge, 1924), where twenty-odd pages on Agricola (79–103) are dovetailed neatly in between those on Guarino Veronese, Leo Battista Alberti, and Matteo Palmieri on the one hand, and Erasmus, Budé, Vives, and Melanchthon on the other. Woodward also has a (helpful) chronological table which confirms this seamless development from Italy to northern Europe via Agricola.

9. There is another candidate for 'best-known work': a letter which became known as the *De formando studio*, first published by Jacobus Faber (Deventer,

1508), and frequently reprinted with corresponding works by Erasmus and Melanchthon.

10. T. Heath, 'Logical Grammar, Grammatical Logic, and Humanism in Three German Universities', *Studies in the Renaissance* 18 (1971), 9–64.

11. Faber brought Hegius's works out in two volumes. The first, containing Hegius's poems, is somewhat confusingly entitled: *Alexandri Hegii Gymnasi / archae iampridem Daventriensis diligentissimi ar / tium professoris clarissimi philosophi presbyteri / poetae utriusque linguae docti Carmina et gracia et / elegantia; cum ceteris eius opusculis quae subiciuntur—De scientia et eo quod scitur contra Academicos / De triplici anima vegetabili: sensili: et rationali / De vera pasche inveniendi ratione Quam ex Isaac / Arguro greco excepisse apparet De Rhetorica De / arte et inertia / De sensu et sensili De moribus / De philosophia / De incarnationis misterio Erotemata.* 'This title is misleading as the volume contains only the *Carmina* and not the *cetera opuscula*' (J. Ijsewijn, 'Alexander Hegius [† 1498], *Invectiva in modos significandi*', in I. D. McFarlane [ed.], *Renaissance Studies: Six Essays* [Edinburgh and London, 1972], 1–20, 2). The second volume *did* contain the *opuscula* (ibid., 3). Faber's prefatory letter explains that the title is deliberate: 'I have deliberately decided to issue [Hegius's poems] in advance of his other productions, even though the latter were far more accomplished, for I shall thereby come to know what reception they can expect. When I perceive that they have won approval . . . I shall then be more ready, without suffering the printer's importunate insistence as I do now, to send his other works to the press to be printed' (CWE 2:65–69 [letter 174], 68). Here, already, we have an early editor (and printer) constructing a story for their readers, while twentieth-century scholarship discards the 'tale' in favour of hard print 'facts'.

12. Allen 1:384–88 (ep 174); 385–86. See Appendices, this volume.

13. As we have already seen, prefatory letters customarily 'tell' the reader pertinent things. We shall see that a good number of prefatory letters to minor works in what I shall call the Erasmus 'circle' advertise connections between that work and forthcoming or promised, doctrinally or intellectually related works.

14. So that we keep the facts straight: Hegius became headmaster of the Deventer school in 1483; he taught the top class. Erasmus was at the Deventer school until some time in 1484, when he was withdrawn because of an outbreak of plague; he had not reached the top class. In my view, the best account by far of Erasmus's life and intellectual influences during the Deventer and Steyn periods is to be found in C. Reedijk, *The Poems of Desiderius Erasmus with Introduction and Notes* (Leiden, 1956), chapter 3, 'His Brethren in Apollo' (42–86). Faber was at the school some time later (but before Hegius's death in 1498), and stayed on as a master.

15. Sixteenth-century editors seem to have been in the habit of pointing out to fellow editors their failure adequately to acknowledge the author they themselves championed. When Gabriel Harvey published his *Ciceronianus* in 1577, Thomas Hatcher, who had recently published the collected works of Walter Haddon, wrote to Harvey expressing surprise at the omission of Haddon from Harvey's list of great Cambridge Ciceronian orators (see V. F. Stern, *Gabriel Harvey: His Life, Marginalia and Library* [Oxford, 1979]). If the account I give here of how such epistolary exchanges were orchestrated is correct, Hatcher (a friend of Harvey's)

may well have expected such a letter to provide a prefatory epistle for a second edition of Harvey's *Ciceronianus*, which would then serve simultaneously as an additional embellishment for the Harvey work, a connecting thread between Harvey's work and other contemporary English scholars, and a 'puff' for Hatcher's own publication.

16. Ibid., 68–69.

17. Erasmus's Libanius did not apparently in fact reach print until Thierry Martens published it in 1519, although the prefatory letter to Nicholas Ruistre is dated 1503 (Allen 1:390–93 [ep 177]). Allen suggests that this was because Martens was not yet in a position to set Greek type in 1503 (1:390). On printers of Greek manuals, see A. T. Grafton and L. Jardine, *From Humanism to the Humanities: Education and the Liberal Arts in Fifteenth- and Sixteenth-Century Europe* (London and Cambridge, Mass., 1986), chapter 5.

18. I am coining this term *purposive* for documents in which authors affirm one thing, but use the occasion to make further connections which give the document a further purpose.

19. On the connection between the Paffraet publishing house and the Deventer school, see Reedijk, *Poems of Desiderius Erasmus*, 25; P. C. van der Meersch, *Recherches sur la vie et les travaux des imprimeurs néerlandais* (Gand, 1856).

20. Huisman, *Rudolph Agricola*, 4.

21. See Appendices for the full text of the 1508 *Quid cani et balneo* adage.

22. Mann Phillips, *Adages* 1.1.1-1.5.100; CWE 31:348–51, 351.

23. W. A. Copinger, *Supplement to Hain's Repertorium Bibliographicum* (3 vols.) (Milan, 1950), items 2430, 2431.

24. There were also editions by Johannes de Westfalia, Louvain, 1483; and edited by Jacopus Canter, published by Peter von Friedberg, Mainz, about 1495 (ibid., items 4768, 4767).

25. Ibid., item 3328.

26. For an account of early Agricola publishing history as I have so far been able to piece it together, see Appendices.

27. 'Quod petis, ut Luciani Mycillum, quem Latinum feci, tibi mittam, dedicemq́[ue] tuo illum nomini, utrunq[ue] si non petisses etiam, facturus era[m]: sed uereor ne tam celeriter illum tibi mittere queam, nondum [enim] recognoui, aut è prima schaeda illum repurgaui, adeo ne respexi quidem, postea quàm traduxi' (Letter to Hegius, reprinted in Alardus, *Lucubrationes*, 185). Nevertheless, it is quite possible that these Lucian fragments will turn up in an early edition (particularly since in the Alardus edition the 'De non facile credendis delationibus' has a prefatory letter by Agricola).

28. 'Accedunt, praeter Latina & Graeca, quae mihi quicunq[ue] possum modo, tuenda sunt, quanquàm & no[n]nihil damni in eis me facere intelligo sed accedu[n]t ad haec (ut dico) studia Hebraicarum literarum, quae mihi nouum & plenum molestiae negocium exhibent. . . . destinaui senectutem meam (si modo me manet senectus) studio sacrarum literarum' (ibid., 185–86).

29. Nauwelaerts, *Rodolphus Agricola*, 165.

30. Huisman, *Rudolph Agricola*, item 3. This *may* be the first printed edition of the important eight-page letter 'De formando studio', but I am not even confident of that. Everything else in the volume I believe to have appeared elsewhere.

This is, nevertheless, an important publishing 'event' for our story, because Faber's prefatory letter to the volume contains a crucial reference to a manuscript of the missing *De inventione dialectica*, and is therefore vital for the story of the retrieval of that work. See Alardus, *Lucubrationes*, 203.

31. *Rhodolfi Agricole. parae / nesis siue admonitio qua / ratione studia sunt tractanda. et qui auctores sunt / euoluendi vna cum epistola eiusdem ad Alexandrum / hegium gymnasiarcham dauentriensem. et parae- / nesis Isocratis ad demonicum Rhodolfo agrico / la interprete e greco traducta /* ❡ *Hermolai barbari patriarchae Aquileiensis / versus in sepulcrum Rodolphi Agricolae grunningensis / Inuidia* [sic Huisman] *clauserunt hoc marmore fata Rhodolfum / Agricolam frisij spemque decusque soli / Scilicet hoc viuo meruit Germania laudis / Quicquid habet latium graecia quicquid habet.*

32. 'Lucubrationes Rodolphi Agricolae, hominis vere diuini, iamdudum expectamus; cuius ego scripta quoties lego, toties pectus illud sacrum ac coeleste mecum adoro atque exosculor' (*De copia*, fol. 2ʳ, reprinted in Allen 2:32 [ep 311]).

33. Allen, 'Letters of Rudolph Agricola', 305. Beatus Rhenanus worked first as corrector for the printer Stephanus in Paris, then did editorial and prefatory work for Schürer, moving to Strasburg in 1508–9 'to take a more active part in Schürer's undertakings'. From 1511 he lived and worked in Basle, with the printing house of Amerbach-Froben (Allen 2:60). See J. D'Amico, *Theory and Practice in Renaissance Textual Criticism: Beatus Rhenanus between Conjecture and History* (Los Angeles, 1988), chapter 2, 'The Novice Critic'.

34. Erasmus and Rhenanus later became close friends; they met in 1515, when Rhenanus was working for the Froben press, and assisted Erasmus in his edition of Seneca's *Lucubrationes* (D'Amico, *Beatus Rhenanus*, 63–65.)

35. 'Salutat te . . . Matthias Schurerius, qui plurimum rogat B. Rhenanum vt aliquando manus Rodolpho adhibeat; nam si castigatus esset, non diutius editionem eius moraretur' (Allen 2:121).

36. Allen 3:19 (ep 606).

37. Allen 3:55 (ep 633).

38. Allen 3:30 (ep 612).

39. And what was the relationship between that first prefatory announcement by Rhenanus and Schürer's (his employer's) printing aspirations in relation to Erasmus?

40. Huisman, *Rudolph Agricola*, 266: *Opuscula aliquot Erasmo / Roterodamo castigatore & interprete: quibus / primae aetati nihil prelegi potest; Neque vtilius neque / elegantius. /* ❡ *Libellus elegantissimus, qui vulgo Cato in- / scribitur, complectens sanctiss. vitae communis / praecepta.* ❡ *Mimi Publiani. /* ❡ *Septem sapientum celebria dicta. /* ❡ *Institutur—Christiani hominis carmine pro pueris. / ab Erasmo compositum. /* ❡ *Parenesis Isocratis Rodolpho Agricola inter / prete, castigatore Martino Dorpio. / Cum gratia et priuilegio. / A. Maximi. Aug. & Car. Aust. / Prostant louanij in edibus Theodorici Martini Alustensis e regione Scholae / Iuris ciuilis.* On this volume see Reedijk, *Poems of Desiderius Erasmus*, 304–6 (introduction to the poem 'Christiani hominis institutum', which was published for the first time in this volume). And note that Dorp, who corrected the Agricola, in fact saw the entire volume through the press, since he too was a Thierry Mar-

tens proof corrector: 'Catonem abs te castigatum mihique creditum castigate impressit, me erratorum vindice. Eam operam magistro Ioanni Neuio [to whom the *Cato* was dedicated], Lilianorum gymnasiarchae, vti iussisti, dicaui; qui te ob hoc beneficium ita complectitur, vt quum redieris, sis profusissime sensurus' (letter from Dorp to Erasmus [1514], Allen 2:10–16 [ep 304], 16).

41. Huisman, *Rudolph Agricola*, 3.

42. Ibid., 4. On Martens see C. Reedijk, 'Erasme, Thierry Martens et le *Julius Exclusus*', in J. Coppens (ed.), *Scrinium Erasmianum* (2 vols.) (Leiden, 1969) 2:351–78 (particularly as specifying a group centred on the Martens printing house, which included Gilles, Dorp, Goclenius, and Alardus, as well as Erasmus [357]); Iseghem, *Biographie de Thierry Martens*; P. C. van der Meersch, *Recherches sur la vie et les travaux des imprimeurs belges et Néerlandais* (Gand, 1856). 'He was a devoted friend and admirer of Erasmus (cf. Ep. 304 and Lond.v.25, LB. 357); for whom he published nearly sixty volumes' (Allen 1:514). The Gilles Agricola collection was reprinted several times, first by Martens, and then by Schürer. The *Cato* volume has a very similar publishing history to the Agricola *Opuscula*: two editions by Martens, followed by one by Schürer (Reedijk, *Poems of Desiderius Erasmus*, 304–6, 372), further suggesting that Erasmus is 'ghosting' the publishing history of Agricola. In 1515 P. Quentell published an edition of the *Cato* collection in Cologne, drawing explicitly to an Agricola connection on its title-page: . . . *Parenesis Isocratis Rodolpho Agricola interprete. castigatore / Martino dorpio. / Epigramma Gerardi Nouiomagi. in laudem D. Erasmi / Roterodami Theologi eloquentissimi / Attica se claram iactat Demosthene tellus / Facundus colitur Tullius Ausonijs / Agricolam Phrysius celebrat Germanus Erasmum /Mellifluum laudet. cantet. ad astra ferat. / Cuius ab ore fluit melliti gurgitis vnda / Oblectat mentes que Cicerone magis / Nam docet ingenuos animos sermone polito / Et recte sapere. & verba diserta loqui* (Huisman, *Rudolph Agricola*, 267; Reedijk, *Poems of Desiderius Erasmus*, 304–6, 372). This volume also went through a number of editions over the following years. From 1522 Agricola disappears from the title page, and the Isocrates is implicitly attributed to Erasmus (Huisman, *Rudolph Agricola*, 282). This may have contributed to the 'slur' of 1523, in which Erasmus was accused of appropriating an Agricola translation of a Euripides play as his own.

43. Allen 3:98.

44. Allen 3:100 (ep 677); CWE 5:139.

45. CWE 5:139.

46. Allen 1:413–14. Gilles was another proof corrector in Thierry Martens's publishing house, whom Erasmus had probably met and befriended around 1504, when he was seeing his *Panegyric* and his *Lucubratiunculae* through the Martens press.

47. Huisman, *Rudolph Agricola*, 4. The configuration is again: scholarly proof corrector associated with Erasmus's printed works; printing house associated with Erasmus's current print output; editor/printer of (derivative) Agricola volume. I am suggesting that this must lead us to the conclusion that Erasmus is 'ghosting' (at the very least by some kind of patronage) Agricola's emergence in print in the volumes edited by Faber, Gilles, and Dorp (see below).

48. 'Petrus Egidius Anuerpianus, Martino Dor- / pio Theologo, Amico iucundissimo. S. D. (Anuerpie pridie Idus decembris.)'. Erasmus apparently did not meet Thierry Martens until September 1515 (Reedijk, *Poems of Desiderius Erasmus*, 336–7), in Antwerp, so one assumes his visits to the Martens shop in Louvain postdate 1515. Erasmus's later estrangement from Dorp over Dorp's criticisms of some of his published works need not concern us here.

49. At least, I have not so far been able to track down an incunabulum printing of this oration.

50. Huisman, *Rudolph Agricola*, 124: *De recta latini grae- / cique sermonis pronuntiatione Des. Era- / smi Roterodami Dialogus. Eivsdem Dialogus cui titulus, Cice- / ronianus, siue De optimo genere di / cendi. / Cum alijs nonnullis quorum ni- / hil non est nouum. / [printer's mark] / AN. M.D.XXVIII / Cum gratia & priuilegio Caesareo.*

51. LB I 1013D–1014A. Hegius and Goclenius (among other Netherlanders) also figure. So the same roll call which caused such offense for slighting French scholars is extremely careful in its mention of 'German' humanists who provide Erasmus with his own immediate pedigree. See Reedijk, *Poems of Desiderius Erasmus*, 74–83.

52. The more I look at the exchange between Faber and Erasmus, the more convinced I become that they are the product of collaboration, and not simply of Erasmus's responding to Faber's published letter. There is a long poem by Cornelius Gerard (Cornelius Aurelius), composed between 1494 and 1497 and dedicated to Jacobus Faber (then a teacher at the Deventer school) which survives in manuscript at Deventer. In the preface Gerard writes that 'Iam enim prime decadis libris absolutis mihi prae animi pusillanimitate in tanto opere pene labenti piae exhortationis manum porrexit quidam canonicus regularis, Herasmus nomine, etate floridus, religione compositus et omnium facile nostri evi tam prosa quam metro praestantissimus', as further evidence of a continuing Faber/Erasmus connection (Hyma, *Youth of Erasmus*, 207; see the whole chapter 'Poems and Orations', 205–19). If I am right about the neo-Latin poetry connection in the 1489/90 letter to Cornelius Gerard (see below), that would also support the link (and see Reedijk, *Poems of Desiderius Erasmus*, chapter 3, passim).

53. The letter, indeed including the adage, is in Alardus's *Lucubrationes*, 205–11. Alardus's commentary (212) quotes the Greek from Erasmus's *Adages*. Hegius had in fact been Agricola's pupil only briefly, around 1474, to learn Greek.

54. Allen 1:580–83.

55. CWE 1. 'Miror autem maiorem in modum cum hunc solum dixeris qui "veterum vestigia seruet." Nam, vt te praeteream, innumeros videre mihi videor nostra hac tempestate literatissimos qui ad veterum eloquentiam non parum accedunt. Ecce occurrit imprimis Alexandri mei praeceptoris quondam praeceptor, Rodolphus Agricola, vir cum omnium liberalium artium egregie eruditus, tum oratoriae atque poeticae peritissimus. Denique et Graecam linguam non minus quam Latinam calluit. Accedit huic Alexander ipse, tanti magistri non degener discipulus; qui tanta elegantia veterum exprimit dicendi stylum, vt si desit carmini

titulus, in autore facile erraueris: sed ne hic quidem Graecarum literarum omnino ignarus est' (Allen 1:105–6 [ep 23]).

56. On the connecting thread of neo-Latin poetry-writing amongst northern humanists see Reedijk, *Poems of Desiderius Erasmus*, chapter 3. In another letter to Gerard written around 1489 Erasmus indicates that he is enclosing some of his own poems, but that he has sent others to his old teacher, Hegius, for his approval: 'Porro aliud quod ad te darem, ad manum habui nihil; quidquid enim reliquum erat, partim ad Alexandrum Hegium, ludi litterarii magistrum, quondam praeceptorem meum, et Bartholomaeum Coloniensem' (Allen 1 [ep 28], cited in Reedijk, *Poems of Desiderius Erasmus*, 48). My surmise is supported by the neat fact that the only *clear* piece of evidence of direct influence of Agricola on Erasmus's own literary production is poetic: in the final ten lines of Erasmus's poem in praise of Saint Anne (1489), 'Rhythmus iambicus in laudem Annae, auiae Iesu Christi' (Reedijk, poem 22, 201–5) Reedijk suggests there is direct influence of Agricola's 'Anna mater' (44–45). For evidence that Erasmus knew the Agricola 'Anna mater' see the 1501 letter to Anna van Borssele (Allen 1:342 [ep 145]).

57. 'Agricola's letter of 1. Nov. ⟨1482⟩, probably as printed in Agricola's translation of Plato's *Axiochus*, Louvain, John of Westphalia, c. 1483 (Campbell, 1420, Copinger, 4768)' (Allen 1:581).

58. In just the same way, Jacobus Faber's account of the intimacy between Agricola and Hegius turns out to be patched together out of textual fragments pillaged from the letters of the two men themselves. I have traced enough of these to be confident that *every* phrase in Faber's affecting account can be found somewhere in their surviving correspondence. Compare, e.g., Faber: 'Quanti autem is ipse nostrum fecerit, hinc profecto clarum; siquidem nostrum sibi persuasit pro eius summo studiorum amore proque eius candore animi (qualem sibi exoptabat) studiorum fuisse acerrimum et exactorem et stimulum et socium, quocum communicaret gratissimum fuit quicquid cogitando inuenerat, quicquid scribendo effecerat, quicquid legendo didicerat, quicquid vel laude vel acriori dignum iudicio annotauerat; que in eius aures ipse, vt itidem in suas ille, deposuit. Semper vel ingerebat aliquid vel contabatur vel dubitabat vel disceptabat, nunc negligentiam liberiori reprehensione castigabat, nunc conatum benigniori prouehebat laude, verum et dicere et audire qui et sciuit et voluit. Itaque quocum etatem vna degere hoc nostro maluerit habuit neminem; id quod per res vtriusque non licuisse tulit egerrime'; and Agricola to Hegius (1480) in Alardus, *Lucubrationes*, 187–88: 'deest enim acerrimus mihi studioru[m]stimulus, exactor eoru[m] & socius, qui [sic] cu[m] co[m]munice[m], in cuius aures ego, ut itide[m] in meas ille deponat q[ui]quid cogita[n]do inuenerit, scribe[n]do effecerit, lege[n]do didicerit, & uel laude dignu[m], uel acriori iudicio annotarit, quiq́[ue] semp[er] ingerat aliquid, perco[n]tetur, dubitet, disceptet, modo neglige[n]tiu[m] liberiori reprehe[n]-sio[n]e co[n]stringet, modo conatu[m] benigniori prouehat laude, utq́[ue] semel syncere omne[m] inter studia beneuole[n]tiae fructu[m] co[m]plectar, q[ui] dicere ueru[m], quiq́[ue] audire sciat et uelit, eu[m] quu[m] te mihi esse persuadea[m]. pro summo tuo studioru[m] amore, proq́[ue] candore animi tui, mihi est omniu[m] quod malim, q[uam] posse unà nos aetate[m] degere' [echoed passages underlined].

59. The passage in the *Compendium vitae* was 'Rodolphus Agricola primus omnium aurulam quandam melioris literaturae nobis inuexit ex Italia; quem mihi puero ferme duodecim annos nato ⟨Dauentriae⟩ videre contigit, nec aliud contigit' (Allen 1:2). For the Melanchthon 'Vita Agricolae', see C. G. Bretschneider (ed.), *Melanthonis opera quae supersunt omnia, Corpus reformatorum*, vol. 11 (Halle-Brunswick, 1843), cols. 438–46, where Melanchthon, unlike Erasmus, is quite unselfconscious about the derivative nature of his biographical material: 'Nos pauca collegimus, sumpta partim ex ipsius scriptis, partim ab iis qui meminerunt sermones senum, quibus in Academia Heydelbergensi cum Rodolpho familiaritas fuit' (439). For the 'Oratio de Erasmo Roterodamo', see *Melanthonis opera . . . omnia*, vol. 12, cols. 264–71. He attributes the anecdote to Erasmus himself: 'Literas Latinas et Graecas Daventriae didicit in Schola Alexandri Hegii, qui familiaris fuit Rodolpho Agricolae. Ac solitus est ipse Erasmus narrare praesagium Rodolphi Agricolae de adolescentis studio. Forte ostenderat Hegius hospiti Rodolpho in scholam ingresso, adolescentum scripta. Cumque tyrocinium illud probaret, et gratularetur studiis, praetulit tamen Erasmiacum scriptum caeteris, propter inventionis acumen, orationis puritatem, et figuras, apte ceu flosculos interspersos. Eoque scripto adeo delectatus est, ut ex lineamentis quoque, de indole coniecturam sumere cuperet. Iubet igitur vocari Erasmum, quem cum pauca sciscitatus esset, contemplans figuram capitis, et charopos oculos, hortatur ad discendum, inquiens: Tu eris olim magnus' (266). Melanchthon has a prefatory letter in Alardus (ed.), Agricola, *Lucubrationes*.

60. Hyma, *Youth of Erasmus*, 48.

61. Allen 1:581. The evidence for the 1484 visit is contained in a letter to Antonius Liberus, printed in Alardus, *Lucubrationes*, 176–77. The letter starts out: 'Annam matrem imprimendam dedi'. It is therefore interesting to juxtapose Allen's hopeful hypothesis of a meeting between Agricola and Erasmus on this occasion with the following (based presumably on the preface to the 'Anna mater' as published in 1484 by Richard Praffaert): 'On 7 April 1484 Richard Paffraet and his wife Stine were honoured by a visit to their home by the great man Agricola. In his luggage the humanist had a panegyric to St. Anne, the mother of the Virgin Mary. Paffraet hastened to his workshop and returned with Agricola's "Anna Mater" in ten pages of print. Agricola, in a hurry to continue his journey, had to overlook the printing errors' (H. D. L. Vervliet, *Post-Incunabula and Their Publishers in the Low Countries: A Selection Based on Wouter Nijhoff's 'L'art typographique' Published in Commemoration of the 125th Anniversary of Martinus Nijhoff on January 1, 1978* [The Hague, 1978], 118). Which does not suggest that any such meeting with a young pupil of Hegius's was leisurely. I am inclined to follow a suggestive remark in Reedijk, and think that Erasmus 'saw' Agricola on some such occasion, but that Agricola never, as it were, *met* him. It is, however, possible that Hegius did show Agricola an early Erasmus poem, for instance the 'Carmen bucolicum' (Reedijk, *Poems of Desiderius Erasmus*, 131–39).

62. 'Apud Dauentriam primum posuit in literis tyrocinium, vtriusque linguae rudimentis imbibitis sub Alexandro Hegio Vuestphalo, qui cum Rudolpho Agricola recens ex Italia reuerso amicitiam contraxerat et ab eodem Graece docebatur;

nam huius literaturae peritiam ille primus in Germaniam importauit' (Beatus Rhenanus to Hermann of Wied, Allen 1:53 [ep III]). For a continuation of this tradition among scholars of Dutch humanism see E. H. Waterbolk, 'Rodolphus Agricola, Desiderius Erasmus en Viglius van Aytta: Een Leuvens triumviraat', in Coppens, *Scrinium Erasmianum* 1:129–50.

63. There are a number of references in the secondary literature to copies of the *De inventione dialectica* circulating in manuscript, or to individuals possessing copies of the manuscript (e.g., Allen, 'Letters of Agricola', 304), but I can find no evidence to support this, nor a single reference to anyone's *reading* the *De inventione dialectica* before it appears in print. We do know that Agricola's personal friends the von Pleningen brothers did own a complete codex (transcribed by themselves), but, as far as we know, they did nothing at all with it. On the important relationship between Agricola and Dietrich von Pleningen (ca. 1453–1520), for whom the *De inventione dialectica* was written, and to whom it was dedicated, see F. G. Adelmann, 'Dr. Dietrich von Plieningen zu Schaubeck', 9–139. Adelmann writes (personal communication, 1977): 'In the Cod. poet. et phil. 4036 Dietrich and his brother state clearly that the contents are collected to be published later on'.

64. I should emphasise how difficult it is, however, to excavate *problems* out of Erasmus's letters in particular, because of the care Erasmus himself took in cosmetically tidying up exchanges for publication (as I am stressing throughout this story, Erasmus's self-conscious command of print communication is an important feature of the narrative). See for instance the letter to Budé of October 1516, published in the *Epistolae elegantes*, edited by Gilles and published by Martens in 1517 (Allen 2:362–70 [ep 480]), where Erasmus writes: 'After [the *De copia*] was published I discovered a certain amount in Rudolphus Agricola'. I take this to be an 'instruction to the reader' (of both Erasmus and Agricola), rather than a fact (it is indeed the link Erasmus's loyal *castigatores* make in their scholia to the Agricola). See the suggestive article by L-E Halkin, 'Erasme éditeur de sa correspondance: Le cas de l'*Auctarium*', *Bibliothèque d'humanisme et Renaissance* 40 (1978), 239–47.

65. On Alardus see above all Kölker, *Alardus Aemstelredamus*. See also B. de Graaf, *Alardus Amstelredeamus, 1491–1544: His Life and Works with a Bibliography* (Amsterdam, 1958); and entry in Bietenholz and Deutscher, *Contemporaries of Erasmus* 1:15–17. Much as in the case of Faber, almost *everything* we know about Alardus is derived from his relationship either with publishing Agricola's works, or with Erasmus, or both. Alardus's own prefaces and title pages regularly introduce both. See, e.g., de Graaf, *Alardus Amstelredeamus*, 52, biblio. item 22: *D. Erasmi / Roterodami Bvcolicon, Le / ctu digniss. cum scholijs Alardi Aemstelre- / dami, cuius studio nunc primum & re / pertum & aeditum est. / Locus communis de uitando pernitioso aspectu, eo- / dem pertinens. / Sacerdotum coelibatus. / Mulier iuxta omneis Inuentionis Dialectic(a)e locos ex- / plicata per Alardum Aemstelredamum* (Cologne, 1539).

66. Kölker, *Alardus Aemstelredamus*, 21: 'Doch uit andere gegevens weten we zeker, dat Alardus reeds in 1514 te Leuvan was. We hebben nl. een hele serie werken, uitgegeven bij Theodoor Martens te Leuven, die door Alardus voorzien zijn van een inleidend gedichtje. Het eerste dateert van November 1514. Heruit

zouden we mogen opmaken, dat Alardus zeker van af die tijd bij deze uitgever, een van de eerste belgische drukkers, minstens af en toe heeft gewerkt, mogelijk als corrector'. Fol. 15ᵛ of Erasmus's *De constructione octo partium orationis libellus* (Louvain, Martens, November 1514) has: 'Alardi Amstelredami in Erasmianam syntaxin ad puerum Dimetrum' (ibid.).

67. See Allen 2:1 (ep 298), dated August 1, 1514, Louvain, and in which he indicates renewed contact with Dorp—also corrector at Martens (lines 42–43).

68. De Graaf, *Alardus Amstelredeamus*, 22. In 1518 Alardus contributed a long Latin poem to Erasmus's *Ratio seu methodus*, celebrating Erasmus's *ordo ac ratio* (Kölker, *Alardus Aemstelredamus*, 22, 34–5.)

69. All the sources for Agricola studies which I cited in footnote 9 accept Alardus's version of the story entirely at face value.

70. Allen, 'Letters of Agricola', says the letter 'was presumably in some book edited by Faber; but I have not been able to trace it' (304). I mention this only because this is the *only* case, in this entire piece of work, where, when I had painstakingly reconstructed the provenance and location of a crucial piece of evidence, I did *not* find that Allen had correctly identified it.

71. 'Quod si quis latius ista et per omnes locos dialecticos fuderit [*sic*], quatenus cuiusque natura capax eorum est, inge[n]s utiq[ue] copia & ad dicendum, & ad inueniendum se praebebit. quod quomodo faciendum sit, maius est, quàm ut epistola id capiat, & copiose est à me ea de re in tribus libris eis, quos de inuentio[n]e dialectica scripsi disputatum' (Alardus, *Lucubrationes*, 199).

72. Alardus's lurid account of the consequences for himself of this announcement are contained in a textual note to this very passage in the 'De formando studio' (Alardus, *Lucubrationes*, 203). Alardus says this copy had belonged to Hegius (it seems eminently plausible that Faber, editing Hegius's works, had found the lost work there). See Alardus, *De inventione dialectica*, 11–12.

73. And that he had insufficient understanding of the material it contained. Without going too far into technicalities at this point: it might appear that a work advertised as containing three books *de inventione dialectica* required a matching 'twin' in the form of three books *de iudicio*. However, in the 'De formando studio' letter, as reprinted in Rivius (e.g.), the phrase in Agricola's letter reads, 'in *sex* libris eis, quos de inuentione dialectica scripsi disputatum'.

74. Alardus claims that it was the reference to six books which drew him to Deventer, implying that this was not the only copy of the work he had access to, but I am inclined to doubt this, and to think that this was the *first* surfacing of any trace of the lost work.

75. Huisman, *Rudolph Agricola*, 11. *Rodolphi Agricole Phrisij Dialectica / Dorpius Studiosis / vt rectis studiis co[n]sulatur studiosi, excusa sunt vobis haec Agricolae dia / lectica: q[ui]bus nihil ce[n]seo vtilius futuru[m] iis: q[ui] vera[m] secta[n]tur arte[m] diserte eloquenterq[ue] dice[n] / di: q[ui]q[ue] no[n] verbis t[a]m[en] inanibus: sed vberi reru[m] copia studeant summa cu[m] admiratione p[er] / suadere: atq[ue] de re qualibet ex p[ro]babilibus apposite: dece[n]terq[ue] ratiocinari: quod noster / ille munus esse dialecticu[m] testatur: hic itaq[ue] garrula sophistar(um) delirame[n]ta ne expectetis: / veru[m] ea expectate: quae a multis-sci[enti]arum limites co[n]funde[n]tibus: rhetoric[a]e tributa: p(ro)pria / t[ame]n sunt dialectic[a]e: quaeq[ue] in Aristotelis Ciceronisq[ue] libris deside-*

ra[n]tur: q[ui]bus certe hic li / ber nihilo est inferior: siue elegantiam filumq[ue]
dictionis spectemus: siue doctrine prae- / ceptorumq[ue] traditionem. Dorp had
already been the addressee of the prefatory letter to Gilles's 1511 volume of Agricola *Opuscula.*

76. Alardus (and subsequent re-tellers of the story like Allen) embellishes his
account with tales of dangerous journeys, failed rendezvous, Faber's deception
and reluctance to show him the manuscript, and subsequent headaches trying to
decipher and transcribe the text. See Allen, 'Letters of Rudolph Agricola', 304–5.

77. For evidence of the unsatisfactory state of this manuscript, see Matthaeus
Phrissemius's graphic description in his commentary on *De inventione dialectica*
(Cologne, 1528, 282–83) 2:16; also Alardus, *Lucubrationes*, sig. *4ʳ⁻ᵛ. On the
handwriting, see Adelmann, 'Dietrich von Plieningen'. Adelmann writes (personal
communication 1977): 'When Alardus Amstelredamus finally published his Cologne edition in 1539 as "ad autographi fidem", according to Alardus himself
rumours were running around in Cologne that he did not possess Agricola's own
signed manuscript. Since Dietrich copied it in 1479 because Agricola's manuscript
was *illegible*, I wonder if Alardus really had Agricola's own manuscript'. See
Allen, 'Letters of Agricola', 312, ep. 18 (1479), to Adolphus Occo: 'The *Dialectica* is just finished and is being copied by Theodoric of Plenningen'.

78. It is striking how many works from the Martens press around this date are
corrected and/or prefaced by Dorp. See Iseghem, *Biographie de Thierry Martens.*

79. On Dorp see Allen 2:11. On his technical competence as a logician see,
e.g., R. Guerlac's treatment of the More/Dorp correspondence in her edition of
Juan Luis Vives's *In pseudodialecticos.*

80. Huisman, *Rudolph Agricola*, item 16. Matthaeus Phrissemius's corrected
version of the text alone (based on the 1515 printed version, which was full of
typographical errors, curious choices of punctuation, and obvious errors of transcription) appeared in Cologne in 1520 (ibid., item 12), and his commented edition in 1523 (ibid., item 14). The supposedly further revised text is substituted in
Phrissemius's commented edition in 1528, but this is not signalled on the title
page until 1535. Ibid., item 27: '*Rodolphi / Agricolae Phrisii de inven- / tione
dialectica libri tres, cu[m]scholijs Iohan / nis Matthaei Phrissemij; & marginalibus
/ annotationibus nunc auctis passim ac reco / gnitis, sublatis etiam multis errori-
bus, qui / cum Rodolpho ipso, tum etiam in scho- / lijs hactenus animaduersi non
fuere* (Cologne, 1535).' In 1529 (a year after the better text of the *De inventione
dialectica* had been retrieved by Alardus, and apparently worked through for
publication by Alardus and Phrissemius together), Phrissemius offered to help get
it published (Allen, 'Letters of Agricola' and Alardus, *Lucubrationes*, sig. †2ᵛ).

81. On the history of the retrieval see Allen, 'Letters of Agricola'; L. Jardine,
'Distinctive Discipline: Rudolph Agricola's Influence on Methodical Thinking in
The Humanities', in F. Akkerman and A. J. Vanderjagt (eds.), *Rodolphus Agric-
ola Phrisius, 1444–1485* (Leiden, 1988), 38–57.

82. '[Pompeius] quicquid habuit Rodolphi Agricolae ab auunculo suo Adol-
pho Occone Sigismundi Archiducis Austriae medico celebratissimo, non tam le-
gitimo Rodolphi Agric[olae]haerede, qua[m] assiduo eiusde[m] studii collega
(neq[ue] enim est sanctius sanguinis uinculo co[n]iungi qu[am] studiis sacrisq[ue]
iisde[m] initiari) relictu[m] candidus impertitus est' (Alardus, *Lucubrationes*, sig.
†1ᵛ), also Protucius's elegy to Agricola, sig. *3ᵛ.

83. And we saw in the case of the similarly vivid and compelling account of the pursuit of Faber's copy, Alardus's version of events is at the very least highly coloured.

84. On Alardus's extended publishing relationship with Pompeius Occo, of which the publication of the Agricola *Opera* forms only a part, see Kölker, *Alardus Aemstelredamus*, and F. J. Dubiez, *Op de Grens van Humanisme en Hervorming: De Betekenis van de Boekdrukkunst te Amsterdam in een Bewogen Tijd, 1506–1578* (The Hague, 1962).

85. Allen, 'Letters of Rudolph Agricola', 308–9. In the end, the *Opera* came out after Erasmus's death.

86. Let alone 'Christian humanism', which will surely now have to enter the story. I note here that while many of Erasmus's works went on to the Index, Agricola's *De inventione dialectica* (in spite of its strenuously Erasmian scholia) not only did not, but was specified as an acceptable pedagogic text in dialectic, at least in Louvain and Paris (whose Index lists I have looked at).

87. 'Rodolpho Agricolo et Alexandro Hegio, quibus ego sane minimum debebam, nonne plenam laudem tribuo?' (*Spongia adversus aspergines Hutteni* [Basle, 1523], ed. C. Augustijn, in *Opera omnia Desiderii Erasmi Roterodami* 9.1 [Amsterdam and Oxford, 1982], 117–210; 196). See Reedijk, *Poems of Desiderius Erasmus* 42. As Reedijk points out, this recantation is confirmed by the phrase 'nec aliud contigit' in Erasmus's *Compendium vitae*, where he states that Agricola visited his school: '. . . quem mihi puero ferme duodecim annos nato ⟨Daventriae⟩ videre contigit, nec aliud contigit' (Allen 1:2).

CHAPTER FOUR

1. See Daniel Kinney's exemplary introduction to Thomas More's 'Letter to Martin Dorp', in *The Yale Edition of the Complete Works of St. Thomas More*, vol. 15. For a full bibliographical portrait see de Vocht, *Monumenta Humanistica Lovaniensia*, 63–348; Bietenholz and Deutscher, *Contemporaries of Erasmus*. See also van Iseghem, *Biographie de Thierry Martens*.

2. For the best account of the conventional version of the Dorp/Erasmus 'quarrel', see Kinney, 'Letter to Martin Dorp'.

3. The first published collection was Faber's of 1508: see previous chapter.

4. 'Petrus Egidius Anuerpian[us], Martino Dorpio Theologo, Amico iucundiss. S. D.' (sig. a ii^r).

5. Sig. a ii^v.

6. For the complete text of this preface, see appendix.

7. See Bietenholz, and Deutscher *Contemporaries of Erasmus* vol. 1, s. v. 'Dorp'.

8. Chapter 1.

9. 'Unum non possum non addere. . . . Primus liber [of the *De inventione dialectica*] ipsius Agricolae manu scriptus, in marginibus multa addita habebat, quae in operae contextum transferenda erant, in ipso vero contextu, multa inducta, multa deleta, quaedam minutissimis lituris potius quam literis annotata, coniecturis ac divinatione assequi oportebat. Quare ego precibus doctissimorum virorum . . . in studiosorum omnium gratiam eum laborem subii, ut primum librum, ordine quo nunc legitur, descripserim Anno Domini (1514)' (Geldenhauer,

'Vita Rodolphi Agricolae Frisi', in Johannes Fichardus [ed.], *Virorum qui . . . memorabiles fuerunt vitae* [Frankfurt, 1536], fol. 86ᵛ, cited in J. M. Weiss, 'Six Lives of Rudolph Agricola', *Humanistica Lovaniensia* 30 [1981], 19–39, 28).

10. See now John Monfasani's excellent survey, 'Humanism and Rhetoric', in A. Rabil, Jr. (ed.), *Renaissance Humanism: Foundations, Forms, and Legacy* (3 vols.) (Philadelphia, 1988), 3:171–235: '*De inventione* seems to have dropped from sight after Agricola completed it. Not even Alexander Hegius, an admirer and compatriot of Agricola, argued for a peculiarly Agricolan conception of logic when he published his *Dialogi* on logic in 1503 [actually Faber; Hegius died in 1498]'.

11. See previous chapter for Alardus's tendency to tidy up the retrospective account of the retrieval of Agricola's works, and his own part in reconstructing them.

12. See Allen 2:379; J. Prinsen, *Gerardus Geldenhauer Noviomagus: Bijdrage tot kennis van zijn Leven en Werken* (The Hague, 1898); J. Prinsen, *Collectanea van Gerardus Geldenhauer Noviomagus* (Amsterdam, 1901); Bietenholz and Deutscher *Contemporaries of Erasmus*.

13. 'Me puero, Alexander Hegius, praeceptor meus, non minus vitae sanctitate quam omnimoda eruditione clarissimus, Rodolphi Agricolae et Wesseli [Gansfort] Friseorum sententiae subscribens, Alexandri Grammaticam non rejecit', in *Institutio scholae christianae* (Frankfurt, 1534), cited in Prinsen, *Gerardus Geldenhauer*, 13. The similarity to Erasmus's account of that introduction goes farther: like Erasmus, Geldenhauer describes Hegius as citing the example of the way Agricola influenced his own Greek studies as an encouragement to his students. In his *Vita Agricolae*, Geldenhauer writes: 'Memini me audire ab Hegio, quum quosdam natu grandiores ad literarum studia hortaretur et ne desperarent admoneret, Ego (inquit) liberalium artium magister et quadragenarius, tum quoque barbarus, perveni ad Agricolam adolescentem praeceptorem meum, a quo quicquid in latinis et graecis literis scio, aut alii me scire credunt didici' (ibid., 14). At the end of the *Vitae Agricolae*, Geldenhauer explicitly attributes the recovery of Agricola's reputation in print to Erasmus: 'Libet hoc adscribere clarissimum encomion, quo Agricola noster, a nunquam satis laudato viro D. Erasmo posteritati commendatus humilitate nauseans, tanti oratoris ac theologi grandiloquentia reficiatur' (ibid., 122).

14. Nijhoff-Kronenburg, 737: Dorpius Martinus, Dialogus in quo Venus et Cupido omnes adhibent versutias, etc. Leuven, Theod. Martinus Alost., (1514). *1a*: Martini Dorpij sacre theo / logiae licenciati Dialogus: in quo Venus & Cupido / omnes adhibent versutias: vt Herculem animi an- / cipitem in suam Militiam inuita Virtute perpella[n] t. / ❡ Eiusdem Tomus Aululariae Plautinae adiectus /cum prologis aliquot in Comediarum actiones: & / pauculis carminibus. / ❡ Chrysostomi Neapolitani epistola de situ Holla[n] / diae viuendiq[ue] Hollandorum institutis. / Gerardi Nouiomagi de Zelandia epistola consi / milis .:. /Cum gratia et priuilegio. / Prostant venales in edibus / Theoderici Martini Alostensis Louanii e regione / Scholae Iuris ciuilis qui & impressit .:. / *1b*: Ornatissimo. ac raro ingenio viro. M. Ioa[n] / ni Neuio Hondiscotano . . . *3a*: ❡ Prologus /SAluete [*sic*] oppido multu[m], . . . *4a r.II*: Dialogus politissimus a M. Martino Dor / pio compositus. / *31b*: ❡ Chrysostomus Neopolitanus Comiti / Nugarolo

S.D.P. /35a r.18: Gerardus Nouiomagus Sebastiano Ciriaci / no amico . . . 36a r.21: . . . Valebis Louanii / in Collegio Cruciferorum. Secundo Kalendas Martias. Anno. M. / .CCCC.XIIII (sic) / ❡ Errata . . . 36b.

15. This volume also already draws Alardus (who claims credit for having retrieved the manuscript of the De inventione dialectica) into the story. In 1516 Alardus contributed the prefatory letter (dated 1515) for Cornelius Aurelius's In Bataviam, sive de antiqvo veroque eivs insvlae qvam Rhenvs in Hollandia facit situ, descriptione & laudibvs; adversvs Gerardvm Noviomagvm, Libri Dvo, auctore Cornelio Aurelio, D. Erasmi olim praeceptore. Boneventvrae Vulcanii opera, nunc primum in lucem edita. Antverpiae, Apud Christophorum Plantinum (Kölker, Alardus Aemstelredamus, 291). '[Alard's preface] invites Cornelius as an authority on the subject to combat a statement, which was being freely made at Louvain and was championed by Gerard Geldenhauer of Nymegen, to the effect that Holland did not correspond to the ancient Batavia' (Allen 1:206). In this case also (as I shall argue in the case of Dorp and Erasmus) there is no sign of a 'real' quarrel about Batavia between Dorp and Geldenhauer, who remain closely associated throughout the surviving correspondences in which they are involved.

16. Allen, 'The Letters of Rudolph Agricola', 305: 'Geldenhauer undertook to write out book i.; the other two were copied by another hand, and corrected for the press by Dorp'. I have found no evidence for the statement that Dorp was castigator for the whole volume, aside from this surmise of Allen's; it could just as well have been Geldenhauer or Alardus (who, we must remember, consistently claimed that he played a major part in this first edition). Geldenhauer and Alardus were both also castigatores for Martens. See in particular H. de Vocht (ed.), Literae virorum eruditorum ad Franciscum Craneveldium 1522–1528, Humanistica Lovaniensia 1 (Louvain, 1928), 609–10: 'Although there is no evidence of Geldenhouwer's having taken any degree, or even of having attended any lectures, it seems probable that he studied at, and was in close connection with, the University; for the Collegium Crucigerorum had been erected for such purposes (Hermans, I, i, 134, 156–9), and he himself was a zealous adept of humanism, and an intimate friend of its chief promoters. It was probably on account of his proficiency in learning and in Latin that, about 1514, he entered Charles of Austria's Court as chaplain. . . . His pamphlet De Situ Zelandiae, [was] dedicated to Philip of Burgundy by a letter signed on Febr. 28, 1514 in the Louvain College of the Crucigeri (Iseghem, 247). His presence in this College implies that Geldenhouwer's office did not monopolize his time. . . . He was a commendator to some, illustrating them with epigrams, and an emendator to others; amongst the latter were Erasmus' Parabolae, 1515, and Opuscula aliquot, 1515 and 1518 (Iseghem, 252, 254, 289), and Thomas More's Utopia (ML, [beta-7] v°; Allen, 2, 487, 1–7; id. The Letters of R. Agricola: Eng. Hist. Rev., xxi, 303). In Martens' office he apparently met Barbirius' collaborator for the Apocalypse, Nicolas van Broeckhoven (Iseghem, 233, 237, 242), as well as Peter Gilles, Cornelius Grapheus, and Rutger Rescius (Iseghem, 262); he himself published there on June 13, 1515, his Satyrae VIII., about abuses, chiefly ecclesiastical, dedicated to his friends Cranevelt, Becker and Cordatus (ML, 419; Collect., 149–176; Iseghem, 248, 251), and on Aug. 31, 1517, a report of Philip of Burgundy's entrance as Bishop in Utrecht on May 19, 1517 (Iseghem, 276; Collect., 215)'. After Philip of Burgundy's ap-

pointment as bishop of Utrecht, Geldenhauer's job became much more arduous, and he gave up his connections with the university and the Martens press. See Barlandus's letter to Cranevelt (1523), de Vocht, *Literae virorum eruditorum*, 157: 'De Nouiomago Gerardo nihil audimus; stat⟨uerat⟩ js remigrare Louanium, sed video hominem sic alligatum aulae ut exp⟨edire⟩ se nequeat. Doleo ingenium studijs natum, in aulicis nugis consen⟨ire.⟩'

17. Geldenhauer's *Vita Agricolae* makes considerable play on the fact that Agricola, chose to take a master of arts at the University of Louvain, as evidence of the high regard in which that university was held throughout Europe. This makes it plain that he considers that Agricola's name enhances the reputation of Louvain, not that there is anything contentious about him. For a reproduction of the opening of Geldenhauer's *Vita Agricolae*, see *Rudolph Agricola, Gronings Humanist, 1485–1985: Tentoonstellingscatalogus* (Groningen, 1985), 119.

18. '❡ Haec exquisitissima Rodolphi Agricolae Dialectica[m] imprimebat / Louanii Theodoricus Martinus Alustensis characteribus / (vt est videre) faberrimis. Anno a partu Virgineo / Millesimo Quingentesimo Decimo quinto; / pridie Idus Ianuarias. Regnan. Cae. / Maximil. Aug. & Car. Aust.'. I have used the copy currently in the New York Public Library, class-mark *KB.pv.16, and the copy in the Bodleian Library, Oxford, class-mark Antiq.d.X.6(S). The volume in the New York Public Library in which the sixty-two-folio work is bound is extremely interesting in its entirety, and looks like an early sixteenth-century compilation. It contains the following: the 1509 edition of Valla's *Dialectice Laure[n]tii Valle libri tres seu eiusdem Reco[n]cinnatio totius Dialectic[a]e & fundame[n]torum vniuersalis Philosophi[a]e; vbi multa aduersus Aristotelem: Boetium: Porphyrium: sed plura aduersus recentiores philosophos acutissime disputata[n]tur: non defore t[ame]n credo a qu[a]e ab illis respondea[n]tur.* 'Venales sunt in [a]edibus Ascensianis & Bibliopolaru[m] de Marnef'; Faber Stapulensis, *In hoc libro contenta / Epitome co[m]pendiosaq[ue] / introductio in libros / Arithmeticos diui Seuerini Boetij: adie- / cto familiari co[m]me[n]tario [Iudoci Clichtovei] dilucidata. / Praxis numerandi certis quibusdam re- / gulis co[n]stricta. / [Caroli Bovilli] Introductio i[n] geometria[m]: sex libris disti[n]cta / Prim[us] de magnitudinib[us] & earu[m] / circu[m]stantiis. / Secu[n]dus de co[n]sequentibus conti-/guis & co[n]tinuis.*, Paris, Henri Estienne, 15 March 1510/11 (See E. Rice, *The Prefatory Epistles of Jacques Lefèvre d'Etaples and Related Texts* [New York and London, 1972], item 96, p. 544). Actually this volume is a hybrid: fol. [i]–fol. xlviii is the 1510 edition, which, as Rice notes, contains only the first two items. Fol. xlix–fol. cxij is from the earlier edition, Rice item 88, p. 543, dated 1503 at the end of the text); *In hoc opere contenta / [Jordani Nemorarij] Arithmetica decem libris demonstrata. / [Jacobi Fabri Stapulensis] Musica libris demo[n]strata quatuor. / Epitome in libros Arithmeticos diui Seuerini / Boetij. / Rithmimachie ludus qui / et pugna numeroru[m] ap- / pellantur.* (Paris, Henri Etienne, 1514) (Rice, *Prefatory Epistles*, item 88, p. 543).

19. See chapter 3.

20. E.g. *problema* and *protasin*, sig. E 5ᵛ. Martens was apparently not able to print entire texts in Greek until 1519 (see chapter 3), so these single words presumably represent early experiments with a freshly cut Greek font. See Iseghem,

Biographie de Thierry Martens, for more details as to fonts. In particular, it appears from Iseghem that Martens only began to use the roman 'cicero' font in 1513; as far as I can judge, all early volumes using this type (as opposed to gothic or an earlier roman) are associated either with Dorp or with Geldenhauer. See, for example, Iseghem, *Biographie de Thierry Martens*, item 81, 246–47, *Martini Dorpii sacre theologie Licenciati opuscula* (1514), in which the cicero font is used for the single work by Gerard Geldenhauer, *De Zelandia epistola*, while an earlier roman type is used for the remainder of the volume.

21. Iseghem, *Biographie de Thierry Martens*, 252.

22. For example (taken at random), here is the closing paragraph of book 3: 'Ista fere sunt: quae de parte illa dialectices quam inuemendi [*sic*] vocant arbitror potuisse dici: nec me latet haec omnia: vt in breuem admodum pr[a]eceptorum summam arctarentur: perfacile fuisse. sed ego (si quid poterunt ista prodesse) malui spaciosius ea dicere: etiam legentium vtilitati consulere: si qui erunt: qui legendis istis fructum aliquem eonsecuturos [*sic*] se credant. quam per capita tantum rerum irem: vidererq[ue] doctos potius quod didicissent admonere: quam docendis disserere: quid & qua via deberent perscribere: rectius itaq[ue] credidi quum possem quidem breuiora dicere: breuiore ducere itinere: sed eo aspero difficiliq[ue] impedito: longo potius flexu: sed laeto magis & molliore: minusq[ue] spinis obsito circuire [*sic*]: nec ista dico quia laudem huius meae rationis captem. quam quidem quum ex omni ingenio meo: tum ex hoc praesertin [*sic*] labore minime ausim sperare. sed quo mihi lectoris aequanimitatem conciliem: si sciuerit non mei facti hac in re: sed vtilitatis profectusq[ue] sui sequutum esse rationem: quam s1 [*sic*] consequimur: boni consultum erit sin minus: voluimus tamen:: [*sic*] conatumq[ue] prestitimus quem [*sic*] (sicut plerisq[ue] in rebus vel solus laudi sufficit) ita mihi eum non arroganter ad veniam sperauerim suffecturum'. A number of the errors in this passage evidently arise from transcription directly from a manuscript. Thus we have *inuemendi* for *inueniendi* (a handwritten *ni* misread as *m*), and *c* misread as *e* to give *eonsecuturos* for *consecuturos*. In addition, we have a contraction missed in *circumire*, which is rendered *circuire*, a redundant punctuation mark (::), and the obvious typographical error *s1* for *si*, all within a single paragraph.

23. CWE 4:275–76. See Allen 2:497–98: 'Est in tua epistola ad Guolphangum Fabricium, Erasme vndecunque doctissime, non procul a fine locus nobis sane omnino inuius, sic incipiens: "Tum audio nonnullos alia quaedam moliri, quae ad Christi cognitionem nihil adferant, sed funcios tantum offendant oculis hominum." Quem quum Paludano et Nouiomago ostendissem, ipsi mecum in eodem haesitantes luto nihilque temere mutandum censentes consuluerunt ipsum locum tibi, antequam imprimeretur, indicandum. Dorpius *fumos tantum offundant* legendum coniectauit. Theodericus igitur hac epistolae parte excudenda relicta in praesentia ad te ipsum exemplar mittit, obnixe orans vt super istius loci lectione sibi quamprimum sententiam tuam aperias. Praeterea cupit, si quid sit quod epistolarum prefationi subiungi queat commode, id ad se dari. Reseruauit enim ei integram pagellam vtrinque mundam, quum dimidiam vix partem occupabit'.

24. A passage in book 1 nearly four times the length of the one above, n. 22 (the opening chapter), yields two minor typos (an *n* for a *u*; *cetre* for *certe*) and two minor readings which differ from Phrissemius's. Other extensive passages

from the first book which I have subsequently compared for typographical and textual errors with books 2 and 3 yield comparable results.

25. 'Quo vobis labores minuam, studiosi, collegi quae in hiis libellis acciderunt errata: non chalcographorum modo, sed eius quoque qui exemplaria transcripsit mendose: nisi forte exemplaria etiam ipsa parum fuerint integra. In plaerisque fretus sum coniecturis quibus nolim ita vos niti, vti tripodos oraculis: quin liberum esto vel sequi vel respuere, modo studium erga vos nostrum agnoscatis' (de Vocht, *Monumenta Humanistica*, 402).

26. I acknowledge that this is a tricky argument to run, and I do not wish to attach too much weight to it. I am confident that the Geldenhauer epigram at the end of book 1 marks the end of his association with the volume, and I would argue that Dorp's intellectual commitment to the volume extended only as far as his co-*castigator* Geldenhauer's portion of the text. On balance, I think that Alardus is probably the person responsible for the remainder of the first edition—another Marten's *castigator*, and perfectly competent, though nowhere near as experienced as Dorp, and nearly ten years younger. That would explain the less satisfactory nature of the text of books 2 and 3, which are, however, it should be stressed, far from being garbled and 'riddled' with errors.

27. Again, checks before and after this point suggest that it is comparatively error-free up to this point, and markedly worse thereafter.

28. 'Copia vero & breuitas in dicendo: quum praesertim istis inter caetera delectamus & offendimus: constantq[ue] etiam inuentione ista: non alienum videtur ab instituto nostro: paucis de his dicere'.

29. *Copia* also occurs in Dorp's commendatory letter on the title page. Chomarat points out that the *copia breuitasque* formulation occurs in Valla's *De voluptate*, which Erasmus certainly knew. See Chomarat, *Grammaire et rhetorique chez Erasme* 2:716–77.

30. See Phrissemius, 1528 ed., 297–98.

31. In book 1, Phrissemius's chapter breaks correspond precisely to the large capitals in the 1515 edition, except that he breaks one long chapter into two (20 and 21 in his edition). Towards the end of book 3 there is no correspondence whatsoever between the 1515 editions paragraphs and capitals and Phrissemius's chapters.

32. See chapter 3.

33. For a brief treatment see L. Jardine, 'Humanistic Logic', 173–98; 181–84; also L. Jardine, 'Lorenzo Valla: Academic Skepticism and the New Humanist Dialectic', in M. F. Burnyeat (ed.), *The Skeptical Tradition* (Berkeley, 1983), 253–86. For a detailed technical treatment of Agricola's *De inventione dialectica* see P. Mack's book (forthcoming).

34. Kinney, 'Letter to Dorp', xxii–xxiv. See also de Vocht, *Monumenta Humanistica*.

35. Kinney, 'Letter to Dorp', xxiv–xxviii.

36. See Kinney, 'More's *Letter to Dorp*: Remapping the Trivium', *Renaissance Quarterly* 34 (1981), 179–207: 'In fact, More's letter is one of the first systematic defenses of humanist method, encompassing a critique of Scholastic grammar, dialectic, and theology, as well as a tightly argued defense of the new philological theology. . . . The history of humanist apologetics is essentially the

history of an endeavor to discredit Scholastic dialectic as the organizational principle of all disciplines and to set forth a sounder alternative, an endeavor which
finds some of its most impressive expressions in More's rigorous answers to Dorp'
(179–81).

37. This was the second printing of Erasmus's letter, in fact. In August 1515
Erasmus added his reply to Dorp to three letters designed to enhance his reputation with Leo X by announcing his intention to dedicate his edition of Jerome to
the pope, in the Frobenius volume, *Iani Damiani Senensis ad Leonem X pont.
max. De expeditione in Turcas elegia* (See 'The Early Publication of Erasmus'
Letters', in CWE 3:348–53, 348).

38. See Iseghem, *Biographie de Thierry Martens*, for Dorp's prominent role in
Martens press publications around 1515.

39. Compare Vives's opening remarks about Louvain in the *In pseudodialecticos* letter, Introduction.

40. 'Habes epistolam prolixam ac ineptam, sed quae tibi ingrata esse non potest, vtpote ab tui amantissimo profecta. Theodoricus Alustensis chalcographus,
qui Enchiridion et Panaegyricum impressit, orauit me, vti se commendarem tuae
humanitati. Cupiuit plurimum videre te, cupiuit hospicio comiter ac liberaliter
excipere, et ea de causa Antwerpiam profectus, vt resciuit te non illic sed Louanii
esse, ilico recurrit, ac totam ambulans noctem venit postridie Louanium
sesquihora ferme postquam abiuisses. Si qua in re potest tibi gratificari, omnia
pollicetur, et haud scio an omnium hominum viuat homo tui amantior. Catonem
abs te castigatum mihique creditum castigate impressit, me erratorum vindice.
Eam operam magistro Ioanni Neuio, Lilianorum gymnasiarchae, vti iussisti, dicaui; qui te ob hoc beneficium ita complectitur, vt qum redieris, sis profusissime
sensurus' (Allen 2:16 [ep 304]. Cited in Iseghem, *Biographie de Thierry Martens*,
256.)

41. See for instance: '[Tu] qui iam olim (vt mihi Dorpius noster narrauit) summopere expetas sententias probati cuiuspiam auctoris ita expoliri vt et animos
adulescentum ad virtutes et linguas ad rectam eloquutionem forment' (Allen 2:3).

42. 'Sed interim clamabit vitilitigator aliquis, Hui, theologum in tam friuolis
versari nugis? Primum ego nihil fastidiendum duco, quantumuis humile, quod ad
bonas pertineat literas, nedum hosce versus tanta Romani sermonis mundicie
tamque ad bonos mores conducibiles. Quamquam cur me pudeat in hoc genere
pauculas horas collocare, in quo non pauci scriptores Graeci non mediocri cum
laude sunt versati? . . . Denique si mihi indecorum esse volunt emendasse haec
tam humilia et explanasse, multo foedius erit eadem et deprauata fuisse et (quod
ex ipsorum liquet commentariis) ista tam puerilia non intellecta fuisse ab iis viris
qui se nihil nescire putant' (Allen 2:2 [ep 298]. CWE 2:3–4).

43. 'Si aliquam tuarum aeditionum domino Meynardo, abbati Egmondano,
Mecenati meo, dicaueris, certo scio gratissimum illi futurum et beneficium haud
illiberaliter pensaturum. Quod vt facias, te eciam atque eciam oro. Hollandus est
et religionis Hollandicae primas, vir doctus quidem, sed religiosior tamen quam
doctior, tametsi doctos omnes non mediocriter amet, et qui tibi, si vsu veniat,
multis in rebus possit esse auxilio' (Allen 2:16 [ep 304]; CWE 2:23). Allen writes:
'Dorp was indebted to [Mann] for a benefice (see the preface to his *Oratio de
laudibus disciplinarum*, Louvain, Th. Martens, 14 Oct. 1513, dedicated to

Mann); and also addressed to him a letter which was printed in the first edition of Adrian of Utrecht's *Quodlibetica*, Louvain, Th. Martens, March 1515' (ibid.).

44. CWE 5:137–39, 138. Allen 3:98–100, 100: 'Vtinam rem pulcherrimam conantem magnatum fauor adiutet! tametsi audio venerabilem virum Menardum Mannium cognatum tuum, Abbatem Edmondanum, vt in caeteris omnibus, ita hac quoque in parte priscorum praesulum exempla referre'.

45. For Alardus's contact with Dorp see Allen 2:270, 378 (letters 433 and 486). The only reference I can find to Alardus's 'kinship' to Mann is this letter of Erasmus's itself.

46. See chapter 1.

47. There seems to be some confusion as to precisely when the *Cato* volume was published. Allen gives August 1514; CWE gives September (which I have followed). Iseghem gives September 1515, but recognises this must be a second edition (*Biographie de Thierry Martens*, item 90, 254–55).

48. CWE 3:111.

49. See chapter 1.

50. 'Dorpius Studiosis / vt rectis studiis co[n]sulatur studiosi, excusa sunt vobis haec Agricolae dia / lectica. q[ui]bus nihil ce[n]seo vtilius futuru[m] iis: q[ui] vera[m] secta[n]tur arte[m] diserte eloquenterq[ue] dice[n] / di: q[ui]q[ue] no[n] verbis t[a]m[en] inanibus: sed vberi reru[m] copia studeant summa cu[m] admiratione p[er] / suadere: atq[ue] de re qualibet ex p(ro)babilibus apposite: dece[n]terq[ue] ratiocinari: quod noster / ille munus esse dialecticu[m] testatur: hic itaq[ue] garrula sophistar(um) delirame[n]ta ne expectetis: / veru[m] ea expectate: quae a multis- sci[enti]arum limites co[n]funde[n]tibus: rhetoric[a]e tributa: p(ro)pria /t[ame]n sunt dialectic[a]e: quaeq[ue] in Aristotelis Ciceronisq[ue] libris desidera[n]tur: q[ui]bus certe hic li / ber nihilo est inferior: siue elegantiam filumq[ue] dictionis spectemus: siue doctrine prae- / ceptorumq[ue] traditionem'. See above, chapter 1.

51. See Iseghem, *Biographie de Thierry Martens*.

52. In that case, Rescius having requested more material to fill the space left by Martens, Erasmus sent too much, and in the resulting printing, the *castigator* had to use all possible contractions to fit the text into the allotted gap.

53. de Vocht, *Monumenta Humanistica*, 404.

54. Ibid.

55. Dorp's letter contains the following passage: '[Martens] has finished printing in correct form the *Cato* which you corrected and entrusted to me, and of which I have corrected the proofs'. Presumably Allen imagined this news would no longer be particularly fresh as late as January 1515. But since Erasmus had left Louvain before the *Cato* was published, there is no real reason why Dorp as the *castigator* should not inform Erasmus of the successful completion of his task on the first occasion on which he wrote to Erasmus after his departure.

56. CWE 3:110. This letter occurs only in the Deventer letter-book (according to Allen). This volume 'was copied by Erasmus' pupils during the years 1517–18' (Allen 1:604), and was perhaps intended for later circulation or publication by Erasmus during that crucial period.

57. Erasmus claimed in a later letter that he had not published Dorp's original letter in August 1515 because a copy was not to hand. The second letter (to which

Thomas More replied), is dated August 27, 1515. This letter was not printed after More had replied, and neither was More's own letter. But Erasmus's published correspondence emphasises the fact that copies of both letter circulated widely (see Introduction). The idea that Erasmus's long, careful reply is 'hasty' is surely another Erasmian contrivance, indicating a certain studied nonchalance, perhaps, about the whole exchange.

58. 'Rem fecisti, mi Noviomage, supra quam dici potest, mihi gratam, quod satyras tuas nuper ad me miseris. Sed te demiror qui me censorem earum adhibueris, hominem jam olim a toto Musarum choro alienum, ac sacrae [theologiae] mancipatum' (Prinsen, *Gerardus Geldenhauer*, 151).

59. On this exchange of letters in relation to Louvain University, see, in addition to the works already cited, J. Lindeboom, *Het Bijbelsch Humanisme in Nederland* (Leiden, 1913), especially 226–37.

60. This is how Erasmus addresses Dorp in the first published letter.

61. See Iseghem, *Biographie de Thierry Martens*, for a checklist of books and *castigatores* for this period.

62. Surtz and Hexter, *Yale Edition of the Complete Works of St. Thomas More* 4:2. The 1517 edition carries the boast that the work is 'ab innumeris mendis vndequaque purgatio [sic]', and the 1518 edition carries a commendatory epistle from Erasmus.

63. This account is closely based on Surtz's admirable summary of events. See Surtz and Hexler, *Yale Edition of the Complete Works of St. Thomas More*, clxxxiv.

64. See in particular the prefatory letter to the *Moriae encomium*.

65. See also below, Conclusion.

66. The 'Dorp' edition is riddled with typographical errors, and contains no chapter breaks; Phrissemius's first edition tidies up, and introduces plausible chapter breaks (and an altered decision as to where book 3 begins).

67. Other than tidied-up typographical errors, punctuation (between the 1515 and Phrissemius editions), and a few quibbles about grammar and syntax, in which Phrissemius emends the text, whereas Alardus leaves it as established in the 'Dorp' text.

68. Bietenholz and Deutscher, *Contemporaries of Erasmus* (3:79) has 1527.

69. I take this biographical account from ibid., 3:79. On Phrissemius's teaching at Cologne see also K. Meerhoff, 'Mélanchthon lecteur d'Agricola: Rhétorique et analyse textuelle', *Reforme Humanisme Renaissance* 30 (1990), 6–22.

70. 'In 1528 (Ep 1978) Erasmus judged Phrissemius to be a promising but somewhat immature young scholar on the basis of his edition of Rodolphus Agricola's *De inventione dialectica*' (ibid.). See Allen 7:368 (ep 1978): 'Opus de Inuentione Rhetorica [sic] quidam onerauit commentariis, iuuenis, vt apparet, nec indoctus nec infacundus; sed insunt multa *parerga*, quaedam etiam odiosiora iuueniliterque destomachata'.

71. Alardus, *Lucubrationes*, sig. †2ᵛ. He also expresses delight that Alardus has apparently just (that is, in 1529) gained possession of a 'truly authentic' manuscript of the work, in place of the corrupt one hitherto available.

72. 'Eramq[ue] hoc quicquid erroris erat, plane assignaturus typographis, nisi pridie q[uam] in hunc locu[m] scribere coepissem, allatu[m] ad me fuisset exem-

plar scriptu[m]. Id in eum usq[ue] die[m] delituerat Dauentriae, primu[m] apud Iacobu[m] Fabrum, deinde apud istos quos uocant fratres. Quid multis? Thesaur[um] aliquem inuenisse mihi uidebar sed posteaq[uam] aperui, postqua[m] coepi euoluere: aliud nihil q[uam] syluam qua[n]dam futuri adhuc operis deprehendi: in ijs praesertim, quae sua manu exararat Rodolph[us]. Quadruplex e[ni]m scriptura, aut si id mauis, character erat: & qu[a]e scripta essent manu ipsius, id iam constabat ex epistola quadam eius ad Langiu[m], cuius nobis legendae copia[m] fecerat anno superiore amicus quida[m]. In ijs ergo alia uelut obeliscis confossa era[n]t, alia rursus ceu asterisci quida[m] in margine notata. Quaeda[m] bis ter'ue paucis interim commutatis uerbis repetebantur: quaeda[m] immutata sic erant ut uix agnosceres. Quoties aut[em] capita tota, uel expu[n]cta omnino, uel in aliu[m] erant locu[m] traducta? quoties pagellae aliquot desiderebant? quoties interlitis medijs, margo occupatus sic erat, ut extrema uerba legi no[n] possent? quoties ita confusa atq[ue] permista omnia, ut nec caput nec pes usqua[m] existeret?' ('Scholia in caput XVI', Phrissemius, *De inventione dialectica*, 282–83).

73. The text is: 'Principem Gr[a] ec[a]e facundiae uirum Demosthenem, cum ad bellum co[n]tra Philippum, Macedonu[m] rege[m], maiori apparatu atq[ue] cura gerendum, populu[m] hortaretur Athenie[n]sem'. I cite the passage from Alardus's 1539 edition. Alardus retains the original version, and makes no comment concerning a possible error, in his scholia to the passage.

74. 'Monui libro superiori, me co[n]iectura quadam adduci, ut credam exemplar illud quo sunt usi chalcographi Louanie[n]ses, scriptum quidem aut dictatum certe fuisse ab Rodolpho ipso, at non in hoc scriptum dictatum'ue ut sic ederetur' (Phrissemius, *De inventione dialectica*, 146–47).

75. Ibid., 120. The marginal note to the * reads 'opposita'.

76. 'Ego tametsi qua[n]to licuit studio id egi, ut mihi uel archetypum ipsum, uel alioqui eme[n]datum aliquod co[m]pararem exemplar: hactenus tamen spe ea frustratus sum: neq[ue] ullum aliud co[n]tigit: q[uam] quod excusum Louanij, infinitis propemodu[m] me[n]dis contaminatu[m] est, quor[um] ut pars maxima reijci in typographos potest. . . . ita quaeda[m] rursus, quemadmodu[m] partim iam indicauimus, partim suis locis indicaturi sumus, non illor[um] uel inscitia uel neglige[n]tia irrepsisse, sed initio par[um] eme[n]date scripta fuisse mihi uidentur. Apparetq́[ue] exe[m]plari illos usos esse, quod aut scripserit, ut sic aut dictarit Rodolphus ipse, uer[um] non in hoc tame[n] dictarit aut scripserit, ut sic prodiret in luce[m]: sed ut post mensem unu[m] aut alter[um], sub incudem reuocatum, emendaretur dilige[n]tius: et si quae adhuc labeculae (ita ut solet) occurrerent, e[a]eq[ue] exactissima cura eluere[n]tur. Ergo ut tande[m] aliqua[n]do ueniamus ad id, quod in praesentia agitur, non negauerim ego, ab Rodolpho scriptu[m] sic esse ut exe[m]plaria habent: sed & illud econtrario ausim conte[n]dere, nihil minus illum scribere uoluisse, quàm quod scripsit' (ibid., 128–89).

77. See previous chapter, and below.

78. Alardus, *Lucubrationes*, sig. †2ᵛ.

79. See chapter 3.

80. 'Is inquam Pompeius per literas me submonuit . . . sibi restitutum esse tandem [autographom] illud inuentionis di[a]lecticae annos minimum duodecim non sine multis & magnis periculis per multorum barbarorum manus sursum

deorsum uersus iactitatum, priusquam esset exhibitu[m]. . . . Nec opinor Proser-
pinam à Plutone abductam ad campos Elysios, à Cerere matre toto orbe diligen-
tius quaesitam esse. Porro autem cum exemplar à Iacobo Fabro Dauentriensi uiro
pio ac docto Louaniu[m] usq[ue] allatum accuratius una cum D. Martino Dorpio
expendissem, deprehendi omnia aut fere omnia perturbatius esse descripta. Alia
enim uelut obeliscis confossa era[n]t, alia rursus ceu asterisci quidam in margine
notata. Quaedam bis terúe paucis interim commutatis uerbis repetebantur,
quaeda[m] sic erant immutata, ut uix agnosceres. Quoties aut[em] capita tota uel
expuncta omnino, uel in aliu[m] era[n]t locu[m] traducta? quoties pagellae aliquot desideraba[n]tur? quoties interlitis medijs margo sic erat occupatus, ut
extrema uerba legi no[n] possent? quoties ita confusa atq[ue] permista o[mn]ia,
ut nec caput, nec pes usq[uam] existeret? Proinde dici no[n] potest, imo ne cogi-
tari quide[m], quo mihi animus gaudio gestierit . . . q[uo]d eae lucubratio[n]es
cognitu dignissime redijssent tandem in manus amici' (Alardus, *Lucubrationes*,
sig. *4^r-v).
  81. 'Vide pensum tuu[m] lepide accures, & opus q[uo]d olim primus
omniu[m] partim mutilu[m], partim deprauatum dedisti excudendum, ia[m] nunc
reco[n]cinnatum emendatius multo, multoq́[ue] locupletius dato, perinde atq[ue]
pri[m]a statim aeditio[n]e pollicitus es. Posteaq[uam] ergo nactus sis [archety-
pum] si q[ui]d forte adhuc ex uaria exe[m]plarioru[m] inter ipsa collatio[n]e,
adhibito sobrio iudicio, exclusaq́[ue] co[n]tentio[n]e muta[n]du[m] putabis, erit
adiume[n]to tibi uir o[mn]ino acris iudicij o[mn]iq́[ue] reru[m] copiam in-
structiss[imus] Iacobus Volcardus Berge[n]sis. Erit D. Herman[n]us à Gauda uir
summa eruditio[n]e, ueru[m] moru[m] integritate neutiq[uam] inferior se. Erit et
Corn[elius] ille tuus Crocus, q[ui] literas aequauit, cu[m] uitae sanctimonia prae-
cipuus iuue[n]tutis institue[n]dae artifex. . . . Alius aliter inquit fortasse, ego ita
sentio' (sig. †1^r). For a commented text of this letter see A. Roersch, *Correspon-*
dance de Nicolas Clénard (2 vols.) (Brussels, 1940) 1:1–7; commentary, 2:1–13.
  82. See Bietenholz and Deutscher, *Contemporaries of Erasmus*.
  83. See above, chapter 3.
  84. At the end of Alardus's text, in the 1539 edition, he prints the date, 1483.
Agricola was in Deventer in 1484, when he gave the 'Anna mater' poem to Hegius
for publication (see above, chapter 3; the evidence for the 1484 visit is contained
in a letter to Antonius Liberus, printed in Alardus, *Lucubrationes*, 176–77, beginning 'Annam matrem imprimendam dedi'). So this date is still consistent with the
single Deventer 'mutilated' manuscript.
  85. Alardus studied in Cologne in 1515–16, during an outbreak of plague in
Louvain.
  86. Reprinted in W. Trillitzsch, *Seneca im Literarischen Urteil der Antike: Dar-*
stellung und Sammlung der Zeugnisse (2 vols.) (Amsterdam, 1971), 2:426. See
below, chapter 5.
  87. Allen, ep 936; cited in Meerhoff, 'Mélancthon lecteur d'Agricola', 6.
  88. I shall return to this idea of a 'circle', with Erasmus at its centre, in chapter 6.
  89. 'Hic praelegebat Ioan. Phryssemius utrumque librum Copiae Eras(mi), de
inventione dialectica lib. Rod. Agricolae tres, orationem Ciceronis pro lege Ma-
nilia, Vergilii Aeneid. posteriores libros VI, epistolam Pauli ad Romanos, isagogen

in literas Graecas et Gryllum Plutarchi. Arnoldus Vuesaliensis exponebat Georgica Vergilii, odas Horatii, Aristot. de syllogismo, de anima etc.' (E. Egli [ed.], *Heinrich Bullingers Diarium [Annales vitae] der Jahre, 1504–1574* [Basle, Geering, 1905], 5). I owe this reference to Kees Meerhoff, 'Mélanchthon lecteur d'Agricola', 5–22, 9. I am extremely grateful to Kees Meerhoff for making his remarkably original work available to me, and for prompting me in fruitful directions in my own work on a number of occasions.

90. For an example of the way in which this pedagogic bracketing together of Agricola and Erasmus has become commonplace by the later sixteenth century, see the Cambridge booklist reproduced in Jardine and Grafton, *From Humanism to the Humanities.*

CHAPTER FIVE

1. As Nauwelaerts puts it: 'Hoe komt het dat Rodolphus Agricola door de eerste generatie van de transalpijnse humanisten bijzonder hoog werd geroemd, dat hij door de Duitse humanisten als een voorloper werd beschouwd en dat zijn invloed zo diepgaande was in West-Europa? Agricola was geen groot schrijver, hoewel taalpurist en verfijnd redenaar; hij heeft geen indrukwekkende rij van boeken nagelaten; hij was geen begenadigd docent, die honderden leerlingen heeft gevormd, zoals Hegius; geen adminstrator of organisator van scholen en schoolwezen, zoals Melancht[h]on; geen beroemd controversist, zoals zijn vriend Johann Reuchlin; geen diepzinnig filosoof, zoals zijn tijdgenoot, de Ockhamist Gabriël Biel' (*Rodolphus Agricola*, 157).

2. As Erasmus romanticised that *traditio* to Botzheim in a self-consciously retrospective letter of 1523: 'When I was a boy, the humanities had begun to put forth fresh shoots among the Italians; but because the printer's art was either not yet invented or known to very few, nothing in the way of books came through to us, and unbroken slumber graced the universal reign of those who taught ignorance in place of knowledge. Rodolfus Agricola was the first to bring us a breath of more humane learning out of Italy; in Deventer, as a boy of twelve or so, I was blessed with a sight of him, and that was all' (CWE 9:294 [letter 1341A]).

3. 'Lucubrationes Rodolphi Agricolae, hominis vere diuini, iamdudum expectamus; cuius ego scripta quoties lego, toties pectus illud sacrum ac coeleste mecum adoro atque exosculor' (*De copia*, fol. 2^r, reprinted in Allen 2:32 [ep 311]). See also CWE 24:289.

4. See Jardine, 'Distinctive Discipline'.

5. On the word *copia*, and the phrases *copia dicendi, copia verborum, copia rerum*, see Terence Cave, *The Cornucopia Text: Problems of Writing in the French Renaissance* (Oxford, 1979), 3–7. I am indebted to Cave's treatment of *copia* in part 1 of *Cornucopian Text*, which stimulated me to think about the topic in relation to humanist dialectic in fresh ways.

6. 'Quod si quis latius ista et per omnes locos dialecticos fuerit [*sic*], quatenus cuiusque natura capax eorum est, inge[n]s utiq[ue] copia & ad dindum, & ad inueniendum se praebebit. quod quomodo faciendum sit, maius est, quàm ut epistola id capiat, & copiose est à me ea de re in tribus libris eis, quos de inuentio[n]e dialectica scripsi disputatum' (Alardus, *Lucubrationes*, 199).

7. Allen 2:362–70 (ep 480).

8. See above, chapter 3. We should note as always that Gilles is involved both with publishing Agricola and with publishing Erasmus.

9. See Jardine, 'Distinctive Discipline'.

10. Cave, *Cornucopian Text*, 16–17. By contrast, for a dismally muddled treatment of the *De inventione dialectica*, displaying the blinkeredness typical of traditional historians of dialectic, and characteristically confused as to what kind of 'tradition' Agricola belongs to, see J. Monfasani, 'Lorenzo Valla and Rudolph Agricola', *Journal of the History of Philosophy* 28 (1990), 181–200.

11. Like most of his contemporaries, Erasmus believed Seneca to be author both of the rhetorical and of the moral works (in fact the work of father and son respectively), though he expressed doubt about his authorship of the tragedies. See Panizza, 'Biography in Italy', 47–98; 52–53.

12. CWE 3:66 (ep 325).

13. On Jerome and Seneca see W. Trillitzsch, *Seneca im Literarischen Urteil der Antike: Darstellung und Sammlung der Zeugnisse* (2 vols.) (Amsterdam, 1971), 1:143–61.

14. 'Ad lectorem. Quia admodum difficule est, in tam deprauatis exemplaribus, cuncta resituere, igitur ubi autorem nimia uetustate corruptum arbitrati sumus, * asteriscum apposuimus. Ubi uero meliora interserenda putauimus, id quoq[ue] suis locis, ubi hoc signum [dagger] uideris annotauim[us]. Proinde haec boni consulito. No[n] enim ubiq[ue] tutum fuit, uel q[uam] leuissimis coniecturis uti' (Seneca, *Lucubrationes*). For a clear account of the evolution of Erasmus's Seneca editions see Trillitzsch, *Seneca* 1:221–50. See also Beroaldus's Tacitus of the same year for these procedures.

15. I have used the copy in the Archives of Speer Library, Princeton Theological Seminary. This copy carries copious annotations, dated 1528, which show that the contemporary reader was aware of some of the glaring anomalies and mistakes in the volume.

16. This story is in the 1523 *catologus* letter to Botzheim, and is repeated in every scholarly study either of Erasmus's Seneca, or of Seneca editions in general. See L. D. Reynolds, *The Medieval Tradition of Seneca's Letters* (Oxford, Oxford University Press, 1965), 5–6; Trillitzsch, *Seneca* 1:225–28. As we shall see, Nesen acted as proof corrector for the 1517 Froben *De copia*, which carried a dedicatory letter to him; Beatus Rhenanus remained closely involved with Erasmus's publications.

17. As we saw, for instance, in his description of the 'Herculean labours' which went into the Jerome edition, or into the *Adagia*. And, for instance, Bruno Amerbach's letter about that edition (CWE 3:139 [ep 337A]): 'The volume of spurious works is going on even better than it deserves, though the manuscripts are so full of mistakes that it would be less trouble to clean out an Augean cowbyre. We shall finish, as far as I can guess, about the first of August. Unless you are content for Jerome to run dreadful risks, you will do well to come back to us soon. As for me, if I have made any mistake from my native ignorance, I will do my best to correct it. In haste, from Messrs Froben's treadmill in Basel. Froben and my brother Basilius send greetings'. See also Bierlaire, *La familia*.

18. See also, for instance, the supposed 'interpolation' by a secretary in the *Adagia*, recounted by M. Mann Phillips, *The Adages of Erasmus: A Study with Translations* (Cambridge, 1964), 162–63.

19. See Reynolds, *Medieval Tradition*, and Trillitzsch, *Seneca*.

20. 'Non hic verbis attollam quantum mihi laboris exhaustum sit. Scio neminem crediturum, nisi priorem aeditionem cum hac contulerit. Id si quis non grauabitur facere, continue fatebitur alium prodisse Seneca' (Allen 8:28 [ep 2091]). The new editions is typographically, as well as textually, a significant improvement.

21. For a concise description of the volume's contents see Trillitzsch, *Seneca*, 235. Beatus Rhenanus also adds the following 'personalising' comment, at the end of his revised commentary to the 'De morte Claudij ludus': 'Habes candide lector annotatiunculas nostras in Senecae libellu[m], quantum quidem in ista temporis angustia scribere licuit. Porro gratulandum est bonis studijs quod que[m]admodum caetera Senec[a]e opera maximis Erasmi sudoribus adamussim castigata, nunc in lucem prodeunt, sic & hoc opusculum aliquanto factum emendatius & magis quam ante scholijs illustratum una cum illis in publicum exit. Quae res absq[ue] labore confecta non est. Bene Vale. Basileae, Calen. Februarijs An. M.D.XXIX.'

22. See A. Grafton, *Forgers and Critics: Creativity and Duplicity in Western Scholarship* (Princeton, 1990), 43. Happening upon this reference to a *De copia verborum* of Seneca's in Tony Grafton's book started off the train of thinking which is represented in this chapter. As always, I am immensely grateful to him for the stimulating discussions which regularly give rise to these kinds of insight.

23. Allen 8:40; cited in Grafton, *Forgers and Critics*, 43.

24. 'Scio te non tam tui causa commotum litteris quas ad te de editione epistolarum mearum [tuarum] Caesari feci quam natura rerum, quae ita mentes hominum ab omnibus artibus et moribus rectis revocat, ut non hodie admirer, quippe ut is qui multis documentis hoc iam notissimum habeam. Igitur nove agamus, et si quid facile in praeteritum factum est, veniam inrogabis. Misi tibi librum de verborum copia. Vale[,] Paule carissime' (Text from Claude W. Barlow [ed.], *Epistolae Senecae ad Paulum et Pauli ad Senecam ⟨quae vocantur⟩* [Horn, Austria, 1938], 131–32; translation, 144). The alternative readings in square brackets are from the more recent Italian critical edition: L. Bocciolini Palagi, *Il carteggio apocrifo di Seneca e San Paolo: Introduzione, testo, commento* (Florence, 1978), 71.

25. The Seneca/Paul correspondence and the *De quattuor virtutibus cardinalibus*, although relegated to the end of the volume, are not explicitly labelled as spurious. A number of other spurious works remain in the body of the volume. By contrast, both the *De moribus* and the *Prouerbia* carried marginal notes declaring them 'non a Seneca fuisse'. On Martin de Braga and the Seneca *spuria* see Claude W. Barlow, *Martini Episcopi Bracarensis Opera Omnia* (New Haven, 1950), 204–50.

26. Erasmus, *Opera Senecae* (Froben, Basle, 1529), sig. a 1ᵛ. I have used the copy in the Rare Books Room of Firestone Library, Princeton University.

27. The English critical edition of the Seneca/Paul correspondence has the following to say about the work specified as a *De copia*: 'Numerous instances of *copia verborum* and *copia dicendi* in Cicero's *De Oratore* and in Quintilian show that to these authors the phrase meant facility in using the Latin language. The same meaning is quite in keeping with the general tone of the present Correspondence, in which Seneca often criticises Paul for not expressing better his fine senti-

ments. Codex Q contains a work which bears the title *De Copia Verborum*, and in other manuscripts, e.g. *Paris lat, 8542*, the heading indicates that scribes believed this to be the very treatise which Seneca sent to Paul' (Barlow, *Epistolae Senecae ad Paulum*, 144). Both the English and Italian critical editions of the letters suggest, on the basis of this preoccupation with the pseudo-correspondence with style and rhetoric, that the author may have belonged to a fourth century rhetoric school, and that the letters may have originated in a classroom exercise, subsequently misidentified as an authentic collection of *epistolae*. We may take it, I think, that Erasmus's own interest in a missing *De copia* by Seneca (contemporary of, if not correspondent with, Paul) similarly arises out of a concern with a kind of *eloquentia* appropriate to Christianity.

28. In the carefully instructive preface to the 1529 Seneca, Erasmus draws attention to Quintilian's comments on Seneca in *Institutio oratoria*, book 10.

29. On 'Quintilian's' *Minor Declamationes*, in particular, see M. Winterbottom (ed.), *The Minor Declamations Ascribed to Quintilian* (Berlin, 1984), xxii–xxv; especially xvi–xvii: 'The *Minor Declamations*, in fact, are pedagogic in purpose; they aim at the production of orators ready to take their part in the law courts. . . . a) The declamations are often equipped with elaborate pointers that make clear the division even where no *sermo* precedes. . . . b) The insistent use of bicolic variation in repetition, with or without anaphora (thus e.g. 266.7 *quis . . . me innocentem, quis dignum conversatione vestra putaret . . . ut in civitate remanerem, ut essem vobiscum . . . ut probarem me innocentem, nihil contra patriam meam esse molitum*) is perhaps more than a trick of style. It showed the pupil how an idea acould be expressed in different ways, how flexible language could be; it built up *hexis*. ⟨It was a better way of teaching synonyms than the learning of lists, condemned by Quintilian at 10.1.7. There is an instructive parallel in Isidore's *Synonyma*. . . .⟩'. On declamations in general see S. F. Bonner, *Roman Declamation in the Late Republic and Early Empire* (Berkeley and Los Angeles, 1949); S. F. Bonner, *Education in Ancient Rome* (London, 1977); R. A. Kaster, *Guardians of Language: The Grammarians and Society in Late Antiquity* (Berkeley, 1988).

30. 'Alium [prodidi] Senecam: non quod nihil resederit excutiendum, sed quod innumera portenta non minus feliciter quam fortiter sustulerimus, idque praesidio diuersorum codicum, inter quos erant aliquot mirae vetustatis. Diuinationi non temere indulsimus, experimento docti quam id tutum non sit. Et tamen alicubo diuinandum fuit, nec raro feliciter cessit coniectura nisi me fallunt omnia. Adiuuit in hoc labore nonnihil industria Matthaei Fortunati Pannonii, hominis, vt res indicat, exacte docti, diligentis, sobrii sanique iudicii. Is enim libros Naturalium Quaestionum accuratissime recognouit: quod operae vtinam et in caeteris omnibus praestitisset! Quem vt in plerisque libenter sequuti sumus, ita in nonnullis ab eo dissentimus, praesertim vbi nostro sensui suffragabantur exemplaria. Profuit et Rodolphi Agricolae codex typis excusus Taruisii, ante annos quinquaginta: quem is vigilantissime videtur euoluisse. Arguebant hoc notulae manus ipsius, quibus innumera loca correxerat, sed in multis, vt apparebat, diuinationem ingenii sequutus magis quam exemplaris vetusti fidem. Incredibile vero quam multa diuinarit vir ille plane diuinus; non enim possum Rodolphi dotes et plurimas et eximias complecti breuius. Eius codicis nobis copiam fecit Hayo Herman-

nus Phrysius, iuuenis tam felici natus indole vt vnus videatur idoneus qui Rodol-
phicae laudis successionem capessat, tantique viri gloriam sustineat; alioqui et
patriam habens cum illo communem et affinitate propinquus. Quin et Sigismun-
dus Gelenius, qui iampridem in officina Frobeniana castigandi praefecturam gerit,
vir citra omnem ostentationem exquisite doctus et, quod in eruditis quoque rarum
est, emunctae naris exactique iudicii, non pauca feliciter deprehendit quae nos in
multa distractos, interdum et defessos, fefellerant. Non enim est mei ingenii
quenquam laude merita fraudare' (Allen 8:28).

31. See Bietenholz and Deutscher, *Contemporaries of Erasmus*, s.v. 'Haio
Herman', 1498/1500–1539/40.

32. See above, chapter 2.

33. 'Gratulor tibi incolumem ex Italia reditum, gratulor felix coniugium, vt
vtrunque perpetuum sit vehementer optans. Dialogis meis de Pronunciatione et
Ciceroniano adieci orationem Rodolphi Agricolae, Mediolani, sic vti videtur,
habitam. Nihil ab illo viro proficiscitur quod non diuinitatem quandam spiret.
Itaque nolim quicquam illius intercidere. Hoc studii, mi Hermanne, debes vel
patriae vel affinitati. Quare te rogo vt in hoc incumbas. Nulli magis congruit hoc
munus quam tibi. Opus de Inuentione Rhetorica [*sic*] quidam onerauit commentariis, iuuenis, vt apparet, nec indoctus nec infacundus; sed insunt multa *parerga*,
quaedam etiam odiosiora iuueniliterque destomachata. Malim scholia docta et ad
rem facientia. Ni tot oneribus essem oppressus, non grauarer hanc suscipere prouinciam; adeo faueo Rodolphi memoriae. Hanc operam si sumpseris, simul et
tuum nomen reddes illustrius. Feret haec aliquam tibi fama commoditatem. Soce-
rum tuum Pompeium Occonem saluta meis verbis diligenter. Tu vale quam optime' (Allen 7:368 [ep 1978]). See also Allen 7:533–34 (ep 2073) (to Haio Cam-
myngha, a fellow Frisian, also published in the *Opus Epistolarum*): 'Vt enim
sileam Canterios et Langios, quid Rodolpho Agricola diuinius? in cuius gloriam
succedit Haio Hermannus, iuuenis nihil mediocre de se pollicens, qui tibi huius
laudis lampadem aliquando traditurus est; nam Viglium, vt scribis, gaudeo in hoc
stadio strenue properare. Haec arguunt non omnino vanum esse quod vulgo nar-
rant, Phrysiam esse felicissimam ingeniorum parentem, sed vitae delicias [non]
obstare quo minus multa ad summam virtutem eluctentur'.

34. Translation of Lucian's *De non facile credendis delationibus* (Louvain,
R. Rescius and J. Sturm, July 4, 1530; NK 558). His prefatory letter is reprinted
in Alardus, *Lucubrationes*, 243–45.

35. There is some difference of opinion in the secondary literature as to the
extent of Haio Hermann's involvement in Agricola publications. Allen, 'The Letters of Rudolph Agricola', suggests that Hermann began as joint editor with Alardus of Agricola's *Opera*, but later dropped out of the project.

36. 'Senecam exorsi sunt; nam ad libros De Beneficiis eramus abunde instructi.
Interim hunc veredarium emisimus nostro sumptu, non ob aliud nisi vt nobis
adferat tuum codicem: cui nihil est quod metuas; praeter vnum me nullus illum
contiget. Tantum obuoluas illum tunicis chartaceis, ita vt summum operculum sit
linteum ceratum; remittetur eadem diligentia. In praefatione dabitur oportunitas
honorifice commemorandi tui nominis, si modo id pateris. Quos codices viderit
Viues nescio, nisi forte tuum, aut eum qui per amicum quendam collatus aliquam-

diu fuit apud Thomam Morum. Verum mihi tanta sylua annotationum congesta est vt nec illius nec tuum codicem metuam' (Allen 7:506 [ep 2056]). Along with the public commendations, Erasmus offered Hermann more practical recompense for his assistance. With this letter he enclosed letters of recommendation to Erard de la Marck and John Carondelet at the imperial court at Mechelin (epp 2054, 2055) (also published in the 1529 *Opus epistolarum*). Hermann's 1530 Agricola Lucian translation was dedicated to de la Marck.

37. 'Remitto codicem tuum—quo nihil, vt scribis, pulchrius—vna cum duobus excusis. Ex pacto mihi dabantur tres; maiorem portionem tibi cedo. Si tuus codex valebat quinquaginta florenis, excusus valet mille: nec tamen inficias eo tuum alicubi profuisse. Non fraudauimus Rodolphum sua laude, vt arbitror. Tui quoque mentionem fecimus in praefatione; et Ciceroniano nomen tuum adiecimus. Si nondum videor animo tuo satisfecisse, quod coepimus implebitur de meo. Nam defuncto Ioanne Frobenio tota officinae ratio mutata est' (Allen 8:66 [ep 2108]).

38. Critics have suggested some sort of tension between Erasmus and Hermann after this exchange of codices and compliments. It seems more likely to me that Erasmus had no further use for (and therefore interest in) Hermann hereafter.

39. There is a further letter in the 1529 *Opus epistolarum* volume advertising the extent of Erasmus's search for further 'codices' of Seneca, via Vives and Thomas More (Allen 7:469–71 [ep 2040]). The letter clearly suggests that there are further 'codices' (printed volumes or manuscripts, which Erasmus wishes to consult). However, Vives's reply (printed in his own *Opera*, but not amongst Erasmus's letters), declines involvement in the project. On Vives and Seneca see Karl Alfred Blüher, *Séneca en España: Investigaciones sobre la recepión de Séneca en España desde el siglo XIII hasta el siglo XVII* (Spanish version, expanded and corrected) (Madrid, 1983), 260–84.

40. As so often, this means that Allen was unable to find it, and subsequent scholars (including myself) have concurred with his view that it is lost.

41. 'Taruisij per Bernadum de Colonia Anno domini M.cccc.lxxviij'. I have used the copy in the Kane Collection, Firestone Library, Princeton University. According to L. D. Reynolds, *Medieval Tradition*, the Treviso Seneca is a reprinting of the *editio princeps* published in Naples in 1475.

42. The phrasing of Erasmus's letter is sufficiently misleading to lead at least one scholar to believe that Erasmus used Agricola's corrections as part of the apparatus for the new version of the *Quaestiones naturales*. See D. F. S. Thompson, 'Erasmus and Textual Scholarship in the Light of Sixteenth-Century Practice', in Weiland and Frijhoff, *Erasmus of Rotterdam*, 158–71, 159. For a suggestive introduction to the whole question of studying Erasmus as a textual editor see P. Petitmengin, 'Comment étudier l'activité d'Érasme éditeur de textes antiques?' in J.-C. Margolin (ed.), *Colloquia Erasmiana Turonensia* (2 vols.) (Paris, 1972), 1:217–22.

43. 'In the Copenhagen MS. are two leaves (151–2) of autograph notes by Erasmus, which were printed in this new edition, pp. 348, 333; they give readings from Agricola's volume' (Allen 8:26).

44. 'Quum epistolarum opus iam aliqua ex parte esset excusum, allatum est exemplar e Brabantia, ex cuius collatione si qua prius fefellera[n]t restituimus. Ea

quoniam in contextu[m] inseri non potera[n]t, hac appe[n]dice subiecimus: no-
tauimus obiter et illa quae operarum incuria com[m]itti solent, praesertim si quid
uidebitur alicuius momenti' (Seneca, *Opera* [Basle, Froben, 1529], 268).

45. For example: 'In librum quartum [epistolarum]. [105] Ver. a fine 22. Quidam sic habebat, quod illi genus insaniae hilare contigerit. Nec dubium quin haec
germana sit lectio. Rodulphus [*sic*] Agricola manu notarat' (ibid., 269); (On book
8, ep 60 'De uero et inani gaudio') '[133] Ver. ab epist. initio 4. pro, ad nostrum
aluum, Rodulphus legendum putat, ad nostrum album, ut intelligas ad iudicium
Stoicorum. Et magnopere placet Rodolphi sententia' (ibid., 270).

46. See M. G. M. van der Poel, *De Declamatio bij de Humanisten: Bijdrage tot
de studie van de Functies van de Rhetorica in de Renaissance* (Nieuwkoop, 1987),
9. In 1529 Bebelius also published Quintilian's *Institutio oratoria* and *Declamationes*, with a prefatory letter by Sichardus (*M. Fabri Quintiliani oratoris eloquentissimi institutionum oratorium libri XII, incredibili cum studio tum iudicio
ad fidem uetustissimi exemplaris recens iam recogniti. Eiusdem Declamationum
Liber*).

47. See Nauwelaerts, *Rodolphus Agricola*, 166. Huisman, *Rudolph Agricola*,
does not record editions of this work at all. See most recently van der Poel, *De
Declamatio*, 9: 'De enige die bij mijn weten over de publicatie van de nalatenschap
van Agricola heeft gepubliceerd is P. S. Allen, *The Letters of Rudolph Agricola*, in:
The English Historical Review 21 (1906), p. 302 sqq. Dit artikel bevat geen gegevens over Agricola's commentaar op de *declamationes*. Evenmin zijn hierover
gegevens te vinden in K. Hartfelder, ed., *Unedierte Briefe von Rudolf Agricola,
Festschrift der Badischen Gymnasien, gewidmet der Universität Heidelberg zur
Feier ihres 500järigen Jubiläums*, Karlsruhe 1886. Ook het voorwoord in de post-
hume editie van Ioannes Bebelius, de drukker en uitgever, bevat geen verhelde-
rende punten voor deze kwestie: van het werkje, "gemmula" zoals Bebelius het
noemt, zegt hij slechts "ab amico quodam doctissimo oblata" (ed. 1529, pp. 3–4;
dit voorwoord is niet opgenomen in de herdruk van 1539)'. On Bebelius see
Bietenholz and Deutscher, *Contemporaries of Erasmus*, s.v. 'Ioannes Bebelius',
'documented 1517–38'; the first record of Bebelius is as a *castigator* for Froben in
1517. The text (but not Bebelius's introduction) is reprinted in Alardus's 1539
volume of Agricola's *Lucubrationes*, 91–118. On Agricola's interest in *declamationes* see van der Poel, *De Declamatio*, 9–14.

48. See W. Trillitzsch, 'Erasmus und Seneca', *Philologus* (1965). See also Trillitzsch, *Seneca* 1:221–50.

49. Or, more surreptitiously, one of the *castigatores* working with Erasmus on
the Seneca was responsible for transmitting the text to Bebelius.

50. E.g., *Precatio dominica in septem portiones distributa* . . . (s.d. [1523]);
De libero arbitrio . . . (s.d. [1524]).

51. The Bebelius volume is extremely rare. I am grateful to Bill Sherman for
transcribing the prefatory letter from the copy in the Bodleian. For the full letter
see Appendices.

52. See J. M. M. Hermans, 'Agricola and His Books', in F. Akkerman and
A. J. Vanderjagt (eds), *Rodolphus Agricola Phrisius, 1444–1485: Proceedings of
the International Conference at the University of Groningen 28–30 October*

1985 (Leiden, 1988), 123–35; F. Römer, 'Agricolas arbeit am text des Tacitus und des jüngeren Plinius', ibid., 158–69.

53. Such inquiries have caused confusion in the secondary literature, which refers to commentaries on a number of these authors as 'lost works' of Agricola's, as if we are talking about completed, structured commentaries, rather than manuscript copies, and occasional marginal notes in printed (or manuscript) texts.

54. Chapter 3.

55. See *Rudolph Agricola, Gronings Humanist, 1485–1985*, 108. The catalogue states that the Pliny 'bevat eigendomskenmerken van Agricola zelf', while the Tacitus 'talrijke randnotities laat zien van Agricola, de Von Pleningens en van een onbekende derde'. See also, more fully, Römer, 'Agricolas arbeit', 163.

56. Römer, 163–69.

57. See reproduction, plate 6, Hermans, 'Agricola and His Books', 125.

58. Unlike the Seneca/Paul introduction, this is not included in Allen's *Opus epistolarum Erasmi*, and has therefore largely escaped the notice of critics. The introduction is printed in Trillitzsch, *Seneca* (2: 441–43). It is reproduced here in the Appendices. As far as I am aware, the only critic to give this introduction any attention is van der Poel, *De Declamatio*, 13:14–16.

59. 'Inter omnes Senecae lucubrationes, nullum opus extare integrum & inuiolatum magis referebat publica studioru[m] utilitas, quam hos declamationum libros' (Seneca, *Opera*, 1529, 485).

60. 'Hae censurae hominu[m] in omni doctrinae genere praecellentiu[m], incredibile dictu, quantu[m] utilitas attulissent, non solu[m] ad bene dicendu[m] ueru[m]etia[m] ad iudicandu[m], siue in forensibus causis, siue in concionibus popularibus militaribusue, siue in co[n]sessibus, siue in omni uitae functione, quae maxima ex parte, linguae prudentis officio temperatur. Ea inuenie[n]di iudicandiq[ue] facultas, si statim pueris tradatur, mihi uidetur multo plus fructus allatura, quam quae nunc in scholis traditur dialectica, qua[m] tamen nec improbo, nec submouendam censeo, modo resectis nugalibus argutijs, ad usum potius quam ad puerilem oste[n]tationem tradatur. Atq[ue] utinam felix aliquis casus hos Senecae libros nobis integros restituat'.

61. See H. D. L. Vervliet, 'De gedrukte overlevering van Seneca pater', *De Gulder Passer* 35 (1957), 179–222, 200–201. The first edition listed by Vervliet which includes the Agricola commentary on the *Declamationes* is dated 1537, i.e., before Alardus's *Lucubrationes* of Agricola were published, but during a period when he had them collected for publication. I have looked at the 1540 Basle edition in the Rare Books Collection, University of Pennsylvania, where the attribution of Erasmus's introduction (and indeed of all the annotations) is unclear, except for the inclusion on page 268 of the original description of the discovery of Agricola's annotated copy. I have also looked at the 1573 Basle edition in Speer Library, Princeton, where Erasmus's introduction appears on page 502, headed: 'Rodolphi Agricolae in primam Senecae declamationem, commentariolum. AD LECTOREM'. The title page of this volume perfectly exemplifies the influence of the Erasmus/Agricola conjunction on sixteenth-century readers of Seneca: 'L. Annaei Senecae Philosophi Stoicorum omnium acutissimi opera quae extant omnia: Coelii Secundi Curionis vigilantissima cura castigata, et nouam prorsus faciem,

nimirum propriam & suam, mutata: Quorum lectio non modo ad bene dicendum, uerumetiam ad bene beateq[ue] uiuendum, prodesse plurimum potest. Post Herculeos insuper C. S. C. labores, Vincentii Pralli H. opera ac studio, innumeris in locis emendata ac restituta. Totius emendationis ratio, quidq[ue] superiori aeditioni accesserit, ex sequentibus statim cognosces. Accessit index Rerum & uerborum copiosus.' Van der Poel reports that the 1557 Basle Seneca (Vervliet, 'De gedrukte', 200–201) also attributes this Erasmian introduction to Rudolph Agricola (van der Poel, *De Declamatio*, 13, note 49).

62. Cologne, H. Alopecius, 1527; Cologne, [F. Birckmann], 1528, (Huisman, *Rudolph Agricola*, items 15, 16).

63. 'Aristoteles certe, Plato, & quor[um] interea in philosophia paribus laudibus eloque[n]tia eruditioq[ue] celebrant[ur], rarissime putaueru[n]t utendu[m] sibi nudis illis & expressis ratiocinationibus, quod ex libris eorum facile perspectu est. At nostri seculi philosophis, qui quaeritur & arguitur primo et secu[n]do, & notandu[m] quarto & quinto, & consequentia tenet in baroco, & reliquas id genus ineptias demas, destitutos prorsus & nihil quod dicant habituros uidebis. Nec haec eo dico, quod ea pute[m] esse contemnenda. Disci enim illa ab incipie[n]tibus in scholis, & quidem exactissima cura, uelim, & exerceri quoq[ue], sed adeo ut intra schola[m] maneant' (Phrissemius, *De inventione dialectica*, 1528, 390).

64. 'Equidem argumentationem in oratione controuersa censeo necessariam esse, tanquam neruos sine quibus ea subsistere non possit. Sed quemadmodum deforme non modo sit corpus, sed nec corporis quidem speciem habeat, in quo soli sint omnique carne nudati nerui, sic nec orationis aut faciem aut nomen iure habent horridae istae & una perpetua specie compositae argumentationes. Apud Graecos quide[m] in prouerbio fuit, ut dicerent, egregia de lente, quoties minor res maiore[m] in modum tolleretur. Quanto nunc rectius hi notabu[n]tur, cum puerilibus etia[m] nugis diuina pertractent? Verte[n]dae sunt igitur formae argumentationu[m], & partes earum uaria collocatione disponendae. Nec t[ame]n adeo uitandus ordo rectus, ut credamus non interdu[m] ratiocinationem tota proferendam. quod & Quintilianus fecit in ea declamatione, quae inscribit[ur]: Ignominiosus co[n]tra tres rogationes. Ergo (inquit) si & ignominiosum uult esse eu[m] q[ui] ter contradixerit nec tenuerit, et hic contradixit ter nec tenuit, quo[niam] non sit ignominiosus, iuuenire profecto no[n] poterit' (ibid., 390–91). In his edition of the *Minor Declamations*, Winterbottom points out this use of the *Declamationes minores* by Agricola, and thanks Michael Reeve for identifying it. We know Erasmus had read this passage, because he includes Agricola's version of *egregia de lente* in the *Adagia* (see Alardus, *Lucubrationes*, 445).

65. 'Quanq[uam] no[n] destiterit eum Aristoteles incessere, tanq[uam] copia effusum, nouitatis cupidum, eloquendo tumidum, orationis ostentatorem. Fama tamen pro Platone stetit, & sicut multor[um] fauore Aristoteles aequauit primu[m]: sic maximorum iudicio Plato hunc proximum quide[m], sed infra se tamen, sicut omnes, reliquit. Quintilianus aute[m], sicut declamationu[m], sic altercationu[m] quoq[ue] proprium co[n]didit uolumen, quod in nostras peruenit manus, egregiu[m] quidem, sicut sunt illius uiri omnia' (Phrissemius, *De inventione dialectica*, 1528, 397).

66. 'Demiror ego, cum nihil ferme tam obrutum fuerit hactenus, quin in nostra hac tempestate in lucem prodeat, q[ui] fiat, ut hoc Fabrij altercationum opus nondum usquam excusum sit' (ibid., 399). Actually, there was a late fifteenth-century edition, but evidently Phrissemius did not know it.

67. Lotzer had inherited Hutten's manuscripts, including the Quintilian. See Allen 8:77. Already in 1515, when Erasmus was preparing the first edition of his Seneca, Rhenanus wrote to him asking that he 'give some thought to . . . emending Quintilian' (CWE 3:83 [ep 330]).

68. 'Habemus varias eruditorum annotationes in Quintilianum, et accepimus tibi codicem esse peruetustum; cuius ab nobis ad paucos dies voles facere copiam, speramus futurum vt autore tam probo studiosi nihil sint desideraturi, et tuus thesaurus incolumis et illibatus ad te redibit cum foenore. Ad haec curabitur ne posteritas etiam ignoret cui hoc beneficii debeat, quemadmodum vides a nobis factum in praefatione castigati nuper Senecae' (Allen 8:77–78 [ep 2116]).

69. The dates of the major authorised, successively revised editions of the *De copia* are 1512, 1514, 1526, and 1534.

70. Thomas Elyot, *The Book Named the Governor* (London, Tho. Bertheleti, 1531; Menston, Eng., 1970), fol. 35ᵛ–fol. 36ʳ.

CHAPTER SIX

1. For another argument that the reception of the *De copia* resulted in readings and uses of it which did not correspond to Erasmus's own plans for it, see T. O. Sloane, 'Schoolbooks and Rhetoric: Erasmus's *Copia*', *Rhetorica* 9 (1991), 113–29.

2. Thus we return to the discussion of paintings and letters which opened chapter 1.

3. As early as 1489, in a letter to Cornelius Gerard, Erasmus writes that he has 'long ago not only read them, but copied out all of them with [his] own hands' (CWE 1:35 [letter 22]; Allen 1:103). Even if these early letters, first published in the *Vita Erasmi* of 1607, are not to be treated as entirely 'genuine', the inclusion of Jerome's *Epistolae* here indicates Erasmus's long-standing commitment to them (and his eagerness to make that commitment appear long standing). See C. P. H. M. Tilmans, 'Cornelius Aurelius [Gerard] (c. 1460–1531), praeceptor Erasmi?', in Akkerman and Vanderjagt, *Rodolphus Agricola Phrisius, 1444–1485*, 200–210, especially 206, and note 33: 'Aurelius' *Vita gloriosi Jheronimi* is preserved in Deventer Athenaeum Library MS I.32. The relation between Erasmus' *Vita* and Aurelius's remains to be studied'. For a succinct account of Erasmus's interest in Jerome see Allen 2:210–11 (introduction to ep 396).

4. On the uniqueness of Erasmus's *Vita Hieronymi* within his own works see, P. G. Bietenholz, *History and Biography in the Work of Erasmus of Rotterdam* (Geneva, 1966), 91: 'The logical conclusion would seem to be that, for once at least, Erasmus positively envisaged a historical science and proceeded to demonstrate its methods in the life of Jerome. Yet if this biography is a historical essay of singular vigour and value, one must say that Erasmus never again availed himself of the model here created'.

5. See also above, chapter 2.

6. See Binns's description of the familiar letter in his discussion of Erasmus's *De conscribendis epistolis*: 'Here belong the news letter, in which distant friends are informed of the writer's personal news; the letter of announcement, which gives information on new developments either in public, private, or even domestic affairs; the letter of congratulation; the letter of lament, deploring the fortunes of the writer or of someone else; the business letter, in which some personal business is entrusted to someone else to be carried out; the letter of thanks for service done; the letter of commendation, giving praise to a servant for doing his duty; the dutiful letter, which of its own accord offers help and goodwill to a friend; and the jocose letter, which delights the mind by its sportive urbanity' (J. W. Binns, 'The Letters of Erasmus', in T. Dorey [ed.], *Erasmus: Studies in Latin Literature and Its Influence* [London, 1970], 55–79, 72).

7. On the publishing history of the *De conscribendis epistolis* see J.-C. Margolin's introduction to the ASD *De conscribendis epistolis* (I–2). For Erasmus's partition of types of letters, see ASD I–2, 224–5. The *Libellus de conscribendis epistolis*, published without Erasmus's consent in 1521, opens with the familiar letter.

8. See J. Rice Henderson, 'Erasmus on the Art of Letter-Writing', in J. J. Murphy (ed.), *Renaissance Eloquence: Studies in the Theory and Practice of Renaissance Rhetoric* (Berkeley, Calif., 1983), 331–55.

9. ASD I–2, 225. On some of Erasmus's indebtednesses in defining letter-writing in the *De conscribendis epistolis* see J. Monfasani, 'Three Notes on Renaissance Rhetoric', *Rhetorica* 5 (1987), 107–18; 'Two Greek sources for Erasmus's *De conscribendis epistolis*', 115–18.

10. 'Hieronymus ad Nitiam: Turpilius comicus tractans de uicissitudine literarum: Sola, inquit, res est, quae homines absentes praesentes facit. Nec falsam dedit, quamq[uam] in re non uera sententiam. Quid enim est (ut ita dicam) tam praesens inter absentes, quam per epistolas & alloqui & audire quos diligas? Nam & rudes illi Italiae homines, quos Cascos Ennius appellat, qui sibi (ut in rhetoricis Cicero ait) ritu ferme uictum quaerebant, ante chartae & membranarum usum, aut in dedolatis e ligno codicillis: aut in corticibus arborum mutuo epistolarum alloquia missitabant. Unde & potiores [portitores?] earum tabellarios, & scriptores a libris arborum librarios uocauere. Quanto magis igitur nos, expolito iam artibus mu[n]do id non debemus, omittere, quod illi sibi praestiterunt: apud quos erat cruda rusticatis, & qui humanitatem quoda[m]modo nesciebant? Ecce beatus Chromatius cum sancto Eusebio non plus natura quam morum aequalitate germano, literario me prouocauit officio. Tu modo a nobis abiens, recentem amicitiam scindis potius quam dissuis. quod prudenter apud Ciceronem Laelius uetat. Nisi forte ita tibi exosus est oriens, ut literas quoq[ue] tuas huc uenire formides. Expergiscere, expergiscere, euigila de somno, praesta unam chartae schedulam charitati. Inter delitias patriae, & communes quas habuimus peregrinationes, aliquando suspira. Si Amas, scribe obsecranti: si irasceris, iratus licet scribe. Magnum & hoc desiderij solamen habebo, si amici literas, uel indignantis accipiam' (Erasmus, *Epistolae Hieronymi* [Froben, 1524], 1:218).

11. 'Qua[m]q[uam] nulla ingenij suo monume[n]ta nobis reliquit, quae quide[m] extent' (fol. 97ᵛ).

12. Erasmus is not alone in finding this letter of Jerome's a compelling example of the *epistola*. There is a 1515 volume, published by Albertus Prafraet, for Murmellius, specially for use in the school at Alcmaar, which contains (alongside a pirated text of Erasmus's *De constructione*) two commentaries by Murmellius on Jerome's letter to Nitias: *In epistolam diui Hieronymi ad Niciam Aquileiensis ecclesie hypodiaconum co[m]mentarioli duo Ioannis Murmellij. in quibus pleraq[ue] traduntur scribendis eleganter epistolis idonea*. The first commentary is a simple gloss on the sense of the letter; the second is a small treatise on letter-writing, using the letter to Nitias as its starting point.

13. 'Is enim debet esse epistolae caracter, tanq[uam] cum amiculo in angulo susurres, non in theatro clames, aut paulo etia[m] liberior. Multa enim epistolae committimus, quae coram pudet expromere' (*Libellus de conscribendis epistolis* [Cambridge, Siberch, 1521], fol. 1ʳ).

14. Allen 4:500–501 (ep 1206): 'Si epistolae carent veris affectibus neque vitam ipsam hominis repraesentant, iam epistolae nomen non merentur. Quales sunt Senecae ad Lucilium: atque adeo inter eas quae olim scripsit Plato, quasque ad Apostolorum, vt apparet, imitationem scripserunt Cyprianus, Basilius, Hieronymus, Augustinus, perpaucae sunt quas non libros rectius appellaris quam epistolas. Porro, quas nobis reliquit nescio quis Bruti nomine, nomine Phalaridis, nomine Senecae ad Paulum, quid aliud censeri possunt quam declamatiunculae? Verum autem illud epistolarum genus quod mores, quod fortunam, quod affectus, quod publicum simul et priuatum temporis statum velut in tabula repraesentat, cuius generis fere sunt Epistolae Ciceronis ac Pliniim et inter recentiores Aeneae Pii'.

15. See Binns, 'The Letters of Erasmus'.

16. Erasmus, *Epistolae Hieronymi*, fol. 97ᵛ: 'Nam comoedia res ficta est. Et tamen in fictis fabulis uerae dicu[n]tur sententiae'.

17. See L.-E. Halkin, *Erasmus ex Erasmo: Érasme éditeur de sa correspondance* (Aubel, 1983); A. Gerlo, 'Érasme éditeur de sa correspondance, le cas de l'*Auctarium*', *Bibliothèque d'humanisme et Renaissance* 40 (1978), 239–47. I have extended the end date here to include the *Vita Erasmi* volume, whose collection of early letters now looks to me as contrived and carefully stage-managed to provide a particular early life for Erasmus as the *Vita Erasmi* itself. On the *Vita* see most recently Tocci, *In officina Erasmi*.

18. 'In memoriam [P. S. Allen]', in H. de Vocht, *Monumenta Humanistica*, vii–xxii.

19. Ibid., xxi.

20. See, for example, his note to letter 867 (3, 393), where he indicates that Rhenanus's prefatory letter to the *Auctarium* must be wrongly dated in the printed text, since it conflicts with the 'facts' of Erasmus's movements in 1518 as described in the letter. My own view would be that the conflict arises from the fact that Erasmus had not already left Basle, as Rhenanus claims, when the *Auctarium* was published.

21. The dates on a number of the letters are altered by Allen so as to make their contents internally coherent, and consistent with the 'autobiography' of the letters as a whole. Individual scholars have challenged the dating of individual letters (for instance, my own questioning of the date of Martin Dorp's first letter to

Erasmus), and generally such challenges are persuasive. But naturally those who work with the volumes as a whole, as a scholarly resource, continue simply to take Allen's dates as definitively correct.

22. CWE 8:98 [letter 1163]; Allen 4:390.

23. For a checklist of editions of Erasmus's letters see *Bibliotheca Erasmiana* (Nieuwkoop, 1961).

24. See above, Introduction.

25. 'Hadrianus Barlandus iuuentuti studiose', reprinted in part in Iseghem, *Biographie de Thierry Martens*, 257.

26. On Rhenanus see most reliably John d'Amico, *Beatus Rhenanus*, although there is relatively little here on Rhenanus's early work with Erasmus.

27. CWE 2:352–53; Allen 2, appendix 11.

28. Rhenanus had been left in charge of a number of Erasmus's publishing projects while Erasmus returned to Louvain. He was responsible for the 1519 Froben *Enchiridion militis christiani*, for which he provided a dedication to John Faber (A. Horawitz and K. Hartfelder [eds.], *Briefwechsel des Beatus Rhenanus* [Leipzig, 1886] 132 [10 Jan 1519]).

29. 'Proinde Lamberti Hollonii Leodiensis docti iuvenis opera familiarium colloquiorum formulas nactus, quas Erasmus ab hinc annos viginti aut amplius in Augustini Caminadi, ni fallor, gratiam, qui Selandos quosdam pueros docebat, per lusum conscripsit, dum Lutetiae degeret, statim excudendas typis apud Frobenium curavi, cum ut nobis in primis gratificarer, tum ut ad alios quoque studiosos hic thesaurus perveniret, apud malignos quosdam hactenus non secus custoditus ac vellus illud aureum a pervigili dracone et ab ipso Caminado semel atque iterum magno venditus. Libellus ipse parentem Erasmum refert stili candore, facilitate et argutia. Praeterea nihil poenitendum, nihil triviale continet, sed ex optimis dumtaxat autoribus decerptos elegantiarum flosculos. Quamquam exemplum ipsum multis locis depravatum erat, quorum nonnulla correximus, quaedam auditori ipsi reservavimus, qui hunc libellum plane periise putavit. Bene valete cum Gulielmo Neseno, praeceptore vestro, viro non minus integro quam erudito' ('Dedikationsepistel aus: Familiarium colloquiorum formulae per Erasmum Roterodamum. Viennae apud Singrenium 1520. Dies ist ein Nachdruck desselben Werkes, das 1519 bei *Froben* in Basel erschien', in Horawitz and Hartfelder, *Briefwechsel des Beatus Rhenanus*, 122–23).

30. Note that Rhenanus had already been pressing Erasmus to prepare a suitable text of the *De conscribendis epistolis* (ibid., 94 [May 1517]).

31. This is consistently Erasmus's argument when he tries to get greater cooperation amongst European printers, to prevent the pirating of editions. Where corrected manuscripts of his works supposedly 'get into the wrong hands', resulting in an edition which is in competition with the printer to whom he has pledged it, Erasmus seems to protest rather weakly, and may well have connived in such controlled double issuing of editions.

32. See most helpfully, H. J. de Jonge, 'Wann ist Erasmus' Übersetzung des Neuen Testaments entstanden?', in Sperna Weiland and Frijhoff, *Erasmus of Rotterdam*, 151–57; on *castigatio*: '*Castigatio* und *castigare* können bei Erasmus auch die folgenden Bedeutungen haben: 2) die pädagogische Zurechtweisung und Bestrafung von Kindern; 3) die textkritische Emendation und Edition eines Textes; 4) die stilistische Verbesserung einer noch nicht vollendeten Prosakompo-

sition oder eines Gedichtes; 5) Korrektur lesen. Die häufigste Bedeutung ist jedoch: das Revidieren, Verbessern und Ergänzen eines literarischen Werkes im Hinblick auf eine sowohl stilistisch, als auch rhetorisch und inhaltlich verbesserte Ausgabe. In dieser letzten Bedeutung verwendet Erasmus *castigare* und *castigatio* in bezug auf seine lateinische Übersetzung des Neuen Testaments: diese Übersetzung soll eine Verbesserung, *castigatio*, der Vulgata sein' (153). See also S. Rizzo, *Il lessico filologico degli umanisti* (Rome, 1973).

33. Allen 2:63 (ep 328).

34. On the Seneca edition see also Reynolds and Wilson, *Scribes and Scholars*.

35. On 'codex' as printed, not necessarily manuscript, source (e.g. Agricola's Treviso Seneca), see Rizzo, *Il lessico filologico degli umanisti*, 7–8.

36. 'In collegio Regali sunt opera Senecae descripta in membranis. Ex his multa subnotaram in codice meo.... [T]e rogo, charissime Aldrisi, sume volumen operum Senecae a Frobenio excusi, et committe aliquibus bonae fidei, qui denuo ascribant in margine quae discrepant. Eum codicem sic notatum mittito ad Thomam Morum, vt per eum ad me veniat. Libros Naturalium Quaestionum scio aeditos. Eam collationem ego peragam' (Allen 6:243 [ep 1656]). This letter was published in the 1529 Froben *Opus epistolarum*.

37. 'In quo peragendo hunc ordinem obseruaui. Illud exemplar quod in nostra Regii Collegii bibliotheca custoditur, solas ad Lucilium Epistolas habet, et eas itidem habet illud volumen Collegii diui Petri; quod ab illa bibliotheca nescio qua nisi vnius Erasmi gratia mutuari permisisset seria seruandorum librorum cura, priuatis etiam legibus decreta. Igitur dum Epistolas ad Lucilium percurro, excusum a Frobenio librum cum duobus illis peruetustis codicibus confero. Que variant, dum marginibus ascribo, duos codices suis ita notis distinguo, vt quod Collegii Regii volumen aliter habet, hac nota subindicem Θ, quod vero volumen Collegii diui Petri, hac nota: *J* Vbi consentiunt illi duo codices, sed a Frobeniano dissentiunt, que variant, ascribo, sed notam nullam facio. Neque quicquam quod vsquam discrepabat, omisi, siquis omnino sensus inerat; et quanquam illud quod Frobenianis tipis excusum erat, multo melius arbitrabar, tamen ascripsi. ... Quorum ego minimus nunc imperata tua facesso, volumina que volebas, contuli. ... Codicem notatum, vt volebas, misi ad dominum Thomam Morum quinto idus Maii, solicite precatus vt in quam posset celerrime ad te transmittendum curaret' (Allen 6:434–36 [ep 1766]). This letter was unpublished.

38. 'Non erat necesse mittere codicem, poterant omnia describi in schedis' (Allen 6:481 [ep 1797]).

39. Erasmus's respect for Aldridge as a textual scholar is indicated by the fact that he later addressed one of his *Apologia* for his editorial works to him (Allen 7:128–41 [ep 1858]).

40. Allen 4:498–502 (ep 1206).

41. Allen 3, appendix 12, 627–29.

42. 'Scis enim quam non dextris auibus exierint Epistolae, quas tu primum aedendas curasti; at quanto peioribus illa Farrago! Cuius aeditionem partim extorsit amicorum flagitatio, partim ipsa necessitas' (Allen 4:498 [ep 1206]).

43. 'Impudenter faciunt qui mea me viuo publicant formulis typographorum; sed multo impudentius qui pueriles etiam naenias meas euulgant. Omnium autem impudentissime qui nugis alienis meum praefigunt nomen: id quod nuper fecit nescioquis, qui libellum emisit De ratione conscribendi epistolas; in quo praeter

pauculas voces furtiuas nihil est meum. Nec vnquam mihi quisquam notus fuit cui nomen esset Petro Paludano' (Allen 4:456 [ep 1193]).

44. See Allen 11:366 (appendix 26). For a clear account of the editions of the *Breuissima formula* see now R. A. B. Mynors's introduction to the text, CWE 25:256–57.

45. 'Vicisti me tandem, humanissime P. Habes toties efflagitatam a nobis scribendarum epistolarum rationem. Sed vide interim, dum tuae morem gero voluntati, quantis me calumniis ipse obiecerim. Quid tandem eritici [*sic*: critici?] dicent, imo quid non dicent, vbi viderint me ausum tractare rem a multis tam diligenter ac scite tractatam? Vis tu, inquient, Penelopes telam retexere? Post tantos autores aut eadem dicas necesse est aut deteriora: quorum alterum superuacaneum est, alterum etiam perniciosum. Ego vero quanquam multa alia habeo quae respondere possum, vnum hoc tamen dico, nullius qui de hac re aliquid conscripserit me vestigiis inhaesurum. Accipe itaque breuissimam maximeque compendiariam conficiendarum epistolarum formulam, tibique hoc vnum persuade, non verbis tantum illas sed arte etiam indigere. Vale. Saluta amicos communes' (Allen 11:366–67). For a further comment on this letter, and on a further letter 'to Fabritius', in which 'nullum verbum est meum, nec est quicquam illa insulsius', see ep 3099 (prefatory letter to *Ioannis Ludouici Viuis Valentini de conscribendis epistolis Libellus vere aureus. Eiusdem argumenti D. Erasmi Roterodami compendium ab ipso autore denuo recognitum* (Basle, T. Platter and B. Lasius, March 1536) (Allen 11:286).

46. I have only so far seen the July 1521 Hillenius, Antwerp, reprint of this unauthorised edition.

47. See Appendices.

48. 'Postquam Holonius ille desierat esse apud superos, eruditissime Beralde, non putabam mihi quenquam alium metuendum, qui naenias, quas iuuenis vel exercendi stili gratia vel obsequundans amicorum affectibus scripsissem, in vulgus aederet, in quiduis potius quam in hoc natas. Et ecce de repente apud Britannos exortus est alter Holonius, qui librum De componendis Epistolis excudit, quem annis abhinc ferme triginta Lutetiae scribere coeperam, cuidam amico parum syncero, cui simili munere gratificari volebam, videlicet vt haberent similes labra lactucas' (Allen 5:63–64 [ep 1284]).

49. See above, chapter 2.

50. CWE 3:265–66 (letter 396). The passage from Jerome's preface to the book of Kings runs as follows (in Erasmus's edition): 'Lege ergo primu[m] Samuel & Malachim meu[m]. Meu[m], inq[uam], meu[m]. Quicq[ui]d e[ni]m crebrius uerte[n]do & eme[n]da[n]do solliciti[us] & didicim[us] & tenem[us], nostru[m] est' (3:13).

51. CWE 9:291 (letter 1341A).

52. CWE 9:356.

53. Erasmus came on the scene late in the progress of the edition, with his own edition of the *Epistolae* to add to the edition-in-progress. Apparently, Reisch stepped down as overall editor, giving way to Erasmus. See most colourfully, P. S. Allen, 'Erasmus' Relations with His Printers', in H. M. Allen (ed.), *Erasmus: Lectures and Wayfaring Sketches* (Oxford, Clarendon Press, 1934), 109–37; P. S. Allen, 'Erasmus's Services to Learning' (Annual Lecture on a Master-Mind, British Academy) (London, [1925]), 12–13.

54. The second book of the original edition (in two parts), containing the spurious letters, Erasmus dropped from this first volume altogether. It forms the first part of the *second* volume, which also carries a brief preface to Warham.

55. See above, chapter 1.

56. See above, ibid.

57. 'Amplissime Praesul, arbitror tibi redditam imaginem pictam, quam misi vt aliquid haberes Erasmi, si me Deus hinc euocarit. . . . Hieronymum ad te mitto; nondum poterat compingi ob recens attramentum. . . . Vehementer gaudio Epistolas Hieronymi feliciter absolutas; nam in his plurima restitui. Caetera quoque volumina sequentur, si conuenerit inter typographos: nam res est immensi sumptus, nec vnius hominis' (Allen 5:534–36 [ep 1488]).

58. See above, chapters 1 and 2.

59. 'Quanquam in prima aeditione sic aduigilatum erat vt vix vlla spes esset posterioribus curis, quas prouerbio dicunt meliores, quicquam adiungi posse, Praesul incomparabilis; tamen ego magnopere cupiens hoc opus, quod nomini tuo ceu monumentum, vtinam victurum, erexeram, omnibus, quantum fieri posset, numeris absolutum exactumque reddere, curaui vt denuo separatim excuderetur et chartis et formulis elegantioribus: quanquam Ioannes Frobenius sic se gesserat antea in excudendo Hieronymo, vt non solum omnium suffragiis antecederet omnes, verum etiam vix ipse sibi locum relinqueret vincendi sui. Nos in Hieronymi scriptis pene nihil deprehendimus quod esset corrigendum. In nostris scholiis nonnulla correximus, quaedam sustulimus, adiecimus non pauca. Restant tamen adhuc loca sed ea perpauca, in quibus mea diuinatio non omnino satisfecit animo meo: quae si quis me felicior, vel ingenio vel exemplariorum copia, restituerit, libenter et hominis industriam exosculabimur et publicae gratulabimur vtilitati. In hoc labore duae quaedam res exortae magnam nostrae laudis portionem decerpserunt. Primum quod per omnes totius orbis regiones sic effloruerunt linguae cum bonis literis, vt in multis non perinde necessaria videatur opera nostra. Deinde quod hoc seculo plurimorum ingeniis ad cruentas istas et gladiatorias *logomachias* auocatis, neque studio neque frequentia pari versantur homines in pratis saluberrimis ac viridariis amoenissimis veterum autorum. Caeterum laudis quidem iacturam facillime ferrem, nisi cum publico dispendio studiorum esset coniuncta. De rerum euentu viderit Christus. Nos certe bonam praestitimus voluntatem: quam et praestabimus vsque ad extremum vitae diem' (Allen 5:493 [ep 1465]).

60. In the first edition, after the opening letter, the scholia preceded the text; in the revised edition, more reasonably, the scholia follow the text.

61. Allen 5:562 (ep 1504).

62. 'Si cui non probatur nostrum iudicium, non habet tamen quod nobis indignetur. Non solum enim habet omnia quae prodita fuerant superioribus aliorum aeditionibus, verum etiam multa illis adiecta sunt; et habet eadem tum nitidus excusa, tum emendatius quam vnquam antea fuerint. Per me licebit vt suo quisque iudicio fruatur' (Allen 5:562 [ep 1504]).

63. 'Tantum ordo tomorum epistolarum mutatus est: secundo, qui complectebatur aliena, in quartum locum translato: ita qui prius erat tertius, nunc erit secundus: & qui quartus, tertius. Libellus de locis & nominibus Hebraicis certo consilio semoueramus a quarto tomo: qui nunc, ut dixi, tertius est: uerum eos nunc separatim excudimus, ut possis pro tuo arbitrio cui uoles tomo annectere.

Adiecimus nouum & elaboratum indicem sententiarum, quem & ipsum adiungere cui commodum erit tomo licebit' (Title page, 1526 Jerome *opera*).

64. In the set of volumes which I used in Cambridge University Library, the *index sententiarum* is bound at the end of the sixth bound volume (i.e., volume 9), the *In loca hebraica* and *De nominibus hebraicis* at the end of the fifth bound volume (volume 8).

65. See above, chapter 2.

66. See Allen 3:256. I have examined two in the British Library.

67. 'Eucharius quidam Coloniensis Ceruicornus quasdam Epistolas Hieronymianas ex archetypo nostro est imitatus. Traximus hominem in ius apud Francofordiam, quippe qui summorum priuilegia neglexerit atque adeo contempserit. Dabit, ni fallor, sue temeritatis penas' (Allen 3:256–57 [ep 802]); CWE 4:352.

68. As Kees Meerhoff points out (Warwick symposium), 'how-to' handbooks—manuals on rhetoric, the art of writing, etc.—are as much instructions on how to *read* as on how to write or speak oneself.

69. 'ARTIS ANNOTATIO: Caeterum quando diuus Hieronymus in proxima epistola fatetur in hac se rhetoricum flosculis lusisse, fortasse non alienu[m] fuerit artis quoq[ue] ratione[m], quam sequutus est, iudicare: sed paucis, neq[ue] nimis anxie, ne duo pariter incom[m]oda nos sequantur: vt & molesti simus lectori, & salubribus huius viri praeceptis pondus ac fidem detrahamus. Minus enim mouere solent animos, quae non ex animo, sed ex arte scripta putantur. Atq[ue] vt primu[m] de argume[n]ti genere no[n]nihil attingamus, exhortatoriu[m] est, sicut ante dictum. Id adeo confine est suasorio, vt Aristoteles no[n] putarit ab eo separandum. Tametsi meo iudicio no[n] parum interest. Suademus enim, vt quis velit: hortamur vt audeat & possit. Suademus haesita[n]ti, hortamur cessantem. Suademus, cum ostendimus quid expediat fieri: hortamur, cum addimus animum. Cum enim imperator co[m]missurus cum hoste, milite[m] exhortatur: no[n] hoc agit, vt miles intelligat esse pugnandum, sed addit calcar, vt quod vult, ausit & possit. Quanqu[am] partes fere conueniunt vtriusq[ue] generis: nempe, honestum, vtile, laudabile, possibile, necessarium, facile, iucundum, & si quae sunt aliae. Ab his enim omnis argume[n]tatio petitur. Habet hoc peculiare exhortatio, quod ardentior est, & multu[m] laudis habet admixtum, quae t[ame]n hic no[n] utitur Hieronymus. Duabus enim rebus homines potissimu[m] exstimula[n]tur, laude, & ignominiae metu. Sunt aute[m] huiusmodi libelli nihil aliud quam Christianae declamationes. Etenim cum videre[n]t eloque[n]tia[m] rem esse pulcherrima[m], simul & vtilissima[m]: neq[ue] decorum existimarent, inter profanos rhetores, in nugacissimis argume[n]tis exerceri: videlicet an Isthmus debeat intercidi: an Alexander Oceanum ingressus, longius progredi debeat: tota[m] declamandi ratione[m] sicuti Socrates philosophiam, ad morum institutionem traxerunt: quoq[ue] res magis esset seria, mutato declamationis nomine, libellos, aut epistolas vocauerunt: vt eadem opera geminam vtilitatem co[n]sequerentur, dum & eloquentia[m] exercent, quae citissime arescit, vt ait M. Tullius: & salubribus monitis ad pietatem exhortantur' (fols. 3ᵛ–4ᵛ).

70. 'Atq[ue] vt primu[m] de argume[n]ti genere no[n]nihil attingamus, exhortatoriu[m] est. . . . Habet hoc peculiare exhortatio, quod ardentior est, & multu[m] laudis habet admixtum, quae t[ame]n hic no[n] utitur Hieronymus. Duabus enim rebus homines potissimu[m] exstimula[n]tur, laude, & ignominiae

metu. Sunt aute[m] huiusmodi libelli nihil aliud quam Christianae declamationes' (ibid.).

71. 'QUID INTER EXHORTATIONEM ET SUASIONEM. Ac primum finitimae admodum inter se sunt, exhortatio, et suasio, quas nos tamen dicendi gratia separauimus; idque fecimus neque sine exemplo, neque citra iudicium, propterea quod et veterum nonnulli in arte dicendi, exhortatorium genus a deliberatiuo disiunxissent, et ipsi nonnihil discriminis perspiceremus. Siquidem nec eodem tendit vtrunque, neque via simili. Nam suadendo id agitur, vt velis; exhortando, vt audeas. Suasio probationis docet: exhortatio stimulus excitat. Suasor sententiam mutat; exhortatio animum addit. Suademus aut errantibus, aut certe haesitantibus; exhortamur cessantes, aut etiam iam currentes. Quare si rem ad viuum excutiamus, exhortatio suasoriae epistolae pars erit, nempe epilogus, qui affectibus constat, non argumentis. Neque enim suadenti sat erit, quid sit optimum factu docuisse, nisi et stimulos subiiciat, ne vel difficultate, vel periculo deterriti, vel ignauia retardati, quod optimum esse viderimus, non sequamur. Sed vt in suasionem fere semper incidit exhortatio, ita in hac non raro continget vti in suasione. Est autem vtrunque officiosum literarum genus, cuiusque vsus maximis, minimisque in rebus quam latissime pateat. Atque hoc maiore cura diligentiaque nobis erit pertractandum' (*De conscribendis epistolis*, in *Opera Omnia Desiderii Erasmi Roterodami* I–2 [Amsterdam, 1971], 315–16). 'DE EPISTOLA SUASORIA. Iam ad suasorium genus veniamus, quod quidem ab illo superiori non admodum abhorret. Nam vt illic, ita hic quoque laudem, spem, expectationem, cohortationi nonnunquam admiscemus. Complectitur autem hoc genus varias epistolarum specias, quas separatim tractabimus. Nam et qui petit suadet, et qui commendat, et qui consulit, et qui monet, et qui consolatur. Suasoriam igitur epistolam hoc pacto licebit instituere. Si res postulabit captanda paucis est benevolentia. Id quemadmodum fieri conueniat, a rhetoribus diligenter monstratum est. Deinde narrationem subiiciemus, in qua omnia ad suadendum accommodabimus, et tanquam argumentorum semina iaciemus. Deinde si res ipsa partes in se continebit, eas cum diuisione proponemus. Quod si simplex erit, ipsi nostro ingenio diuisionem faciemus, et rationum capita, a quibus potissimum sumus suasuri, sub distributione, vt diximus, enumerabimus. Deinde de singulis rationibus varie copioseque tractabimus. Si quid vehementer nostrae rationi videbitur officere, id statim in principio destruemus, aut vt quicque inciderit, ita confutendum erit. Sed de rationum inuentione prius, postea de earum tractatione praecipiemus. Sumuntur autem rationes ab his potissimum partibus, honesto, vtili, tuto, iucundo, facili, necessario' (ibid., 365–66).

72. See this introduction in full for a clear discussion of *suasoria* and *declamatio* in the context of this work.

73. 'Est et inter Hieronymianas epistolas, exhortatoria ad Heliodorum, quae vniversum eius generis artificium vna complectitur' (*De conscribendis epistolis*, 353).

74. See above, chapter 2.

75. Mann Phillips, *The 'Adages' of Erasmus* 161–63.

76. 'Affixi signum meum, quod quidam ceperunt imitari manum meam, sic vt discerni vix possit. Id factum es(t) Romae. Erasmus Rot. mea manu' (Allen 11:145 [ep 3028]).

77. Ibid., 10:313–34 (ep 2874).

78. See above, chapter 5.

79. E.g., for the Barlandus volume, see above, chapter 5.

80. Rice, 'Erasmus on the Art of Letter-Writing', 339. I am myself increasingly troubled about the status of many of the early letters which Allen publishes in the first volume of the *Opus epistolarum*. Several of these present the youthful Erasmus in the process of producing impeccable programmes for his future interests. They were first published in the 1607 *Vita Erasmi* volume (long after Erasmus's own death), and seem literally too prescient to be true. See, for example the letter to Cornelius Gerard, which Allen identifies as 'June 1489? Steyn'. This letter is itself a classic exercise in letter-writing ('crescit scribendo scribendi studium', line 5). It includes the Turpilius reference from Jerome's letter to Nitias: 'Siquidem, si fidem habemus Turpilio,literarum vicissitudo vna res est quae absentes coniugat amicos' (Allen 1:104 [ep 23]). My own feeling is that at the very least this letter has been updated much later in Erasmus's life, to provide some juvenilia to add to the *Vita*.

Conclusion

1. As Pierre Bourdieu points out: 'When the book remains and the world all around changes, the book changes' ('La lecture: Une pratique culturelle', in Chartier, *Pratiques de la lecture*, 218–39).

2. See most recently, S. L. Hindman (ed.), *Printing the Written Word: The Social History of Books, c. 1450–1520* (Ithaca, 1992).

3. For a description of the volume see Surtz, and Hexter, *Utopia*, vol. 4 of *Yale Edition of the Complete Works of St. Thomas More*, clxxxiv: 'The copy in the Yale University Library is extraordinarily fine. It is bound with other works published between 1508 and 1514 in Reggio, Paris, and Vienna. The elaborate Netherlands binding of calf over oak boards is contemporary. The autograph inscription on the title page of the *Utopia*, the first work in the volume, reads: *Sum Tunstalli* ("I am Tunstall's book"). These words appear again on pages 152, 153, and 497. The copy measures 8 1/4 × 5 1/2 inches'.

4. See ibid., clxxxiv; Allen 2:339.

5. See the descriptive notes boxed with the volume at Yale.

6. CWE 4:103 (letter 480). In 1517, Erasmus orchestrated a correpondence between Budé and Tunstall, the focus of which was their mutual expertise in Greek. See Allen 2:459 (ep 531), 538–42 (ep 571), 542–43 (ep 572), 560–83 (ep 583).

7. CWE 4:163–64 (letter 499): 'his opinion of my republic [*Utopia*], so frank and so favourable, cheered me more, dearest Erasmus, than a nugget of pure gold.' He acknowledged this praise in a grateful letter to Tunstall himself (More, *Correspondence*, 84–85).

8. See the title page of the 1526 Froben *Adagia* in the Vatican Library, heavily annotated by Erasmus and his *famulus* Nicholas Cannius, which is inscribed 'Cannius est dominus, sed magni munere Erasmi' (reproduced in Tocci, *In officina Erasmi*). This volume was given by Erasmus as a gift to Cannius. Other volumes of Erasmus's which he gave away are inscribed 'Sum Erasmi'.

9. See Dominic Baker-Smith, *More's 'Utopia'* (London, 1991), 181.

10. See the preface to the 1514 edition, CWE 24:284–88.

11. For a reproduction of Colet's hand, see CWE 24 [*De copia*], 286–87. See also Sears Jayne, *John Colet and Marsilio Ficino* (Oxford, 1963), appendix A ('The Identification of Colet's Hand'), 135–37 (I find it hard to believe that the hand in plate 5 is not a copyist's version of the inscriptions reproduced in the CWE *De copia* volume—it is certainly unlike any of the other hands reproduced as 'Colet's').

12. Allen 2:257 (ep 423): 'Nam nunc dolor me tenet quod non didicerim Graecum sermonem, sine cuius peritia nihil sumus'.

13. CWE 4:80; Allen 2:347 (ep 468). In a prefatory letter to Colet of 1517, Richard Pace also refers to Colet's learning Greek, and attributes to Erasmus the influence which encouraged him to start these studies so late in his life (Dedicatory letter to *De fructu qui ex doctrina percipitur*, cited in G. Marc'hadour, 'Érasme et John Colet', in *Colloquia Erasmiana Turonensia: Douzième stage international d'études humanistes, Tours, 1969*, 2 vols. [Limoges, 1972], 2:761–79, 766).

14. Allen 2:198.

15. On Clement as Greek scholar see K.-L. Selig and R. Somerville (eds.), *Florilegium Columbianum: Essays in Honor of Paul Oskar Kristeller* (New York, 1987).

16. Surtz and Hexter, *Utopia*, 41: 'As you know, John Clement my pupil-servant, was also present at the conversation. Indeed I do not allow him to absent himself from any talk which can be somewhat profitable, for from this young plant, seeing that it has begun to put forth green shoots in Greek and Latin literature, I expect no mean harvest some day'.

17. Ibid., 47.

18. Reproduced ibid., plate 2.

19. See above, chapter 1.

20. Compare also the discussion of Erasmus's 'customising' of presentation volumes for specific patrons in chapter 1.

21. See above, and Kinney, 'Letter to Dorp' xxii–xxiv. See also de Vocht, *Monumenta Humanistica*.

22. On Rhenanus see John d'Amico, *Beatus Rhenanus*, and Bietenholtz and Deutscher, *Contemporaries of Erasmus*.

23. CWE 3:79–82 (letter 328).

24. CWE 3:77–79 (letter 327). The dedication is an elaborate play on 'Beatus', and Rhenanus's appropriate designation as *beatus vir*—a blessed man.

25. See above, chapter 5.

26. CWE 3:81 (letter 328).

27. CWE 3:83 (letter 330).

28. I. Bezzel, *Erasmusdrucke des 16 Jahrhunderts in Bayerischen Bibliotheken* (Stuttgart, 1979), 362–63 (item 1302).

29. See above, chapters 1 and 2. 'For the printing was going on at Bâle of the *Adagiorum Chiliades*, so amended and increased that the new edition cost me as much trouble as the previous one which had been produced in Venice by Aldus Manutius, and at the same time they were printing the complete works of St

Jerome in which I had undertaken the largest and most difficult part' (Margaret Mann Phillips, *Erasmus on His Times: A Shortened Version of the 'Adages' of Erasmus* (Cambridge, 1967), 18–31, 30. For the reference to Listrius as *castigator* of this volume see Allen 2:407, also ep 269, and the letter from Listrius to Amerbach in the Amerbach correspondence.

30. CWE 3:30–31 (letter 305).

31. Bezzel, *Erasmusdrucke*, 363 (item 1304).

32. Ibid., 81 (item 150).

33. Iseghem, *Biographie de Thierry Martens*, 255 (item 91). Martens's letter runs: 'Quo vestris non iam studiis modo, verum et crumenis consulam studiosi, (quod quotus est typographus qui faciat?) idcirco haec nobis separatim impressimus, vt nummulo emi possint. Nam quae in Germania sunt hiis coimpressa, plurimos scio vestrum olim comparasse. Eadem denuo ob tantillam appendicis accessionem emere, vobis (si vos noui) graue foret. Omnes siquidem optimos libros vultis, vultis et multos, sed qui paruo constent. Atqui nos nihil emimus paruo, non vilissimarum rerum vllam, librorum comparatione. Proinde vos nostram industriam adiuuate, qui contra Mimi illius sententiam, Magno emimus, et vendimus paruo Valete, Louanij Theodoricus Martinus Alustensis suis typis excudebat'.

34. As Allen points out, Listrius's commentary so obviously serves Erasmus's purpose that it has often been attributed to Erasmus himself (compare the similar function of 'E.K' 's commentary on Edmund Spenser's 'Shepheard's Calender'). 'The question of authorship is solved by the following statement by Erasmus in an unpublished letter to Bucer, dated 2 March 1532 (Copenhagen MS. G.K.S. 95 Fol., f. 172): "Conuenerat vt Lystrius in ⟨Moriam⟩ adderet scholia. Quum ille tantum polliceretur et vrgeret tempus, quo viam illi aperirem, cepi quedam annotare paucis ab ipso fusius tractanda. Quum ne ⟨si⟩c quidem prouocaretur et iam officina flagitaret exemplar, coactus perrexi donec ille iuuenem hoc ambire gloriae quo facilius emergeret, cuius humanitatis fuisset et illum frustrari suo voto et mihi totum vendicare quod aliquanta ex parte erat alienum?"' (Allen 2:407).

35. We should note, however, that Listrius's commentary on Peter of Spain, in which Peter Mack has shown the clear influence both of Valla's and of Agricola's dialectic, needs, on this kind of reading, to be considered as crucially influenced by the Erasmus circle. Its version of dialectic, in other words, forms part of the story I told in chapter 3, of the construction of a specifically Agricolan frame for northern humanist argumentation in the curriculum. See P. Mack, 'Valla's Dialectic in the North: A Commentary on Peter of Spain by Gerardus Listrius', *Vivarium* 21 (1983), 58–72.

36. 'Scarabeus aquilam quaerit' ('the beetle searches for the eagle' or 'the beetle is midwife to the eagle') discourses with effortless virtuosity on beetles and on eagles in relation to ancient culture; 'Sileni Alcibiadis' (the Sileni of Alcibiades) likewise discourses on things which seem slight and contemptible, but which, when opened, are revealed to contain profound riches. The two adages are conveniently available in translation in Mann Phillips, *Adages*, 229–63, 269–96.

37. 'Dabo operam strenue vt Copia quam ocyssime simul et nitidissime Frobennianis typis excusa in lucem exeat. Moria tua quouis theologo prudentiore iam propemodum est absoluta. Beatus Rhena⟨nus⟩ eam sub incude aliquamdiu remoratus est cum suo Gryllo a se Latinitati donato quem adiicere cupit. Schure-

rius Enchiridion denuo impressit. . . . Frobenius rogat te plurimum, si quid habeas quod vel a te castigatum vel de nouo compositum sit, vt sibi mittas; et diligenti opera et pecuniis gratiam referet' (Allen 2:352–53 [ep 473]).

38. Allen 2:126.

39. Allen 2:126.

40. See above, Introduction, for some discussion of humanist 'quotation'.

41. This is the aspect of the letters which is beyond the scope of this work to take further. Elizabeth Clark has argued brilliantly, in the case of Saint Jerome, that the surviving correspondence, and the doctrinal quarrels it preserves, suggest a kind of contrivance among and between the participants. These participants are connected to one another, and to the issues, by too many overlapping links (kinship, patronage, geographical proximity, national affinity) to be considered spontaneous. She bases her work on contemporary sociological network theory. I have begun a data base for Erasmus's letters which will ultimately, I hope, allow me, in a gingerly fashion, to make some similar suggestions for Erasmus's correspondents and surviving correspondence. See E. Clark, 'Elite Networks and Heresy Accusations: Towards a Social Description of the Origenist Controversy' (manuscript lent by the author). See also Clark, *Jerome, Chrystostom and Friends: Essays and Translations* (New York and Toronto, 1979).

42. Allen 2:407–9, 414–15, 422–23.

43. See above, chapter 3.

44. 'Quid omnino sine te Listrius aut facere aut tentare potuisset? Omnia mea, qualia sunt, tibi accepta refero. Nam cum tot lucubrationibus, tot Herculeis laboribus omnem posteritatem, nedum praesens seculum tibi demeruisti, tu de me vno peculiarissime bene meruisti' (Allen 2:409).

45. For Listrius's part in the 1515 *Adagia*, see Allen 2:407; Bietenholtz and Deutscher, *Contemporaries of Erasmus*.

46. 'Tua longitudo est breuitas. Crescit appetitus, modo stomachus sit sanus, in lectione tuorum amantibus Scripturas. Si aperueris sensus, quod nemo te melius faciet, magnum beneficium conferes et nomen tuum immortalitati commendabis. Quid dico, immortalitati? Nomen Erasmi nunquam peribit' (Allen 2:258 [ep 423]). Allen notes: 'The manuscript of this letter only goes as far as *studia tua* (l. 7), at which point the copyist discovered his error and added in the margin 'impressa est' [the letter was printed in *Epistolae aliquot ad Erasmum*, Martens, 1516—the first collection of Erasmus's letters]' (257). This suggests to me that the copyist was putting together a collection of 'familiar letters' by Erasmus, of the type represented by all the letters discussed here, for publication, but that such a volume did not in the end appear.

47. *De copia*, CWE 24.

APPENDICES

1. CWE 2:65–69 (letter 174).

2. See J. Monfasani, 'Besarion, Valla, Agricola, and Erasmus', *Rinascimento* 28 (1988), 319–20, for this borrowing.

3. 1508–23. This was altered in the 1526 edition to read: 'There were lying hidden in some people's possession his treatises on dialectic, and they have recently appeared, but in a mutilated state'.

4. LB 2:166A–167D; M. Mann Phillips, *Adages* 1.1.–5.100; CWE 31:348–51.

5. Vervleit, *Post-Incunabula and Their Publishers*, 118. Presumably based on a prefatory letter, which I have not seen.

6. The problem in straightening out the publishing history of Agricola's works seems, indeed, to stem almost entirely from the complete separation of bibliographies of incunabula printing (pre-1500) from bibliographies of post-1500 printing. Agricola's works crucially straddle the 1500 dividing line in a bibliographically inconvenient way.

7. Hain, *Repertorium Bibliographicum*, items 15921 and 15922 are further editions of this work by de Breda and Paffraet, respectively (who frequently exchanged sheets, publishing the same works in the same or consecutive years). For Huisman, see Huisman, *Rudolph Agricola*, 129. 15921 (undated) runs: 'Vita divi Antonii. F.Ia: Vita divi Antonii au sanctissimum Eugenium papam quartum: per Mapheum Vegium laudensem. Incipit una cum dialogo quodam de nativitate Christi a magistro Sandero Hegio Schole Daventriensis olim rectore composito et edito . . . Impressum Daventriae per me Iacobum de Breda'. The 15922 entry runs: 'Vita divi Antonii. F.Ia. tit: Vita diui Antonij ad Sanctissimum dnm Eugeni \\ um papa[m] quartu[m]. p[er] Mapheu[m] vegium laudensem . . . Impressum Dauentriae. In platea episcopi Anno d[omin]i. Mcccc.yc. . . . 11ff. (Rich. Paffroed.)' Both these editions may contain the Agricola 'Anna mater' as well as the Hegius dialogue as part of the customary padding which Paffraet and de Breda had at hand.

8. Allen, 'Letters of Rudolph Agricola', 310 (letters 3 and 4).

9. van Thienen, *Incunabula in Dutch Libraries* 375, items 2514, 2515.

10. CWE 3:137.

11. Iseghem, *Biographie de Thierry Martens*, item 62 (231): 'C'est la traduction faite par Agricola de trois opuscules grecs, à savoir: *Isocrates de Regnô; Luciani libellus de non credendis delationibus; Luciani micyllus sive gallus*'.

12. Sig. a ii^{r–v}.

13. *L. Annei Senecae Declamationes aliquot, cum Rodolphi Agricolae uiri doctissimi co[m]mentariolis, antehac non excusis* (Basle, Bebelius, 1529), 3–4 (a2^r–a2^v).

14. *Libellus de conscribendis epistolis, autore D. Erasmo, opus olim ab eodem coeptum, sed prima manu, mox expoliri coeptu[m], sed intermissum, Nunc primum prodit in lucem*, sig. A i^v.

15. Sig. A iii^r.

16. 'Dedikationsepistel zu: *C. Plinii Secundi* Novocomensis Epistolarum libri Decem, in quibus multae habentur epistolae non ante impressae etc. Am Schlusse: Argentorati ex aedibus Schurerianis Mense Februario an MDXIIII', in Horawitz and Hartfelder, *Briefwechsel*, 61–62.

Index

DATE DUE

APR 20 1994
